Advances in Distributed Processing Management

VOLUME 2

WILEY–HEYDEN ADVANCES LIBRARY IN EDP MANAGEMENT

Edited by Thomas A. Rullo

Other Advances Series in the Library

ADVANCES IN DATA PROCESSING MANAGEMENT Volume 1
ADVANCES IN DATA BASE MANAGEMENT Volumes 1 and 2
ADVANCES IN COMPUTER PROGRAMMING MANAGEMENT Volume 1
ADVANCES IN DATA COMMUNICATIONS MANAGEMENT Volumes 1 and 2
ADVANCES IN COMPUTER SECURITY MANAGEMENT Volumes 1 and 2
ADVANCES IN DISTRIBUTED PROCESSING MANAGEMENT Volume 1

Advances in Distributed Processing Management

VOLUME 2

Edited by
P. S. Fisher
Kansas State University
Manhattan

Jacob Slonim
GEAC Computers International, Inc.
Markham, Ontario
Canada

E. A. Unger
Kansas State University
Manhattan

A Wiley Heyden Publication

JOHN WILEY & SONS
Chichester · New York · Brisbane · Toronto · Singapore

Library of Congress Catalog Card No.: 81-649059

British Library Cataloguing in Publication Data:

Advances in distributed processing management.—Vol. 2.
—(Wiley Heyden advances in EDP management)
1. Electronic data processing—Management—Periodicals 2. Electronic data processing—Distributed processing—Periodicals
00.64 QA76.9.M3

ISBN 0 471 26232 3

Typeset by Pintail Studios Ltd, Ringwood, Hampshire.
Printed by The Pitman Press, Bath, Avon.

CONTENTS

LIST OF CONTRIBUTORS

WILLIAM P. AIKENS, U.S. Army, Fort Huachuca, New Mexico, U.S.A. (p. 251).

CHARLES T. BAKER, IBM Corporation, P.O. Box 390, Department CO2, Building 702, Poughkeepsie, New York 12602, U.S.A. (p. 183).

W. T. COTTRELL, Major, U.S. Army, CACDA, Fort Leavenworth, Leavenworth, Kansas 66027, U.S.A. (p. 221).

LIONEL E. DEIMEL, Jr., Ph.D., Department of Computer Science, North Carolina State University, Raleigh, North Carolina, 27650, U.S.A. (p. 93).

PAUL S. FISHER, Ph.D., Department of Computer Science, Kansas State University, Manhattan, Kansas 66506, U.S.A. (p. 145).

ROBERT J. FORNARO, Ph.D., Department of Computer Science, North Carolina State University, Raleigh, North Carolina 27650, U.S.A. (p. 93).

JAMES N. GRAY, Ph.D., Tandem Corporation, 19333 Valco Parkway, Cupertino, California 95014, U.S.A. (p. 1).

WILLIAM J. HANKLEY, Ph.D., Department of Computer Science, Kansas State University, Manhattan, Kansas 66506, U.S.A. (p. 267).

DAVID F. McALLISTER, Ph.D., Department of Computer Science, North Carolina State University, Raleigh, North Carolina 28650, U.S.A. (p. 93).

RICHARD A. McBRIDE, Ph.D., Department of Computer Science, Kansas State University, Manhattan, Kansas 66506, U.S.A. (p. 117).

L. H. MacRAE, NDX Corporation, P.O. Box 7028, Station A, Toronto, Ontario, Canada M5W 1X7. (p. 117).

FRED MARYANSKI, Ph.D., Digital Equipment Corporation, Corporate Research Group, 9 Highfield Drive, Lancaster, Maryland, 01523, U.S.A. (p. 15).

RALPH MAURIELLO, Manager Computer Design Systems, Litton Data Systems, 8000 Woodley Avenue, Van Nuys, California 91109, U.S.A. (p. 73).

C. MOHAN, Ph.D., IBM Research Laboratory, K55/281, San Jose, California 95193, U.S.A. (p. 45).

MOON JIN HAN, Department of Computer Science, Kansas State University, Manhattan, Kansas 66506, U.S.A. (p. 145).

A. SILBERSCHATZ, Ph.D., Department of Computer Sciences, University of Texas at Austin, Painter Hall 3.28, Austin, Texas 78712, U.S.A. (p. 45).

JACOB SLONIM, Ph.D., Geac Computers International Corporation, 350 Steelcase Road West, Markham, Ontario, Canada L3R 1B3. (p. 15).

E. A. UNGER, Ph.D., Department of Computer Science, Kansas State University, Manhattan, Kansas 66506, U.S.A. (p. 117).

P. A. VIGLUCCI, Major, U.S. Army, Ft. Devons, Maryland 01433, U.S.A. (p. 221).

V. E. WALLENTINE, Ph.D., Department of Computer Science, Kansas State University, Manhattan, Kansas 66506, U.S.A. (p. 267).

PREFACE TO THE WILEY–HEYDEN ADVANCES LIBRARY IN EDP MANAGEMENT

Information, to be of value, must be timely, accurate, and accessible. By addressing each of these criteria, the *Wiley–Heyden Advances Library in EDP Management* has proved to be a unique and valuable source of information for managers.

The timeliness of the material is maintained by issuing additional volumes within each series. These volumes build upon the base of previous ones to provide new insights and add topics of current interest. Because we continue to generate new ideas our readers receive the most up-to-date information.

The second attribute of useful information is accuracy. To create the *Wiley–Heyden Advances Library in EDP Management*, we assign a separate editor to each volume as an expert in the field, that editor being responsible for the overall content of the volume. Each chapter is in turn developed by an expert in a specific area and then submitted to the volume editor for review. Wherever necessary, additional technical review support is obtained. Because of this detailed editorial and review process, a high degree of accuracy can be assured.

The third attribute that makes information of value is accessibility. This feature is the least commonly discussed and the most difficult of the three to accomplish. In fact, the lack of easy accessibility to information was the main reason for developing the *Wiley–Heyden Advances Library in EDP Management*. Our primary role as developers and managers of this base of material is to provide our users with the information they want in a form in which they can readily use it. This task is accomplished through the selection of relevant topic areas, maintenance of a consistent level of content, and organization of material in line with its intended use. Although we have achieved our timeliness, accuracy, and accessibility objectives, we strive to improve the library through the added dimension of communication with our end users. Thus we welcome any suggestions for improvement of our current series or expansion into new areas.

Thomas A. Rullo
Executive Editor

PREFACE

The opening of this decade finds the computer milieu strongly flavored by commercially available computer networks. The integration of cooperative distributed processing into the computer systems is a reality for many large- to medium-sized organizations. The geographic distribution of the ultimate users of data has been a driving sociological force in distributed processing while the existence of reasonably priced hardware and adequate software has provided a permissive background. Distributed processing is also imposing several new challenges for the professionals involved. These challenges include those emanating from a changing management role—the central control mechanisms of the past are no longer adequate to control and guide distributed processing systems. Another concern is the creation and maintenance of global knowledge while providing uniform views of secure, efficient, correct data and functional bases to all users. These crucial issues formed the basis for the selection of topics in the volume; authors were selected for their knowledge and experience and for their ability to communicate that knowledge to EDP managers and their staffs.

We have divided the volume into four sections: standards, planning, local distribution, and geographical distribution. Each section contains tutorials which address both the state of the art as well as perspectives on the future. James Gray was selected as an author for his broad knowledge of distributed systems. In the first chapter he provides an example of a distributed data base management system, and defines concepts useful in understanding data bases, data communications, networks, data and function distribution, transaction and function routing, and remote procedure calls. An extensive annotated bibliography is included for the reader who wishes to pursue this topic further.

The second chapter, written by Fred Maryanski of Digital Corporation and Jacob Slonim, of GEAC Computers International, is designed to provide the reader with a terminological basis for data base technology and distributed information system environments and describes the common data models and hardware/software distribution environments found in use and in the literature. The authors describe and categorize these models and thus provide the reader with both a definitional base for the terminology of this field and a survey of actual and proposed models and environments.

The effective application of cooperating distributed processing systems is dependent on the development of languages for programming within these environments. Current high-level production languages like FORTRAN are not suitable. C. Mohan of the IBM Research Laboratory and A. Silberschatz of the University of Texas at Austin were selected to address this topic. Chapter 3 examines the design issues in creating languages for use in distributed processes and the alternatives. Having provided the reader with this background, they survey the languages/language proposals currently available. An extensive bibliography is included.

The five chapters of Section II concentrate on the concerns of individuals planning for a distributed processing system. Ralph Mauriello presents a general method for designing and evaluating distributed systems. The distribution of functions and data are addressed in terms of the sizing of computer memory and communications capability to achieve a cost-effective design that satisfies the response time criteria of the organization.

The fifth chapter uses the design of the integrated photo grammetric instrument network (IPIN) currently being implemented for the Defense Mapping Agency Aerospace Center as a case study of the application of the state-of-the-art distributed system design methodologies., A number of geographically distributed distinct designers effected this design solution using the method, thus giving further credence to its usefulness. Distributed systems arise generally from the interconnection of existing nodes so these global systems are heterogeneous. In Chapter 6, Richard McBride has described the work progressing on the problem of interconnecting dissimilar systems into a network which appears homogeneous to the end user. An elaboration of this topic is included in Chapter 7 where the issues of design alternatives and problems are elaborated.

Nodal application autonomy is measured by the amount of application work that a node can provide without depending on the data or services at another node. Charles T. Baker of IBM provides a tutorial on how to distribute data and applications to maximize local node autonomy and to minimize interdependency support requirement and functions.

Geographically distributed systems are the subject of the last three chapters of this volume. An approach to the distribution of the management function of such a network is described in Chapter 9. The authors suggest a model based upon current distributed management plans of the U.S. Army for use in the mobile computerized battlefield system. The discussion distinguishes between strategic and tactical decision-making requirements and the concept of minimum essential information. Although based upon the military environment, this model has many parallels to the management of any distributed system, and managers may find that this approach is the logical extension of their current decision support strategies.

The question of system resiliency to loss of model hardware/software data is explored by William Aikens and Elizabeth Unger in Chapter 10. Trade-offs in storage for replicated data and programs and maintenance of the integrity of that information are discussed. The restoration of a node to service after a failure is a problem that Aikens has considered. The solution he proposes involves a recuperating node status, which he introduces and describes.

In the final chapter the authors discuss ways to determine the performance of a distributed system through mathematical models and simulation studies. This tutorial is aimed at the information systems manager—thus the authors have provided definitions and concepts for developing simple models which can be used to characterize the performance of real systems of great complexity. The indicators of system viability are throughput and response time. The level of detail includes host processors, data base machines, communication subnets and processors, communication levels, and data resource frames. The use of the models in discrete event simulation for analysis of the dynamic behavior of distributed systems is proposed as a practical in-house tool for management analysis. The chapter concludes with a discussion of the problems encountered in simulating large distributed data management systems.

The editors wish to express their appreciation to the various contributors for the quality of their insight and their willingness to impart concise, comprehensive information. Special thanks are also extended to Russell William Hultgren for his indefatigable efforts in compiling and combing the manuscript.

Section I
A STANDARD

Advances in Distributed Processing Management, Volume 2
Edited by P. S. Fisher, J. Slonim, and E. A. Unger

Chapter 1

A DISCUSSION OF DISTRIBUTED SYSTEMS*

James N. Gray
Tandem Corporation, Cupertino, California 95014

HISTORICAL PERSPECTIVE

The decade of the seventies is over. During that decade we have seen the maturation of data management systems. Fifteen years previously, each such system was handmade. Only 12 years ago, commercial systems began to appear. Today such systems actually work and are being installed at the rate of ten a day.

Not only have data management systems become workable and commonplace in the last ten years, but the topic itself has become a popular if not respected research area. Charlie Pachman received the Turing award for his work with IDS and DBTG, the ACM has begun a journal on data management, and several universities have included the topic in their curriculum.

I point out this information because I believe that things will continue in this way. I believe that *by looking at current advanced systems one can safely predict the state of computing over the next ten years.*

By all accounts, the airlines have the most sophisticated data management system. It involves:

1. Multiple corporations
2. Diverse data management systems
3. Diverse terminal types
4. Diverse computer architectures
5. Diverse operating systems
6. Activity on six continents

In addition, the systems are highly available on a 24-hour basis and support highly respectable transaction rates. A typical node has duplexed processors, upward of 10^{10} bytes of disk (over 100 spindles of disk) and runs an average of

* This chapter is the text of an invited lecture at the Congresso Annuale of Associazione Italiana per il Calcolo Automatico, Bari, Italia presented in 1980 which appeared in the proceedings of the conference.

100 transactions per second. Large systems and peak loads double these numbers. The nodes are connected via a special network that carries over 30 messages per second among them.

Although each airline generally operates its own data management system, a common protocol allows them (and charted travel agents) to submit transactions from any system to any other system.

The airlines system is definitely special-purpose. Its techniques are not immediately applicable to other problems. On the other hand, I expect that the next decade will be devoted to making such systems so simple that they too can be installed at the rate of ten a day.

By contrast, present data management systems are generally constructed as centralized systems serving a network of terminals. Such systems are relatively easy to construct and to manage; however, both social and technologic forces are at work to change this architecture.

WHY DISTRIBUTED SYSTEMS ARE ATTRACTIVE

Sociological Forces Toward Distributed Systems

The users of data management systems are rarely centralized. More typically, users are geographically distributed and may be from different organizations within a parent company or from different companies within an industry. Organizations have become increasingly interested in having local control of their own data and data processing resources. Terms such as 'reflect organizational structure,' 'local autonomy,' and 'local accountability' are often used in this context.

Technological Forces Toward Distributed Systems

Historically, the high cost of main frames (millions of dollars) has precluded decentralized data management systems constructed from several geographically distributed mainframes. However, as the cost of computing declines, users are beginning to install several small interconnected systems rather than a single central complex. Another trend is to install front-end processors to a preexisting central complex. This approach results in 'division of labor' along organizational lines. It allows load shedding to be rationally accounted for (used only where productivity increases or cost reductions are visible to an accountable entity). Applications and data with either *functional* or *geographic* locality of reference allow decentralization. If the application has geographic locality, then distribution can also reduce communication costs and response times by putting the data and computing 'near' the users. For example, banks and credit validation have strong geographic locality of reference (most transactions are on local accounts). In addition, decentralization may have a positive effect on both availability and reliability. In a loosely coupled system, the failure of one system should not affect the operation of other systems. This localization of failures enhances availability. Conversely, by replicating data and programs, systems may act as backup for one another during periods of maintenance and failure. Finally, decentralization allows for modular growth of the system. When more storage or processing is needed, it may be justified and added in small units.

TECHNICAL PROBLEMS OF DISTRIBUTED SYSTEMS

So far I have sketched the rationale for distributed systems. Distributed data also pose some difficult technical problems. The main problem *unique* to a distributed system is the lack of global (centralized) knowledge. It is difficult (probably impossible) for one node to know everything about the rest of the network. Yet global knowledge seems to be required to answer questions such as, 'Where is file A?' or 'Is there a deadlock?' or 'What is the best way to answer the question . . .?' Most other problems of distributed data management are also present in a centralized data management system. It is simply a matter of degree. Messages in a distributed system travel more slowly, less reliably, and more expensively than in a centralized system. Whereas in a central system a data item is rarely more than a disk seek away (about 30 ms), in a distributed system it may be one or more satellite hops away (600-ms round trip per hop). Moreover, the communication system sometimes loses messages and always charges quite a lot to deliver one. This communications aspect associated with the lack of global knowledge adds an entirely new dimension to the problems of data placement and program execution (where to keep the data, where to run the program).

CONCEPTS AND TERMINOLOGY

Several concepts promise to be fundamental to the architecture of distributed (and centralized) data management systems:

1. Partitioned data
2. Replicated data
3. Location transparency
4. Replication transparency
5. Data currency
6. Transaction
7. Transaction routing
8. Remote procedure call
9. Network virtual data manager
10. Function shipping

I will try to interpret each of these terms.

A data management system may be viewed in terms of its four major components:

1. Data dictionary
2. Data base
3. Data communications
4. Transaction manager

The *data dictionary* contains a description of each system object. For example, it describes files, terminals, users, and transactions. It is the central repository for all information about such objects. It contains natural language (e.g. Italian) descriptions, as well as precompiled (source) and compiled (control block) descriptions. The data dictionary has two major subcomponents:

1. The *directory* maps symbolic names to network-unique names for objects.
2. The *catalog* contains descriptive information about system objects.

It is not yet clear whether location information should be kept in the directory or catalog or both. Ten years ago it was strongly felt that the data dictionary was separate from the data base. In fact the CODASYL task forces have separate languages for data definition and data manipulation. Current wisdom is that the data dictionary is simply metadata. Best viewed as part of the data base, it can be manipulated by the data manipulation commands or by transactions supplied with the system. This practice reduces system complexity and allows a more powerful dictionary facility. Several systems (notably INGRES, SDD-1, and System R) have implemented this approach.

The data base is organized into *files* of *records*. The data management system supports *actions* which insert, delete, and modify these records. In general, the data management component extends the base access mechanisms (e.g. VSAM) to support data base concepts.

The data communications system supports the notions of *message* and *session*. A session is a bidirectional communication path between an agent (task) or terminal and another agent (task) or terminal. Messages travel on sessions. The data communications component gives device-independence to the application (the equipment at the other end of the session can be any kind of computer or terminal) and provides message-editing (matting and decoding of messages). In general, the data communications component extends the network operating system (e.g. VTAM + NCP) to support data management.

The transaction management component is responsible for scheduling (system startup, transaction startup, and concurrency control), for system recovery (logging), and for authorization. The transaction management component allows collections of actions to be grouped to form atomic *transactions*. It ensures either that a transaction *commits* and its effects survive forever or that the transaction *aborts* and its affects are forgotten. The transaction manager insulates the application programmer from the problems of failures (via logging and recovery) and concurrency (locking). In addition, the transaction manager enforces restrictions on who may run each transaction type. In essence, the transaction manager extends the base operating system (e.g. MVS) to support transaction management concepts.

The entire system is viewed as a collection of *nodes* (computers and terminals) connected via a *communications network* (lines and carriers).

Against this broad setting it is now possible to define the terms listed at the beginning of this section.

PARTITIONED AND REPLICATED DATA

A file is usually stored entirely at one node of the network, but any file may be partitioned into *disjoint fragments*. The fragmentation criterion can be any function which, given a record, computes a fragment name. Typically it has the form:

⟨ selection expression ⟩ = ⟩ ⟨ fragment ⟩

where selection expression is defined by the data manipulation language. If the expression evaluates true, then the record is part of the fragment. For example:

AREA CODE = 415 = ⟩ SAN FRANCISCO
AREA CODE = 617 = ⟩ BOSTON
AREA CODE = 202 = ⟩ WASHINGTON

The file is said to be *partitioned* if its fragments are distributed among several nodes of the network but each fragment resides at exactly one node. Alternatively, the file is said to be *replicated* if some of its fragments are represented at several nodes of the network.

Data are partitioned in order to put them close to the sites that use them (e.g. accounts might be stored at their home branch). This practice reduces message traffic, message delay, and distributing work. In the case of the airlines system, data are fragmented by corporation. Most transactions submitted by American Airlines deal entirely with American Airlines' data and so run in only that node. Some transactions deal with other airlines and so are routed to other nodes. Less than 5 per cent of the airlines' transactions are nonlocal.

Data replication brings the data closer to the user. In addition, data replication may contribute to data availability. If there are several replicas of a file, then one may read any current copy of the file. For example, each airline can keep a schedule of the flights of the other airlines. This feature allows each airline to plan tickets even if the other airlines' computers are down. Such replication is very attractive for read-only data. The only cost for such replicas is the extra storage they occupy. On the other hand, each replica increases the cost of updating the file. If there are ten replicas of a file, one must update all ten whenever any one is updated. If any one replica is unavailable, it may be impossible to update the file. Several solutions have been proposed for this problem. Generally they require that a *majority* of the replicas be available. These algorithms are quite subtle and costly; to my knowledge, none have been implemented.

DATA CURRENCY

Another promising approach is to abandon the notion of replicas and postulate that the files are *time-stamped copies* (*versions*) which are immutable or are periodically refreshed from a master copy. Most organizations operate in this way already; notably, banks balance their books at night, invoice systems do monthly billing, and phone companies publish phone books once a year. The problem is that we do not at present understand how programs can deal with 'stale' data. One proposal would have transactions run with

CURRENCY = 'YES'

which means that the transaction wants the current version of the object or with

CURRENCY = 'NO'

which means that the transaction wants the closest available version and is willing to tolerate inconsistencies which may arise from reading noncurrent data. Non-current versions cannot be updated.

DATA BASE DESIGN AND QUERY COMPILATION

Determining how to fragment a file is a subtle decision and adds a new dimension to the data base design problem. At present good systems are available for doing data base design for centralized systems. They work by having the designer specify the system traffic to a modeling system which then evaluates the performance of various designs and proposes good ones. These models include network design (how to lay out the telephone lines to minimize delay and cost) and data placement on disk (what data organizations are appropriate). Once the system is installed, its traffic is measured and the process is iterated. It appears that existing tools can be generalized to distributed systems.

Query compilation is a related problem. Given a fixed design, what is the best way to perform a given transaction? This question is the counterpart of the question: What is a good design? An algorithm to answer one of these questions can be adapted to answer the other.

LOCATION AND REPLICATION TRANSPARENCY

Current data management systems insulate application programs and users from the *organization* of data. The data may be hashed, indexed, or accessed via pointers. Indeed, the organization of the data may change without affecting the logic of application programs (although it may change the cost of running the program). This feature is known as *data independence.*

If data are distributed in the network, many programs will not want to be aware of the exact location of the data. Data independence requires that the application program be able to view a partitioned file as a single entity. The system is responsible for locating and addressing the fragments of such a file. Otherwise, application programs will have to be rewritten each time a file is repartitioned. The ability of a program to be independent of the location of a file (local or remote) and of its fragmentation is called *location transparency.*

If a file is replicated, the logic to read and write the replicas of the file may be quite subtle. One wants to read the closest currently available replica. One wants to write all current replicas. Again, data independence (and integrity constraints) imply that the system is responsible for locating and manipulating replicas. The program should continue to work if replicas are added to or subtracted from the system. The application program should have the impression that only single copy of the file exists. The ability of a program to be insensitive to data replication is called *replica transparency.*

A system which provides both replica and location transparency prevents application programmers from being aware that the system is in fact distributed. Certain companies may not want to pay the cost of this feature and may want to explicitly address fragments for their applications, but I suspect that most will be perfectly happy to take advantage of these features.

At present several systems provide location transparency (CICS/ISC, INGRES, and SDD/1(. SDD-1 also provides replication transparency).

TRANSACTIONS

A data management system provides primitive objects (records and messages) and primitive actions which manipulate these objects (read and write record, send and receive message). A particular user of this application (e.g. an airline) maps such abstractions as flights, tickets, and customers into the system by representing them as records. Application procedures are mapped into programs which invoke a set of primitive actions; e.g. ordering a ticket might update flight information, create a customer ticket record, and send several messages.

The common business term for such an operation is *transaction.* A key property of transactions is that either all the actions of a transaction occur or the transaction is nullified (either I get the ticket and you get the money or the deal is off). It is also the case that transactions are usually independent of one another. I am surprised that many data management systems do not have a clear or general notion of transaction. Some systems insist that a single data base action is a transaction. Others insist that the receipt or transmission of a message implicitly delimits a transaction. Needless to say, these assumptions become quite a liability when one tries to generalize a system to a distributed environment.

A simple and apparently general model postulates that a program may issue a

BEGIN TRANSACTION

action which causes all subsequent actions issued by this program to be considered part of the transaction. The program may then read and write data at will.

At any point the program may issue the action:

ABORT TRANSACTION

which will cancel the effects of the transaction (will 'undo' all its updates and cancel pending messages). Alternatively, the program can issue the action:

COMMIT TRANSACTION

which completes the transaction and makes its results public. Prior to commit, the outputs of a transaction are not made public to other transactions because these outputs may be revoked by an abort or by subsequent updates.

TRANSACTION ROUTING

The execution of a transaction is effected by the arrival of a message from a terminal or by an event (e.g. clock tick or threshold). If the transaction is started by a terminal, the terminal and input message become parameters to the transaction. The transaction may then converse with the terminal and access the data base and finally commit the final output message to the terminal and any updates to the data base. This approach is called *direct transaction processing* because the terminal is connected directly to the transaction.

Another approach is to put arriving input messages and pending output messages into message queues. Such queues must be recoverable so that messages are not lost. Queued messages are processed *asynchronously*; i.e. the transaction is run at some later time and its response is routed via a queue to the originating terminal.

Queued transaction processing does not lend itself to conversational transactions (a queued transaction has one input and, optionally, one output message, and the terminal may not be available when the transaction runs). However, *queued transaction processing does lend itself very nicely to processing simple transactions in a distributed system.* Suppose that each transaction can execute entirely at a single node; i.e. all the data needed by a transaction are at one node, called the *destination node.* Then running the transaction is best done by routing the input message to the destination node, running the transaction, and then routing the response to the originating terminal. In a queued system, an arriving message is always put into queue space. However, if the transaction is nonlocal, the message is routed to the destination node. When the destination node acknowledges receipt of the message, the message is dropped from the queue space of the originating node. This technique is called *transaction routing.*

The fact that queued processing is asynchronous means that one does not need to reserve a session between the destination node (transaction) and the terminal so that they can converse. Rather, the terminal is free to do other work and will be informed when the asynchronous transaction is complete. To give a specific example, local transactions are processed directly by the airlines systems, but transactions which must be forwarded to another airline are treated as queued transactions.

This situation exposes another advantage of queued processing: in a transaction routing system, the interface between two nodes is simply a collection of message formats. The nodes may have completely different data management systems, machine architectures, and terminal types. However, as long as they have a common format for transaction input and output messages, they are completely compatible. In particular, no node needs to understand how to support the terminals connected to a second node. Each node can process the transactions in any way it chooses consistent with the semantics of the messages.

Transaction routing is the cornerstone of the airlines system and most commercial data management systems now support it. Although transaction routing is very limited (transactions can only do work at one node), it is also quite popular, being ideal for communication among systems belonging to separate organizations—they need only agree on common message format and settle accounting and authorization problems. Transaction routing is an easy way to connect inhomogeneous data management systems.

DISTRIBUTED TRANSACTIONS

In a centralized system it is possible to confuse the notions of process (task), program, and transaction. However, in a distributed system a transaction may involve several nodes and hence several programs and tasks. For this reason one must distinguish three aspects:

1. *Transaction* is a unit of recovery which transforms the system from one consistent state to another.
2. *Agent* is the representative of a transaction at a node. An agent subsumes a process, a program, and all bookkeeping necessary to integrate the agent into the global transaction.
3. *Program* is the algorithm followed by an agent at a particular node.

The agents of a particular transaction are collectively called its *cohorts*. Complex algorithms are required to ensure that all cohorts of a transaction commit or abort together. Also, resource management issues such as locking and deadlock detection must be aware that cohorts are related parts of one transaction and must be treated as a unit in making scheduling decisions. No system has confronted all these issues, but the SDD-1 system, distributed INGRES, and the Inter-Systems Communications Feature of CICS have each recognized the need for agents and each has taken an interesting approach on some of these issues.

REMOTE PROCEDURE CALLS

From the point of view of the application programmer, the simplest way to program a system which accesses distributed objects is to take advantage of location transparency and simply write the program as though all data were centralized in a single node. It is then the responsibility of the system to execute this program.

Remote procedure calls are an elegant way to execute such a program. As stated before, the system provides actions on objects. A typical action invocation has the form:

$$\text{ACTION, OBJECT, } P_1, P_2, \ldots, P_n$$

where $p_1, p_2, \ldots, p_n$ are parameters to the action. If the object is local, the action is performed locally. If the action is not local, the system *packs* the parameter list and *ships* it to a cohort at the node holding the object (this action may require creating such a cohort). This cohort *unpacks* the call, *invokes* it, *invokes* the action on the object, *packs* the response to the action, and then *ships* the response to the requesting cohort. The requesting cohort *unpacks* the response and returns it to the invoking program as though it were the response to a local action. This pack, ship, unpack, invoke, pack, ship, unpack process is called a *remote procedure call.* It allows nonlocal actions to masquerade as local actions. It is quite general and may be applied recursively.

NETWORK VIRTUAL DATA MANAGEMENT SYSTEM

The notion of remote procedure calls requires that each action have an architected linear syntax (a collection of message formats and a specification of their semantics). Perhaps the most sophisticated version of this syntax is the IBM system network architecture protocols for type 6 sessions, which architects actions on queues (e.g. get-put, . . .), DL/1 data bases (e.g. get unique within parent, replace), and other models as well as the notion of transaction and the two-phase commit protocol. Any system willing to understand this linear syntax can talk to any other system. At present only CICS understands this syntax, but many systems are expected to write an adaptor for it since it would then allow them to connect to many other systems.

Such a protocol is similar to the network virtual terminal protocols being fostered by various standards groups. Any system supporting such a protocol can talk to any terminal which can understand the protocol. Thus, I have chosen the term *network virtual data management system.*

Standardizing such an interface is likely to create an intense debate reminiscent of the data model debates of the sixties. Aside from the religious issues of graphs versus relations versus trees, some substantive issues have appeared in this debate. The architecture must define both the data model and the semantics of the operators on the data.

For some applications it seems to be much better to ship fairly complex operations to a destination node for execution rather than doing all that work over a slow communication line. Such an approach requires a fairly high-level data exchange language which allows the expression of complex operations. SQL or an SQL derivative may be a solution to this problem. For example, a record at a time interface to update an account requires the sequence:

```
OPEN ACCOUNTS FILE:
FETCH ACCOUNT (325A42);
ACCOUNT.BALANCE <= ACCOUNT.BALANCE + 100;
REPLACE ACCOUNT (325A42):
```

which involves six messages. If the destination node supported SCL, one might execute the single command:

```
SET ACCOUNT.BALANCE <= ACCOUNT.BALANCE + 100
WHERE ACCOUNT.NUMBER = 325A42;
```

which involves two messages (a request and an acknowledge). This approach has the virtue of reducing communications and of offloading work.

The XNDM group as well as the System R group are pursuing this approach.

FUNCTION SHIPPING

In talking to users of data management systems, I am impressed that they have a clear notion of their application. They feel quite comfortable introducing another level of abstraction into the system and programming at that level rather than at the action level. I would call this higher level of abstraction *functions on entities*, rather than actions on objects.

A particular industry (e.g. funds transfer) could architect a set of functions and entities appropriate to that application. Cohorts would be expected to execute functions rather than actions. It is presumed that this approach would be the optimal mix between transaction routing (in which function is a transaction) and a high-level data manipulation language (in which function is an action).

A specific example proposed by Bob Good of the Bank of America is a system for manipulating bank accounts. The entities are accounts, tellers, branches, and customers. Functions include operations such as:

DEBIT ACCOUNT *x* BY *y* DOLLARS.

Such a system has the virtues of:

1. Easy-to-write applications
2. Minimal communications

It may well be that most production systems are constructed based on function shipping. Observe that a function is a collection of actions; thus, a need still exists for the facilities described earlier. The functions are simply an application specific data model.

SUMMARY

Unfortunately, the 'Buzzwords' used in this chapter seem to be necessary to talk about the subject of distributed systems. Several experimental and commercial systems offer the features described here although no single system offers them all.

It seems clear that transaction routing will be the way that systems are connected together in the next few years. Also, for reasons of independence, authorization, and accounting, transaction routing is likely to be the way that independent organizations (e.g. the airlines) share data. Such systems are already in common use.

Function shipping may be adopted within certain industries as appropriate functions and entities are defined. However, the emergence of such protocols will require careful analysis and is more likely to come from computer users than from computer manufacturers.

At least one network virtual data management system already exists and other protocols are likely to appear in the next few years. This setup will allow any node to get data from any other cooperating node. Such protocols will no doubt be adopted by most data management systems.

Location and replica transparency as well as distributed transaction management are available from several systems (although none provides all three features). These mechanisms will be fundamental to function shipping and to network virtual data managers.

Hence, at the level of discussion of this chapter, distributed data management is a solved problem. It is now 'simply a matter of programming.' Needless to say, programmers have their work cut out for them.

BIBLIOGRAPHY

Alsberg, P. A., and Day, J. D.: *A Principle for Resilient Sharing of Distributed Resources.* Center for Advanced Computation Report, May 1976. *Comment.* Points out the availability possible through careful use of redundancy.

Bernstein, P. A., Shipman, D. W., Rothnie, J. B., and Goodman, N.: *The Concurrency Control Mechanism of SDD-1: A System for Distributed Database (The General Case).* Computer Corporation of America, Technical Report CCA-77-09, December 1977, 172 pp. *Comment.* SDD-1 gives replica and location transparency. It has attacked the problems of a distributed data dictionary, tolerance of missing replicas, and query evaluation in a distributed system. Papers on SDD-1 tend to be rather long. A seven-paper set is about to appear in the *ACM Transactions on Database Systems.* Preprints are available from CCA.

Blasgen, M. W., *et al.*: *System R: An Architectural Update.* IBM San Jose Research Report RJ 2571, June 1979, 38 pp. Submitted to *IBM Systems Journal. Comment.* System R is not a distributed system, but I have included it here because it is interesting.

Chamberlin, D. D., *et al.*: SEQUEL2: a unified approach to data definition, manipulation, and control. *IBM J. of R&D*, **11**, No. 6, 560–575, November 1976. *Comment.* As mentioned in the text, a high-level data manipulation language like SQL may be appropriate for a network interface.

CICS-Inter Systems Communication: *CICS/VS System/Application Design Guide*, Chap. 13, Version 1, Release 4, pp. 379–412. IBM Form Number SC33-0068-1, June 1978. *CICS/VS Introduction to Program Logic*, Chap. 1.6, Version 1. *Comment.*

Describes CICS, which provides transaction routing and location transparency via remote procedure calls.

Epstein, R. S., *et al.*: Distributed query processing in a relational database system. *Proc. 1978 ACM-SIGMOD Conf. on the Management of Data*, May 1978. *Comment.* Something very much like this feature has been implemented on INGRES. It gives location and replica transparency. At present the implementation supports only reading data (no updates).

Gray, J. N.: Notes on data base operating systems. In *Operating Systems: an Advanced Course* (Eds. R. Bayer, R. M. Graham, and G. Seegmuller), pp. 393–481, Springer Verlag, New York, March 1978. *Comment.* A tutorial on transaction management in centralized and distributed systems.

Hoffman, G.: *SNA Architecture Reference Summary*, pp. 218–248. IBM Palo Alto Systems Center Technical Bulletin, DAPS Code C895, Form number G320-6024, December 1978. *Comment.* Describes IBM's System Network Architecture (in bit terms). In particular, it describes the message model (queue model) and data model (DL/1) which CICS uses in doing its remote procedure calls. Also architects the notion of transaction and two-phase commit.

IMS Multiple Systems Coupling: *IMS/VS Version 1.4 System/Application Design Guide*, Chap. 5, pp. 5.1–5.18. IBM Form Number: SH20-9025-5, July 1977. *Comment.* Describes IMS transaction routing.

Kimbleton, S. R., Wang, P., and Fong, E. H.: XNDM: an experimental network data manager. *Proc. of the Fourth Berkeley Conf. on Distributed Data Management and Computer Networks*. Lawrence Berkeley Laboratory, August 1979. *Comment.* A network virtual data manager based on SQL being implemented by the National Bureau of Standards (United States). It is to map to an inhomogeneous collection of data management systems.

Lamport, L.: The implementation of reliable distributed multiprocess systems. *Computer Networks*, **2**, No. 2, 95–114, June 1978. *Comment.* A difficult and little noticed paper which explains how to tolerate failures in a redundant system.

Lampson, E. W., and Sturgis, H. E.: *Crash Recovery in a Distributed System.* Unpublished Xerox Research Report, Palo Alto, 1976, 34 pp. *Comment.* An underground classic which proposes an algorithm to coordinate atomic commit.

Lindsay, B. G., *et al.*: *Notes on Distributed Database Systems*. IBM San Jose Research report RJ 2571, June 1979, 57 pp. *Comment.* A tutorial on authorization, query evaluation, updating replicas, and transaction management in distributed systems.

Manning, E., and Peebles, R. W.: A homogeneous network for data sharing and communications. *Computer Networks*, June 1977. 211–224, **1**, No. 2. *Comment.* Describes a system which provides processes and remote procedure calls. It has been used in several applications.

Marill, T., and Stern, D. H.: The datacomputer: a network utility. *Proc. of AFIPS National Computer Conf.* Vol. 44. AFIPS Press, 1975. *Comment.* The database machine which supports SDD-1.

Obermarck, R. L.: *Distributed Database* IPM Palo Alto Systems Center Report DAPS Code 0932, Form Number G320-6019, September 1978, 81 pp. *Comment.* A pragmatic paper which explores the limitations of transaction routing, sketches an architecture for a distributed system, and gives much good advice.

Rosenkrantz, D. J., Sterns, R. E., and Lewis R. E.: System level concurrency control for distributed database systems. *ACM Trans. on Database Systems*, **3**, No. 2, 178–198, June 1978. *Comment.* This paper describes an effective model and some elegant proofs. I am told that it is the theoretical underpinning of an interesting (but unpublished) system constructed by General Electric Research called MADMAN. Do not follow this paper's advice on deadlock; deadlock detection is cheap and guessing wrong is expensive.

Stonebraker, M., Wong, E., Kreps, P., and Held, G.: The design and implementation of INGRES. *Trans. on Database Systems*, **2**, No. 3, 189–222, September 1976. *Comment.* Another system which is not distributed but is interesting.

Stonebraker, M., and Neuhold, E.: A distributed database version of INGRES. *Proc. Second Berkeley Workshop on Distributed Data and Computer Networks*, May 1976, pp. 19–36. *Comment.* The first proposal for distributed INGRES (see Epstein *et al.*).

Stonebraker, M. M.: *Concurrency Control and Consistency of Multiple Copies of Data in Distributed INGRES*, Memo. No. UCB/ERL M78/24, May 1978, Third Berkeley Workshop on Distributed Data and Computer Networks, August 1978. *Comment.* A companion to the Epstein paper which discusses transaction management issues.

Stonebraker, M. M.: *MUFFIN: A distributed Database Machine.* Memo No. UCB/ERL M79/28 May 1979, 34 pp. *Comment.* This paper explains why data base machines are a bad idea. Then it goes on to propose an architecture for a data base machine! It makes interesting reading. The first part of the paper is 'right on.'

Thomas, R. H.: *A majority Consensus Approach to Concurrency Control for Multiple Copy Data Bases.* BBN Technical report, Nov. 1977, 58 pp. To appear in TODS. *Comment.* Presents an algorithm which will tolerate the failure of a minority of the nodes of a network.

Advances in Distributed Processing Management, Volume 2
Edited by P. S. Fisher, J. Slonim, and E. A. Unger

Chapter 2

DATA MODELS AND THE INFORMATION SYSTEM ENVIRONMENT

Jacob Slonim

GEAC Computers International, Inc., Markham, Ontario

Fred Maryanski

Digital Equipment Corporation, Corporate Research Group, Lancaster, Maryland

Data, the building blocks of information, are fundamental to the existence of any organization. The generation, manipulation, and consumption of data have evolved over a period of years into a specialized and identifiable element within organizations. In order to meet the demands of increasingly complex environments, relationships, and narrowing response requirements, the development and utilization of data base management systems have begun in earnest. Part of this effort has been concerned with the development of models to express logical relationships and to accommodate the user-views required within the surrounding organization. The purpose of this chapter is to explore the various models. Each model attempts to express important and necessary information, yet all are considerably different. Some closely resemble implementations; others are useful for their expressive capabilities. It is clear that, in this complex area, a model is an important tool.

Along with models comes a consideration of the environment. One can approach the implementation of information resources in a variety of ways. The standard, single-system approach could be modified to permit the functionalization of responsibilities and activities. The environments considered in this chapter will include the single machine environment, front ends, back ends, and functional organizations.

DATA MODELS[1,2]

Organizational data are derived from a data model and used to structure informational data according to the model (see Figure 2-1). Data models are of two basic categories: *structured* and *unstructured*. Each of these categories contains a number of specific models.

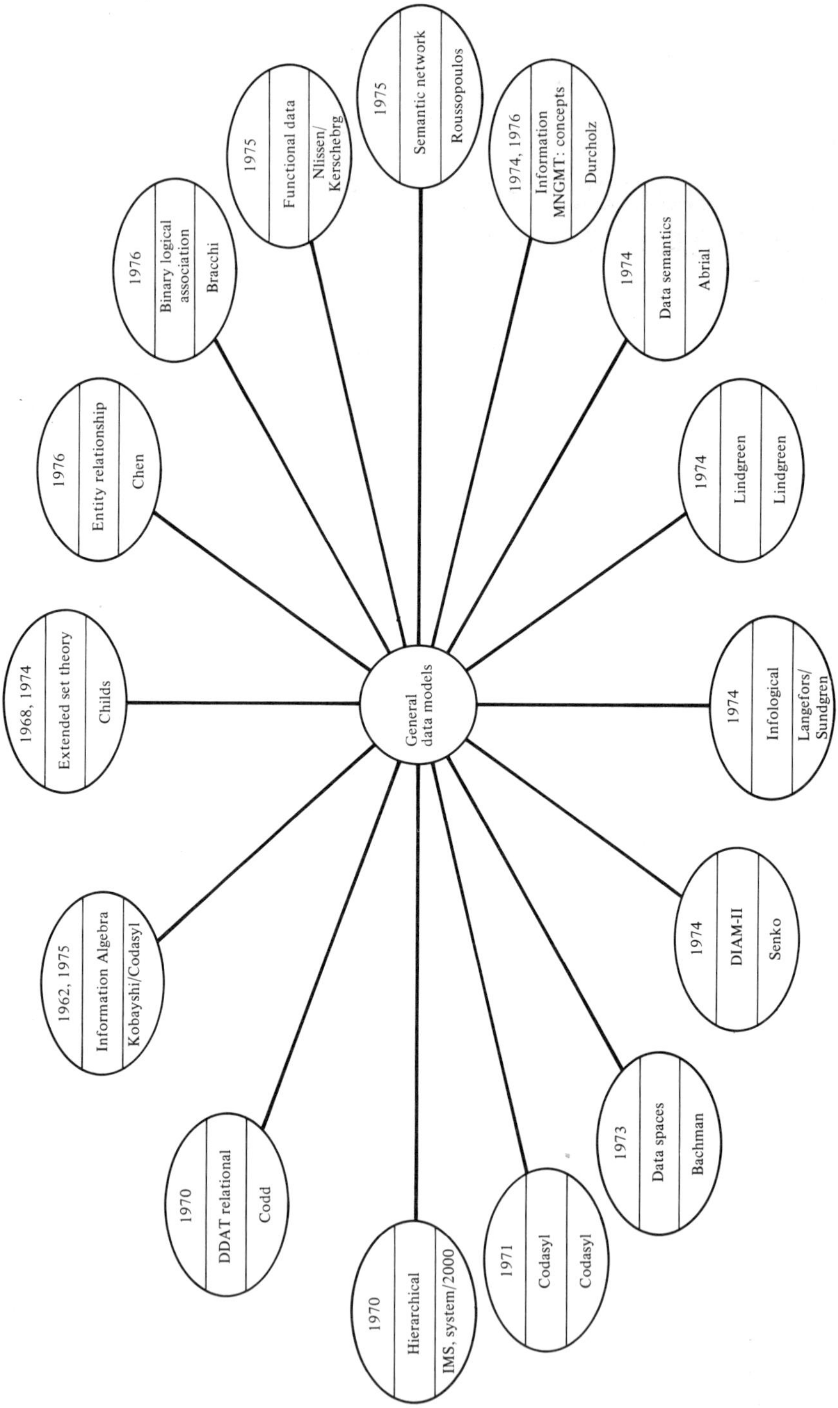

Figure 2-1. Contemporary data models.

MODELS BASED ON GRAPH THEORY

Structured models are based on *graph theory*, while unstructured models are based on *set theory*. It is possible to map a structured model into an unstructured model; in order to do so, it is necessary to introduce one unstructured data model for each *field* of the record type (a field is the smallest data unit in a record) and to identify each of the terms of the original structured model. *Edges* are binary relations within models of the structured class. (A binary relation between any set A and another set B can be viewed either as a mapping of elements of A to elements of B or as a subset of ordered pairs of the Cartesian product A and B.) Each class can be seen as a set. Movement from one class of data model to the other is accomplished by establishing an identity between each edge in the structured model and a role name in the unstructured model.

Four of the common structured data models have functional edges: the hierarchical, functional, and entity-relationship models, and the model devised by the data base task group of CODASYL (the DBTG model). A *directed edge* is a nonfunctional edge; all four of the data models cited contain such directed edges. Since a directed edge cannot be expressed as a binary relation, it cannot be automatically mapped into an unstructured data model. Its place in the unstructured model must be designated by an arrow. Models embodying directed edges are classified in Table 2-1.

MODELS BASED ON SET THEORY

Although a tuple can be used to represent a data relationship in graph-class models, in set-class models the tuple is the *principal vehicle* for the representation of relationships. Two parameters are used in subdividing data models of the set class: they are grouped according to tuple size and according to set nesting. Each model has either a nested or a flat structure. (A 'nested tuple' contains one or more elements which can also be sets.)

The three data models with a nested structure are:

1. The information management concept[3]
2. The extended set theory model[4]
3. The hierarchical relational model[5]

When a data model has a flat structure, the elements of its tuples are 'simple' objects. Flat models are further divided according to the size of the tuples they use.

The next three models discussed use triplets to define basic data. The data space model[6] and Lindgreen's model[7] are similar. The components of their respective triplets are ⟨ ENTITY, ATTRIBUTE, MEASURE ⟩ and ⟨ ENTITY, PROPERTY, VALUE ⟩, respectively. DIAM-I[8] is similar to these two. These three models (presented in Table 2-2) can be stored according to their treatment of the three coordinates where entity sets (ES) are mapped to the value set (VS), the

TABLE 2-1
Graph theoretic models

	Model	Class	Class element	Edge	Functionality
Structured class element	DBTG	Record type	Record	Set type	Member → owner (against arrow)
	Hierarchical	Segment type	Segment	Parent/child relationship	Child → parent (against arrow)
	General network	Record type	Record	Link	None
	Information algebra	Area	Point	Arc	None
Unstructured class element	DIAM-II	Identifier	ID value	Association pair	None
	Binary logical associations	Set of concepts	Concept	Logical association	None
	Abrial's	Category	Object	Relation	None
	Functional	Set	Value, entity, abstract entity	Function	Domain → range (with arrow)
Multiple class type	Entity relationship	Value set	Value	Attribute	Attribute: ES → VS
		Entity set	Entity		Attribute: RS → VS
		Relationship set	Relationship	Role	Role: RS → ES
	Semantic network	Value node	Value		
		Concept node	Entity	Characteristic	CH: Char. class → concept
		Event node	Event	Role	CH: Char. class → event
		Characteristic node	Property	Characteristic	V: Char. class → value

TABLE 2-2
Set theory models

Model	Tuple size	Nesting
Relational	Arbitrary	Flat
Infological	Arbitrary	Flat
Information algebra	Arbitrary	Flat
IMC	Arbitrary	Nested
Extended set theory	Arbitrary	Nested
Hierarchical relations	Arbitrary	Nested
DIAM-I	Triplet	Flat
Data space	Triplet	Flat
Lindgreen's	Triplet	Flat

attribute of relationship set (RS) maps to value set, and the attribute of role relationship set maps to entity set. The data space model is the most homogeneous—the ENTITY, ATTRIBUTE, and MEASURE coordinates are treated on an equal basis. In Lindgreen's model, ENTITY and PROPERTY are treated equally, while VALUE is subordinate. A homogeneous information set may be factored as a collection of isonymous information sets or as a collection of isotypic information sets. In DIAM-I, ENTITY has precedence. No primitive notion corresponds to an isotypic information set.

MATHEMATICAL STRUCTURES

Instead of classifying data models according to their structures in graph or set theory, it is possible to relate entities, data items, values, etc., within each model. The contents of a data model can be related in three ways.

Through Binary Relations

Entities, data items, and values are related in pairs only. The main distinction between the graph-subclass and the set-subclass of the resulting binary group is that the set models maintain asymmetric concepts of 'being described' and 'describing,' while the graph models treat these two related concepts as equally important. Another characteristic to be noted in binary relations is the presence or absence of directed edges.

Through *N*-ary Relations

The relational model,[9,10] CODASYL's information algebra model,[11] and the infological model[12] can be so related. Things (i.e. entities, data items, values, etc.) are related through various forms of the tuple. In the information algebra and relational models, *data items* are related by tuples. The infological model relates *objects* by tuples (Table 2-3).

TABLE 2-3
Mathematical structure binary and/or +*N*-ary

Binary	*N*-ary	Binary + *N*-ary
Data space	Relational	DBTG
Lindgreen's	Information algebra (CODASYL)	Information algebra (Kobashi)
DIAM-I	Infological	General network
DIAM-II		Semantic network
Binary logical association		Hierarchical
		Hierarchical relations
Abrial's		Information management concepts
Functional		Extended set theory

Through a Combination of Binary and *N*-ary Relations

As in the binary group, subclasses of set class and graph class models are grouped together (see Figure 2-2). At the top of the binary/*N*-ary list are the general network,[13] semantic network,[14] DBTG,[15] and information algebra[11] models. The *N*-ary relationships are represented by event classes, record types, and areas. The binary relationships are the areas, links, and structures. Between any two record types (areas), any number of links (structures) may be defined. In the middle of the list is the hierarchical model.[16] This model has certain qualities mentioned in relation to other subcategories: it is similar to the extended set theory and information management concept models in that there can be one binary relationship at most between two segments or relations. On the other hand, the existence of the superior segment is not predicated upon the existence of its subordinate segments.

At the bottom of this list are the IMC[3] and extended set theory models. The single binary relationship is set membership. Set membership defines the nature of the enclosing set as the identity of the enclosing set, depending on its members. Only one membership relation can exist between any two sets.

INFORMATION SYSTEM ENVIRONMENTS

There are five basic types of information system environments. Four of these, the *front-end host*, *single machine*, *back-end host*, and *functional* receive separate treatment in this section. The other, the *bifunctional machine*, is defined in terms of the others. It should be noted at the outset that the name 'front-end host' does *not* imply a single front-end and a single host (and so on for the other combinations). Any number of front-ends can be interfaced with any number of hosts, depending on system requirements.

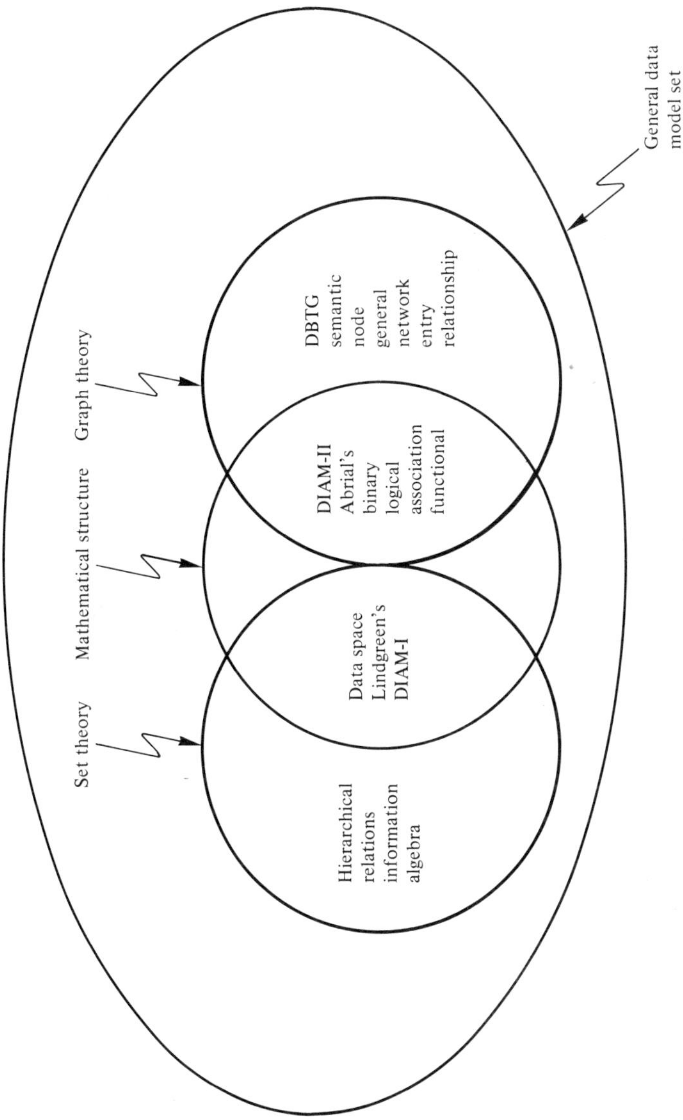

Figure 2-2. Classes of data model.

Single Machine

A knowledge of the operation of a single-machine environment (Figure 2-3) makes it easier to understand the enhancements required to distribute an information system. Figure 2-4 illustrates the flow of data through the system; it can, however, be used to define the position of the information system in relation to application programs and operating system functions.

Information can stand in three positions relative to these functional levels, each of which has advantages and disadvantages:

1. The information system can be an integrated part of the application

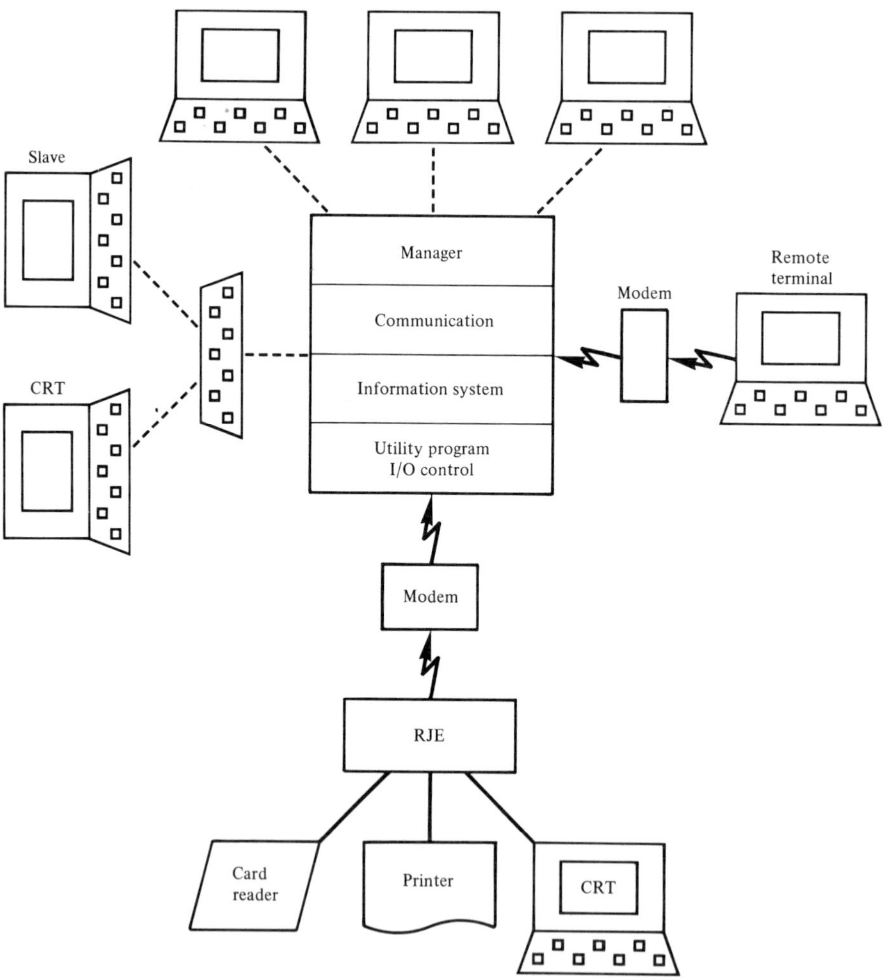

Figure 2-3. Single-machine environment.

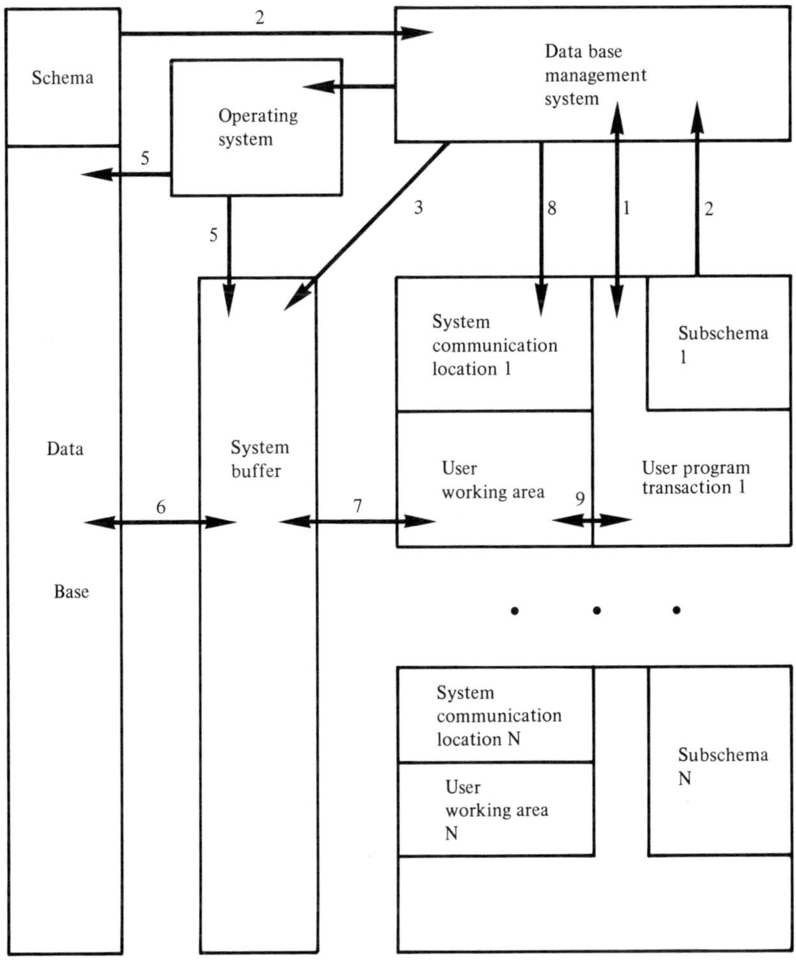

Figure 2-4. Conceptual data flow in data base management system.

programs. In a time-sharing environment, this arrangement can be useful, especially when the application to which the information system is linked is an *asynchronous* process. In this position, the system must employ a multiprogramming operating system to support the shared segment–code feature. If this requirement is satisfied, a number of applications can run simultaneously. Each application is, in effect, linked to its own information system, but only one information system is physically present. Note that in such cases the information system *must be reentrant*.

The linking of the information system to the application programs causes some distinct problems for concurrent processing. Because the *virtual* information systems are not aware of each other's existence, they cannot take the necessary precautions for concurrent processing, except through the facilities offered by the operating system. The result is that only one application can have access to the files at a time.

2. The information system can be an *independent job* under the operating system. This arrangement solves the concurrency problems of the first example. Indeed, it solves all such problems. Unfortunately, the arrangement offers no efficient way of transferring control through the operating system. Time sharing demands extra controls, which must be maintained at three levels: first, the operating system controls the programs running under it; second, the information system controls the application program running under it; and third, the application program is controlled by asynchronous processing techniques from the operating system. This arrangement causes high system overhead because it imposes controls which operate more or less independently at three levels.
3. The information system can be an *integrated part of the operating system*. This arrangement offers a solution to all the previous problems. In this case, the operating system assumes responsibility for all problems of concurrency, including resource allocation and input/output. A difficulty is that the operating system must control very small units of data which may be structured according to various complex data models. Moreover, a generalized operating system forces overhead upon the information system unrelated to its own functions. However, new developments in the areas of firmware and microprocessing are making this arrangement increasingly attractive in terms of both cost and efficiency.

Figure 2-4 represents the memory layout, data flow, and sequence of actions of a typical information system. This sequence, corresponding to the numbers in the figure, is explained below:

Step 1. The data base command is encountered in the application program and issues a call to the information system.

Step 2. The DBMS analyzes the call and verifies the request against the object versions of the schema and subschema, which contain a description of the data base storage—the data structure (schema) and the ways in which users see the data (subschema).

Step 3. The contents of the system buffer (the loading and unloading zone between the DBMS and the operating system) are checked by the DBMS.

Step 4. If necessary, the DBMS requests the operating system to perform a physical I/O transfer.

Step 5. Data are transferred between secondary storage and the system buffers by the operating system.

Step 6. The operating system initiates and controls the I/O operation in Step 5.

Step 7. The DBMS transfers the data between the system buffer and the user working area (the loading and unloading zone between the DBMS and the application) as required by the application for user query.

Step 8. The DBMS provides information on the status of the now-completed operation to the system communication location (1).

Step 9. The data in the user working areas can be processed by the application program.

Front-end Host

A front-end machine[17,18] is a small digital processor of limited capabilities programmed to replace the hard-wired input functions of a central computing system (a host). The front-end processor (see Figure 2-5) permits the host com-

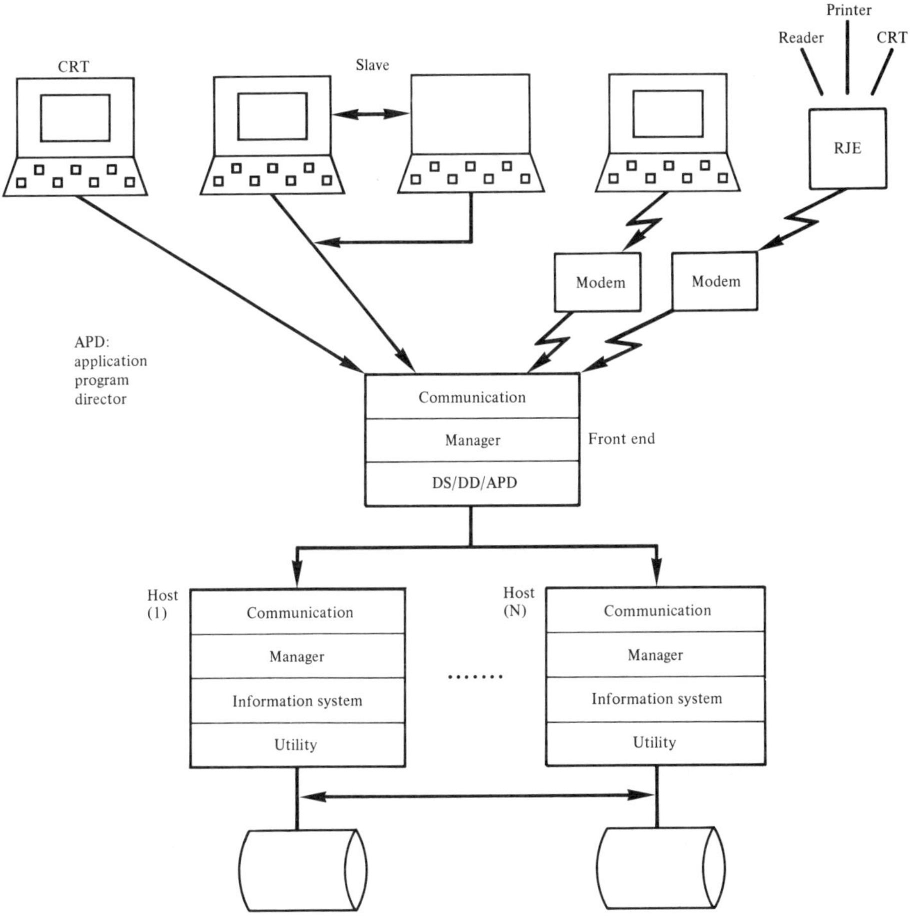

Figure 2-5. Front-end multiple-host environment.

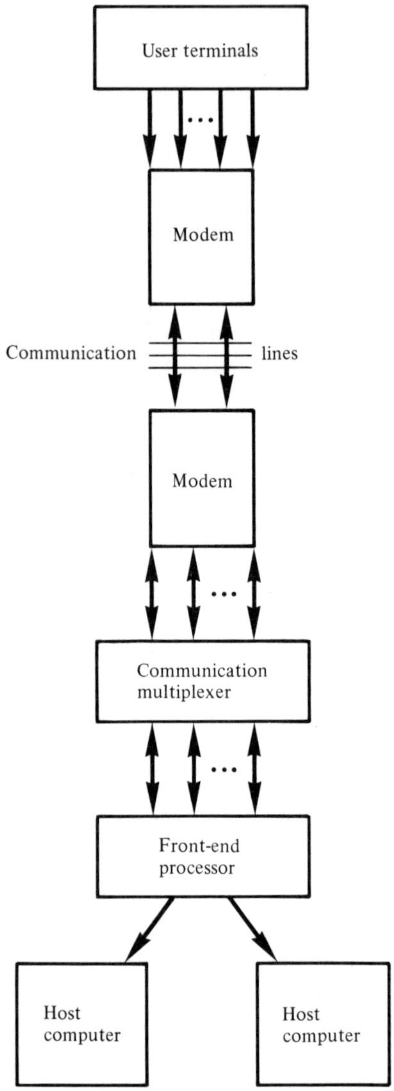

Figure 2-6. A front-end message switcher.

puter to perform its primary function with little regard for the slower I/O activities of a large-scale multiprogrammed computing system.

In addition to receiving and transmitting all data passing through the host, the front-end processor supports a wide variety of functions which include the following:

1. *Data and/or format conversion.* The conversion of incoming data codes and formats to those of the host system.

2. *Polling.* The determination by a front-end processor of a terminal's readiness to send or receive data.
3. *Assembly of characters and messages.* The assembly and disassembly of all data, input at various speeds and in synchronous or asynchronous formats, to ensure that the host system receives only complete messages.
4. *Error control and editing.* The detection and possible correction of transmission errors, as well as corrections initiated at the terminals, prior to the reception of messages by the host system.
5. *Fail-safe functions.* The ability of the front-end processor to keep part of the system (such as the terminals) operating when a major element of the system has failed.
6. *Queuing.* The placing of incoming messages in order of transmission for processing by the host system or, in some cases, the queuing of messages on auxiliary storage devices (spooling).
7. *Message system.* A function of a front-end processor which allows it to service more than one host system, i.e. a front-end message switcher (Figure 2-6).

The front-end processor can be a powerful and economical means of relieving a central processor of its time-consuming overhead activities by placing these activities under the control of an independent unit.

Back-end Host

Important early work on back-end processors (Figure 2-7) was carried out at Bell Laboratories.[19] A prototype (XDMS) was constructed using Univac 1108 as a host and a digital scientific META 4 as the back end. As a result of this investigation, Canaday[19] concluded that not only is back-end data base management feasible, but it can also be expected to make a substantial improvement in the cost performance of information systems, even if an off-the-shelf minicomputer is used as the back-end. These results were corroborated by Heacox[20] in a similar test vehicle. He found that the simplicity of the system software in the dedicated back-end was a decisive factor in its economy.

The U.S. Bureau of Census has been designing a back-end host system in which multiple Univac mainframes share a very large data bank (in excess of 900 billion characters).[21] In this system several back-end minicomputers will operate in parallel, each computer managing its own disk resources.

Anderson[22] discusses the technical objectives of back-end processors and incidentally examines the hardware and software requirements for a back-end host configuration. Maryanski[23] and Rosenthal[24] provide much more detail about desirable features in such processors, stressing the importance of a large address space, multiple paths to memory, and multiprocessing capabilities. It has also been suggested that a back-end processor requires a larger instruction set and interrupt mechanisms than are offered on most minicomputers.[24]

Throughout the evolution of computer systems, a primary tenet has been that

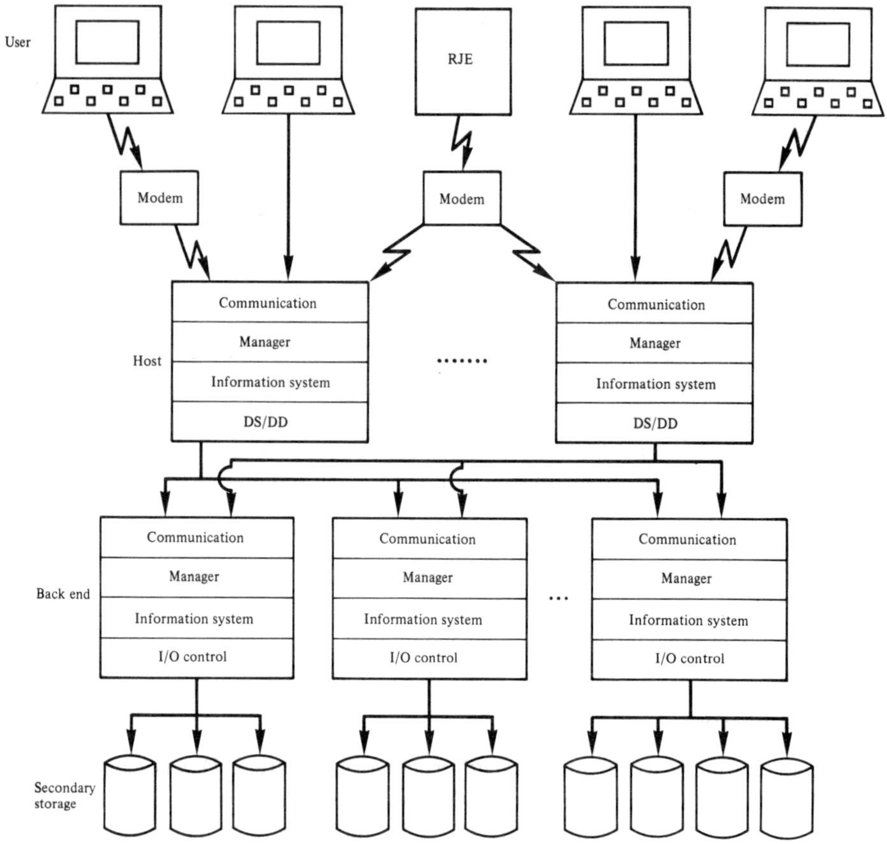

Figure 2-7. Multiple-host/back-end environment.

system resources should be used as continuously and fully as possible. With the advent of data base management systems, the amount of manipulation and management by computer systems has increased dramatically. For the user, a typical DBMS makes such extensive data manipulation relatively simple. However, a single command from a user may result in several I/O operations. Each I/O operation must be initiated by the host CPU. In addition, the CPU may have to perform computations or decision operations between I/O operations. In a multiprogrammed environment, such conditions require the seizing and releasing of the CPU several times in succession to carry out a single user command. The probable result is excessive overhead due to task switching.

In a back-end host configuration, a minicomputer dedicated to data base management functions is incorporated into the system. When a data base command from a user is encountered by the host CPU executing an application program, a message is transmitted (through the message system) to the back-end machine, instructing it to perform the necessary data base functions. The back-end machine carries out all such functions, including both I/O and intervening computations. The results of the user's command in terms of data and/or status information are then transmitted to the CPU in the host.

Since the task of managing the data base has been delegated by the application CPU to the back-end processor, the host CPU has additional time to devote to other tasks in the system. Moreover, a single user command demands only one task switch in the host. This fact considerably reduces the level of task-switch overhead for the host.

The operational sequence of a back-end DBMS is described next (see Figure 2-8):

Step 1. When a data base request is encountered in the host, a request is sent to the message system for a line to the back-end.

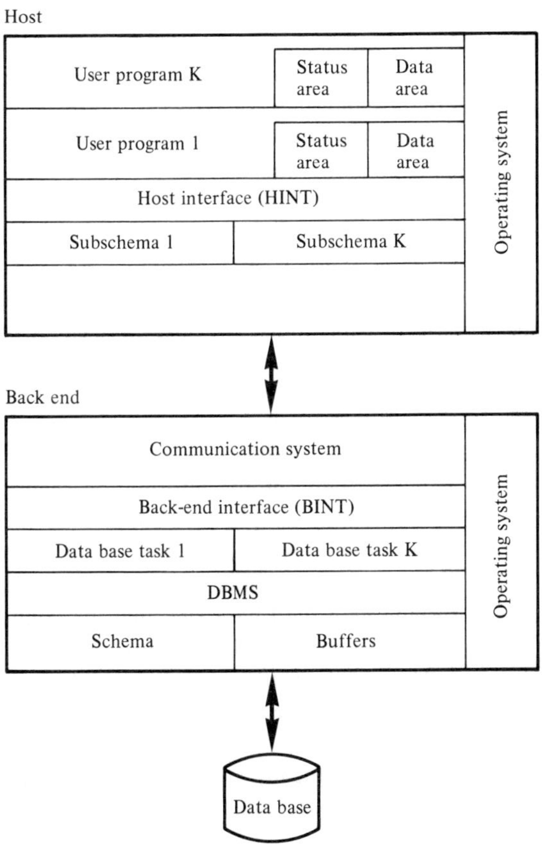

Figure 2-8. Conceptual data base management in back-end/host environment.

Step 2. When the message system has a line available, the DML statement is sent to the back-end.

Step 3. A task is created on the back-end to perform the DML statement. Tasks may be queued in the BINT (back-end interface) until partitions are available for them.

Step 4. When a task is activated (ready to run), it must wait for the back-end CPU.

Step 5. When the back-end CPU becomes available, the task is given to it and executed there until either an I/O operation must be performed or the DML statement has been completed.

Step 6. If an I/O operation must be performed on the task, the CPU of the back-end issues an I/O command and relinquishes the task.

Step 7. Steps 5 and 6 are repeated until the complete DML statement has been performed.

Step 8. The task may have to queue in BINT until the message system has a free line to the host.

Step 9. Depending on the nature of the result of the DML operation, a new data page may have to be sent to the host machine.

Step 10. When the transmission from the back-end to the host has ended, the task on the host enters the host interface (i.e. HINT).

Step 11. Steps 1 to 11 are repeated for each DML statement encountered by the host CPU in the application program.

The *advantages* of the back-end host configuration include the following:

1. *Low processor costs.* By removing the data base software load from the central processor, it is possible to use the host more effectively to service the remaining workload of the system. Forty to fifty per cent of the central processor's workload can be so delegated.[20]
2. *Shared back-end facilities.* Back-end processors can serve as shared repositories for information accessible to a group of related host machines. In this case, the back-end can enforce information security constraints.[25] The Datacomputer,[26] operating as a loosely coupled back-end processor (a communications system to a physically remote system of hosts) through the ARPANET, is a useful example. In such an environment, multiple back-end processors, each serving as a data base site, may be connected to provide processing capabilities for a distributed data bank.
3. *Low storage costs.* This configuration can pool the storage requirements of many computers and permit the use of more economical high-volume storage devices.
4. *Modularity.* A single, mechanically independent back-end processor can make possible the sharing or exchange of information among a number of *disparate* computers.
5. *Security.* Since, in this configuration, application programs (in the host) and

data base facilities (in the back-end) are physically separated, there is no direct communication between the user and the data.

One *disadvantage* lies in the area of communication, which is normally an important factor in determining response times. More communications links are required than can be handled by introducing efficient and fast communications facilities. Another possible disadvantage is that BINTs are not always easily implemented.

Functional Information Systems

The INFOPLEX[27] system architecture proposed by Madnick is a specialized data base machine for effective high-performance processing of information. It takes advantage of the parallelism inherent in multiple requests to achieve a very high level of performance. This concept takes advantage of new memory and processor technologies to organize a 'smart' memory hierarchy which can store and retrieve large volumes of information.

The key to the INFOPLEX architecture is the hierarchical ordering of functions. A highly parallel information system architecture can be implemented through a hierarchical decomposition which is both functional and physical. Figure 2-9 illustrates this conceptual structure in INFOPLEX. Similar techniques have been used successfully in operating systems[28] and file systems.[29] The New England energy information management system (NEEMIS)[30,31] uses an analogous concept:

> It is important to note that each functional level of the hierarchy is implemented in terms of the functions provided by the next lower level. This strictly hierarchical approach results in an extremely powerful, flexible, and modular data base management system. In addition, the conciseness of the structuring generally reduces the complexity of the system, making optimization and debugging much more effective.[31]

The technique of hierarchical decomposition has been found very effective in INFOPLEX.[32] A detailed explanation of this approach is presented by Madnick in his general account of the project.[27] Briefly, information is moved to storage levels which automatically depend on actual or anticipated use. Information most likely to be used in the near future is kept at the highest, fastest access level. Figure 2-10 shows the general structure of such a hierarchical storage system.

Two important types of parallelism can be exploited in an information system—functional and physical. The INFOPLEX system concentrates on the advantage of physical hierarchical decomposition. Current technologies aimed at achieving a low cost per byte in storage devices have reached this goal by providing relatively slow access to the data. Higher performance can be combined with a lower cost by combining expensive higher performance storage devices. It is clear

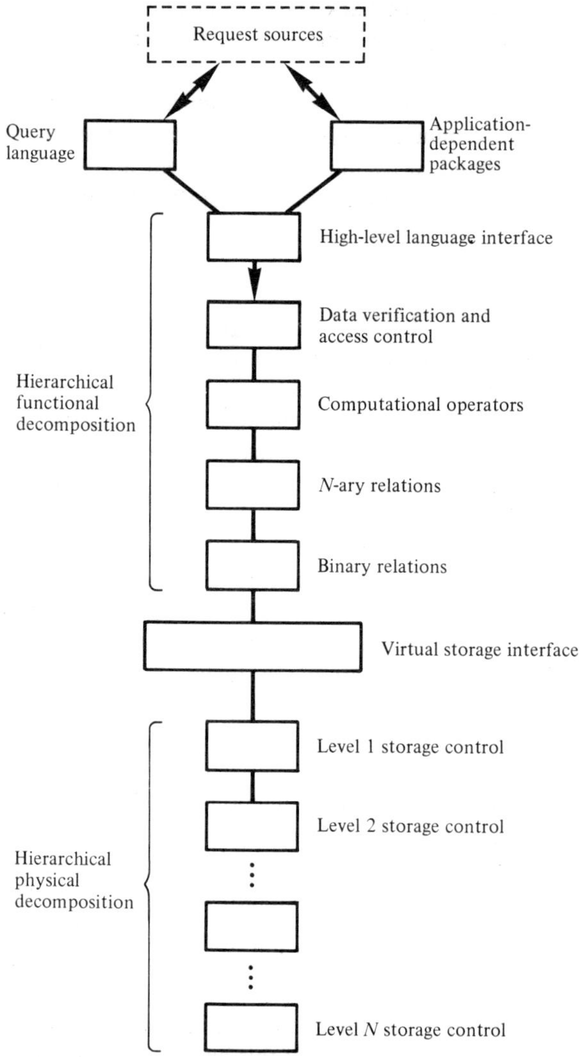

Figure 2-9. The conceptual structure of INFOPLEX.

that the range of performance and cost per byte for typical present-day storage technologies span six orders of magnitude in both cost and performance.

If all references to information in the system were *random* and *unpredictable*, there would be little need for combinations of devices with middling cost and performance. However, most practical applications result in *clustered* references. During any sample interval of time, only a small portion of the data is actually used, especially when indices and other control information are available. This common phenomenon is called *locality of reference*,[33,34] and under these

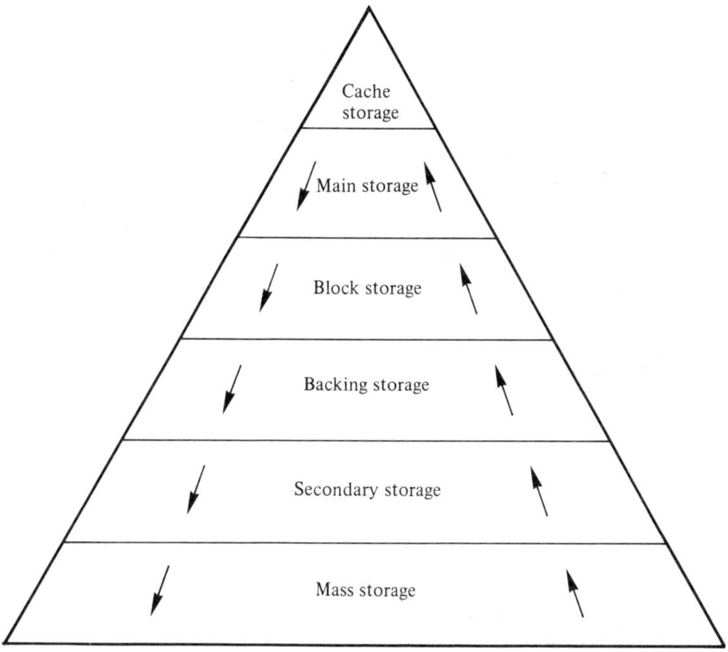

Figure 2-10. Hierarchy of storage devices organization.

circumstances, intermediate-level storage devices can be used as *paging* devices to hold these clusters of information.

In the INFOPLEX system, the storage devices are decomposed into a hierarchy of storage levels operating under local controls with only limited coordination between levels. Various physical storage management and movement techniques (page splitting, read through, store behind) can be distributed through the levels (see Figure 2-11). This strategy can lead to a parallel and asynchronous operation of great reliability.

In a *read through* strategy, when data currently stored at level i (and all lower performance levels, $k > i$) are referenced, they are automatically and simultaneously copied and stored in all storage levels $j > i$ (i.e. all higher performance levels). The data themselves are moved among levels in standard transfer units (pages) whose sizes $N(i - 1, i)$ depend on the storage level from which they are being moved (Figure 2-11). Since all upper storage levels receive this information simultaneously, no change is required if a storage level must be removed from the system. Since all data available at level i are also available at level $(i + 1)$ (and all higher levels $j > i$), no information is lost. We expect that performance may decrease as a result of the missing storage level.

In a *store-behind* strategy, all modified information is initially stored in $L(1)$, the highest storage level. This information is marked 'changed' and is copied into $L(2)$ as soon as possible, usually during a time of no activity between $L(1)$ and

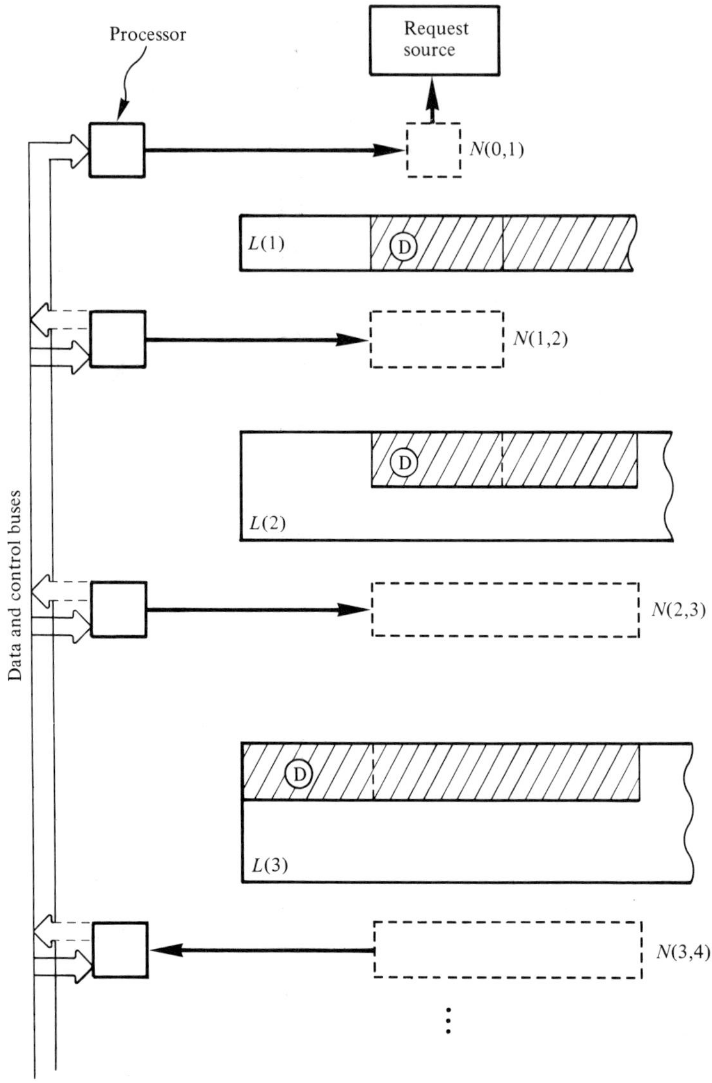

Figure 2-11. Example of read-through with page-splitting.

$L(2)$. Later, the information is copied from $L(2)$ to $L(3)$ and all lower performance levels. A changed page must not be purged from a storage level until the next lower level has been updated. In some cases, two levels of acknowledgment are preferable, ensuring at least two copies of each changed piece of information at levels i and $(i + 1)$ in the hierarchy. A considerable amount of work is required to manage this storage hierarchy. Work can be distributed by means of multiple processors servicing separate physical storage levels.

The INFOPLEX architecture presents, in hierarchical decomposition, a good,

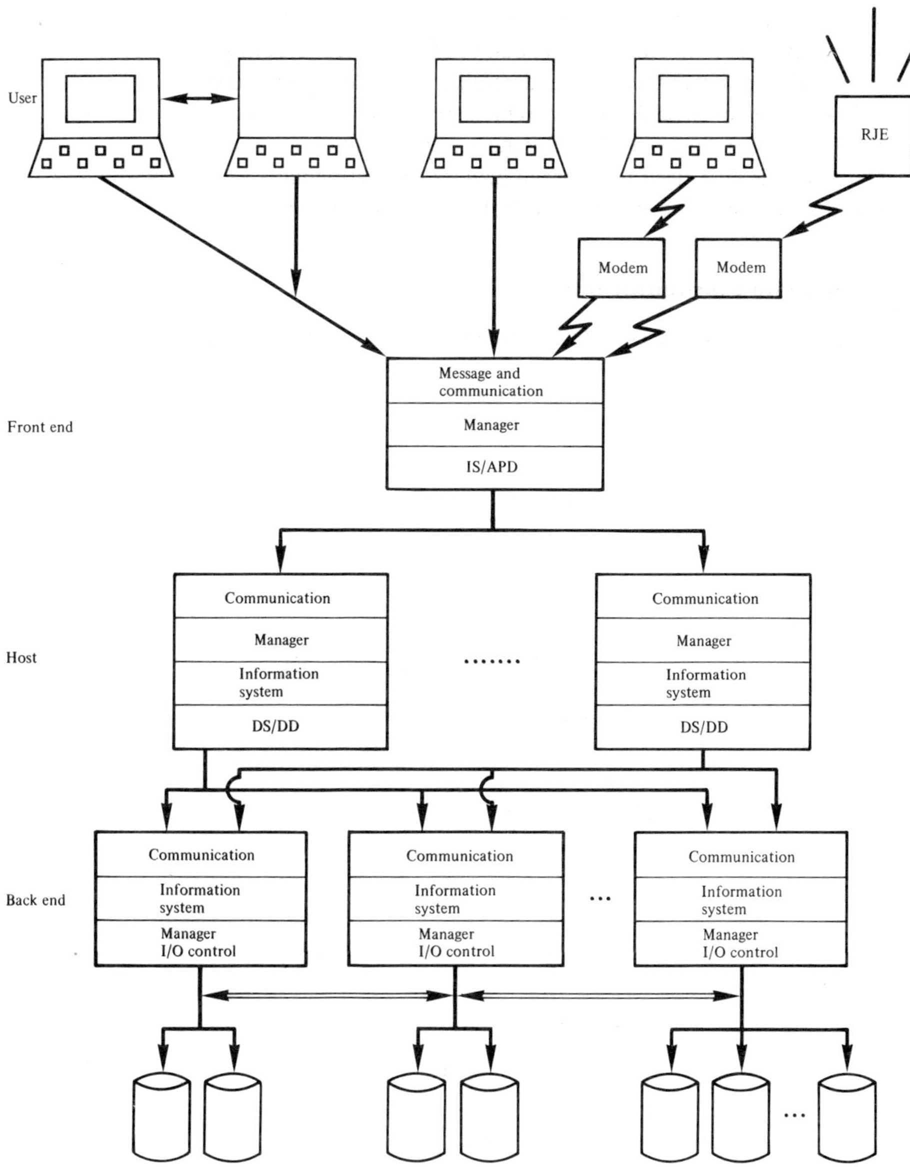

Figure 2.12. Front-end/multiple-host/back-end environment.

straightforward basis for a decentralized control system. Decentralized controls are essential to the development of an information system capable of managing extremely large memory, as well as secondary storage and a large number of requests. Moreover, the components of a hierarchically decomposed system can be implemented by means of a complex of microprocessors. If any hierarchical level malfunctions or must be serviced, it can be removed from the system without causing a loss of information. In addition, hierarchical ordering of a system results in improved performance and lends itself to considerable parallelism of functions.

The major drawback of hierarchical physical decomposition, as embodied in INFOPLEX, is that when all references to information are random and unpredictable, there is little need for storage devices of intermediate cost and performance. Finally, management of the INFOPLEX storage hierarchy is complex and costly.

Composite Configurations

Figure 2-12 presents a *front-end/host/back-end* configuration, in which the

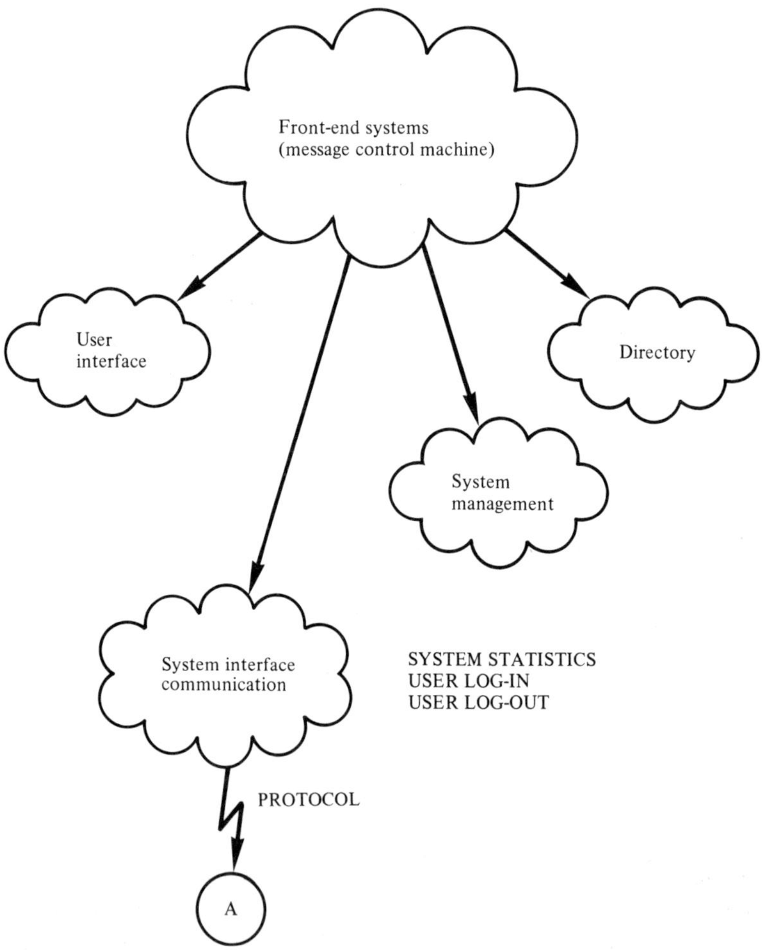

Figure 2-13. Distribution of functions in the front-end machine for front-end/host/back-end environment.

functions delegated to the front-end in the front-end/host section and those delegated to the back-end in the back-end/host section are all assigned to independent processors.

Figure 2-13 shows the functions of the front-end in a front-end/host/back-end configuration. The 'cloud' figures indicate that the arrangement is not a fixed one and can be altered according to the particular environment.

Figure 2-14 shows the functions of the host in the same configuration.

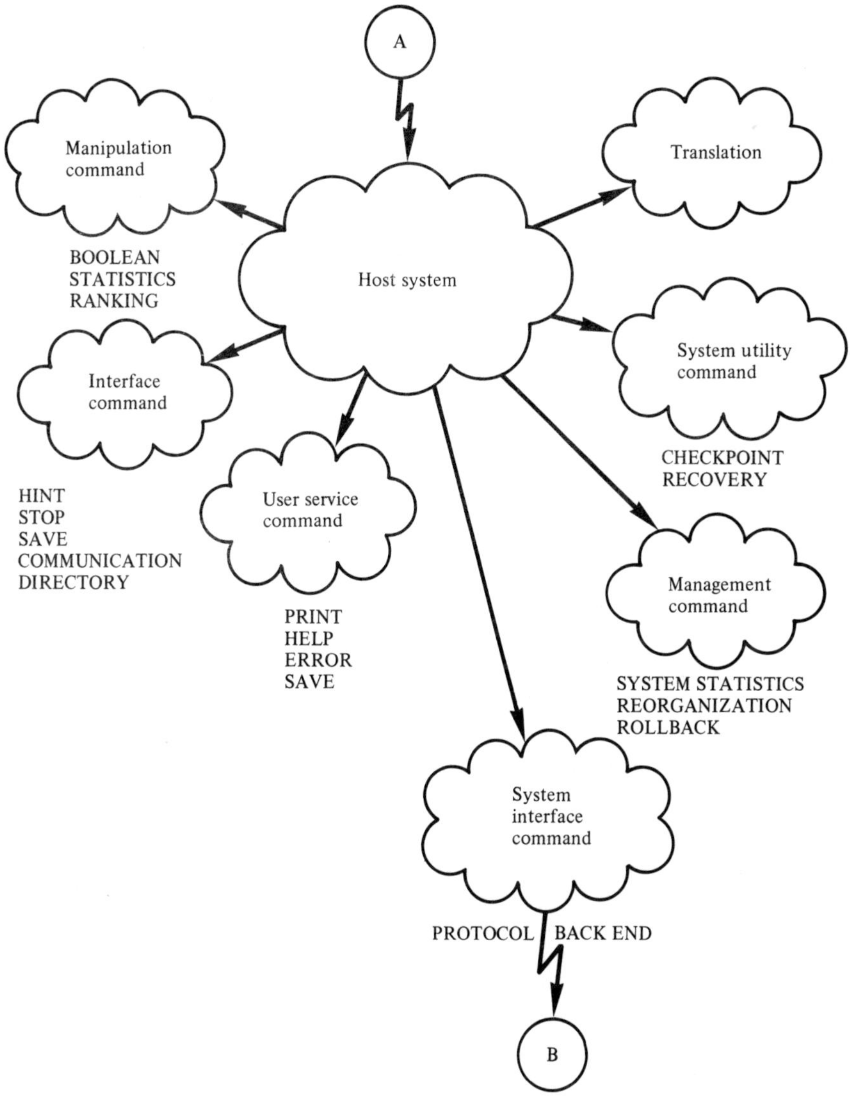

Figure 2-14. Distribution of functions in the host machine for front-end/host/back-end environment.

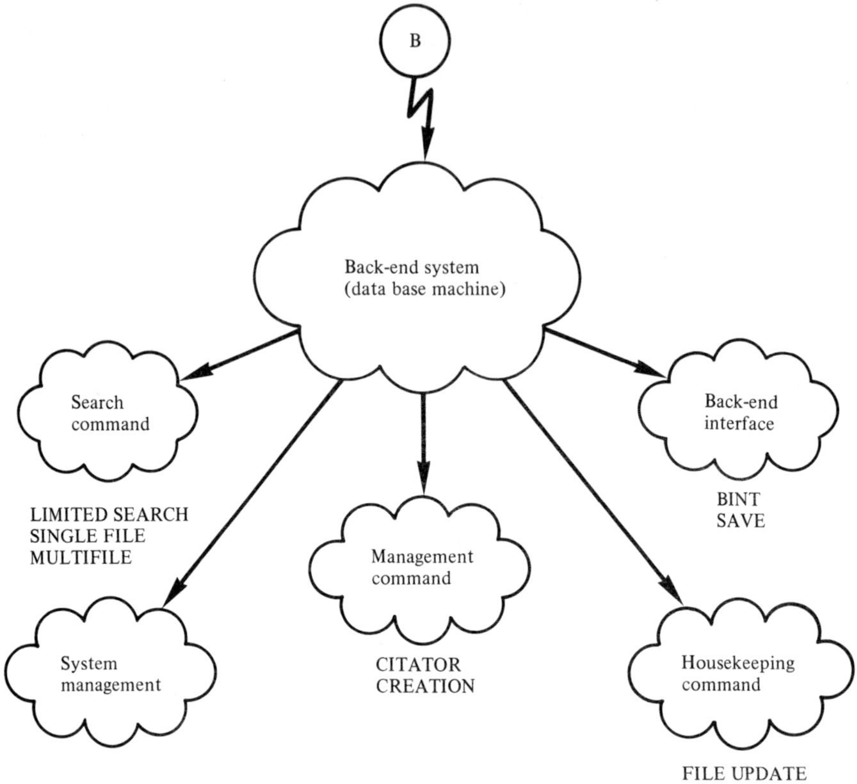

Figure 2-15. Distribution of functions in the back-end machine for front-end/host/back-end environment.

Figure 2-15 shows the function of the back-end in this configuration.

Figure 2-16 presents a *bifunctional environment*, which is a network of computers, each of which has its own application programs, data bank, and system interfacing devices. These computers may directly share each other's data banks plus a data bank on a data base machine independent of all computers in the network (e.g. ARPANET).

SUMMARY

Organizational data are derived from a data model. Data models are of two basic categories, graphic and set. Graphic (or structured class) data models are based on graph theory, and pertain to files in which the information possesses a structure of its own which must not be affected by mechanical manipulation. Set (or unstructured class) data models are based on set theory, and pertain to files in which informational data are independent of organizational data. Each of these categories contains a number of specific models.

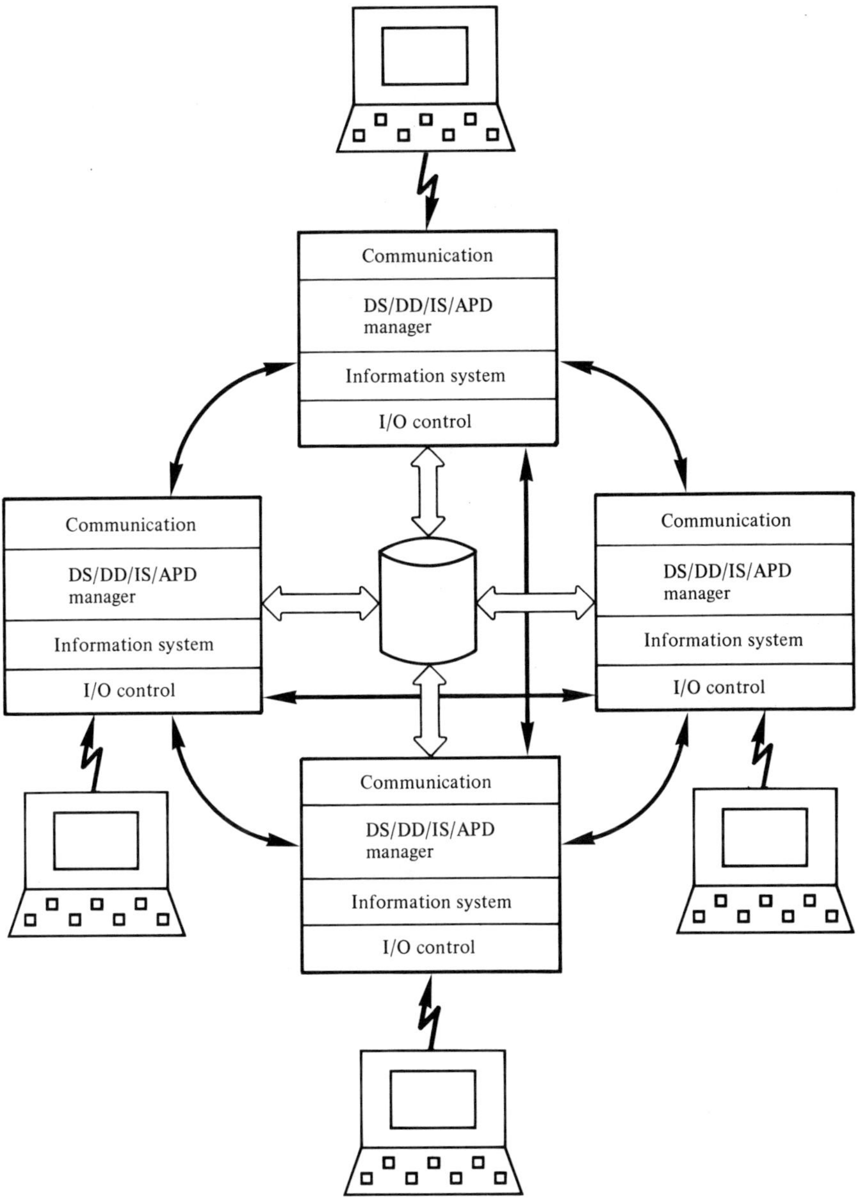

Figure 2-16. Bifunctional environment.

An information system must have the characteristics of a public utility. It must be able to support shared and concurrent access while enforcing the integrity and security constraints specified by users. Several data base environments have appeared in reports of recent research. Each of the environments described in this chapter is highly specialized; all are primarily devoted to solving the I/O and communication problems associated with data bases. The approach taken to solve the problem described in this chapter stems from the realization that centralized systems lose efficiency because of bottlenecks in communication and input/output. The solution is to remove communications and I/O responsibilities from the central processing machine and delegate these responsibilities to peripheral devices. The purpose of this delegation of functions is to balance the workload of the computing elements of the data base while maximizing access and throughput.

Clearly the system's architect may construct hardware solutions from a variety of possibilities. The architecture selected will impact the selected data model since it is necessary to express required data redundancy as well as organizations appropriate for the selected environment. For the most part, the model must represent the user's views and will divorce logical organization from architectural considerations. Practically, however, the data model must account for its hardware environment at some level.

REFERENCES

1. Kerschberg, L., Klug, A., and Tsichritzis, D. C.: A taxonomy of data models. In *Systems for Large Data Base* (Eds. P. C. Lockemann and E. J. Neuhold, 1976. North-Holland, 1976.
2. Lockemann, P. C. and Neuhold, E. J.: System for large data base. *Proc. of the Second Int. Conf. on V.L.D.B.*, North-Holland, 1976.
3. Durchholz, R., and Richter, G.: Information management concepts (I) for use with DBMS interface. *Proc. IFIP*, TC-2-WC, Black Forest, 1976.
4. Childs, D. L.: Description of a set-theoretical data structure. *AFIPS*, *National Computer Conf.*, 37, 756–763, June 1968.
5. Tsichritzis, D. C., and Lochovsky, F. H.: Hierarchical data base management. *ACM Computing Surveys*, **8**, No. 1, 105–123, March 1976.
6. Bernstein, P. A., Goodman, N., Rothnie, J. B., and Papadimitriou, C. A.: Analysis of serializability in SDD-I: a system for distributed databases (the fully redundant case). *Proc. First Int. Conf. on Computer Software and Applications*, IEEE Computer Society, Chicago, Illinois, November 1977.
7. Lindgreen, P.: Basic operations on information as a basis for data base design. *Proc. IFIP-74*, North-Holland, 1974.
8. Senko, M. E.: Specification of stored data structures and desired output results in DIAM-II with foral. *Conf. on Very Large Data Base*, 1975.
9. Chamberlin, D. D.: Relational data base management systems. *ACM Computing Surveys*, **8**, No. 1, 43–66, March 1976.
10. Codd, E. F.: A relational model of data for large shared data banks. *Communication of the ACM*, **6**, 377–387, June 1970.
11. Kobyashi, I.: Information and information processing structure. *Information Systems*, **1**, 39–49, 1975.

12. Sundgren, B.: Conceptual foundation of the infological approach to data base. In *Data Base Management* (Eds. J. W. Klimbie and K. L. Koffeman). North-Holland, 1974.
13. Tsichritzis, D. C.: Feature of a conceptual schema. *Conf. on Very Large Data Base*, 1975.
14. Roussopoulos, N., and Mylopoulos, J.: Using semantic networks for data base management. *Conf. on Very Large Data Base*, 1975.
15. CODASYL: *Data Base Task Group Report*. ACM, New York, 1971.
16. Taylor, R. W., and Frank, R. L.: CODASYL data base management system. *ACM Computing Surveys*, **8**, No. 1, 67–103, March 1976.
17. Canning, R. G.: Distributed intelligence in data communication. *EDP Analyzer*, **11**, No. 2, pp. 130–142, October 1980.
18. Reside, K. D. and Seiter, T. J.: The evolution of an integrated data base. *Datamation*, **20**, No. 9, 57–60, 1974.
19. Canaday, R. E., Harrison, R. D., Iwie, E. L., Ryder, J. L., and Wehr, L.A.: A back-end computer for database management. *Communication of the ACM*, **17**, No. 10, 575–582, October 1974.
20. Heacox, H. C., Cosloy, E. S., and Cohen, J. B.: An experiment in dedicated data management, *Proc. Int. Conf. on Very Large Database*, September 1974, pp. 511–513.
21. Simonson, W. E., and Alsbrooks, W. T.: A database management system for the U.S. Bureau of the Census. *Proc. of the First Int. Conf. on V.L.D.B.*, ACM, 1975.
22. Anderson, D. R.: Data base processor technology. *Proc. of AFIPS National Computer Conf.*, **45**, 811–818, June 1976.
23. Maryanski, F., *et al*: Evaluation of conversion to backend data base management system. *Proc. of the Annual Conf. of the ACM*, October 1976, 293–297.
24. Rosenthal, R. S.: An evaluation of a backend data base management machine. *Proc. of the Annual Computer Related Information System Symp.*, U.S. Air Force Academy, 1977.
25. Baum, R. I., and Hsiao, D. K.: Database computers: a step towards data utilities. *IEEE Trans. on Computers*, **C-25**, 1254–1259, December 1976.
26. Marill, T., and Stern, D.: The datacomputer—a network data utility. *AFIPS Conf. Proc.*, **44**, 389–395, 1975.
27. Madnick, S. E.: INFOPLEX: hierarchical decomposition of a large information management system using a microprocessor complex. *AFIPS Conf. Proc.*, **44**, 581–586, 1975.
28. Madnick, S. E., and Donovan, J. J.: *Operating Systems*, McGraw-Hill, New York, (1974).
29. Gray, J.: Notes on data base operating system In *Operating System: An Advanced Course* (Eds. R. B. Ayer, R. M. Graham, and G. Seedmuler), pp. 394–481. Springer-Verlag, 1978).
30. Donovan, J. J.: Database system approach to management decision support. *ACM Trans. on Database Systems*, **4**, No. 1, 344–369, December 1976.
31. Donovan, J. J., and Jacoby, H.: *A Hierarchical Approach to Information System Design.* MIT Sloan School of Management, Report CISR-5 and WP 762–75, January 1975.
32. Madnick, S. E.: The future of computers. *Technology Review*, **75**, No. 8, 34–45, July/August 1973.
33. Conti, C. J.: Concepts for buffer storage. *IEEE Computer Group News*, 1969, 6–13, March 1969.
34. Denning, P. J.: Virtual memory. *ACM Computing Surveys*, **2**, No. 3, 153–190, September 1970.

Section II

PLANNING FOR A DISTRIBUTED SYSTEM

Advances in Distributed Processing Management, Volume 2
Edited by P. S. Fisher, J. Slonim, and E. A. Unger

Chapter 3

A PERSPECTIVE OF DISTRIBUTED COMPUTING: LANGUAGES, ISSUES, AND APPLICATIONS

C. Mohan
IBM Research Laboratory, San Jose, California

A. Silberschatz
Department of Computer Sciences, University of Texas at Austin, Austin, Texas

This Chapter concerns distributed applications and languages which are intended for networks of processors. It does not consider those concurrent programming languages which are intended only for uniprocessor systems or shared-memory multiprocessors. Hence the emphasis is on message or procedure invocation-based systems, with an underlying notion of a collection of cooperating processes. A distributed program consists of a group of tasks, modules, or processes—possibly distributed over a network of computers—cooperating with each other in order to achieve a common objective.

The following section discusses some criteria that may be used in evaluating the suitability of any language proposals for distributed computing. In the next section the distributed programming applications are classified by outlining their characteristics and the requirements that they place on a language needed for implementing them. This effort, we hope, will provide some insights into which language proposal(s) may be well suited for a given type of application. Also, this work may be used by language designers as a basis to develop future languages specifically meant for a given type of application. We believe that a language which would suit all kinds of applications is not likely to evalue. The existence of different types of languages for sequential programming partially supports this belief. Different types of applications are sometimes likely to place conflicting demands on languages used for their realization.

The next section contains an enumeration and discussion of the various issues involved in the design of a language for distributed programming. A look at the literature reveals that the various issues involved in distributed programming are not thoroughly understood. The pros and cons of some language features are presented, and some of our ideas on certain issues which have not yet received much attention are also given.

The last section briefly touches upon the performance aspects of distributed programs, while the Appendix gives the salient features of many recent language proposals and a tabular comparison of them. The analysis of the various proposals is based on the identification of some dimensions.

EVALUATION CRITERIA

A great deal of work remains to be done in the development of evaluation criteria. The criteria ought to be expressed more formally, and a well-defined methodology (based on these criteria) for evaluation of distributed programming languages must be developed. There is a dearth of highly objective techniques.

Some possible evaluation criteria are:

1. *Expressive power or richness.* This criterion refers to the ability of the model/language to express certain behaviors, i.e. the ability to model certain computations like recursion and nondeterminism. This property is also referred to as completeness or adequacy. An increase in expressive power is likely to be accompanied by an increase in the difficulty of proving programs. While it is desirable to have simplicity as one of the goals, it is not advisable to have that as the overriding criterion.
2. *Provability.* One may be interested in proving many properties, such as partial correctness, freedom from blocking, termination, and fairness. The presence of some constructs would make it extremely difficult, if not impossible, to prove certain properties. For example, at the current state of the art of program-proving, the presence of time-outs could make the achievement of tractability of proofs almost impossible. Moreover, an important consideration is the power of the language used for specifying assertions about program properties. The assertion language or the logic used should be rich enough to be able to specify various desired properties formally.[1–9]

   Formalization of the semantics of language constructs is an important prerequisite for program-proving. The functional or denotational approach to semantics[10] is gaining wider acceptance.[6,11–14] The semantic domain of (communication) history trees has been used in the work of Francez and others[6] for defining the denotational semantics of a slightly restricted version of CSP.[15] While researchers have been talking about all of the previous properties for a long time, few well-defined techniques or formal methods are available to show the existence of the necessary properties. Keller[16] presents a concise overview of proof methods for concurrent programs. The three major approaches are: axiomatic, denotational, and operational. The notion of independence of process proofs has also been advanced.[3,7,17] Message histories or traces are turning out to be important in proving certain properties of distributed programs.[6,7,11,18,19]
3. *Efficiency of implementation.* It is not sufficient merely to define primitives whose functionality makes them worth implementing. It must also be

possible to deliver that functionality with reasonable efficiency. In most applications, efficiency or costliness is likely to be an important consideration. While some constructs might be easily implemented, the efficiency of such implementations may not be good. Practicality of mechanisms would be measured by the efficiency of their implementations. For example, a discussion of the problems involved in facilitating the use of both input and output statements (i.e. message SEND and RECEIVE statements) in the guards of guarded commands in CSP[15] can be found in several articles.[20–23] Some interesting discussions concerning the management of buffers can also be found.[24]

4. *Ease of use.* With the increasing cost of software development programming language user convenience is gaining more and more importance. The presence of powerful features does not mean that they would be easy to use. Normally high-level constructs and good abstraction capabilities make things easier. Ease of use and expressive power are complementary criteria. A model/language being rich enough to express a certain type of computation does not automatically mean that such computations would be easily expressible—ingenious, awkward, and obscure ways may be required. Constructs which reflect the intuitive abstractions of humans might be appealing to the user.

   While writing programs, language primitives should be combinable in a coherent way. Orthogonality should be exhibited by the primitives. Avoidance of subtle interactions among primitives would make them easier to use and help reduce errors. Flexibility of the constructs is also an important factor in the ease of their use.

5. *Understandability of resulting programs.* Any proposal for new language features should be closely scrutinized to determine the effect of the proposed facility on program structure. The mechanisms should discourage complex and confusing structures. Reasoning about programs should be made easy. The presence of high-level and very powerful constructs could lead to easily understandable programs, but, of course, this may not always be the case. Simple features do not automatically contribute to the writing of easily understandable programs. The ability to perform hierarchical composition of the process structure should be of great benefit. In general, constructs that are easily verified are likely to be easily understood.

6. *Impact of changes.* If the constructs do not induce/force a high degree of modularity, a change in the definition of one process may necessitate changes throughout the rest of the system. These changes might be highly undesirable, particularly if the number of processes involved is quite large. Permitting a high degree of autonomy in the definition of processes would reduce and localize the impact of changes.

7. *Extent of concurrency possible.* Constructs which permit higher degrees of concurrency are more desirable. The overhead involved in supporting such concurrency should not be such as to offset the advantages gained through the increased parallelism.

The criteria set forth previously could be used not only for evaluating already existing language proposals but also for stating design goals for new proposals. Once the design goals have been clearly defined, the discussions in the section on issues and design alternatives would be applicable in making specific choices of constructs when several alternatives exist.

A set of criteria greatly simplifies the evaluation of proposals for distributed computing. Nonetheless, the criteria cannot/should not be applied independently of any other considerations. Other considerations are as follows:

1. The application which needs to be modelled: the 'size,' complexity, criticality, etc.
2. The operating environment of the application in the real world: the way in which inputs or outputs are received from or sent to the environment, whether the interactions are predictable, etc.
3. The likely future evolutions of the application: the nature of the evolutions—predictable or unpredictable.
4. The design and configuration of the distributed computing system on which the language is to be implemented: the hardware, the operating system's features, etc.
5. The performance requirements that would be placed on the distributed program.

APPLICATIONS

In the past, quite often language design efforts in the distributed area do not seem to have been application driven. It is not clear whether this aspect is desirable. Problem analysis should precede studies for defining tools to express solutions to problems. One major exception to the preceding general trend is the ADA effort.[25] Another exception is the research being done at the University of Massachusetts at Amherst.[26] The PCL work[27] being done at UMASS is motivated by the desire to implement distributed artificial intelligence applications as functionally accurate cooperative distributed systems.

The distributed applications can be separated into three categories: distributed simulation/modeling applications,[18,28,29] real-time or systems applications,[30,31] and non-real-time or nonsystems applications.[26,32,33] Let us denote these as type 1, type 2, and type 3 applications, respectively. Table 3-1 gives the characteristics of these applications, the requirements that they place on the languages, and a few examples of such applications.

Some consequences of this classification are that, in terms of increasing difficulty of proving programs, the applications could be ordered as follows: type 3, type 1, type 2, because the type 3 language requirements do not have any time-dependent features.

The preceding classifications are preliminary and are likely to undergo many refinements as a result of insights obtained through further studies.

ISSUES AND DESIGN ALTERNATIVES

This section identifies and discusses various issues and provides some guidance for choosing among several alternatives by pointing out the advantages and disadvantages of many features. Many of the issues are closely related, as seen from the following analysis. The reader should note that the ensuing discussions do not purport to be exhaustive. The Appendix contains a summary of the important features of various language proposals referred to in this section. The interested reader can also find additional information in Rao's technical report.[34]

The requirements (those presented in the last section) placed by various applications on the programming languages need to be kept in mind while reading what follows. They would serve as the motivations for the consideration of alternatives given next.

Type of Communication

Communication between two entities could be either direct or indirect. If the direct communications discipline is adopted, then each entity which wants to send a communication (or message) has to explicitly name the recipient(s) of the communication, i.e. the direct addressing scheme is used. The disadvantage of this scheme is the reduction of modularity of the resulting process definitions. The descriptions of the interfaces between processes are spread out. Changing the name of a process might entail examination of all other process definitions to determine references to the old name in order to modify them to the new name. This practice is not desirable from the viewpoint of separate compilation. (Libraries of processes cannot be supported easily.) Further, it would be difficult to provide multiple channels of communication between two processes. (In PLITS/ZENO,[35,36] which supports direct communication, multiple channels can be realized by using its 'transaction' concept.) Communicating sequential processes (CSP)[15] and the network system language (NSL)[37] employ this mode of communication.

With indirect communication the messages are directed at ports (also sometimes referred to as gates) or received through ports.[23,38–41] If the statements of a process reference only ports attached to (or defined as part of) that process itself, the ports of that process are designated as output or input ports, respectively. The linking (or binding) of ports of different processes is external to the process definitions (PARLANCE[39] has adopted this scheme). By associating a type with each port, one can restrict the messages that can be sent/received through that port to only those that are of that type. Further, only ports of the same type would be allowed to be linked together. Adherence to these requirements is checkable at compile or link time.

In another approach, named buffers/channels are definable as system entities. In this case, the buffers/channels have an existence of their own; i.e. they are

TABLE 3-1
Distributed applications

Distributed simulation/modeling (type 1)	Real-time/systems (type 2)	Nonsystems/Non-real-time (type 3)
Characteristics		
Predictable process structures.	Unpredictable process structures.	Predictable process structures.
Protection issues unimportant.	Protection issues important.	Protection issues unimportant.
Nondeterminism is exhibited.	Nondeterminism is an inherent characteristic	Nondeterministic interactions among processes are likely to be minimal.
Performance and reliability characteristics are of importance.	Efficiency and reliability are important issues.	Reliability is not an important issue.
On-line functional enhancements (evolutions) are not necessary.	On-line functional enhancements are likely to be necessary (i.e. unpredictable evolutionary behaviors).	On-line functional enhancements are not necessary.
Life span of software is likely to be short.	Life span of software is likely to be long	Life span of software is likely to be of medium length.
Requirements placed on languages		
Support for static process structures is likely to be sufficient.	Support of dynamic process structures is essential.	Only static process structure support facilities are needed.
Nondeterministic message primitives are necessary.	Protection/security related constructs need to be present.	Only minimal support for nondeterminism is likely to be needed.
Support of mechanisms to specify performance and failure characteristics in a probabilistic way.	Good mechanisms to handle failures and efficiently implementable constructs are essential.	Efficiently implementable constructs may be essential.

Clock and timeout primitives should be provided. Priorities (and consequently scheduling decisions) should be specifiable. Forced (external) termination of processes may need to be specifiable.	Incremental combining of new software with already running software should be supported (in an on-line mode). Clock and timeout primitives should be provided. Priorities (and consequently scheduling decisions) should be specifiable. Forced (external) termination of processes should be possible. Testing for the presence of messages should be feasible. Nondeterministic process interaction primitives are necessary.	
Example applications		
Discrete event simulation. Specification and analysis of protocols.	Distributed data base software. Kernel software. Ballistic missile defense (BMD) real-time system. Process control in industries. Command and control applications in the military. Distributed office information systems.	Numerical software. Distributed interpretation systems (speech, image, and signal interpretation applications). Combinatorial algorithms.

independent and not 'attached' to any particular process. The right to read or write such a buffer could be propagated to other processes by the creator of the buffer. LIMP[42] takes this approach to interprocess communication, which could result in multiple readers and writers for each channel. Since all processes with access rights to a buffer may ultimately terminate, after some time a buffer may no longer be accessible by any process. Hence, garbage collection is necessary.

In terms of power, both the direct and indirect schemes are equivalent. The preceding schemes exhibit a kind of symmetry in their addressing, i.e. both the sender and the receiver have to name one another (in the direct case) or, equivalently, a port (in the indirect case). Still another way of addressing is the asymmetric way. Here only the sender names the recipient (or the name of a procedure or operation in the recipient process). The recipient is not required to name the sender. ADA,[25] Cell,[43] Distributed Processes,[44] *MOD,[45] and Synchronizing Resources (SR)[46] have this asymmetric direct addressing feature. The semantics of this type of communication is akin to that of procedure invocations in sequential programming languages—also a great similarity to the way monitors operate. The calls represent a two-way communication link. Some information is passed by the caller first, and after a certain amount of delay the caller gets back information. This discipline of communication has been termed remote operation or remote invocation paradigm.

It is possible to achieve asymmetric addressing through the primitives provided by PLITS/ZENO. ACTORS[47,48] employs the direct asymmetric addressing scheme, but in PLITS/ZENO and ACTORS message transfers take place instead of procedure calls. When a procedure or operation is invoked, the caller is not always suspended until the called procedure or operation terminates. Some languages (like MESA[49] and SR) permit concurrent execution of the invoker and the invoked computation.

In the case of the indirect asymmetric mode, each process directs its messages at the input port of another process (instead of an output port of its own). If this is done, then all ports will be of both input and output types. The total number of ports will be half that in the previous scheme (assuming that in the previous scheme each port is linked to only one other port). The disadvantage of this scheme is that port names must be unique throughout the system. (E-CLU[38] requires this.) Alternatively, if the process names are made to be unique, then only port names within a process would need to be unique. In this case the port references will be made unique by giving the process name and the port name for each such reference. However, this action results in the scheme being no longer indirect. The scheme of PARLANCE is preferable since it provides better modularity.

Reports in the literature have discussed messages versus procedure calls, for both centralized and distributed systems.[50,51] The send/receive paradigm (which requires using message transfer statements explicitly) provides more concurrency than the remote operation paradigm.

Buffers

Buffers are also known by other names, e.g. links and channels. They are relevant for both direct and indirect communication. In the context of message-passing, the presence of a buffer between two communicating entities means that the sender of a message need not wait for the recipient to receive the message in order for the sender to proceed with his subsequent work (the NO-WAIT SEND). When the buffer is of finite capacity, the sender is forced to wait if the buffer happens to be full when he tries to send a message. Some proposals do not provide for buffers explicitly. (In such cases buffers must be implemented using processes.) They require the sender and the receiver to be synchronized for message transfers to take place (SYNCHRONIZED-SEND). It is not clear what could be gained by placing this restriction.

In fact, the proof techniques of Chandy and Misra[3] do not require this kind of synchronization. As for deadlocks, in the absence of nondeterminism, increasing the size of buffers between two communicating processes will reduce the possibility of deadlocks involving those processes. When constructs with non-deterministic features are present, an increase in buffer size could result in some previously unreachable statements becoming reachable. As a result some deadlock situations might become possible.

In a concurrent programming language designed for specifying systems for simulation, buffer or link types should be specifiable so that one could define the characteristics of a link. For example, if a communication network is to be simulated, a link type could represent a physical link in the network, and characteristics of the link could be the capacity, the probability of error, and the type(s) of messages that could be sent.

If buffers could be declared explicitly, then multiple writers and readers for a single buffer would be possible. LIMP,[52] Gypsy,[7] and PCL[27] provide this generality. Extended POP-2[53] allows multiple readers and a single writer per channel, while Roscoe[24,54] permits multiple writers and only a single reader per link. These facilities complicate program proofs.

Process Network Structure

The application of modularity principles leads to the definition of a number of processes. Since these processes are intended to achieve an objective in a cooperative way, they might be interconnected. These interconnections are likely to exhibit a network structure. The more explicit the expression of this structure, the better it would be for an easy understanding of the activities of the communicating processes. This structure could either remain static or change as execution proceeds. The flexibility available in the composition of compound processes from simpler ones is an important feature of any distributed programming language. Efforts are underway to formalize the notion of process composition by defining various operators intended for effecting such compositions.[11,13,55]

With indirect communication, i.e. communication through ports only, static structure means that ports cannot be created dynamically and that the port linkages will remain unaltered throughout the execution of the network. PARLANCE programs have to be structured in this way. Dynamic configurations could be obtained if the binding sections (which link ports) themselves are treated as processes, thus enabling dynamic bindings to be accomplished. In a language which permits the definition of buffer types (and hence instances with distinct names), dynamic network structures can be obtained if names of buffers are allowed to be passed in messages or as parameters to newly created processes or previously existing ones, as is possible in LIMP, Roscoe, and Gypsy. If processes with ports could be created dynamically and if the new port names could be passed in messages or as parameters, dynamic structures would also result, as in Extended POP-2.

E-PARLANCE[56] does not permit newly created processes to communicate via messages with already existing processes because of the restriction that while a procedure call is permitted to result in the creation of new processes, ports cannot be passed as parameters of the procedure call. In this respect, compared to E-PARLANCE, the preceding languages are more flexible and provide for a higher degree of concurrency, while at the same time not requiring too many processes to be in existence at any given time.

In the case of direct communication, i.e. communication using process names explicitly, static structure might mean that the knowledge of each process about the existence of other processes would remain unchanged during the execution of the program. This approach rules out the possibility of the transmission of names of processes in messages. CSP processes have to follow these restrictions. Dynamic structures might be possible if processes could be created dynamically and their names could be passed in messages. Process names obtained through messages should be usable to send future messages. PLITS/ZENO and ACTORS[57] exhibit these features. PCL provides capabilities for defining complex dynamic configurations and evolutionary characteristics using static descriptions.

The problem with dynamic structures is that it may not be possible to *avoid* deadlocks among their components. On the other hand, it might be possible to avoid deadlocks if one is restricted to having only static structures, as is true for necessary and sufficient conditions for deadlock-freeness.[4] Another problem with dynamic structures is that, if names of processes could be transmitted in messages, then, depending upon the way message construction is performed, static type checking may be impossible. Our contention is that, for programming certain complex applications, dynamic structuring facilities would be essential, e.g. when the functional capabilities of a network of processes have to be enhanced on-line (without reinitiating the system) by the introduction of new processes into the existing process network. Depending on what the application designer's primary objective is, he may have to trade off ease of proving for the sake of expressive power or efficiency of functioning of the distributed program.

In most proposals the process structure is implicit in the descriptions of the processes themselves. Notable exceptions are PARLANCE and PCL.[27] Explicit specification of the process interconnection structures would enable effective allocation and scheduling decision-making.

Later, while comparing language proposals, we refer to the ability to communicate port/process/link names in messages or as parameters (for subsequent use to send messages) as port/process/link name propagation capability.

In the languages which permit only static network structure, one can clearly identify two phases: network setup and network activation. Milne and Milner also mention these two phases.[13] This identification would not be easy to perform in those languages which permit dynamic network structures.

Priorities

Any language which is intended for writing concurrent programs that control access to resources should permit the user to specify priorities for message receptions/transmissions and processes, thus enabling the programmer to specify scheduling decisions. These facilities would increase the expressive power of the language and would not force the user to write complicated and obscure programs to achieve certain objectives.

This fact has been recognized by the designers of ADA, Cell, *MOD, SR, and the scheme of Test.[41] Discussions concerning this topic can be found in Stark's article.[58] Extensions to CSP for incorporating priorities have been proposed by Schneider and Bernstein.[59] The extensions relate to the specification of the order of evaluation of the guards in guarded commands.

In this regard, it is useful to quote Andrews.[46] 'Since efficient scheduling is a major concern of parallel systems, it is important to have adequate mechanisms *in* the language rather than to have to build them *using* the language.'

The priorities could be either static or dynamically variable. In the static case, the priorities for message communication statements would be assigned (at process creation/definition time) based on the types of messages involved. In the dynamic case, the priorities could be made to be a function of various types of information pertaining to or part of the given process. In SR the contents of the waiting messages (different invocations of the same operation) at a process could be used to determine their priorities. (Thus, messages may not get served on a first-come-first-served basis.) SR does not provide means to specify priorities of different operations in relation to each other.

The notion of priorities being associated with message communication statements makes sense only if nondeterministic message communication constructs are permitted (as, for example, when message communication statements are allowed to appear in the guards of guarded commands). Thus, when multiple message communication statements within a process are eligible for execution and only one of them should be executed, the choice of which one to execute would be determined by the associated priorities.

Language outlines like CSP assume that the underlying kernel would make sure that fair scheduling of input operations (message reception statements) in guarded commands would be done to prevent starvation. Other proposals like PARLANCE try to get away, in some sense, from the need for fair scheduling by not permitting guarded commands. It should be noted that in those latter proposals the burden has now been shifted from the underlying kernel into the hands of the user. Now he has to write his program in such a way that each process would receive inputs from all ports connected to it in a fair way. The fair scheduling algorithm has to be embedded in the program text. This is not simple as it requires the user to be aware of the frequency with which messages would arrive at the different ports. The important distinction is that if the user has to do the fair scheduling, he has to make use of *a priori* knowledge; whereas if the underlying system does it, it can make use of dynamic knowledge (i.e. the latter would be able to examine the message queues and then make a fair decision). The former would make the programmer's job complicated and would result in obscure programs.

Reliability

Along with its advantages, distributed computing brings with it a host of reliability problems. Dealing with reliability problems is intellectually more taxing in the distributed area than in the centralized context.

In almost all the proposals that we have come across, little attention has been paid to the robustness issue. For some applications (see previous section), reliability will be a critical issue. In coming up with a language proposal for distributed computing, the designer has to take reliability considerations into account from the beginning since, in most instances, it would be extremely difficult, if not impossible, to add on good reliability features at a late stage in the design process. Addressing this issue at a late stage would result in *ad hoc* and clumsy mechanisms. A look at the sequential programming languages would provide considerable support to this claim. There is evidence to that effect in the distributed data base area also.[60–62,75–76] Kain[63] discusses a few of the problems associated with dynamic recovery mechanisms for interprocess communications schemes and suggests system designs to deal with them.

Recently, extensions have been proposed to the PARLANCE model of distributed computing.[56] These extensions permit a group of interacting processes to be considered as a parameterized procedure (similar to what could be achieved in Extended POP-2[53]). As in sequential programming, the caller of a procedure waits until the called procedure has completed. We propose that, for recovery purposes, a procedure be considered as a commitment unit, i.e. if the procedure does not complete normally, due to unrecoverable faults or deadlocks, then the parameters of the procedure should be restored to the value which existed at the time of the call and the caller should be given an error return, describing the type of problem encountered. It is to be hoped that the caller would be able to resort to remedial action.

Process/Processor Mapping

Some languages require this binding to be fixed (e.g. PLITS/ZENO and E-CLU). This feature is undesirable since it reduces the reliability of the system and also precludes dynamic load-sharing in a distributed environment (even where the total number of processors is fixed[77]). This restriction would be all the more disadvantageous in an environment where the number of processors varies dynamically (not necessarily because of failures but also, possibly, because of dynamically reconfigurable network architectures).

Network Visibility

Network visibility refers to the issue of whether the physical network, on which the distributed program would function, should be made visible at the language level. Visibility is said to exist if the language has primitives which refer to physical sites/nodes and of variables of type site/node are allowed in the language. NSL[37] provides this type of visibility. This feature is necessary if one wants to write network protocols using distributed programming languages. The developers of E-CLU also propose to provide for network visibility.

Provision of network visibility would allow specification of dynamic process migrations (from one site to another). For example, forms in an office information system could be modeled as processes which migrate from one work station to another.[30]

Specifications

An abstract specification of the function of a process (or process-type) would help a great deal in understanding the activities of that process. It would also help in organizing a library of processes, which could be used later on (as off-the-shelf components) in new applications. One way to characterize a process is to specify the predicates/constraints that the inputs to the process (from other processes, possibly through ports) and the parameters of the process (the parameters get their values at process instantiation time) should satisfy. Then the relationships of the outputs of this process to its inputs and parameters could be specified, in order to characterize the behavior of the process abstractly. A formalism for the specification of the semantics of any process has been presented by Francez and his colleagues.[6] A language based on traces for the specification of communication systems has been presented[64] as well as a methodology for the specification of the functionality of asynchronous communication modules.[65]

This type of abstract specification could not only be produced after a process has been implemented, but could also be given as a design specification to programmers for writing the code of the process.

Tools and Programming Methodologies

Much more work remains to be done in the area of programming methodologies for distributed systems although attention has been paid to proof techniques for such systems for quite a long time. A program development methodology which combines a concurrent program proof technique needs to be formulated. Several benefits would accrue if such a methodology were to be synthesized.

A great deal of work needs to be done toward the development of design and analysis tools, debugging aids, and so on. When teams of programmers are involved in the design and implementation of distributed systems, it is crucial that techniques and procedures be developed for the proper management of the programming activity and for the subdivision of the work. Unfortunately, in the sequential programming area, this important topic has received little attention from researchers until recently, even though practitioners of computing in the real world have noted a pressing need for good techniques. It is to be hoped that such a situation does not recur with respect to distributed programming.

Development of diagrammatic techniques for the representation of process network interconnections would go a long way toward the easy understanding of distributed programs. Realizing the importance of diagrams, Milner has treated the notion of a diagram algebraically and has come up with an algebra of nets.[14] Hoare also feels that it is illuminating to picture the behavior of a process in terms of graphs.[11] Arguments in favor of diagrams can be found in Milne and Milner's report.[13]

A debugging tool for distributed programs could be designed to provide at least the following facilities: constructs to record a trace of message transfers, process creations, and process terminations (normal and abnormal).

Termination

The issue of achieving termination of distributed programs has not been studied extensively. With respect to CSP's facilities for achieving this goal, it is useful to quote Hoare:[15]

> The automatic termination of a repetitive command on termination of the sources of all its input guards is an extremely powerful and convenient feature but it also involves some subtlety of specification to ensure that it is implementable ... But the dangers of convenient facilities are notorious. For example, the repetitive commands with input guards may tempt the programmer to write them without making adequate plans for their termination; and if it turns out that the automatic termination is unsatisfactory, reprogramming for explicit termination will involve severe changes, affecting even interfaces between the processes.

An algorithm for achieving distributed termination of certain classes of CSP programs has been proposed by Frances[66] and was revised and improved by Francez and his colleagues.[5] Another approach to termination detection is presented in Dijkstra and Scholten's article.[67]

Forced (external) termination of processes would normally require that process names be visible in the executable part of process definitions as is the case with TASK, NSL, and ADA. (A few examples of languages in which process names are invisible are PARLANCE, Extended POP-2, E-CLU, and LIMP.) The language which does not obey this requirement is PCL, but from the description by Lesser, Serrain, and Bonar[27] it is not clear how PCL handles forced termination of processes.

More information on the salient features of the different language proposals can be found in the Appendix.

PERFORMANCE EVALUATION/ANALYSIS

One of the important advantages often attributed to distributed computing is that use of multiple computers could decrease reponse times. Much more experience remains to be gained before this claim can be validated. It is quite difficult to state analytically the expected performance or complexity of a distributed algorithm, i.e. an algorithm defined using multiple communicating processes. In contrast, many techniques and theories exist to evaluate sequential algorithms for their computational complexity. If an algorithm is defined as a collection of processes communicating through messages only, then the greatest problem in evaluating its performance seems to be in being able to predict the delays involved in the execution of message send and receive statements. The presence of constructs which permit nondeterminism is likely to further complicate matters. Solely by looking at a process code, one would not be able to characterize its performance accurately if that process were interacting with other processes. A network of communicating processes would have a complex impact on the performance of each of its constituent processes.

The number of processes to be employed in solving a certain problem should not be based solely on qualitative considerations; it should be based on performance considerations also.

While many correctness measures have been thought of for distributed programs, hardly any algorithmic complexity/performance measures exist. Traditionally, the functional objectives of algorithms have been separately examined from their performance aspects. However, with respect to protocols, Yemini and Cohen[68] state that the separation of functionality from performance cannot be taken for granted.

PRESENT-DAY LANGUAGES

The reader can convince himself about the inadequacy of present-day (widely available) languages for use in implementing distributed programs by evaluating languages like FORTRAN, COBOL, and PL/I against the requirements placed on distributed programming languages (see Table 3-1). Further, the evaluations should also be done with respect to the issues/features discussed in the preceding section. The languages commonly available to the data processing community were all designed for the uniprocessor environment, even though languages like PL/I do support multitasking. Only primitive synchronization mechanisms are supported, even in the more sophisticated of the commonly available languages. Even less well-known languages like Concurrent PASCAL and MODULA are suitable only for the shared-memory environment. The material presented in the Appendix should shed some light on the features for distributed computing which the present-day languages lack.

APPENDIX

This appendix presents a brief description of the key features of various proposals that have been put forth in recent years.

Most of the proposals that we have reviewed do not state explicitly the assumptions that they have made about the facilities provided by the run-time support environment, i.e. the underlying kernel. The attributes of the kernel are important to decide whether certain issues need to be dealt with at the language level. This problem further complicates the language comparison task. Also, it needs to be borne in mind that almost none of the language proposals discussed here have yet been implemented or have been implemented only recently. As a result, in a majority of cases the languages have been used to program only 'toy' examples. The works have been based more on intuitions than on 'hard' experiences. A consequence of all the previous observations is that our comparisons are confined to only qualitative considerations and are not based on any quantitative measures.

It is interesting to note that of the proposals surveyed, only the ADA language has been designed in response to a comprehensive set of requirements. The requirement definition and language design activities were completely decoupled; in fact, different teams of people were involved in the two activities.

CSP[15]

Distributed program: processes, with mutually disjoint address spaces, communicate directly using typed messages. Arrays of processes can be defined.

Sends and receives of messages are termed as input and output operations, respectively. Sender and receiver are to be synchronized for message transfer.

Nondeterminism is permitted through guarded commands. Input statements can appear in guards. A parallel command permits simultaneous initiation and execution of several processes. During such an execution the parent process is suspended.

Note. Various papers have presented proof techniques for CSP[2,8] and implementation issues concerning CSP have also been discussed.[20–23,69]

PARLANCE[39]

Distributed program: processes communicate using messages through typed ports.

Hierarchies of processes can be defined, but only the processes at the lowest levels can have executable code.

Binding of ports is done external to the process definitions. Each port of a process is connected to only one port of some other process. The bindings are static. Sender and receiver are to be synchronized for message transfer (input/output), as in CSP.

A parallel command which involves only input and/or output statements is permitted; i.e. AND-WAIT on multiple ports—all message transfers, in any order, must be completed before the command execution is deemed to be complete.

Non-determinism cannot be handled.

TASK[70]

This extension of BLISS is based on the 'object model' supported by the STAROS operating system for Cm*.[71]

Different object types: task force, module, process, basic, stack, deque, device, mailbox.

A TASK specification affects only creation and initialization of objects.

One codes algorithms in BLISS and specifies logical structures in TASK.

Implements both procedure invocations and message-passing capabilities. A procedure invoked by a process could be executed in parallel with the execution of the caller. Communication is through mailboxes.

Dynamic definition and creation of task forces is possible.

NSL[37]

A high-level definition language to be used for specifying the detailed requirements on any particular layer or group of layers in the ISO model of a distributed system, i.e. a language for specification of protocols.

Processes communicate through typed messages. Dynamic creation of processes at a desired physical site/node of the network is possible. Destruction of a process by its creator is permitted. Destruction of a process results in destruction of all its descendent processes.

Network data objects like files can be shared.

Certain protection mechanisms are provided.

PCL[27]

Distributed program components: processes, memory segments, ports, and links. Components can be in five states (uninstantiated, bound, expanded, initialized, and executing) and can be shared.

Ports are connected by links. Various types of links can be defined (including some performance attributes). Presence of a message at a port can be tested.

Highly dynamic process configurations can be instantiated during execution, using a static description of the process structure. Hierarchical structuring of processes (called clusters) is also possible. Process structure descriptions can be given in terms of static or structural characteristics, evolutionary characteristics, and creation characteristics.

Distributed Processes[44]

Processes contain local data, initialization statements, and common procedures, which are able to be called by other processes. Those calls are termed external requests.

Unsymmetric communication: procedure call semantics for message transmission.

Initial statements and external requests of a process are executed serially. They terminate or wait for some condition to become true. The execution of a process is similar to that of a monitor.

Guarded commands and guarded regions provide nondeterminism. The latter can delay the execution of an operation.

Arrays of processes are possible.

ADA[25]

Tasks (which are similar to processes) consist of entries (which are similar to procedures of a monitor), which are able to be called by other tasks.

Intertask communication is through entries, which can be dynamically and selectively enabled. Such a communication through an entry call is called a 'rendezvous'. The caller task and the called task are synchronized (as in CSP) during a rendezvous.

Tasks can be initiated dynamically and they can have program-modifiable priorities associated with them. The parent task and the child tasks can execute in parallel. Every task can be aborted by other tasks which 'know' its name.

Synchronizing Resources[46]

Distributed program: a set of resources, each of which encapsulates a set of processes and shared variables.

Processes contain declarations of externally callable operations, which can have priorities associated with them. If an operation is invoked by a CALL, then the caller gets suspended until the operation completes. It is also possible for an operation to be invoked by a SEND. In this case the caller continues execution along with the called operation, but cannot receive any values back from that operation.

Intraresource process communication, through operations or shared variables.

Interresource process communication, through operations.

Multiprocess. Multiple numbers of those operations defined in a multiprocess can be in execution simultaneously.

Note. Synchronizing resources has been implemented. The translator produces Modula source code.

Extended CLU[38]

Distributed program: one or more 'guardians' (a guardian is similar to the managers described by Jammel[72,73]).

Guardian: processes + objects. Each guardian is expected to provide synchronization, security, backup, and recovery for the resources it protects. Each guardian exists entirely in a node of the underlying physical network.

Objects: passive. Direct manipulation by processes only through invocations of predefined operations.

Dynamic creation of guardians is possible, but they are immovable from the nodes where they are created.

Interguardian communication, only through messages. Timeouts are permitted in message reception statements to handle some exception conditions.

Intraguardian communication, through shared objects.

Buffered messages sent to typed ports. Compile-time type-checking can be quite comprehensive.

*MOD[45]

Derived from MODULA. Separate compilation is possible.

Processor modules: contain processes and message types used by those processes. Variables can be shared by processes in a processor module. Similar to guardians of E-CLU (Extended CLU). Messages are directed at ports.

Network module: links processor modules and declares global types and constants.

Interface module: similar to monitor—mutual exclusion across all the contained procedures.

A process is initiated for every message. (*Note*. The semantics of this are not clear. We foresee problems.)

Processes have dynamically variable priorities associated with them.

Extended POP-2[53]

An extension of the artificial intelligence language POP-2.

Parameterized process types with input and/or output ports can be defined. Parallel processes (with connecting ports, either new and/or old ones) can be dynamically created, thus facilitating shrinking or expansion of process hierarchies (Gypsy's features are quite similar[7]).

Recursion is permitted, but nondeterminism cannot be handled.

Ports are connected by channels. Each channel can have multiple readers (with only one writer), and all of them receive all the messages sent along the channel.

ACTORS[47,48,57]

Distributed program: dynamically creatable actors (which are somewhat like processes), communicating through buffered messages. Messages may transmit actors' names.

Nondeterminism, recursion, and timeouts can be specified.

Serializers are used to control access to protected resources. The serializer mechanism is a generalization and improvement of the monitor mechanism.

Note. To our knowledge, no consistent and complete description of the syntax and semantics of ACTORS is available.

PLITS/ZENO[35,36]

Distributed program: multiple modules (which are similar to processes) communicating solely through buffered messages.

Modules: can be created dynamically, but cannot be destroyed by other processes.

Messages: all components/fields of a message may not be visible to the recipient of that message. Module names as well as transaction names could be used for controlling message receptions and dispatches. Transaction names could be considered as dynamically created mailboxes.

Types: parts of PLITS/ZENO are intentionally left not strongly typed.

Flowgraphs[13]

Processes communicate through typed ports, of channels, with unbuffered messages.

Recursion and nondeterminism can be expressed.

Processes and channels can be dynamically created.

Note. This is only a model, not a language.

LIMP[42,52]

Distributed Program: processes communicating solely through unbuffered messages.

Processes can be dynamically created.

Typed channels (with, possibly, multiple readers and writers) link processes for message transfers. The read capability for a channel is called a 'source' and the write capability a 'sink.'

Channels, sources, and sinks can be dynamically created and passed around in messages.

TABLE 3-2
Proposals for distributed languages

	NO-WAIT SEND	OR-WAITS	Direct communication	Process/link/port name propagation	Shared objects	Only self-destruction of processes	Process types	Dynamic process creation
Distributed processes[44]	N	Y	Y	N	N	1	Y	N
Synchronizing resources[46]	Y	Y	Y		Y	Y	Y	Y
PLITS/ZENO[35,36]	Y	Y	2	Y	N	Y	Y	Y
Extended POP-2[53]	Y	N	N	Y	N	Y	Y	Y
ACTORS[47,57]	Y	Y	Y	Y	N	Y	Y	Y
PARLANCE[39]	N	N	N	N	N	Y	Y	N
Flowgraphs[13]	N	Y	N				Y	Y
Roscoe[54]	Y	Y	N	Y	N	N		Y
E-CLU[38]	Y		N	Y	Y	Y	Y	Y
PCL[27]	Y	Y	N	N	Y	N	Y	Y
TASK[70,71]	Y	Y	2	Y	Y	N	Y	Y
NSL[37]	N	Y	Y	N	Y	N	Y	Y
LIMP[42]	N	N	N	Y	N	Y	Y	Y
CSP[11,15]	N	Y	Y	N	N	Y	Y	N
*MOD[45]	Y	N	Y	N	Y	Y	Y	Y
ADA[25]	N	Y	Y		Y	N	Y	Y

Notes.
1. Processes exist forever.
2. Both direct and indirect communications are possible.

Y = Yes.
N = No.
Blanks indicate lack of information.

Table 3-2 presents a comparison of many of the proposals found in the literature. The comparison is done along many dimensions, most of which have been discussed earlier. These dimensions can be considered as the features of a model for a distributed programming language. Identifying such a model of programming helps to abstract away from syntactic distinctions among languages. There are many descriptions of models of distributed computing[11,13,53,57,74]. A look at Table 3-2 should provide the reader with a quick overview of the various proposals. Detailed information about the proposals can be found in the papers listed in the references section. The existence of a large number of recent proposals is a reflection of the widespread attention that this area has been receiving of late.

REFERENCES

1. Abrahamson, K.: Modal logic of concurrent nondeterministic programs. *Proc. Int. Symp. on Semantics of Concurrent Computation*, Evian (France), July 1979.
2. Apt, K., Francez, N., and de Roever, W.: A proof system for communicating sequential processes. *ACM Trans. on Prog. Lang. and Systems*, July 1980.
3. Chandy, K. M., and Misra, J.: *An Axiomatic Proof Technique for Networks of Communicating Processes*. IEEE Transactions on Software Engineering Vol. SE-7, No. 4, July 1981. (Also Tech. Rep. TR-98, Distributed Systems Group, University of Texas at Austin, May 1979).
4. Chandy, K. M., and Misra, J.: Deadlock absence proofs for networks of communicating processes. *Information Processing Letters*, **9**, No. 4, November, 1979. (Also Tech. Rep. TR-105, Distributed Systems Group, University of Texas at Austin, June.)
5. Francez, N., and Rodeh, M.: *Achieving Distributed Termination Without Freezing*. Tech. Rep. 072, IBM Israel Scientific Center, Haifa (Israel), July 1979.
6. Francez, N., Hoare, C. A. R., Lehmann, D., and de Roever, W.: Semantics of nondeterminism, concurrency and communication. *J. of Computer and System Sciences*, **19**, No. 3, December 1979.
7. Good, D., Cohen, R., and Keeton-Williams, J.: Principles of proving concurrent programs in Gypsy. *Proc. sixth Symp. on Principles of Programming Languages*, January 1979. (Also Tech. Rep. ICSCA-CMP-15, Certifiable Minicomputer Project, University of Texas at Austin, January.)
8. Levin, G.: *A Proof Technique for Communicating Sequential Processes* (with an example). Tech. Rep. TR 79-401, Cornell University, 1979.
9. Pnueli, A.: The Temporal Semantics of Concurrent Programs. *Proc. Int. Symp. on Semantics of Concurrent Computation*, Springer-Verlag, Evian (France), July, 1979.
10. Scott, D.: Logic and Programming Languages. *CACM*, September 1977.
11. Hoare, C. A. R.: *A Model for Communicating Sequential Processes*. Oxford University Computing Lab., Oxford (England), December 1978.
12. Hoare, C. A. R.: *Towards a Theory of Communicating Sequential Processes*. Oxford University Computing Lab., Oxford (England), February 1979.
13. Milne, G., and Milner, R.: Concurrent processes and their syntax. *JACM*, April 1979. (Also Internal Report CSR-2-77, University of Edinburgh, February 1978.)
14. Milner, R.: *Algebras for Communicating Systems*, Internal Report CSR-25-78, University of Edinburgh (England), June 1978.
15. Hoare, C. A. R.: Communicating sequential processes. *CACM*, August 1978.
16. Keller, R. M.: Proof methods for concurrent programs. In *Research Directions in Software Technology* (Ed. P. Wegner). The MIT Press, Cambridge, Mass., 1979.

17. Owicki, S.: Specification and Verification of a Network Mail System. In *Program Construction*, LNCS, Vol. 69, Springer-Verlag, 1979.
18. Chandy, K. M., and Misra, J.: Distributed simulation: a case study in design and verification of distributed programs. *IEEE Trans. on Software Engineering*, September 1979.
19. Hauser, C.: *Specification and Verification of Communication in Parallel Systems*. Ph.D. Thesis, Tech. Rep. TR 80-420, Cornell University, May 1980.
20. Bernstein, A. J.: Output guards and nondeterminism in 'communicating sequential processes,' *ACM TOPLAS*, April 1980.
21. Kieburtz, R., and Silberschatz, A.: Comments on 'communicating sequential processes.' *ACM Trans. on Programming Languages and Systems*, October 1979.
22. Silberschatz, A.: Communication and synchronization in distributed systems. *IEEE Trans. on Software Engineering*, November 1979.
23. Silberschatz, A.: Port Directed Communication. *Computer Journal* (in press).
24. Solomon, M., and Finkel, R.: Roscoe: a multi-microcomputer operating system. *Proc. Second Rocky Mountain Symp. on Microcomputers*, August, 1978. (Also Tech. Rep. 321, University of Wisconsin—Madison, May.)
25. ADA: Reference Manual for the ADA Programming Language—Proposed Standard Document, U.S. DoD, July 1980.
26. UMASS: Working Papers in Distributed Computation—I. *Cooperative Distributed Problem Solving*. Distributed Computation Group, University of Massachusetts at Amherst, July 1979.
27. Lesser, V., Serrain, D., and Bonar, J.: PCL: a process-oriented job control language. *Proc. First Int. Conf. on Distributed Computing Systems*, October 1979.
28. Bryant, R.: Simulation on a distributed system. *Proc. First Int. Conf. on Distributed Computing Systems*, October 1979.
29. Nutt, G.: *An Experimental Distributed Modeling System*. Tech. Rep., Xerox PARC, January 1980.
30. Ellis, C.: *An Office Information System Based on Intelligent Forms*. Memo, Xerox PARC, 1980.
31. Fitzwater, D. R.: *The Formal Design and Analysis of Distributed Data Processing Systems*. Tech. Rep. 361, University of Wisconsin—Madison, August 1979.
32. Davis, L., and Rosenfeld, A.: *Cooperating processes for Low-Level Vision: A Survey*. Tech. Rep. 123, University of Texas at Austin, January 1980.
33. Smith. R. G.: The control net protocol: high level communication and control in a distributed problem solver. *Proc. First Int. Conf. on Distributed Computing Systems*, October 1979.
34. Rao, R.: *Design and Evaluation of Distributed Communication Primitives*. Tech. Rep. 80-04-01, University of Washington, April 1980.
35. Ball, J., Williams, G., and Low, J.: *Preliminary ZENO Language Description*. Tech. Rep. TR 41, University of Rochester, January 1979.
36. Feldman, J.: High level programming for distributed computing. *CACM*, June 1979.
37. Tarini, F., Sharp, R., Martelli, M., and Endrizzi, A.: A network system language. *Proc. First Int. Conf. on Distributed Computing Systems*, October 1979.
38. Liskov, B.: Primitives for distributed computing. *Proc. seventh Symp. on Operating Systems Principles*, December, 1979. (Also Computation Structures Group Memo 175, MIT, May.)
39. Reynolds, P.: *Parallel Processing Structures: Languages, Schedules, and Performance Results*. Ph.D. Thesis, University of Texas at Austin, 1979.
40. Stiegler, H. G.: A unified interface for process communication. *Proc. First Int. Conf. on Distributed Computing Systems*, October 1979.
41. Test, J. A.: An interprocess communication scheme for the support of cooperating

process networks. *Proc. First Int. Conf. on Distributed Computing Systems*, October 1979.

42. Hunt, J. G.: Messages in typed languages. *ACM Sigplan Notices*, January 1979.
43. Silberschatz, A.: *Cell: A Distributed Computing Modularization Concept*. Tech. Rep., University of Texas at Austin, 1980.
44. Brinch Hansen, P.: Distributed processes: a concurrent programming language. *CACM*, November 1978.
45. Cook, R.: *MOD—a language for distributed programming. *IEEE Trans. on Software Engineering*, November 1980.
46. Andrews, G.: *Synchronizing Resources*. ACM Trans. on Prog. Langs. and Systems, Vol. 3, No. 4, October 1981. (Also Tech. Rep. TR 79-20, University of Arizona, December 1979).
47. Hewitt, C., Attardi, G., and Lieberman, H.: Specifying and proving properties of guardians for distributed systems. *Proc. Int. Symp. on Semantics of Concurrent Processes*, Evian (France), Springer-Verlag, July 1979.
48. Hewitt, C., Attardi, G., and Lieberman, H.: Security and modularity in message passing. *Proc. First Int. Conf. on Distributed Computing Systems*, October 1979.
49. Lampson, B., and Redell, D.: Experience with processes and monitors in Mesa. *CACM*, February 1980.
50. Lauer, H., and Needham, R.: On the duality of operating system structures. *Proc. Int. Symp. on Operating Systems*, IRIA (France), October 1978. (Reprinted in *ACM Operating Systems Review*, April 1979.)
51. Peterson, J.: Notes on a workshop on distributed computing. *ACM SIGOPS Operating Systems Review*, July 1979.
52. Hunt, J. G.: An introduction to LIMP: an experimental language for the implementation of messages and processes. *Proc. Fifth Conf. on Programming Languages of the Gesselschaft fuer Informatik*, Technische Universitaet Braunschweig (West Germany), March 1978.
53. Kahn, G., and MacQueen, D.: Coroutines and networks of communicating processes. *Proc. Information Processing*, before 77. IFIP, 1977.
54. Solomon, M., and Finkel, R.: The Roscoe distributed operating system. *Proc. Seventh Symp. on Operating Systems Principles*, December 1979.
55. Milner, R.: Synthesis of Communicating Behaviour. *Proc. Seventh Symp. on Mathematical Foundations of Computer Science*, Springer-Verlag, Zakopane (Poland), Lecture Notes in Computer Science, Vol. 64, 1978.
56. Chandy, K. M., and Misra, J.: *A Simple Model of Distributed Programs Based on Implementation-Hiding and Process Autonomy*. Tech. Rep. TR-127, Distributed Systems Group, University of Texas at Austin, January 1980.
57. Hewitt, C., and Baker, H.: Laws for communicating parallel processes. *Proc. Information Processing*, Vol. 77. IFIP, 1977.
58. Stark, E.: A unified interface for process communication. *Proc. First Int. Conf. on Distributed Computing Systems*, October 1979.
59. Schneider, F., and Bernstein, A.: *Mechanisms for Specifying Scheduling Policies*. Tech. Rep. TR 79-365, Cornell University, January 1979.
60. Mohan, C.: An analysis of the design of SDD-1: a system for distributed data bases. In *Distributed Databases*, Infotech State of the Art Report, Infotech International, Maidenhead, England, 1979 (Also Tech. Rep. SDBEG-11, University of Texas at Austin.)
61. Mohan, C., and Popescu-Zeletin, R.: *Impact of Distributed Data Base Management on the ISO-OSI and ANSI/SPARC Frameworks*, Proc. 15th Hawaii International Conference on System Sciences, Honolulu, January 1982.
62. Mohan, C.: Distributed data base management: some thoughts and analyses. *Proc.*

ACM 1980 Annual Conf., 1980. (Also *Tech. Rep.* TR-129, Software and Data Base Engineering Group, University of Texas at Austin, May.)
63. Kain, R., and Franta, W. R.: Interprocess communication schemes supporting system reconfiguration. *COMPSAC 80*, November 1980.
64. Darondeau, Ph., Le Guernie, P., and Raynal, M.: Abstract specification of communicating systems. *Proc. Fist Int. Conf. on Distributed Computing Systems*, October 1979.
65. Kramer, J., and Cunningham, R. J.: Towards a notation for the functional design of distributed processing systems. *Proc. Int. Conf. on Parallel Processing*, 1978.
66. Francez, N.: Distributed termination. *ACM Trans. on Programming Languages and Systems*, **2**, No. 1, January 1980.
67. Dijkstra, E., and Scholten, C. S.: *Termination Detection for Diffusing Computations*, Information Processing Letters, Vol. II, No. 1, August 1980.
68. Yemini, Y., and Cohen, D.: Some issues in distributed computing. *Proc. First Int. Conf. on Distributed Computing Systems*, October 1979.
69. Jazayeri, M., *et al.*: CSP/80: a language for communicating sequential processes. *Proc. COMPCON*, Fall 1980.
70. Jones, A., and Schwans, K.: TASK forces: distributed software for solving problems of substantial size. *Proc. Fourth Int. Conf. on Software Engineering*, September 1979.
71. Jones, A. *et al.*: StarOS, a multiprocessor operating system for the support of task forces. *Proc. Seventh Symp. on Operating Systems Principles*, December 1979.
72. Jammel, A., and Stiegler, H.: Protection based on decentralized control. *Proc. Second Int. Symp. on Operating Systems Theory and Practice*, Rocquencourt (France), October 1978.
73. Jammel, A., and Stiegler, H.: Structural decomposition and distributed systems. *Proc. First European Conf. on Parallel and Distributed Processing*, Toulouse (France), February 1979.
74. Lynch, N., and Fischer, M.: On describing the behaviour and implementation of distributed systems. *Proc. Int. Symp. On Semantics of Concurrent Computation*, Springer-Verlag, Evian (France), July, 1979. (Also Tech. Rep. 79-06-01, Georgia Institute of Technology.)
75. Mohan, C., and Lindsay, B.: Efficient Commit Protocols for the Tree of Processes Model of Distributed Transactions. *IBM Research Report*, IBM San Jose Research Laboratory, February 1983.
76. Lindsay, B., Haas, L., Mohan, C., Wilms, P., and Yost, R.: Computation and Communication in R*: A Distributed Database Manager. *IBM Research Report RJ3740*, San Jose Research Laboratory, January 1983.
77. Mohan, C., Strong, H. R., and Finkelstein, S.: Method for Distributed Transaction Commit and Recovery Using Byzantine Agreement within Clusters of Processors. *IBM Research Report*, San Jose Research Laboratory, February 1983.

BIBLIOGRAPHY

Atkinson, R., and Hewitt, C.: Synchronization in actor systems. *Proc. ACM Symp. on Principles of Programming Languages*, January 1977.

Clark, D., Greif, I., Liskov, B., and Svobodova, L.: *Semantics of Distributed Computing.* Progress Report of the Distributed Systems Group, Laboratory for Computer Science, MIT, September 1978.

Fitzwater, D. R., and Zave, P.: The use of formal asynchronous process specifications in a system development process. *Proc. Sixth Texas Conf. on Computing Systems*, November 1977.

Honda, M.: *The Design of a Parallel Programming Language for Artificial Intelligence Applications*. Ph.D. Thesis, Tech. Rep. 331, University of Wisconsin—Madison, August 1978.

Luniewski, A.: *Relation Between Multiple Ports and Multiple Processes*. Distributed Systems Group Note 29, MIT, December, 1978.

MacQueen, D.: *Models for Distributed Computing*. Tech. Rep. RR No. 351, IRIA (France), April 1979.

Mohan, C.: Survey of recent operating systems research, designs and implementations. *ACM SIGOPS Operating Systems Review*, January 1978. (Also Tech. Rep. TR-75, University of Texas at Austin, October 1977.)

Mohan, C.: An overview of recent data base research. *ACM SIGBDP's DATABASE*, Fall 1978. (Also Tech. Rep. SDBEG-5, Software and Data Base Engineering Group, University of Texas at Austin, April.)

Advances in Distributed Processing Management, Volume 2
Edited by P. S. Fisher, J. Slonim, and E. A. Unger

Chapter 4

SIZING ACTIVITIES AND RESOURCE REQUIREMENTS IN A DISTRIBUTED PROCESSING SYSTEM

Ralph Mauriello
Litton Data Systems, 8000 Woodley Avenue, Van Nuys, California

The two major aspects of distributed design to be considered are:

1. Creating a distributed system for application to various functions
2. Applying an existing distributed processing system (DPS) to a particular task or function

The first of these design aspects involves such tasks as:

1. Identification of a portion of the marketplace
2. Analysis of each potential application
3. Identification of the requirements of each application
4. Postulation of candidate distributed processing configurations
5. Evaluation of the configurations versus the requirements for each of the identified applications
6. Selection of those features which apply to the greatest dollar volume of the potential market

A review of the preceding list reveals that an entire book could be written on the creation of a DPS for applications to various functions. Therefore this chapter is limited to the application of an existing DPS to the solution of a particular set of problems.

DISTRIBUTED DESIGN METHODOLOGY

The methodology for design of a DPS is no different than that for the design of a large centralized processing system. The steps to be followed, listed in Table 4-1, are applicable to the design of any system in an orderly manner. The relative

TABLE 4-1
Distributed processing system design methodology

1. Determine objectives.
2. Identify requirements.
   (a) List system functions.
   (b) Determine processing load.
   (c) Identify response time requirements.
3. Define approach.
   (a) Select candidate hardware approaches.
   (b) Propose partitioning.
4. Develop and apply model to evaluate proposed hardware and partitioning versus requirements.
5. Repeat step 4 until optimum solution determined.

newness of distributed processing design make the use of a preestablished procedure mandatory.

What are the objectives of the system and what are the constraints? Is high performance or low cost the key objective? Is ultrareliability 'no matter what it costs' the objective? What physical factors, such as size, weight, and power, are important? What is the environment in which the equipment must operate—air-conditioned room or outdoors? The system objective(s) must be identified, classified, and prioritized. The answers to these and other questions of the same type are required to establish the evaluation criteria needed for step 5 of Table 4-1.

Next, the system requirements must be identified, categorized, and quantified. What are the primary system functions? What processing is needed to provide the functions? What stimuli activate the functions? How fast must the system respond?

The approach must consider the various design choices available. What node intercommunication should be used? Which CPU offers the best architecture for the problem at hand? How are tasks to be allocated and distributed? How should the data base be partitioned? What is the system control approach?

Because of the complexities of the interactions, manual analysis is limited to preliminary evaluations. Therefore, a computer program which models the system and its responses to the various stimuli is required. The 'optimum' solution is obtained by applying the criteria determined in step 1. The proposed hardware and partitioning are evaluated and iterated to achieve an optimum solution. It is assumed that objectives (and their relative priorities) will be established, to a large extent, by the customer. Therefore, this discussion will be limited to items 2 through 4 of Table 4-1.

ESTABLISH THE REQUIREMENTS

This task is the key in any system design. Failure to translate the customer objectives correctly into system performance requirements can be catastrophic. By its very nature a DPS is more 'forgiving' than a conventional centralized

TABLE 4-2
Establishing system functional requirements

1. Identify all system functions.
2. Determine system processing load.
   (a) Identify all types and frequency of system stimuli.
   (b) Trace functional flow in response to each stimulus.
   (c) Determine processing requirements for each function (including interfaces).
3. Identify response requirements for each stimulus.

approach. If designed properly, the addition of more computing resources is easily accommodated. The keywords in the sentence are 'designed properly.' The major factors in arriving at a 'properly' designed system are functional partitioning and the internode communication, which will be considered later.

The first step in any design is identification of the system requirements. Considerations should include, but not be limited to, those in Table 4-2. All system functions, and the processing required for each, must be determined. System stimuli types, and frequency of each, must be identified along with the allowable response time to each stimulus.

An aid in listing all the required system functions is the classification of the various functions into three categories:

1. Primary functions
2. Support functions (subfunctions)
3. Interface functions

The primary functions are those tasks that must be performed to accomplish the overall objective of the system. For example, in an air traffic control system, primary functions would include correlation, tracking, display, and communication. Support or subfunctions exist only to support the primary functions. These subfunctions may create and maintain files and/or tables that are used during the execution of the primary function and/or support more than one primary function.

Interface functions provide service to both the primary functions and subfunctions within the system. They generally fall into three major categories, two of which are routines (such as math subroutines) and centralized file update control and maintenance. A third and most significant interface function in a distributed system is the distributed executive which resides at each node. In addition to the usual services, it provides communication between the nodes in such a manner that applications programs may call for resources without knowledge of the physical location of the resource being called.

Referring once again to Table 4-2, after identifying and classifying all functions, the next step is to determine the system processing load. The first step in determining the system processing load is the identification of all external stimuli and their frequency. Only external stimuli (e.g., a radar report in an air traffic control system) are considered, because internal stimuli (e.g. a program call of subroutine) are the result of the interfaces between functions.

The next step is to define the interrelationships of all primary functions, subfunctions, and interface programs. Functional flow diagrams, which trace the interaction of the functions in response to each stimulus, must be created. A careful tracing through all functions, of all three categories, is necessary to obtain an accurate system model that can be used for candidate system evaluation.

Finally, the processing time requirements for each function must be determined. This step involves identification of all inputs and outputs for each function as well as estimates of the program execution time, size, and data base requirements. The input and output requirements can be obtained directly from the functional flow diagrams developed in the previous step.

The sizing and throughput studies undertaken will be governed by whether a totally new application is being solved on a distributed processing system or whether the distributed processing system is being used to provide a more cost-effective solution to an already existing application. It is apparent that much less risk is involved in reimplementing an existing application, as the software and hardware that are already operational may be analyzed in great detail to assure an optimum solution to the problem. By contrast, a new application requires the added task of a complete conceptual design, including, for example, definition of requirements, identification of stimuli, and specification of response times, all of which are usually well defined in an existing system.

Frequently, many of the functions required of the system have been previously provided, usually on a different computer architecture from the one(s) available in the DPS to be applied to the task. Sample coding of several critical tasks can yield a 'conversion factor' between architectures to permit relatively accurate estimates of program and data base size and the execution rates required. Often, even when one is applying a distributed system to an existing application, the potential user will demand additional capabilities for his system. This special need then forces the sizing task to be broken into two phases: analysis of the existing functions and synthesis of the new capabilities.

If the application is a totally new one a comparable set of functions must be identified and analyzed to determine program sizes, processing speeds, and data base needs. Even with comparable functions available for analysis, considerable experience is needed to estimate required program sizes and throughput. Without comparable functions, reasonable estimates are extremely difficult, if not impossible. Selection of the tasks for sample coding is critical. Estimates based upon the wrong set of sample programs can be disastrous.

Finally, and perhaps most important of all, the response time to each external stimulus must be determined. My experience is limited to the application of distributed processing concepts to the tactical military environment. This limited set of well-defined functions is a mixed blessing. On one hand, it permits certain simplifying assumptions, while on the other hand, it imposes unyielding response time requirements. The 'luxury' of a statistical response time approach permitted in a large time-sharing network is not available in a military real-time system. Although the number and frequency of the stimuli make a large contribution to establishing the required processing throughput, in a real-time command and control system, the response time is the final determining factor.

While all of the preceding information is important in the design of a centralized system, it is absolutely critical in the design of a distributed system. In fact, as will be shown later, the response time requirements force the partitioning of programs and data bases along certain lines and are a critical factor in determining the node intercommunication data rates.

DEFINE THE APPROACH

Now that the requirements have been detailed, the next step is to define the approach. The system designer is always confronted with design choices. Table 4-3 lists three critical choices to be made in the design of a distributed system. These choices make a significant impact in the sizing and partitioning of programs and data bases.

INTERCONNECTION OF THE DATA PROCESSORS

Two basic configurations which have been the object of considerable effort are the star and loop configurations, shown in Figures 4-1 and 4-2, respectively. In the purest form of the ring architecture, the system is designed to provide

TABLE 4-3
Three critical design choices

1. Interconnection of nodes
   (a) Type
      — Ring or loop
      — Star or net
      — Linear bus
   (b) Protocol
      — Command response
      — Polled contention
      — Token passing
   (c) Media
      — Radio
      — Wire
2. CPU selection
   (a) New architecture
   (b) Emulation
3. Allocation of functions to processors
   (a) On-line tasks allocation (load-balancing)
   (b) Processors dedicated to selected task
   (c) Combination of above

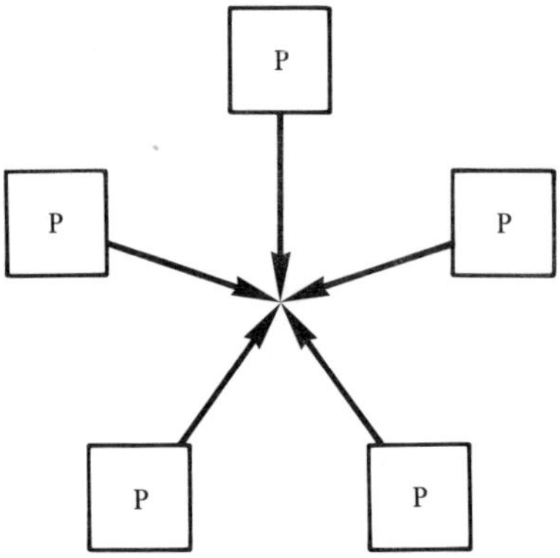

Figure 4-1. Star configuration.

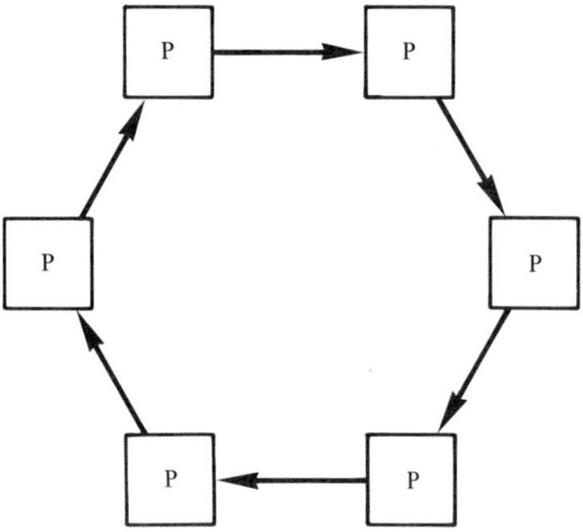

Figure 4-2. Loop configuration.

autonomous user access (no central polling), and processor intercommunications are implemented through a unidirectional loop connecting the processors. In the star configuration, one processor is usually in full control of the system, and may be dedicated to that role. However, autonomous user access has been implemented in at least one star configuration.

The ring and star structures can probably be considered to be at the opposite extremes of the computer interconnection spectrum. Some intermediate architectural concepts are the global bus concept (Figure 4-3) and the complete interconnection concept (Figure 4-4).

The global bus can be viewed as a 'distributed' star in that both have the characteristics that all processors 'see' all messages on the bus and only one message may be on the bus at a time.

The complete interconnection and loop configurations can permit simultaneous multiple transmissions. (The loop is, after all, a series of point-to-point links tied in a ring.) It should be noted that the loop can also be designed to provide the same

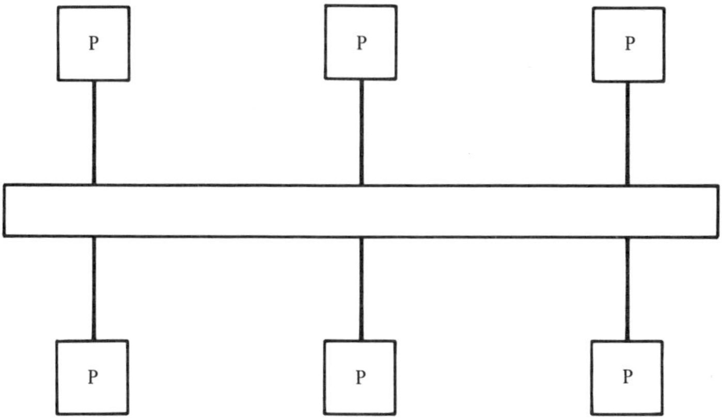

Figure 4-3. Global bus.

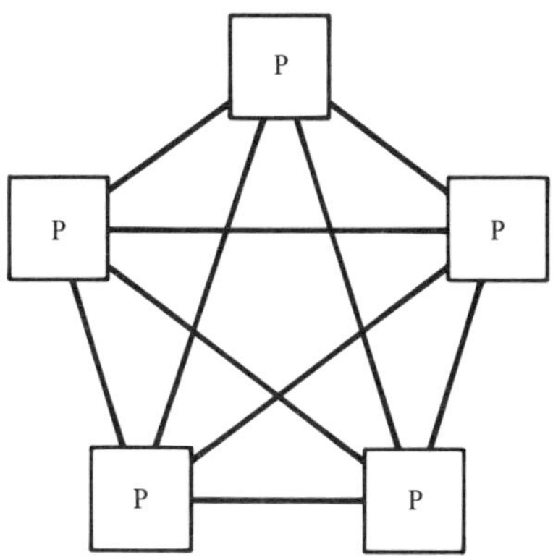

Figure 4-4. Complete interconnection.

characteristics as the star and global bus; i.e.

1. All processors 'see' all messages.
2. One message appears at a time.

The highest data transfer exchange rate as well as the ability to continue operation in the event of a failure(s) is provided by the complete interconnection approach. However, as the number of processors increases, the complete interconnect scheme quickly becomes too expensive in all but very special cases. Therefore, further considerations will be limited to the first three bus types.

Choice of Protocol

The three major techniques in use (Table 4-3) may be applied to all bus types. The command response protocol requires a bus master with total control. 'Slaves' transmit only when commanded. Slave transmission may be directly to another slave or to the master which stores and forwards the message to the intended recipient.

The polled contention technique also requires a master which controls all bus traffic. Each of the slaves is polled in turn and given a chance to transmit. If it has no message to transmit, the next slave is polled.

The token passing scheme provides autonomous user access and thus limits the bus controller function to that of issuing a 'token' to one of the processors. (The token is a permit to transmit.) The token is passed sequentially to all processors. Upon receipt of the token, if a node has nothing to transmit, the token is passed to the next processor in the sequence. If a node must transmit a message, it does so and then appends the token to the end of the message. Note, in the star or global bus, the token must be addressed, whereas in the loop the sequence is determined by the interconnection.

Type of Media

To a large extent, the decision of media type is governed by the geographic distribution between nodes and is therefore beyond the scope of this chapter.

The preceding discussion has made no attempt to evaluate the relative merits of the type, protocol, or media used for node interconnection. The model evaluates these choices after distribution of the programs and data base.

CPU Architecture

A low-risk approach to a distributed implementation of an existing system is afforded by the technique of emulation. While it is true that the updating of any system to state-of-the-art hardware will be accompanied by new functions, the sizing of which is always difficult, the vast majority of the applications programs may be used unmodified, making program-sizing estimates very accurate, since only a small portion of the programs will be new. Processing speed requirements may also be accurately estimated for the same reason; i.e. a relatively small portion is new. The throughput performance of existing application programs may be accurately measured, as can the speed of the emulator.

At first glance, one may feel that while all the preceding description applies very well to application programs and their supporting subroutines, the executive from the previous system should provide little, if any, carryover to a distributed system. That concept is true if the new system is implemented with a new computer architecture. However, once again, the technique of emulation permits the salvaging of major portions of the executive. It must be remembered that all the application programs were designed and coded in expectation of the support provided by the executive.

I know several cases in which this technique was successfully applied. The cost is the extra memory and execution time required at each node to store and execute a much larger and more comprehensive executive than would otherwise be required. The savings are the elimination of the effort required to develop a new and 'more efficient' (less memory space and faster execution) executive.

Studies in the early seventies showed that system development costs were predominately those for software (60 to 85 per cent.). With the advent of truly cheap hardware during the latter part of the decade, costs were skewed even more, making the choice of emulation even more attractive for distributed implementation of existing functions. It is still necessary to modify the existing executive. These modifications take two forms: (1) the elimination of unneeded support functions and (2) the addition of a capability that would permit an application program to call for a resource without knowledge of the physical location of the resource.

Allocation of Tasks

A key factor in the design considerations for the application of the DPS is the philosophy of the design approach. For example, does the system provide the ability for users in various nodes to request functions of other users without the knowledge of the location of the resource? Is load-balancing provided in the system? Are the requirements such that statistical response times are permissible as opposed to worst-case response times? Are degraded modes considerations for failures only or is battle damage a consideration? (Military systems must consider battle damage.) Finally, will the design approach be simulated exclusively, or will the simulation be augmented by experimentation on an available set of hardware?

The most notable of the preceding considerations is 'load-balancing.' This concept employs on-line monitoring of the load of each processor within the system, and uses that information to assign tasks to the 'least busy' processors. The primary goal of this approach is to reduce the number of processors required by using all computing resources efficiently. Such a concept, in my opinion, is no longer viable for the following reasons:

1. Hardware is cheap, and the cost of an added processor or two will be much less than the cost of developing the load-monitoring and load-balancing software.
2. Software schemes of that type require a centralized system executive which will be much more vulnerable to failures than a system with distributed control. In addition, the 'overhead' for such a generalized scheme may preclude satisfaction of response-time requirements.

PARTITIONING THE SYSTEM

Having determined all requirements, selected several candidate approaches, identified all external stimuli, and developed the functional flow diagrams, which show the interrelationships of the software modules, it is now time to proceed to distributing the system.

The initial attempt of distributing a design throughout a network of processors is based upon the information gained during the requirements definition phase of the functional design. The design for distribution should be attacked in three phases. Phase 1 is an allocation of system functions and subfunctions to each of the nodes within the system. Phase 2 considers distributing the associated data base, and phase 3 involves redistribution of both the programs and the data as the response time bottlenecks become apparent.

Phase 1—Functional Distribution

Ideally, the programs which perform the appropriate functions required at a particular node will be resident within that node. Although this situation means replication of the programs to perform that particular function (if that function is required at multiple nodes), the rapidly decreasing hardware costs encourage that approach as a first partitioning for the instructions.

During the requirements definition phase of the design, all system functions were classified into one of three categories: primary, support, and interface. Each of these categories must be treated differently in the partitioning process. Response times to external system stimuli (e.g. operator action at a console) are usually specified in relation to primary functions. Therefore, in a real-time distributed system, a primary function software module should almost always be placed at the node where the function is required. Achieving this goal often requires replication of a program at several nodes.

Subfunctions exist only to support one or more of the primary functions. The number of nodes which require the subfunction and the response time are the key factors. If a subfunction is required in very few nodes, then consideration should be given to placing the subfunction at all those nodes where its support to the primary function is needed, independent of its size. Natural redundancy is obtained with this approach. However, if the subfunction is large, replication in all nodes requiring this subfunction may be costly.

On the other hand, if the subfunction is required in support of many primary functions, then program size and response time are the key factors. If the size of the subfunction is small enough, then this subfunction may be replicated throughout the system independently of response-time requirements. If the system stimulus, which requires use of this subfunction, has a high frequency and/or a short response-time requirement, it may be necessary to place this subfunction in the same node as the primary function. If the subfunction is quite large, the minimum number of copies permitted by the response time and survivability should be kept.

Interface functions, such as math subroutines and file update control, are typically small programs, and it is best to replicate these functions at each node to minimize data exchange between nodes. The last major interface function provided by the executive, internode communication, must be replicated at all nodes.

In summary, functional distribution is performed based on:

1. Functional relationship to primary system mission
2. Frequency of stimuli
3. Response time to stimuli

Phase 2—Data Base Distribution

The partitioning of the data base is far more complex than the partitioning of the functions. Since the data bases are typically much larger than the programs, the placement of the entire data base in each of the nodes is immediately determined to be impractical. Even reducing the data base to only that portion which is relevant to that particular node will require far more memory in each node than may be economically feasible. It should be noted, at this point, that the maintenance and data retrieval problem of a distributed data base is, in itself, a nontrivial task and the subject of many textbooks. Suffice it to say that the partitioning of the data base is critical because it determines, to a large extent, the system memory requirements and the amount of data that will be required to be exchanged between the nodes. The ideal situation limits the internode exchange of data to responses to queries and update of the data base.

The distribution of the data base, to support the previously selected partitioning of the functions, must take into consideration the factors listed in Table 4-4. Reviewing these items reinforces the fact that the response time is the forcing function in a distributed design of a real-time system.

Response time to each external stimulus, that requires access to the data base, must be determined. The frequency of the stimulus and the type of data base access also must be determined. For example, does the stimulus require data base query or update? What are the percentages of each and how do these figures relate to system response times? Where response times are not specified, values must be assumed to permit evaluation of the data base partitioning. The trade-off is cost of replication versus response time. For example, replicating a function and its required portion of the data base at every node may provide a response time in milliseconds, whereas system requirements may permit 2 or 3 seconds. This 'leisurely' response will permit a single copy of the data base and probably a single copy of the program.

Therefore, the first two considerations regarding the allocation of portions of the data base to each of the nodes are the desired response time to each of the external system stimuli and the location of the using function. Those that need immediate reaction, i.e. a visible, immediate response to the operator, will require local storage of that portion of the data base necessary to provide that response. On the other hand, those stimuli which permit delays on the order of 1 or 2 seconds may permit the system to contain a single copy of that portion of the data base, thereby reducing the amount of memory required to satisfy the total system requirements.

It should be noted that degraded mode requirements will almost always demand that a second safety copy of all data and programs be stored somewhere within the system. Therefore, even those portions of the data base that are required only once—to satisfy system response time requirements—will have to be stored a second time owing to degraded mode requirement. However, those portions of the data base which require their replication, to ensure the appropriate response time, have a natural redundancy built in and, therefore, need not be specifically replicated for degraded mode operation.

The next three factors of Table 4-4 are also closely related. If the maximum number of accesses and the percentage of query versus update is known, a trade-off between replication of the data versus a single-system copy can be made. The percentage of query versus update is critical because the more dramatic the reduction of query time (through file organization methods), the greater the time required to update the file. Therefore, a major decision at this point involves file organization, access techniques, and program design.

For example, if a direct access method is used, a useful technique is the file retrieval prediction. When it is known that a file must be accessed once halfway through the processing, this file could be located at another node; then prior to starting the process, it is possible to request a copy of the record required within the file. When the function requests the data, the data have already been returned or are on their way.

However, for sequential file access, it is not realistic to contemplate a search of the file across a network structure. Therefore, if sequential file processing is required in support of a primary function, the data usually must be colated. If the response time permits, the file may be remotely located. However, the file search mechanism must be colocated with the file, thus limiting the network exchange to a query and the return of requested data.

Indexed or inverted files can be used effectively in distributed systems to reduce access times. Based on element/primary mission requirements, indexed files or inverted files can be colated with the using function. Information contained within the index or inversion scheme is sufficient for the function to compute the key to the data required for completion of the processing. The result will be direct access to a specific set of records that may be local or located at another node. Again, the eventual decision of replication versus one copy is based on the data set size as well as response time.

This decision returns us to consideration of the rate of queries versus updates.

TABLE 4-4
Data distribution considerations

1. Response times to external stimuli
2. Location of using function
3. Type of data base access required
4. Percentage of queries versus update
5. Location(s) of the data base maintenance function

Basically, as the data are distributed over a greater number of nodes, update time increases and query time decreases. On the other hand, reducing the number of nodes maintaining a set of data results in increased query time while decreasing update time. Since response time to external stimuli is the final criterion, the system model must be used to determine a satisfactory and low-cost partitioning.

PHASE III—REDISTRIBUTION THROUGH MODELING

The initial partitioning process described earlier must now be subjected to verification to determine whether the system response time to each of the external stimuli is satisfactory. An excellent technique is stimulus-tracing, using a computer model which simulates system reaction to each stimulus. The key factors to be included in the model are listed in Table 4-5.

The first item is fixed by system requirements and the second is provided by the functional flow diagrams. The remaining items are parametric in the model to permit iteration of the partitioning. (It is very unlikely that the initial partition will satisfy all response-time requirements.)

Using the model and the estimates of program size and throughput required, determine for each partitioning:

1. The throughput required at each node
2. The size of the programs
3. The amount of data transfer required between nodes to perform all mission functions within the specified response times

The stimulus trace method referred to earlier can be illustrated by an extremely simple example. Figure 4-5 depicts three nodes in a distributed system which contain three functions and four data items, as shown after the partitioning. Based on the assumptions of Figure 4-5, Table 4-6 is a stimulus trace of S1, which results in two external outputs, E1 and E2.

Assumption 1 of Figure 4-5 deserves comment. The initial pass at partitioning will be based upon manual estimates of the size and speed required of the programs. The stimulus trace model will probably render the first cut invalid

TABLE 4-5
Key factors in distributed system model

1. Identification of stimuli and frequency of each
2. Interrelationships among all functions (functional flow diagrams)
3. Physical location of functions and associated data base
4. Processing time for each function
5. Data base access time
6. Interface time between functions
   (a) Executive calls
   (b) Data bus access time
   (c) Data bus transfer rates

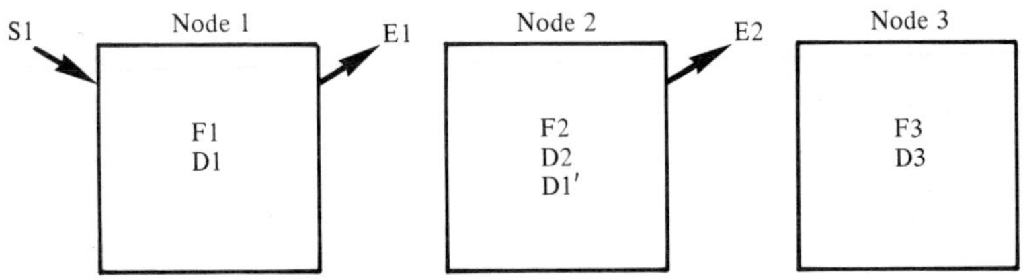

Assume:

1. Initial partitioning satisfies throughput and memory size requirements at each node.
2. Three functions (F1 through F3) and four data segments (D1, D2, D3, and D1′).
3. Stimulus S1 causes two outputs, E1 (at node 1) and E2 (at node 2).
4. F1 needs D1;
   F2 needs D2 and D1′ (subset of D1);
   F3 needs D3, D1′, and D2.

Figure 4-5. Sample partitioning of distributed system.

TABLE 4-6
Stimulus trace of system response to stimulus S1

Stimulus S1 trace

- Node 1
  - Receive stimulus S1
  - Activate F1
  - Access D1
  - Process
  - Update D1
  - Output update data to other nodes
- Node 2
  - Input from node 1
  - Activate F2
  - Update D1′ with node 1 output
  - Process
  - Access D2 and D1′
  - Process
  - External output E2
- Node 3
  - Input from node 1
  - Process
  - Access D3
  - Access D2 from node 2
  - Process
  - Output result to node 1
- Node 1
  - Input from node 3
  - Process
  - External output 1

because the interaction of all programs is too complex to deal with manually. Typically, the model will expose the need for redistribution of the program and data base to increase system performance. This usually requires additional replication of the program and/or data base at the nodes closest to the user. The result is reduced response time. In addition, the model will identify areas wherein replication actually exceeds the requirements for appropriate performance. In these cases, replication can be reduced, thus decreasing memory costs. After review of the model output, redistribution is submitted to the model. It is exercised once again, and the result is evaluated.

Unfortunately, in the real world of system requirements, it is frequently impossible to satisfy all requirements simultaneously. Even when the addition of more hardware is possible, cost is always a salient factor. Therefore, at this point negotiations with customers are required to prioritize response times. This permits the system design to satisfy the requirements identified by the customer as most critical.

INTERNODE COMMUNICATION REQUIREMENTS

It is axiomatic that a well-partitioned distributed system not only satisfies all response-time requirements but also minimizes the amount of data transferred between nodes. Since a distributed system, by definition, requires physical separation of computers and memories, sizing of the communication requirements is critical in achieving a cost-effective design. In fact, a poor sizing of the bus throughput may result in an inoperable system at less than specified loads. However, minimization of data bus loads does not ensure success. Two items of information are needed:

1. The total system data throughput that the bus must provide to satisfy maximum system loading requirements within the required response times.
2. The data throughput rate provided by the bus.

The first of these, system data throughput, is one of the significant outputs of the model described earlier. System data are defined as useful system information exclusive of overhead for synchronization, protocol, addressing, error checks, and other features. The second item, bus throughput, was considered by Schenk, Hileman, and Fischer,[1] who applied queuing analysis to digital data buses to determine the relative merits of different bus protocols. While the initial goal of selecting the most efficient bus was satisfied by the study, a side benefit was the exposure of the criticality of the typical message length in determining bus performance. It is intuitive that longer messages result in better bit-rate bus efficiencies. However, when real-time response requirements are considered, the message lengths become critical. Data for the study were obtained from existing programs in a military combat system. Simulated inputs representing maximum load conditions were used to drive the system while data flow between program modules was recorded. The results were:

1. The average length message was 120 bits (70 per cent. were 96 bits).
2. Transactions occurred in spurts resulting in peak loads five to eight times the nominal maximum.

Two charts are reproduced from that report to show the significance of message length and response time in relation to system data throughput (Figures 4-6 and 4-7). In these figures, the vertical axis is the average delay time for servicing a message. This delay time is equal to the message transmission time plus the average time spent waiting for the bus. The horizontal axis is the average message length in words when one word is equal to 16 bits of data. The dashed vertical lines correspond to average message lengths of 50 bits (3.1 words) and 120 bits (7.5 words). The average message lengths correspond to the average messages for existing systems which were studied. The dashed horizontal lines represent message-servicing delays of 200 and 20 μs respectively, identified as requirements in the system under study.

Figure 4-6 shows the characteristics of a 20-Mb token-passing bus operating in a system with only 5 Mb/s of system throughput data. The family of three curves shows the sensitivity to the number of nodes on a loop, with curves for 5, 10, and 15 nodes plotted. The lower three curves show actual message transmission times (time to transmit a message once the sending node gains bus access) as a function of message length. The difference in time between the lower three curves and the upper three curves is the average time that a node will have to wait for bus access (as a function of the average message length).

As can be seen, for short message lengths, the high ratio of protocol (overhead) to data causes the delay to increase rapidly as a function of decreasing message lengths while keeping the total throughput constant. When the delay becomes too large, the system buffers will overflow and data will be lost. None of the three loops shown (5, 10, or 15 nodes) is capable of transferring 5 Mb/s of data within the specified 20 μs, whereas the 5- and 10-node loops can handle both 50- or 120-bit average message length in the 200-μs delay time. The 15-node system can handle the 120-bit but not the 50-bit message within the 200-μs criterion.

Another view of the same data is presented in Figure 4-7, which holds the number of nodes constant at 10 and varies the bus throughput requirements from 2 to 12 Mb/s. This graph shows that 3 Mb/s is the maximum achievable requirements throughput capable of satisfying the 20-μs delay time. The 5-Mb/s system throughput requirement (this curve is repeated from Figure 4-6) can handle the 50-bit message length in less than 200 μs, whereas the 8-Mb/s requirement can only handle a 96-bit average message within the 200 μs constraint.

The significance of the information presented in Figures 4-6 and 4-7 is highlighted by the fact that the bus under study had a nominal 20-Mb/s transfer rate. The degradation in system data throughput is due to bus protocol and overhead bits. Furthermore, the bus examined was a token-passing bus, the most efficient of the candidate protocols identified earlier in Table 4-3.

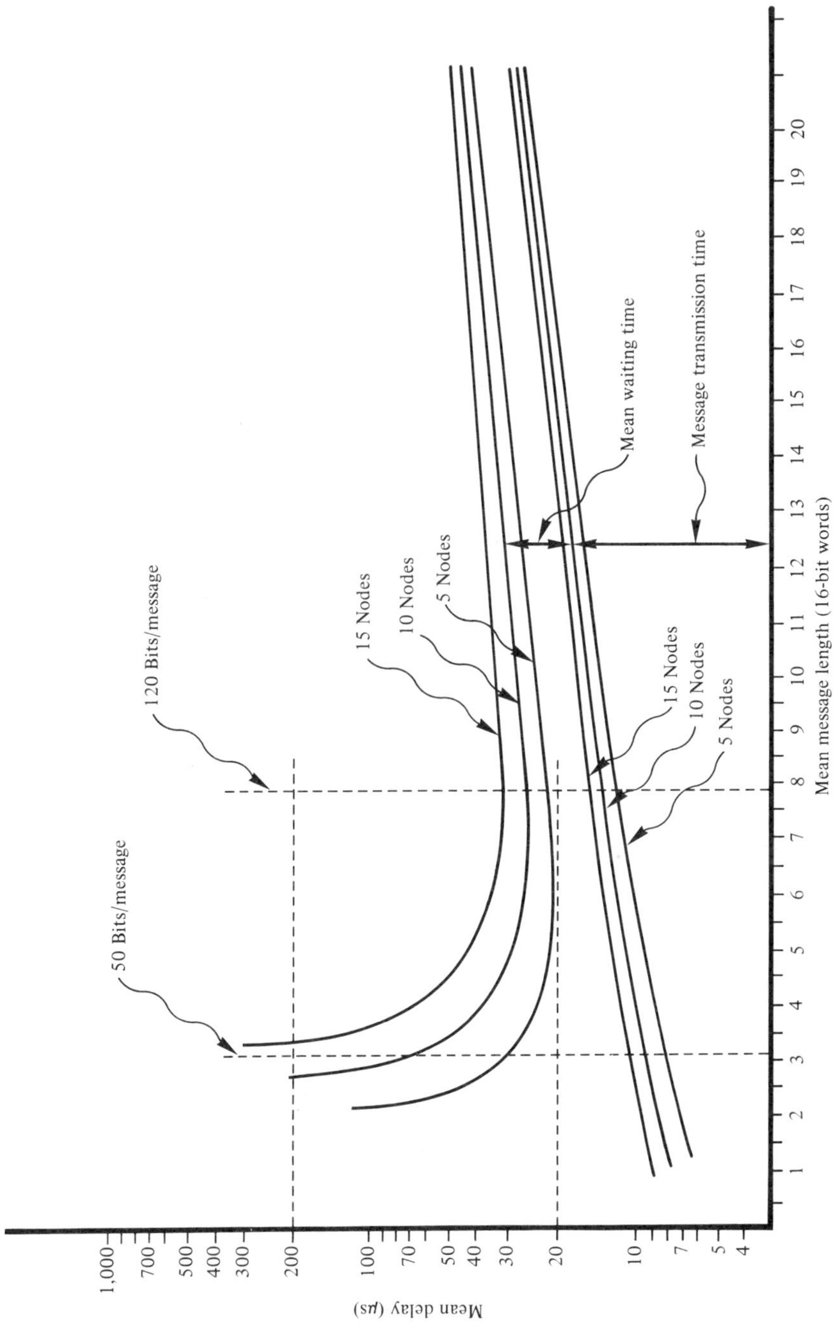

Figure 4-6. Data bus for 5 Mb/s of throughput. (From Schenk, Hileman, and Fischer.[1])

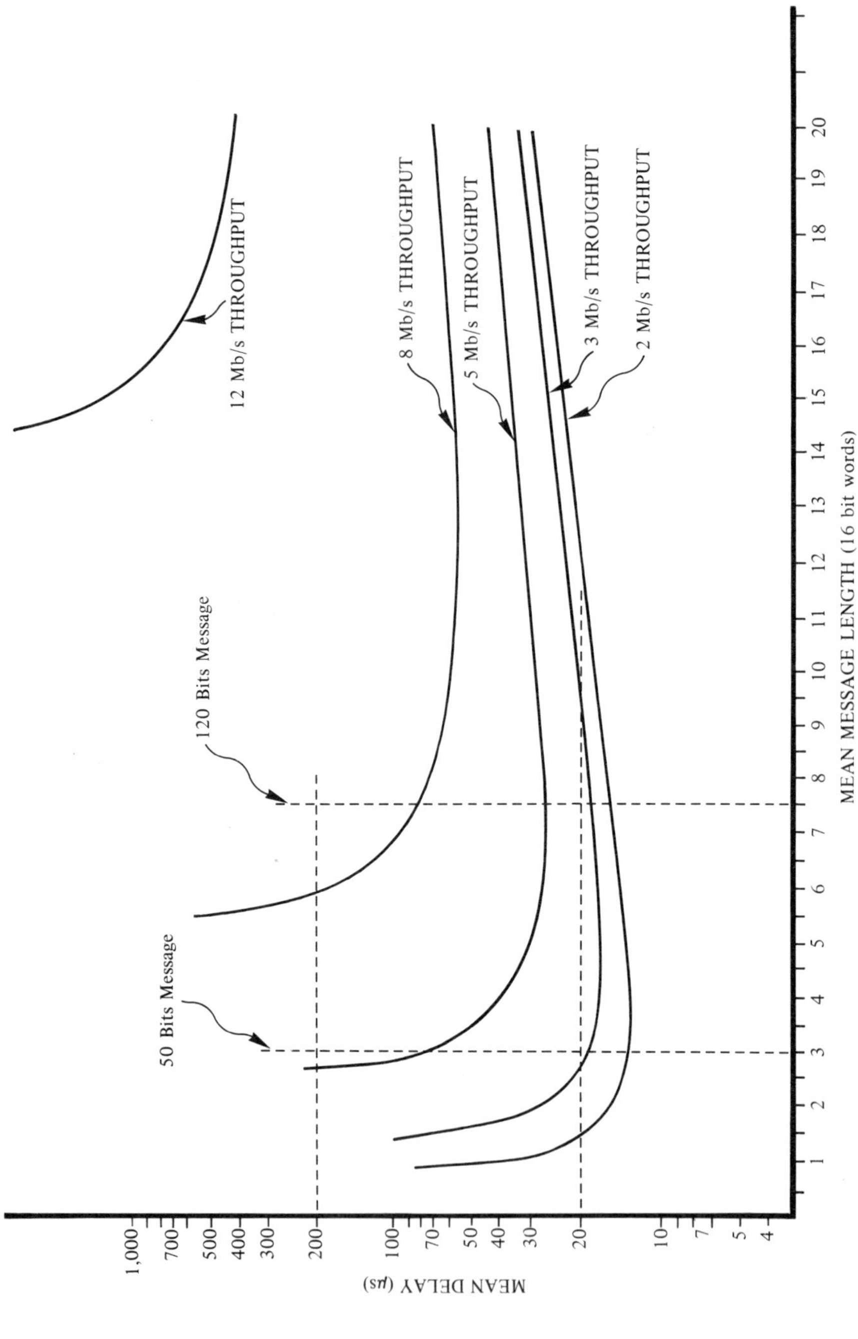

Figure 4-7. Ten-node loop bus. (From Schenk, Hileman, and Fischer.[1])

ITERATION

Using the results of the bus transfer model, parameters must now be changed in the system stimuli trace model, e.g. new partitioning to reduce data transfers and recorganization of data files to reduce access time and, therefore, response time.

SUMMARY

A disciplined methodology must be applied to the design of a distributed processing system. One such approach has been identified in this chapter.

BIBLIOGRAPHY

Advanced Data Communication Control Procedures (ADCCP). Draft 6, October 15, 1976.

Aircraft Internal Time Division Command/Response Multiplex Data Bus. MIL-STD-1553A, April 30, 1975.

Boehm, B. W.: Software and its impact: a quantitative assessment. *Datamation*, May 9, 1973.

Bold, N. T., Wapner, M., and Blackwell, L. M.: Shipboard data multiplex system (SDMS)—a new design for lower ship cost and improved flexibility. *Naval Engineers J.*, April 1976.

Donnan, R. A., and Kersey, J. R.: Synchronous data link control: a perspective. *IBM System J.*, No. 2, 1974.

Kleinrock, L., and Opderbeck, H.: Throughput in the ARPANET—protocols and measurement. *Proc. Fourth Data Communications Symp.*, Quebec City, Canada, 1972.

Mauriello, R.: A distributed processing system for military applications—a four part series. *Computer Design Magazine*, September 1980, October 1980, December 1980, January 1981.

Schenk, R., Hileman, R., and Fischer, H.: *Queuing analysis in digital data buses. ACM Pacific 1980 Conf. Session on Real Time Issues in Network Performance*, November 1980.

Wiley, K.: *Distributive Design Methodology*, Internal Litton Memorandum, December 18, 1976.

Advances in Distributed Processing Management, Volume 2
Edited by P. S. Fisher, J. Slonim, and E. A. Unger

Chapter 5

DISTRIBUTED COMPUTING SYSTEMS: METHODOLOGY AND CASE STUDY*

Lionel E. Deimel, Jr., Robert J. Fornaro, and David F. McAllister
Department of Computer Science, North Carolina State University, Raleigh, North Carolina

Distributed processing has had a significant impact on the field of computing. An example of a distributed system—and the subject of this chapter—is the integrated photogrammetric instrument network (IPIN), which is currently being implemented for the Defense Mapping Agency Aerospace Center (DMAAC). As in any state-of-the-art design effort, several mistakes were made during the design process, some of which were identified early in the process and some of which were not identified until implementation was begun. Our purpose is to describe those principles which we feel should be an integral part of the design of a distributed system and to show how these principles relate to the design of IPIN. We begin by presenting a brief overview of distributed systems.

A primary factor responsible for the burgeoning interest in distributed computer systems is the favorable price/performance ratio achievable when minicomputer systems and groups of minicomputer systems are used in certain computation and data base applications. The driving force behind the cost-effectiveness of this computing hardware is the advance in semiconductor and integrated circuit technology. Even under the most conservative predictions, this trend will continue for some time to come. Very Large Scale Integration (VLSI) technology will, within the next several years, produce processors and memories equivalent in computational power to those of the state of the art ten years ago, but at a small fraction of their cost and size.

The price/performance of hardware is only one component of a complete system. As Wirth[1] has pointed out, it is the software that allows the potential of the hardware to be realized. Unfortunately, as is widely recognized, the capabilities of software have not kept pace with hardware advances. This lag has primarily occurred because early computing systems were inherently large and expensive and they depended on economies of scale. The generality and complexity demanded of a virtually nonexistent software technology forced towering

* Supported in part by Rome Air Development Center Post Doctoral Program.

and inscrutable programmed structures to be built before anyone really understood the nature of the foundation of this discipline. Recently, however, there have been fundamental advances in perspective and technique, especially in the areas of software engineering and operating systems. These advances, in concert with VLSI innovation, promise to keep distributed computing a productive and active area.

The realm of distributed computing is already quite broad. Enslow[2] has characterized a distributed system as a point in three-dimensional space whose degree of distribution is measured along an axis of hardware decentralization, an axis of control decentralization, and an axis of data base decentralization. In fact, several authors have published their interpretation and explanation of the term 'distributed computing system.'[3–7] Overall, their collective concern is to identify precisely what is to be distributed and to formalize reasonable limits concerning the way in which these items are distributed. Specific candidates for distribution are hardware (processors), software (operating system and applications), data, and control.[2] Techniques are sought to aid in the solution of partitioning and assignment problems, especially for software. Simply stated, the partitioning problem involves the division of an application into subsets of activity in such a way as to minimize interaction among these subsets.[4] Once a partitioning has been accomplished, the assignment problem deals with mapping these partitions onto the desired (or required) hardware configuration.

A developing research area relevant to distributed computer systems is that of distributed control. Current activity in this area is concerned with defining and understanding appropriate generalized control primitives wherein distributed control is viewed as a more general case of centralized control. Specific research areas include the study of synchronization primitives and, recently, nondeterministic and probabilistic programming.[8]

We choose to partition the distributed computing field into two classes. In all cases, we are concerned only with hardware configurations that involve more than one autonomous computing subsystem. Typically, this configuration would comprise a processor, memory, and perhaps a disk subsystem or other peripheral devices. We distinguish to which class a given distributed system belongs primarily by characterization of the volume and behavior of traffic within the system. Broadly described, elements of these two classes are:

1. Large-scale systems that provide a variety of functions to many users. Such systems typically have high traffic volumes that are statistically well behaved.
2. Special purpose, real-time, or other limited function systems. The behavior of these systems is best characterized as 'bursty.' The systems may have extensive periods of idleness followed by short periods requiring maximum performance.

The first type of system continues to depend on economies of scale, primarily because the application demands large scale. Examples of such systems include the airlines reservation system, the Bank of America distributed computing facility, and others.[7,9,10] The second type of system takes advantage of the price/computing performance revolution in a unique way. No overriding economic reason exists for such systems to conserve (share) historically scarce resources such as processor cycles or memory. Entire computing subsystems can be dedicated to a specific portion of an application, if necessary, with the understanding that the resulting 'underutilization' is more than compensated for by increased modularity, simplicity, and flexibility.

The primary reason for this particular characterization of distributed systems has to do with our ability to understand and model them, and thus to predict and control their behavior. The consistent volume of traffic present in large systems makes it possible to use powerful mathematical tools, such as queuing theory, to abstract and model performance and interactions within such systems. Although open questions and difficult problems are present within this discipline, queuing theory is recognized as an indispensable tool in systems modeling and design, especially when designers are confident that system behavior is adequately reflected by a known, or mathematically tractable, formulation.

On the other hand, it is generally impossible for an individual programmer to comprehend all the programming details of a large-scale system; hence, programming responsibility is shared among a group of such programmers. This approach complicates comprehension of the system because of the problem of proliferation of interaction pairs, described by Brooks.[11] So, in the case of large-scale systems, although reasonably powerful tools are available for design, the connection between these tools and the implementation of the system has remained somewhat murky. This cloudy relationship is due in part to modeling abstractions, but in larger measure to the lack of an adequate notation or language for describing operating system details, and also to the lack of a consistent framework for software engineering. Deficiencies in operating systems and software engineering disciplines are especially evident in the case of large-scale systems.

The preceding discussion identified two issues central to the design and implementation of large-scale distributed computing systems:

1. The form and nature of design tools
2. The form and nature of implementation tools

A curious dichotomy emerges when these two issues are examined in the light of small-scale distributed systems. Because these systems are not driven by economies of scale, the volume of traffic in the system is relatively small or subject to occasional bursts. The transient behavior that results cannot be formulated into a tractable queuing model. Thus, many of the standard analytical modeling techniques cannot be used as design tools. By contrast, however, the bulk of recent results in operating systems construction and software engineering have been demonstrated in—indeed evolved from—the environment of small-scale systems. Hence, in effect, increasingly powerful notation and techniques have become available for operating systems implementation. This situation is exactly the opposite of circumstances holding for large-scale systems.

There is a growing sense that innovations in integrated circuit design and production are going to precipitate fundamental changes in the nature of computer science and computer engineering. However, exactly what the nature of these changes may be remains a subject of speculation. Bowen and Buhr[9] suggest that 'old rules about economies of scale . . . need to be replaced by . . . new ones about economies of specialization.' Our experience leads us to echo their sentiments. At this juncture, we cannot be sure exactly what the new rules about economies of specialization might be. We are certain that pursuit of the design and implementation of special-purpose distributed computing systems along the lines discussed here will eventually lead to the formulation of some of these new rules.

In the discussion that follows, we restrict our topic to the class of small-scale, real-time systems described previously. The development history of the special-purpose distributed computer system IPIN is reviewed, with emphasis on design and specification. IPIN is a distributed network of instruments and minicomputers intended for high-volume digitizing and manipulation of terrain data obtained from photographic source materials. The design methodology in the case study emphasizes hierarchical design, workload characterization, performance prediction and sizing based on multiserver and single-server simulation models, and operating system code specification as a concurrent program written in terms of high-level programming language constructs.

DESIGNING DISTRIBUTED SYSTEMS

A review of recent operating system literature clearly indicates that the field of design and implentation of operating systems is evolving into two areas—centralized and distributed. The distinction is not always clear. Distributed computer systems always contain more than one processor, yet some systems which have been classified as centralized contain multiple processors. Techniques known to be useful in one context may not be useful in the other. It has been suggested that since the current body of operating systems theory was developed primarily from centralized designs, a re-evaluation of accepted theory and practice may be necessary to accommodate distributed systems.[12]

The search for design concepts appropriate to distributed systems should begin with conventional approaches, but should also examine ideas which previously seemed limited in value. A growing number of papers and texts report on concepts, techniques, and experiences in operating system design. We are particularly interested in works which attack the mystique of the design process and suggest methodologies and tools that appear most useful in the context of distributed systems. A recurrent theme in the literature is advocacy of the use of three important tools, which form the basis for a distributed operating design methodology:

1. Performance prediction
2. Hierarchical design
3. High-level programming languages

Performance prediction is an extension of computer performance evaluation into the realm of design. Graham[13] and Ferrari[14] both discuss the application of performance evaluation techniques during the design process. Lockett[15] gives a specific example which illustrates the use of performance metrics to assist system design. Simulation frequently plays a central role in performance prediction, as designs seldom lend themselves to tractable mathematical formulation. The value of simulation is widely recognized, although its use may be discouraged by the effort and costs involved. A benefit of simulation, often unrecognized, is its value as a design aid reflecting developing system structure and as documention.[16–18] In fact, several authors report on the development of language-based design systems which integrate design, simulation, and implementation, and also provide a basis for design evaluation. One such example is the design and evaluation system (DES), discussed by Graham.[19] Another interesting approach, functionally oriented system simulation (FOSS), is described by Scallon and Grupe.[20] FOSS is a FORTRAN-based system which provides for model construction based on pictorial specifications of system software. It produces operating system design information in terms of static interface analysis and levels of task parallelism, and generates a FORTRAN simulation of the proposed configuration. Workload characterization is a concomitant activity which is required to obtain meaningful results in the modeling or simulation process. A detailed workload characterization can be exceedingly difficult for general-purpose systems. Distributed systems are often dedicated systems built for a specific environment, a situation which simplifies the task because functional and performance requirements are usually quite specific early in system development.

Another element of methodology that is evident in recent literature is that of hierarchical design—a top-down design of systems, analogous to the top-down design of programs. This technique allows clear definition of system functions while postponing implementation concerns—possibly including actual hardware configuration—as long as possible. Notice that 'hierarchical design' and 'hierarchical structure' are not synonymous, a fact emphasized by Ferrari,[14] and by Parnas and Siewiorek.[21,22] 'Hierarchical design' refers to the stepwise refinement process used to produce the ultimate design. 'Hierarchical structure,' on the other hand, refers to the nature of the final design itself, namely, a layered system such as that described by Dijkstra.[23] The design of distributed systems appears to benefit from the 'information hiding' principles that underlie hierarchical design (see Parnas and Siewiorek,[22] Quaynor and Bernstein,[24] and Unger[17]).

The final element of a methodology that seems especially well suited to distributed designs is the use of high-level programming languages for operating systems. The concepts contained in Concurrent PASCAL[25] and Modula[26] provide excellent specification and implementation aids to complement the principles of hierarchical design mentioned previously. Certainly it is generally agreed that such languages should eventually replace the large assembly code base of most operating systems. For the time being, however, we may have to be satisfied with using the abstractions provided by these languages for precise specification of how a system should operate. In the current state of the art, implementation continues to be governed by immensely practical issues, not the least of which is the reasonable doubt that these new language concepts are viable in a wide variety of circumstances. In particular, Keedy[27] expresses serious reservations about the practical applicability of monitors in medium- and large-scale systems. He concedes that monitors can be useful in implementing 'toy' operating systems, but argues strongly their unsuitability for 'real' systems. Not all authors show such pessimism. Weitzman,[7] for example, reports a successful implementation of a distributed signal processing system using Concurrent PASCAL and monitors. The designers of ADA conclude that semaphores are too primitive and monitors too confusing and offer yet another evaluation of a language mechanism, the concept of rendezvous, to express and control concurrency.[28]

We conclude that a reasonable design methodology for a distributed computer system should contain the following:

1. Hierarchical design concepts applied to the definition of system components
2. A workload characterization in terms of functional requirements, which can be translated into events or computing resource requirements
3. A performance model to aid in performance prediction, sizing, partitioning, allocation, and design documentation
4. A formal specification of the operating system and applications software as a concurrent program written in terms of a high-level programming language such as Concurrent PASCAL, Modula, or ADA

Weitzman[7] also suggests that the result of top-down software design—which is driven by a functional decomposition that characterizes the original application—can usually be mapped into a physical distribution of processors. His 'multiminicomputer system design methodology' closely resembles the design methodology that we have suggested previously.

The following sections discuss the development of the integrated photogrammetric instrument network (IPIN) in the context of our four design elements for distributed systems.

CASE STUDY

A History of IPIN

The Defense Mapping Agency Aerospace Center (DMAAC) in St. Louis, Missouri, produces maps used by the military. Much of the data with which the agency works is obtained by means of photogrammetry, i.e. from the analysis of aerial photographs. Pairs of such photographs taken some distance apart can provide a stereoscopic image from which depth information may be extracted. With appropriate reference points, this information may be translated into terrain elevation values.

The primary instrument for collection or *compilation* of terrain data in this manner is the analytical stereoplotter, a large optical device with a binocular viewer which allows an operator to examine the stereoscopic image produced by pairs of photographs. The photographs themselves are mounted on two mechanical stages which an operator can move relative to the optical system by means of wheels or cranks. In this way, he may examine any desired area of the terrain represented in the photographs. The operator likewise has control over a spot which can be moved vertically within the stereoscopic image. By adjusting this spot so that it appears to be on the surface, he can obtain an elevation value. By keeping the spot on the surface as he follows a feature such as a ridge line, the operator can collect three-dimensional coordinates of that feature. By keeping the spot on the surface while moving in a straight line, he can compile a terrain profile. By keeping the spot elevation constant and moving the photographs laterally so that the spot is kept on the surface, he can trace contour lines.

Manual operation of the analytical stereoplotter is slow and tedious. For this reason, the process has become increasingly automated by the addition of correlation circuitry to adjust spot elevation and control computers to assist the operator in the collection and storage of data. For some time DMAAC had been collecting these data on magnetic tape and processing them in batch mode on a large computer for incorporation into a data base of digital terrain models. (A digital terrain model is a representation of a geographic region as a collection of elevation values at regularly spaced grid points.) The retrofitting of stereoplotters with their dedicated computers produces instruments which can be described as semiautomatic, at best. A parallel project, on the other hand, has developed a truly automatic device. This advanced stereoplotter, known as automatic compilation equipment (ACE), has been developed under contract by Bendix Research Laboratories for DMAAC through Rome Air Center (RADC) of Rome, New York. The instrument performs rapid laser scans of the two photographs and digitally correlates the images, in order to generate closely spaced elevation values along so-called epipolar lines in a camera-oriented coordinate system.

Long before any ACE was delivered, it became clear that the then-current mode of operation was inadequate for handling the quantity of data which could be generated by the new devices. The matter of the quality of the data base was also an issue. The more automated equipment was faster than human workers, but also introduced both systematic and random errors. The batch processing environment was not well suited to correcting such errors. In fact, it was ill-suited to *any* error correction, so what was needed was an editing capability that would be independent of the development of the ACE. Further, the quantity of information to be processed presented logistical and managerial problems. The system sought would be able to handle increasing quantities of data without physical movement of storage media, would allow more sophisticated processing by introducing an interactive man–machine interface, and would automatically schedule and monitor work flow. This concept and the realization that a number of stereoplotters could share tape drives and other peripherals by tying them into a central computer were the beginning of IPIN. In 1975, a systems analysis was performed by DMAAC, which defined the required process stereophotographs at an acceptable rate for incorporation into a high-quality digital terrain model data base.

Through RADC, a group at Clarkson College of Technology in Potsdam, New York, was selected to design an appropriate computer system to meet the requirements set forth in the DMAAC systems analysis. The Clarkson group was to design but not implement the desired system. Whatever design emerged was clearly to involve distributed processing, as the collection of instruments contained numerous computers. Clarkson completed its software specification for IPIN in 1976.[29] The design methodology employed is discussed in a paper by Meyer and Moellman.[30]

The Clarkson design was heavily influenced by the fact that the ACE (two such devices were planned) produces bursts of data which need to be saved and which require a coordinate transformation, sorting, and later processing (interpolation). The collection, coordinate transformation, and sorting were treated as real-time tasks. It was then decided that a network of minicomputers would be cheaper and simpler than using a single mainframe. Major processing tasks were assigned to specific computers of the network, namely real-time data collection, data collection from other stereoplotters, file management, interpolation, and editing. Results of timing simulations of critical routines from application algorithms dictated the number of computers and their interconnections. (The system configuration was basically a star with the file management/job control computer at the network center—Figure 5-1.) An important feature of this design was the absence of a conventional operating system. Instead, the message-switching scheme adopted for the network transmitted both control information and data in 128-word packets called 'message units.' (The packet size is that of a disk sector.) Each computer utilized a buffer pool of message units, memory-resident application and control programs, and associated queues. Interprocessor links also used 128-word messages. A major reason for adopting the message-switching framework was that no available operating system for the hardware to be used had nearly the amount of throughput required by the real-time tasks. Therefore, it was important that overhead be kept low. The Clarkson group verified the feasibility of its design by means of a fairly detailed simulation written in SIMSCRIPT II.5. This effort provided evidence that the design was viable and adequately insensitive to load fluctuations and design parameter estimation errors.

The final Clarkson software specification differs in detail but not in principle from the design described by Meyer and Moellman.[30] It is presented in the form of an informally described, semistructured pseudo-code. The pseudo-code is organized into 'modules' which communicate with one another through message

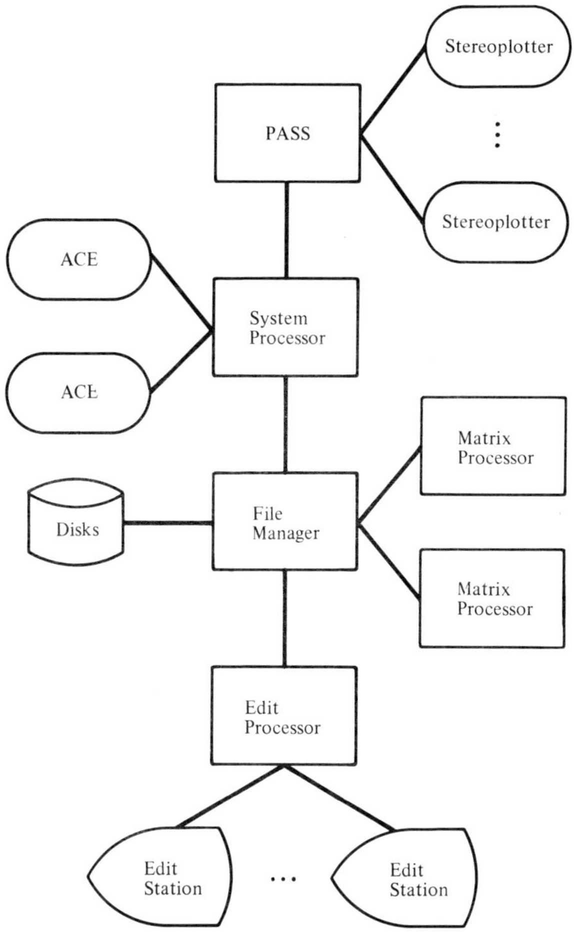

Figure 5-1. Simplified block diagram of IPIN.

units. The specification document is several hundred pages long and was produced without the aid of a text-editing system, a fact no doubt in part responsible for numerous inconsistencies. It was decided that DMAAC would assume responsibility for that part of the network dedicated to controlling and communicating with collection devices other than the ACE subsystems and that the edit subsystem would be designed separately. The Clarkson design applied to what came to be called the postprocessor of IPIN (i.e. post-data collection processor, less the interactive data editing capability). The excluded data collection network nodes were designated the pooled analytical stereoplotter system (PASS—there were to be several such systems) and the edit component was designated the edit processor (EP).

In parallel, design and implementation of the PASSs was begun by DMAAC, postprocessor implementation was begun on the basis of the Clarkson design by Bendix Research Laboratories, and a group headed by the authors at North Carolina State University (NCSU) began a design study of the edit processor. The existence of the postprocessor design provided a framework for development of the edit processor. However, the lack of clarity of some pseudo-code modules and document inconsistencies made interpretation difficult.

The recognition of the need for extensive editing facilities evolved slowly, so the Clarkson design had not specified the edit processor function in detail. By the time NCSU became associated with the IPIN effort, additional application algorithm planning had been done by DMAAC. A hardware configuration for the edit processor had been proposed and needed to be evaluated. It was assumed that edit processor software was to be as much like the software elsewhere in the system as possible. The implementation language had been specified to be FORTRAN, so far as practicable. It was decided early in the process to use simulation in the evaluation of the EP. The following section discusses the procedures used to construct the workload which was used to drive the simulation.

Workload Characterization

A major portion of any computer system simulation effort is the proper characterization of the workload to be placed upon the system. It is important that the workload characterization obtained from the functional specifications of the system be as independent of the system design as possible. The EP's workload is essentially the result of requests originating at 12 edit stations. The edit stations each include two graphics CRTs, a data tablet, and other devices. They were to be interfaced to the EP through six minicomputers designated edit minis. The tasks required of the EP have been summarized[31] and presented in detail.[32]

Once a model (job) is submitted to the EP, it must pass through a series of four major editing steps for each model:

1. Geomorphic edit
2. Epipolar edit
3. Matrix edit
4. Precise-point edit

One and only one of these steps may be in progress at a given edit station at a time. Each of the major edit steps is further subdivided into a series of tasks to be performed, called demands, which define the details of the edit. For example, one such demand in the geomorphic edit is to plot the geomorphic file. Demands may be further analyzed into functions or operations that must be completed in order to satisfy the demand. (Figure 5-2 shows the operations that must be completed to satisfy the demand to plot the geomorphic file.) These operations are the lowest

– Transfer geomorphic file to EP.

– Write geomorphic file to disk (save locally for later access).

– Read geomorphic file from disk.

– Generate plot vectors.

– Plot file.

Figure 5-2. Demand: plot geomorphic file.

level entities in the functional system description. Typical functions are:

1. File transfers. Transfer a file from file manager to EP, transfer a file from EP to edit station, transfer a file from edit station to EP, and write file to tape.
2. Plot functions. Compute plot vectors for contour plot and plot vector file.
3. Computational tasks. Compute lake fill and convert geographic coordinates to plotter scale.

In total, the four edit steps place about 30 distinct demands upon the EP. The frequency and order of occurrence of these demands depend on the number and type of major edit steps occurring at the edit stations and on decisions made by edit station operators based upon the nature of the data being edited. The exact role of the EP operating system in this context is to map each of the demands onto appropriately defined system modules.

Resource and processing requirements of each operation had to be estimated so that a design-independent workload could be constructed for input to simulation models reflecting various system designs. Hence, in constructing the simulation workload, it was necessary to (1) generate a typical stream of demands and (2) for a given demand, in the absence of an actual operating system configuration, assign processing requirements to the operations involved in servicing the demand.

The first objective was treated as follows. DMAAC production requirements demanded approximately four completed DTMs per 8-hour shift. DMAAC made available detailed charts illustrating the expected allocation of operators and devices to the major edit steps. Unfortunately, the amount of processing required in each step is influenced by such variables as the number of lakes in a given geographic area. As a result, a single simulation workload was judged insufficient to test a design adequately. It was decided therefore to construct workloads reflecting three levels of load on the system—light, medium, and heavy. The light workload assumed six edit stations in operation working on various combinations of edit steps. For each edit step, a list of likely demands was also prepared. The medium workload was constructed in a similar fashion for ten edit stations. The heavy workload was based on concurrent operation of all 12 edit stations.

The second objective was resolved by estimating or measuring computational times and such other characteristics as instruction path lengths, input/output rates, wait time, and file sizes. Since many of the application algorithms had already been implemented in a high-level language and since the available hardware components were given, this task was a straightforward mapping of operations to processing requirements.

The model for the edit processor had to contribute to the design effort in several ways. In particular, the model would be used in four ways:

1. To estimate the CPU power that would be required (a single 16-bit minicomputer might not be sufficient).
2. To estimate memory requirements.
3. To identify functions which might better be processed elsewhere in the network.
4. To help develop hardware and software structure.

The Simulation Model

During the design process, the simulation model required needed to have the following properties:

1. Ease of implementation
2. Sufficient flexibility so that many designs could be studied
3. Execution costs that would not be prohibitive

Since several of the problems mentioned in the preceding section required resolution early in the design process, it was necessary to construct the simulation model in the most expeditious manner possible. Modeling the system as a multiple server fulfilled this requirement.

The discrete simulation model treating the EP as a multiple server queuing system was developed in several stages. Message units were the customers that required service. Independent servers were associated with six abstract processes. This configuration is illustrated in Figure 5-3. Details of the simulation are presented elsewhere by Anderson.[33] The anticipated hardware configuration for the EP included:

1. A single 16-bit 64K-word CPU
2. On-line disk storage (2 × 42M words)
3. Twelve edit stations interfaced, two each, through six edit minis
4. A high-speed link to the file manager
5. An XY plotter
6. A magnetic tape drive

Five of the six abstract processes correspond, roughly, to servicing the last five hardware items just listed. The sixth process consisted of computational tasks.

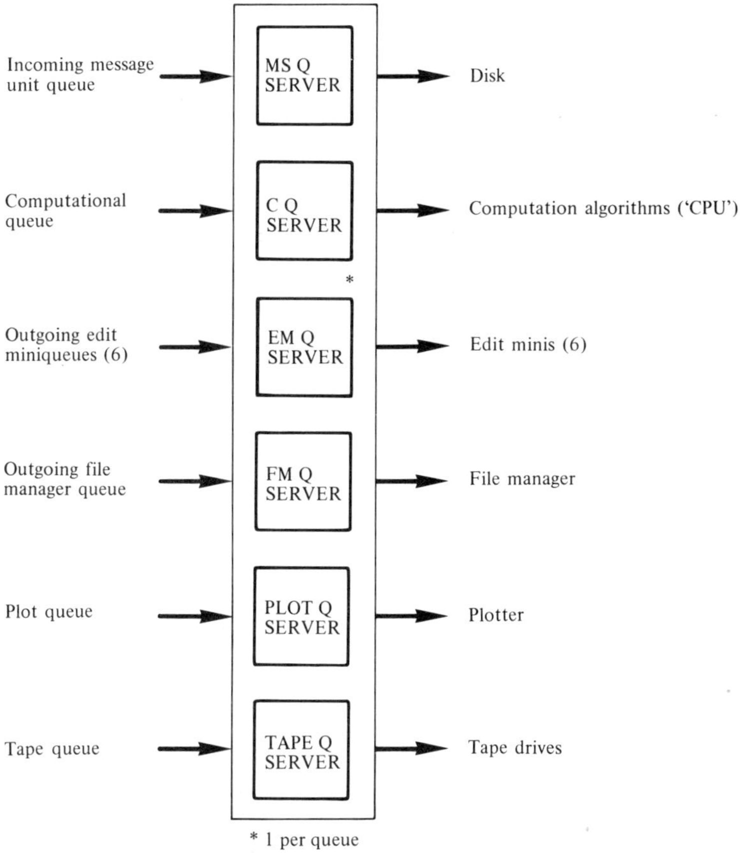

Figure 5-3. Initial EP simulation model.

The disk server was also called upon to handle all incoming message units, thus functioning as a message-switcher. Further decomposition of the model at this stage of development was avoided. Counting six instances of the edit mini handler gives a total of 11 servers in the model. Each server had an associated queue, queues being established based on functional similarities. Since several designs were being considered, assigning input queues to processors made the performance evaluation more flexible and modular. Arrival of message units and their service in simulated time was driven by the workload characterization described previously. The model was coded in SIMSCRIPT II.5 and run in a 500K-byte region of OS-MVT on an IBM 370/165.

The first version of the simulation treated the servers as concurrently executing processes whose activities were overlapped in real time. This approach had several advantages. The simulation model was relatively easy to design and code, and upper bounds on the best performance to be expected of the real system could be obtained. Also, the simulation was relatively inexpensive to run. Since it was expected that the EP would be implemented as a single CPU, estimates of response time and throughput derived from the multiple-server model would not be reliable. However, in the initial design stages, it was important to quantify the relationship between the functional workload and corresponding system behavior. If, for example, the simulation indicated that bottlenecks were present or that parts of the workload caused violent behavior in the model, then system designers would have some means of assessing and correcting the problems.

Notice that the initial simulation model reflects a hierarchical approach to the design. The model reflects an open-minded (or, if you prefer, skeptical) view of the implementation. Certain hardware/software trade-offs were expected, but it was anticipated that simulation results might indicate that the line between hardware and software should be drawn at some point other than the anticipated one.

The simulation computed three performance parameters. A measure of required CPU power was obtained by establishing service times and operating system overhead in terms of processors that execute 1,000,000 instructions per second (1 m.i.p.s.). The average and maximum number of cycles per second used were recorded for the 11 processors for each of the three workloads. In addition, the percentage of time more than one server was busy, T, was also recorded. Note that $T = 0$ implies that only one server is busy at a time. In this case, the multiple server *should* be an accurate predictor of an actual single server operating at 1 m.i.p.s. Memory requirements for data and control messages within the system were estimated by simply finding the average and maximum number of message units queued for each server each second.

Under medium load, simulation results showed average CPU utilization to be relatively light. About 10 per cent. of the time, more than two processors were busy, and hence results could not be extrapolated to the behavior of a single server. Memory requirements under the medium load were considered to be acceptable. Figures 5-4 and 5-5 depict typical results under medium load. In addition, occasional bursts of activity could exceed available memory and make the

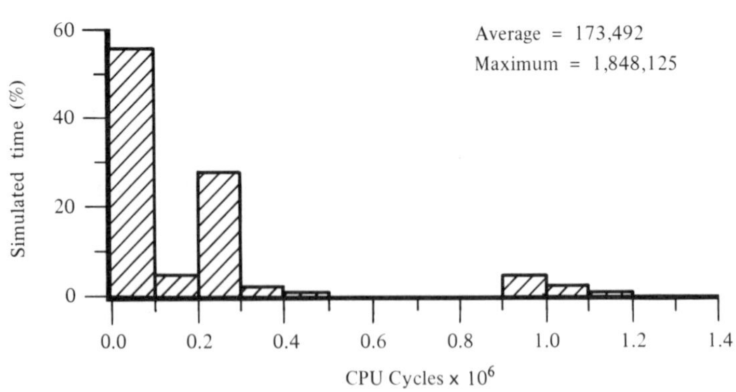

Figure 5-4. CPU utilization—multiple-server model under medium load.

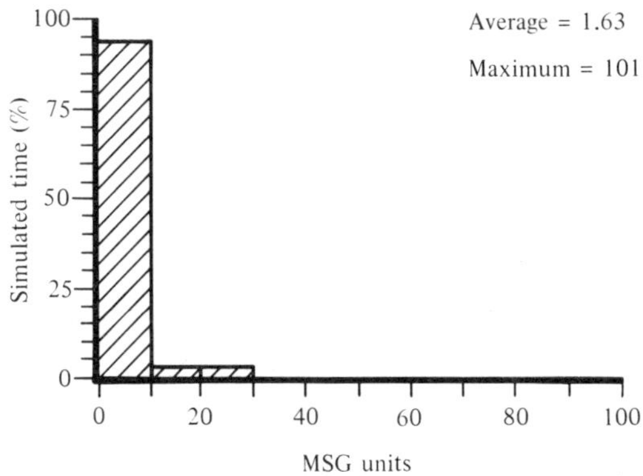

Figure 5-5. Memory utilization—multiple-server model under medium load.

percentage of server overlap uncomfortably high (20 per cent.). Closer examination showed plotting and computational functions to be the cause. This finding cast serious doubts on the ability of a single CPU to handle the load. A single-server simulation model which serviced the 11 queues in cyclic fashion later confirmed this fact. The CPU and memory capacity were judged to be marginally adequate, assuming that the operating system was perfectly designed and tuned. This judgement led to the recommendation that the EP be configured as a dual processor. Plotting and computational functions were to be offloaded to a second CPU. Message-switching and buffering could then be handled by the first CPU, and the impact of plotting and computation confined to a more suitable separate operating system environment. The resulting structural simplicity of the distributed operating system was seen as a major advantage. The NCSU-recommended EP dual-CPU configuration is shown in Figure 5-6.

The simulation model was then modified to reflect the recommended architecture, so that more accurate response-time estimates could be obtained. To model the dual-CPU configuration, the single-server model, which was a refinement of the original model, was expanded into two servers. The second server had all the computational and plotting functions assigned to it. The first server continued to service the remaining queues. In this dual-server model, both processors used a modified round-robin scheduling and had a capacity of 1 m.i.p.s. It was interesting to note that response times under light-load conditions, as measured by the multiple-server and dual-server models, were generally close. The dual-server model predicted an increase in response time of about 9 per cent. over the prediction of the multiple-server model. Under medium-load conditions, the dual-server prediction increased to about 15 per cent.

The dual-port disk configuration represented in Figure 5-6 was unique within IPIN. Bendix suggested the use of a single-port disk attached to the message-switching CPU (EP-I) and having computational CPU (EP-II) requests for disk I/O routed through EP-I. At first, there was concern that this change would have

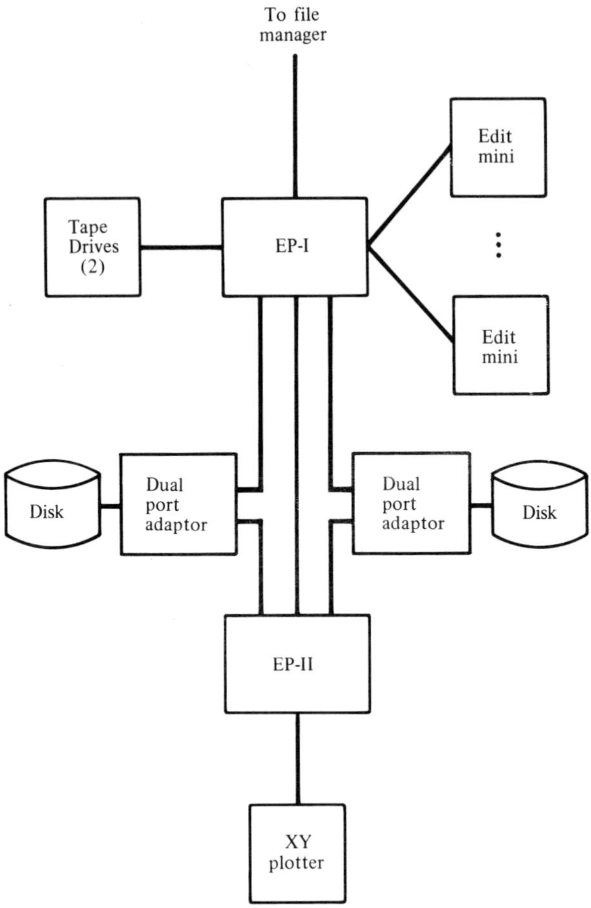

Figure 5-6. Dual-CPU EP configuration.

a significant impact on response time. The dual-server model was easily modified to reflect the suggestion, and the difference in response as a result of this change was not significant. In many cases, performance parameters showed slight improvement over those recorded earlier in various configurations. Turnaround times appeared fairly robust under configuration changes, while memory utilization proved to be the most volatile.

Implementation

As mentioned earlier, Bendix began implementation of the postprocessor while NCSU was producing a design for the edit processor. This scheduling, resulting from a desire to put IPIN into production as soon as possible, produced a period of some confusion. The NCSU group had expected to produce a design specification analogous to that for the postprocessor. It was clear, however, that many details of the underlying software philosophy were going to change as implementation proceeded.

It is obvious that the Bendix task of providing the operating system for IPIN was critical. The original plan to implement the operating system by routinely coding the software specification was quickly recognized as impractical. It soon became evident that some early design decisions were counterproductive. Important lessons of this case study hinge on this point, so it is worthwhile to examine the relevant issues in detail—by looking at postprocessor evolution from the implementors' perspective.

The postprocessor had been conceived as a network of minicomputers, each dedicated to a particular computational task. The machines formed a real-time processing pipeline in which embedded functions were designed to handle maximum data rates achievable by the feeding subsystems. Each processor's software was a monolith of message-driven application programs owing in part to the need for low overhead, coupled with an initial reluctance to design a lower level, special-purpose operating system. Early design methodology focused on real-time constraints, perhaps at the expense of more modular decompositions of the application. Additionally, the design approach was strongly affected by the notion of each physical computer as a site for specific dedicated processing. Although this notion is a valid component of application-driven hierarchical design, it was determined later that it had the effect of degrading reliability, performance, and the ability to modify the system.

The implementation group at Bendix Labs raised two questions. First, was the application inherently real time or could the data collection task be decoupled from data reduction? Second, could the cost of writing a more general uniform network (distributed) operating system be justified?

These two issues were resolved in a redesign phase. The arrival rates of real-time data messages from the subsystems were high relative to the processing times per message, but were relatively low compared to the rate at which they could be written to a disk file. Further, if tasks for collecting real-time data from subsystems could be assured high priority, tasks performing reduction of data previously collected could probably operate in the background. This philosophy can lead to creation of a backlog of unprocessed files. Once it is established that a one-to-one correspondence need not exist between data-delivering subsystems and the set of programs which process the data, however, the designer is free to incorporate multiple copies of certain programs which can be invoked when a backlog exists. The addition of program overlay techniques allows the network the flexibility to respond to any given workload, whereas the dedicated processor approach can result in severe underutilization of resources. Handling priorities and managing program overlays almost certainly dictates a basic operating system. The Bendix group felt that a uniform operating system with a companion file interface was required to provide the throughput and flexibility the post-processor demanded. Once the decision to develop a network file operating system was made, additional advantages of the network configuration became apparent. The postprocessor could consist of a file management processor surrounded by three 'general processors' in a star configuration. Each general processor could be equipped to perform all required data processing so that the loss of any general processor would result in throughput degradation only instead of a hard stop. The number of processors could easily be expanded without major software redesign. Redefining the application strictly in terms of data file processors would leave no unresolved scheduling problems due to the inherent exclusivity of files. The behavior of the network under a uniform operating system could be examined through simulation.

The redesign was undertaken after the following guidelines were selected. The configuration of the application software—processor to which it is assigned and decision on whether it is resident or overlayed—should be delayed as long as possible (preferably until it is coded). All data entering the postprocessor from its subsystems should be written immediately to disk to decouple the system from real-time problems. The operating system and file interfaces should be specified early, including calling formats and functional descriptions in an application coder's manual.

The postprocessor software, as delivered, consists of two distinct parts—a network operating system and a set of application programs (tasks which run under supervision of the operating system). The operating system can be partitioned into three parts—a task-scheduling and device-supporting kernel, an interprocessor I/O and message switch, and a file management system with network-wide access.

The kernel is composed of interrupt-driven handlers for devices, a task scheduler which supports overlays, a mechanism for dynamic allocation of pools of both small 'nodes' and larger data buffers, and interfaces to support FORTRAN, assembler, and device symbiont task activities. The kernel was sufficient to support stand-alone testing of virtually all the application tasks when a file simulation package was used. A dynamic debugger (a system option) is included in the kernel of all the processors in both the postprocessor and the edit processor. The time spent developing the debug package yielded great savings in development time and wear and tear on the implementors' nerves.

The retained message-switching mechanisms are in a self-contained layer placed functionally below the kernel's device and I/O handlers. As the reception and transmission of data buffers between processors are totally interrupt-driven, I/O packets consisting of many buffers (or single buffer messages) can pass invisibly through a processor on their way to a destination device (or task) in a specific processor. The accessibility of a given task (or device) by other tasks is explicitly determined by that task's (or device's) level of definition in the structured system. A task (or external subsystem) has no idea where the devices and tasks with which it communicates actually reside. Postprocessor tasks can be moved about in the network without invalidating them by a simple modification of the system. This feature is important because it allows the final configuration to be extensively 'tuned' to actual production demands while saving the immense analysis that would have been required had it been decided to 'design-in' consideration of these factors.

The file interfaces consist of FORTRAN-callable subroutines for basic file access with optional error control parameters. Because the message switch automatically routes I/O to the correct destination, the users do not concern themselves with the whereabouts of either the physical disks or the symbiont tasks which perform the actual reads and writes. Provisions for multiple self-contained disk volume sets and tape volumes to be accessed through the same uniform interface simplified application task development while centralizing the tricky performance-oriented file handling software. Writing to a file unit involves a 'fast' return to the caller, leaving data queued for later service by a writing task. When serviced, the entire queue is written in a continuous operation (disk seek and transfer). Thus, writing efficiency increases with queue length, as the larger I/O blocks result in less average disk latency time due to fewer seeks. The number of write-queue servers is actually load- and system-dependent, and can be adjusted for optimal queue lengths. The file system performs well, even when many files are to be handled. During final acceptance testing, as many as 50 distinct files were open simultaneously.

A major function of the postprocessor is 'number-crunching' on files. To this end, the major application tasks have been implemented as checkpointable file processors. Multiple copies can exist in the three general processors because of their processor independence. Under the direction of a job control task, any or all of these tasks in the general processors can be concurrently executing without any knowledge of each other. Benchmarks taken on the system as delivered demonstrate a throughput at least four times greater than that originally specified as necessary and three times greater than what is needed today—for two reasons. Most important is the ability to run multiple copies of the long-running interpolate and sort tasks. Second, the highly localized nature of the file system upon which these tasks depend allows tuning performance without worrying about disturbing the tasks' behavior.

For several reasons, edit processor implementation proceeded more smoothly than that of the postprocessor. The original intent was that the Clarkson document would provide a design and specification for uniform operating software that should be used wherever possible throughout the network. The NCSU design effort verified that edit processor operating system requirements were not substantively different from those of the postprocessor. Therefore, it was reasonable at the design level to uncouple specification of edit processor application software from the developing operating system. This decision to separate allowed NCSU to concentrate on applications algorithms. Presumed operating system interfaces were treated in the NCSU specification using pseudo-code. This approach allowed needed overlap of the initial design of the edit processor with the final stages of postprocessor design. The pseudo-code modules for application algorithms in the edit processor specification invoke lower-level modules whose exact nature is purposely vague, yet intended to be appropriately interpretable by system implementors whatever the particular implementation details. This practice is in contrast to analogous modules in the postprocessor specification, which integrate application code and operating system services.

The edit processor software specification produced by NCSU[31] bears a certain similarity to the Clarkson book. Certainly some lessons were learned from the earlier document. First, the pseudo-code used for module specifications was more rigorously defined than that used by Clarkson. The pseudo-code was based on ALGOL-60 with borrowings from PL/I and ALGOL-68. Bendix likewise found it useful to use a better-specified intermediate language when implementing the postprocessor, namely PASCAL. The EP specification document also greatly benefitted from the use of a text-processing program (University of Waterloo's Script). The use of such a program led to a much more consistent document than would have otherwise been possible, as changes were easier to make and could be made on the text globally without error.

Pattern Analysis and Recognition Corporation of Rome, New York, subcontracted to do the edit processor applications software and was able to begin study of edit processor applications as contained in the NCSU specification while Bendix was working on the operating system implementation. The EP applications software utilized the Bendix operating system and was delivered about 7 months after the postprocessor. As of early 1981, IPIN is complete except for some of the software being written internally by DMAAC—that for PASS and the edit stations and edit minis.

SUMMARY AND CONCLUSION

Several lessons about designing distributed systems can be learned from the IPIN experience.

In the hierarchical design of a distributed system, the primary function of a performance model should be to aid in the partitioning and assignment process of determining processing sites, interconnections, and the required number of processors, rather than merely verifying performance of a final design. Models also have the obvious function of identifying proposed configurations which cannot possibly be made to yield required performance. Such rejected proposals require a rethinking of the entire design, but this rethinking must occur before work has progressed to the point that much effort must be discarded. Performance models presuppose existence of a workload description, and in this case, because the system was special purpose and well defined, the construction of such a detailed workload was tractable. This step was performed for the edit processor. The flexibility of the simulation model constructed for that subsystem allowed for rapid and straightforward testing of various design alternatives and produced bounds on resulting performance. This approach led to an efficient configuration for the edit processor. It is important to stress the role which a workload characterization plays. Not only does it facilitate understanding of system dynamics, but it acts as implicit specification, analogous to a user's manual written prior to the software system it describes.

The most important lesson to be learned from IPIN is the value of conducting the design in a hierarchical fashion. On the whole, the IPIN project was conducted hierarchically. This fact is evidenced by the number of distinct groups of contributors and the well-defined responsibility of each group:

	Group	*Responsibility*
1.	DMAAC St. Louis, Missouri	Owners and users; application definition
2.	RADC Rome, New York	Project management
3.	Clarkson College of Technology Electrical and Computer Engineering Potsdam, New York	Overall IPIN structure; postprocessor design
4.	NCSU Computer Science Raleigh, North Carolina	Edit processor design
5.	Bendix Research Laboratories Southfield, Michigan	Postprocessor and edit processor system implementation
6.	PAR Corporation Rome, New York	Edit processor applications; implementation.

It is interesting to observe that, from a global view, the design project itself was distributed both functionally and geographically. This distribution occurred as a matter of administrative evolution and because of the existence of pockets of expertise and experience. In retrospect, this 'design distribution' was itself a significant factor in project success. It imposed a global modularity on project phases and forced a clear definition of module interfaces to emerge as the project evolved. It is important to note that the life of this project has spanned some six years and that at no time were all six participants actively engaged. Some overlap did exist, but as each new group became involved, its specific task was to build on what went before. Hence, in a sense, the output from one phase was input to the next. This feature created the climate for successive refinement of IPIN subsystems that improved the probability of success, in spite of an early weakness that almost proved disastrous.

The postprocessor software specification evidences an undue concern for detail early on. Details such as data formats, disk file formats, and data encoding procedures were assigned to processors, and a simulation of the system was performed to show that performance was acceptable. The temptation to determine network interconnections and processing sites too early can (and did) lead to an inefficient solution in terms of performance, implementability, and reliability. It is easy to become bogged down in the minutiae of obtaining required performance too early in the design process. This insistence on too much detail too soon may lead to design solutions which have to be altered as the system becomes better understood, causing disruptive ripples throughout the design. The cardinal rule must be to defer difficult or poorly understood decisions until later in the design refinement if they are not crucial to understanding the system at a given level of abstraction.

In retrospect, the single issue that created the most problems in the IPIN design was the lack of an adequate programming language (or, as Wirth describes it, 'program notation') for the description of multitask systems. This lack is more a reflection on the state of the art than it is a criticism of IPIN design methodology. Since most of the IPIN project was completed or well under way before the advent of recent systems implementation languages (Concurrent PASCAL, Modula, ADA), it is impossible to describe with certainty what difference, if any, such a language would have made. There are, however, several issues that these languages would have helped separate. Throughout IPIN design phases, constant consternation existed about 'where the design stopped' and 'where the implementation started.' The environment created by a language such as one of those listed effectively separates these concerns. Multiprocessor systems are particularly vulnerable to this confusion of decisions because of concurrent events and the need to synchronize these events within and across processors, provide mutual exclusion, and determine processor allocation strategies. To minimize the danger of misdirected decisions, a sound approach is to establish very early the mechanisms and guidelines for dealing with these complexities. This course should produce task descriptions which are easier to implement and have more predictable behavior owing to the uniform support mechanisms upon which they are built.

The use of a language that contains accepted constructs for expression of concurrency and synchronization (e.g. process, monitor), even if only as a design specification language, should minimize the risks to the design involved in implementation. As mentioned earlier, although we have such languages at our disposal, significant problems remain concerning efficient implementations of these languages and their constructs.

Finally, the IPIN experience suggests that, where possible, a mechanical means (such as a word processor and/or a compiler) should be used to prepare the specification documents and check them for consistency. This suggestion extends particularly to the concept of separate compilation to ensure syntax and type consistency across independent modules.

REFERENCES

1. Wirth, N.: The module: a system structuring facility in high-level programming languages. *Proc. Symp. on Language Design*, Sydney, Australia, September 1979.
2. Enslow, P. H.: What is a 'distributed' data processing system? *Computer*, **11**, No. 1, January 1978.
3. Baker, C. T.: Logical distribution of applications and data. *IBM System J.*, **19**, 2, 1980.

4. Jensen, E. D., and Boebert, W. E.: Partitioning and assignment of distributed processing software. *Proc. Fall COMPCON 76*, New York, 1976.
5. LeBlanc, R.: Research issues in 'fully' distributed systems. *Proc. Eighteenth Annual S.E. Reg. ACM Conf.*, ACM, New York, 1980.
6. LeLann, G.: An analysis of different approaches to distributed computing. Proc. First Int. Conf. on Dist. Computing Syst., IEEE, New York, 1979.
7. Weitzman, C.: Distributed Micro/Minicomputer Systems, Prentice-Hall, Englewood Cliffs, N.J., 1980.
8. Lehmann, D., and Rabin, M. O.: On the advantages of free choice: a symmetric and fully distributed solution to the dining philosophers problem. *Proc. SIGPLAN Conference on Prog. Lang.*, ACM, Williamsburg, Va., January 1981, pp. 133–138.
9. Bowen, B. A., and Buhr, R. J. A.: The Logical Design of Multiple-Microprocessor Systems. Prentice-Hall, Englewood Cliffs, N.J.
10. *Proceedings Fall COMPCON 80*, IEEE, Washington, D.C., September 1980.
11. Brooks, F.: *The Mythical Man-Month.* Addison-Wesley, Mento Park, California, 1975.
12. Levin, R., *et al.*: Distributed systems. In *New Directions for Operating Systems: A Workshop Report* (Ed. J. C. Brown). *Op. Syst. Rev.*, **II**, No. 1, January 1977.
13. Graham, R. M.: Performance prediction. In *Advanced Course in Software Engineering* (Eds. Goos and Hartmanis). Lecture Notes in Computer Science, 30, Springer-Verlag, Heidelberg, 1973.
14. Ferrari, D.: Computer Systems Performance Evaluation. Prentice-Hall, Englewood Cliffs, N.J., 1978.
15. Lockett, J.: Using performance metrics in system design. *Perf. Eval. Rev.*, **7**, Nos. 3 and 4, November 1978.
16. Peters, L.: Relating software requirements and design. *Perf. Eval. Rev.*, **7**, Nos. 3 and 4, November 1978.
17. Unger, B. W.: Programming languages for computer system simulation. *Simulation*, **30**, No. 4, April 1978.
18. Zurcher, F. W., and Randell, B.: Interactive multi-level modelling—a methodology for computer system design. *Proc. IFIP Congress 68*, North-Holland, Amsterdam, 1968.
19. Graham, R. M., *et al.*: A software design and evaluation system. *Proc. SIGOPS Workshop on Syst. Perf. Eval.*, ACM, New York, 1971.
20. Scallon, G. M., and Grupe, J. A.: Functionally oriented system simulation for computer aided design of software/hardware systems. *Proc. Ninth Annual Simulation Symp.*, IEEE, New York, 1976.
21. Parnas, D. L.: On the criteria to be used in decomposing systems into modules. *Comm. ACM*, **15**, No. 12, December 1972.
22. Parnas, D. L., and Siewiorek, D. P.: Use of the concept of transparency in the design of hierarchically structured systems. *Comm. ACM*, **18**, No. 7, July 1975.
23. Dijkstra, E. W.: The structure of the THE operating system. *Comm. ACM*, **11**, No. 5, May 1968.
24. Quaynor, N., and Bernstein, A.: Operating systems for hierarchical multiprocessors. *Proc. Seventh Texas Conf. on Computing Syst.*, IEEE, New York, 1978.
25. Brinch Hansen, P.: *The Architecture of Concurrent Programs.* Prentice-Hall, Englewood Cliffs, N.J., 1977.
26. Wirth, N.: Modula: a language for modular multiprogramming. *Software Practice and Experience*, **7**, 1, January 1977.
27. Keedy, J. L.: On structuring operating systems with monitors. *Australian Comp. J.*, **10**., No. 1 February 1978.
28. Ichbiah, J. D., *et al.*: Preliminary ADA reference manual and rationale for the design of the ADA programming language. *SIGPLAN Notices*, **14**, No. 6, Parts A & B, June 1979.

29. Electrical and Comp. Engineering Dept.: *Integrated Photogrammetric Instrument Network (IPIN) Computer Network Software Specifications.* Tech. Report. ECE 76-1, Clarkson College, Potsdam, N.Y., October 1976.
30. Meyer, R. A., and Moellman, D. E.: Application of distributed processing to the production of digital terrain data. *Proc. 1976 Int. Conf. on Parallel Processing*, IEEE, New York, 1976.
31. Elphingstone, G. M., and Woodford, G. F.: Interactive graphics editing for IPIN. *Proc. Digital Terrain Models (DTM) Symp.* (supplement), Am. Soc. of Photogrammetry, May 1978, pp. 597–609.
32. Department of Computer Science: *Integrated Photogrammetric Instrument Network (IPIN) Edit Processor System Performance Analysis and Software Specification.* North Carolina State University, June 1978.
33. Anderson, I. C.: *The Performance Evaluation of the Edit Processor System in the Integrated Photogrammetric Instrument Network.* M.S. Thesis, Operations Research, North Carolina State University, Raleigh, N.C., December 1978.

BIBLIOGRAPHY

Anderson, I. C., *et al.*: A top-down approach to the use of simulation in computer system design. *Proc. Summer Comp. Simulation Conf.*, Soc. for Comp. Simulation, La Jolla, Calif., 1980.

Champine, G. A.: *Distributed Computer Systems.* North-Holland, New York, 1980.

Courtois, P. J.: Decomposability, instabilities, and saturation in multi-programming systems. *Comm. ACM*, **18**, No. 7, July 1975.

Deimel, L., and Fornaro, R.: The edit processor component of IPIN. *Proc. DTM Symp.*, Am. Soc. of Photogrammetry, Falls Church, Va., 1978.

Doss, C. L.: *High-level Language Implementation of Operating Systems.* M.S. Thesis, Computer Studies, North Carolina State University, Raleigh, N.C., January 1979.

Engleberg, G. P., *et al.*: A real-time simulation of a hierarchical computer network for process control. Simulation, **30**, No. 2, February 1978.

Fornaro, R., *et al.*: *IPIN Edit Processor—Performance Analysis and Software Specification.* Computer Science Dept., North Carolina State Univ., Raleigh, N.C., June 1978.

Hoare, C. A. R.: Monitors: an operating system structuring concept. *Comm. ACM*, **17**, No. 10, October 1974.

Advances in Distributed Processing Management, Volume 2
Edited by P. S. Fisher, J. Slonim, and E. A. Unger

Chapter 6

MEDIATOR: AN APPROACH FOR PROVIDING A GLOBAL USER VIEW IN A DISTRIBUTED INFORMATION ENVIRONMENT

R. A. McBride and E. A. Unger
Department of Computer Science, Kansas State University, Manhattan, Kansas

J. Slonim
Geac Computers International, Inc., Markham, Ontario

L. H. MacRae
NDX Corporation, Toronto, Ontario

This chapter deals with a study of the integration of a generalized information management system into a distributed network environment. It proposes the following solutions to the problems associated with such integration.

1. A methodology for the distribution of the components of a generalized information management system network
2. A detailed quantitative description of the communication and interaction among information management system components and data objects over a network.
3. Creation of a site-selection algorithm for satisfying each query through the use of a distributed system.

Neither literature focusing on information management systems nor that concerned with network interfaces has offered much insight into these issues. Thus, we have decided to consider the general problems of distribution of an information management system over a general network topology and of a query within such a distributed information system. A pragmatic view of solutions has been considered in the light of cost and time factors.

Let us first establish a basic terminology for information technology. A *generalized information system* is a collection of devices which stores, updates, and retrieves information of various kinds in a collection of files constructed according to disjoint models. The data in the files consist of conventional symbols of any kind in diverse combinations. These data are of two kinds, informational and organizational. Organizational data are derived from a *data model* and are used to structure informational data according to the model. Data models are of two basic categories: graphic and set. Each of these categories contains a number of specific models.

In graphic data models, which are based on graph theory, the organizational data are derived from the informational data. In other words, graphic (or structured class) data models pertain to files in which the information possesses a structure of its own which must not be affected by mechanical manipulation. Set (or unstructured class) data models are based on set theory and pertain to files in which the informational data are independent of the organizational data.

A *data base management system* (DBMS) is an information system which processes data arranged according to the requirements of the system itself. A DBMS uses records or tuples as basic data fields. From these basic fields it builds larger units which define data from two points of view. From the data administration viewpoint, it creates a schema (structured class) or a base relation table (unstructured class). From the user's viewpoint, it creates subschemas and subtables ('user's views'). Each record in such a schema or relation table contains predefined sets of abstract data arranged in fixed formats. One or more items in each record serve as a primary key or unique identification. Data are manipulated through data manipulation languages. These languages provide links to the logical data model, which in turn is 'mapped' into the physical storage structure.

A *textual information system* processes information arranged in any format. It must maintain both the integrity of the information and the structure of the text. It imposes no limitations on the size of texts processed. The basic data field is of variable length and format: it can be any or all occurrences of a single word or any defined unit of text, e.g. a word, sentence, or paragraph. A textual information system contains files based on various data models. Information is retrieved through physical linkages among these files. All retrievable units of data are uniquely identified. All files are 'self-organizing'; no identifiers outside the structure of the text are used to construct files.

A generalized information management system (GIMS) is a textual information system containing as a subset a DBMS. The data provided by a GIMS are described in terms of object collections. A *collection of objects* is said to be any combination of alphanumeric characters which has predefined physical and logical interpretations in regard to structured, unstructured, and/or textual data models.

In any information management system, several hierarchically organized categories of objects can exist. Data base systems allow for two levels of subject category; the first level corresponds to a schema (which represents the view of an entire user community) and the second level is a set of subschemas (which corresponds to the view of a particular group of users). Textual management systems can have several levels of subject categories; however, it is assumed in the material which follows that textual systems are limited to two subject levels. This simplification permits the same representation to be used in directories for both data base and textual management systems. For the purposes of this paper a first-level subject heading is termed a *cluster*, while a second-level subject category is described as a *subcluster*.

A *query* is a command issued by the user, and may be thought of as a call to any application program or any management procedure which acts upon objects maintained by the GIMS. In a distributed system, such programs or procedures represent control points which may be located at convenient sites in a network.

A *generalized distributed information management system* is a GIMS which makes use of a data bank which is distributed over a network of computers, which can be distributed locally or geographically. To the user, this data bank appears as a single collection of files; all data are available to all sites, subject to the access constraints of the network. Although the system is distributed, it cannot be totally decentralized: a system-wide discipline is required and is enforced at all times. Although a distributed system may consist of heterogeneous hardware and software, ideally, all queries and all data are transparent to all users at all sites in the network.

A generalized distributed information management system offers several advantages:

1. It can process all types and combinations of data files.
2. A distributed system can be more reliable than a centralized system.[1]
3. Since this type of system resides in multiple sites, it is possible to store portions of the data and application programs at sites where they are more heavily used.[2]
4. A distributed architecture makes it possible to store a very large data bank on several small machines rather than on a single large machine.[3]
5. If the power of a distributed systsm must be augmented, because of an increase in the number of users or the size of the data bank, new sites can be added or the power of existing sites increased by the addition of new resources.[3]
6. The concept of a distributed system is attractive from a managerial point of view, since it enables a manager to gather information from all locations of his company or organization.
7. By the very fact that it resides at a number of locations, valuable information is more secure in a distributed system. Moreover, in this type of system, data files remain isolated from application programs; no one, not even the system designer, can have access to data without authorization.[2,3]
8. Since it is likely to use a number of smaller machines, a distributed system is in many cases less costly than a centralized system on a single large machine.[1]
9. From a technical viewpoint, it is much easier to work with modular subcomponent functions than with the complex integral structure of a centralized system.

The disadvantages of a distributed system are:

1. Communications software costs are high.[4]
2. Personnel qualified to maintain and develop a distributed system are of necessity scattered among a number of sites.[4]
3. Some technical points concerning the design of complex networks using heterogeneous hardware have not yet been adequately resolved: the problem of data or data model translation, for example.[2]
4. The existence of a network necessarily imposes a degree of standardization on all sites. No single site possesses quite the freedom that it would have if it were on its own.[2]
5. Adequate operating systems for use in network environments have not yet been developed.[5]

Major recent advances in the technology of memories, storage devices, and processors have made feasible the on-line storage, access, and management of very large data banks. These advances have gone hand in hand with an increase in the understanding of the needs of the users and of the most basic problems which affect the design of information systems. In the past five years, much fruitful research has been devoted to networks, data models, the definition, manipulation, and independence of data, queries, and I/O[6]. One research effort resulted in CONIT, a software device which provides user access to multiple textual systems.[7,8]

MEDIATOR

MEDIATOR is a mechanism which provides users with a uniform view of a distributed, generalized IMS. The user interface (see Figure 6-1) consists of a friendly, English-like language which allows local users to access objects held in distant data banks. The vocabulary of this friendly user language is chosen so that it contains terms already familiar to the users. The user language allows distant and heterogeneous information management systems to be accessed in a simple, standardized manner. Thus, MEDIATOR must contain translators which carry the user language into commands for each possible destination information management system. Destination systems are selected in accordance with information concerning the user, his query, and directories kept by MEDIATOR. Another portion of MEDIATOR is the network interface (see Figure 6-1), which has the responsibility of ensuring the delivery of management system commands which have been generated for a user. Also, any data that are received in response to a user's query must be translated into a form which the user can understand and must then be delivered to the user.

In order to minimize the effects on users, and for reasons of economy, a generalized distributed IMS should utilize both the hardware and software which already exist at each of the sites that are being linked together by means of a com-

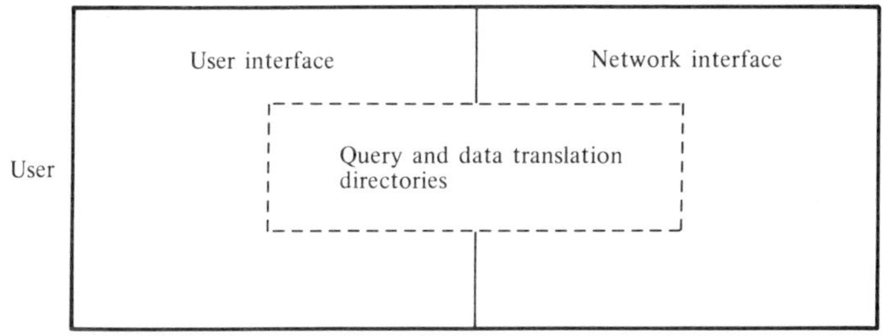

Figure 6-1. A simple view of MEDIATOR.

munications network. Such a transitional environment can be expected to exist for an indeterminate period of time. The concept of MEDIATOR represents an attempt to provide users with a global view of information which is available in such a system.

MEDIATOR represents an extension of the existing network's communication system components at a site. Requests are accepted by the MEDIATOR from any local tasks which may correspond to either users or elements of the distributed IMS. Each such request is divided into subcommands; if a subcommand cannot be serviced locally, then it is put into a form that is acceptable to the site's communication system modules. Thus, under this scheme, the reception and coordination of responses are done under the direction of MEDIATOR.

Nonlocal costs which are incurred by the remote execution of the user subcommand are determined by three factors:

1. The transmission of the subcommand to the program responsible for overseeing its execution.
2. The transmission of the data, resulting from the subcommand's execution, back to the user.
3. The actual execution of the subcommand by the controlling program.

Formulas for determining the costs of the first two factors are provided in Figure 6-2, while the third factor reflects a cost which is calculated as the subcommand is executed and is returned along with the data results.

We now proceed to a more detailed description of each of the tasks constituting MEDIATOR (see Figure 6-3). The module labeled 'user interactive' represents the vocabulary which is to be employed by a group of users in framing their queries. The terms contained in this vocabulary should capture the particular jargon which the users employ in their business. Further, this module can be so tailored that the vocabulary can easily be changed.

The user interactive module provides a friendly interface, first, by the use of subject menus reflecting the information available at all locations on the network and, second, through a set of commands which offers a common, unified view of

t = translation cost per byte

p = priority weight

n = number of data records to transfer

c = transmission cost per byte

b = bytes per record

l = length of command (in bytes)

a = the set of programs selected for executing subcommands

(a) *Communication cost factors*

C_C = cost of transmitting a subcommand to a control program that executes it

$= (t + p \cdot c) \cdot l$

C_D = cost of a data transfer

$= (t + p \cdot c) \cdot n \cdot b$

C_E = cost of executing a subcommand by a control program

Accounting information for a user is updated by

$$\sum_a (C_C + C_D + C_E)$$

(b) *Component factors*

Figure 6-2. A list of communication factors.

all information systems to which the user can have access. Both the menus and the command language can be altered quickly and easily to reflect changes in the nature of available information and changes in the nature and needs of users.

It is appropriate to provide a sample 'scenario' for the interaction of a user with the network communications system. As a user logs onto the system, he is presented with a menu of available subjects, listing the general areas of knowledge covered by all information bases to which he has authorized access. Thus, as a user selects his areas of interest, he also determines the specific information systems to be employed in his searches.

A second menu will then list classifications covered by information banks available in the information systems he has chosen. This second menu is a subject directory (see Figure 6-4); information concerning any given subject may be contained in several different information banks.

After the user has selected what he requires from the second menu (and keep in mind that in more complex situations there could be a hierarchy of three or four menus), he is presented with a list of information banks which are to be searched for an answer to any query he submits.

Associated with the name of each information bank is an estimated cost per

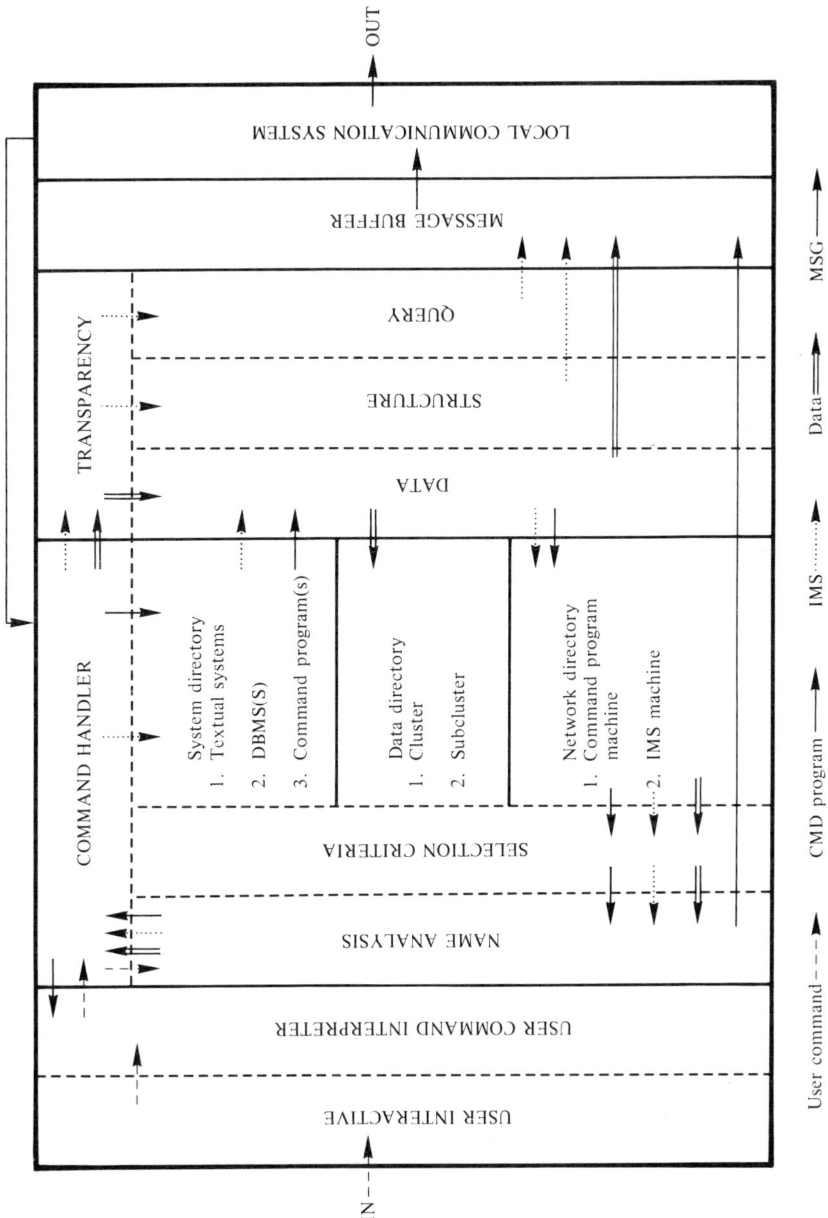

Figure 6-3. Layout of MEDIATOR.

Subject	Data bank name	Basic cost

Figure 6-4. Format of an entry in the subject dictionary.

article retrieved. Since various levels of information are available from most information banks, these estimates will cover several levels such as (in the case of a textual bank):

1. A response in the form of the number of 'hits,' or citations which fulfill the user's criteria
2. A thesaurus search.
3. The author(s), title, and data of each citation
4. The abstract of each citation
5. The full text of each citation

COMMAND INTERPRETER

The command interpreter (CI) is an executive-level task responsible for providing an interface whereby local tasks, including both users and local IMS components, are potentially capable of interaction with all elements of a generalized distributed IMS. The CI establishes and maintains a message list header for each such task (see Figure 6-5), which maintains information about each command that concerns a task.

The CI must possess the facility for interrupting a task with either a return code reflecting the status of a command or the notification of an incoming command. Also, the CI should allow a user to retrieve information about the current state of queries with which he is involved. A certain amount of modification to previously submitted commands is also allowed by the CI (e.g. permitting more data to be retrieved than was previously specified). In an effort to conserve both time and space, the CI is given the ability to read and write directly into the storage area of any local task.

Three events drive the CI:

1. A local task's request is sent to the MEDIATOR.
2. An incoming command is destined for a local task.
3. One of the subcommands which make up a local task's command has been completed.

Local task ID	List of inbound command buffers	List of outbound commands

Figure 6-5. Message list header.

The command interpreter maintains a *profile* for each authorized user of the system. This profile contains system information relating to the user (see Figure 6-6) as follows:

1. A *password:*
   (a) Establishes the user's authorization to employ the network's communication system.
   (b) Identifies those information systems to which the user has authorized access.
   (c) Within these systems, identifies those information bases to which the user has authorized access.
   (d) Restricts, as necessary, the commands by which the user is authorized to gain information from particular information banks.
2. An *identifier* provides a unique, network-wide name for each user.
3. A *priority level* defines the rapidity with which a particular user's commands are to be executed. A high-priority command will be executed quickly, while those of lower priority may be delayed and batched together, in order to secure favorable communications and processing costs.
4. An *accounting field* maintains a record of the costs incurred by the user in both his local use of the system and his queries to remote information banks.
5. A *list of messages* fall into three categories:
   (a) Results of commands submitted previously.
   (b) Messages from other users. (Messages of this type will be typically between the user and a local information specialist who acts as a consultant.)
   (c) System messages informing the user of any modifications either to the local system or to remote information banks.
6. A list of *user files* permit the user to store commands which he uses frequently and temporarily to store results.

Note that the amount of space required by a user command cannot be determined until a response is received detailing how many data bytes are to be transferred. It is assumed that sufficient buffers have been reserved by

Password
Identifier
Priority
Accounting information
Message list
File list

Figure 6-6. Format of a user profile.

MEDIATOR so that each command is able to gain requisite space. This assumption precludes the possibility of deadlock due to reassembly lockup, but in practice would accomplish this end by wasting space.

The user friendly language which is input to MEDIATOR allows:

1. Commands directed to a specific DBMS.
2. Commands oriented toward the objects in several DBMSs. These commands must be implemented through the use of functionally equivalent application programs available on the different DBMSs.
3. Commands (based upon the commonality of queries to textual management systems) that may be translated into queries targeted for a specific textual system.
4. Commands unique to a particular textual information system.

Each query or command issued by the user has the following format:

$$\langle \text{Command} \rangle \text{ [IMS]} \cdot \text{[Cluster} \cdot \text{Subcluster]} \cdot \text{[object]*}$$

where ⟨ ⟩ indicates a field which is required, while [ ] indicates a field that may be supplied by the user in the command; otherwise it will be provided by the system. Also, * denotes that zero or more objects may be named in a command.

User commands are decomposed into subcommands based on the manner in which the requested objects are spread among the management systems. The MEDIATOR at the user's site must combine the objects retrieved by the subcommands in a way which is consistent with the user's original command. With regard to data bases, this concept assumes the existence of application programs which allow objects at various levels of granularity to be retrieved.

COMMAND HANDLER

The command handler (CH) performs three major functions on each command that is accepted by the CI:

1. *Name analysis*. The user command is first compared to entries in the command program directory (Figure 6-7) in order to derive a list of application programs and their associated DBMSs (or a list of actual textual commands and the management systems in which they are implemented). Along with each pair of command and management system names is included a sequence of local cluster names. Only those clusters are allowed which are compatible with any schema and subschema specified by the user in a command directed for data bases or which match the clusters specified in the user's profile. Next, the data directory of Figure 6-8(a) is used to map the local cluster names into their network, global equivalents. The directory of Figure 6-8(b) is used to provide the global synonyms for each local object identifier and to eliminate any management system and cluster that does not hold any of the objects required.

Local names				Partially global name	
CMD PGM	IMS	Cluster	Subcluster	CMD PGM	IMS
Payroll	IMS	Personnel	Burser	Division payroll	IBM IMS
Payroll	IMS	Personnel	Burser	Division payroll	UNIVAC DMS

(a) Command program subdirectory

Local names				Partially global name	
IMS	CMD PGM	Cluster	Subcluster	IMS	
IMS	Payroll	Personnel	Burser	IBM IMS	Division payroll
DMS	Payroll	Personnel	Burser	UNIVAC DMS	Division payroll

(b) IMS subdirectory

Figure 6-7. System directory.

Local names		Global names	
Cluster	Subcluster	Cluster	Subcluster
Personnel	Burser	Finance	Comptroller
Personnel	Checks	Finance	Auditor
Manufacturing	Equipment	Budget	Tangibles

(a)

Local	Global		
OBJ	OBJ	IMS Cluster	Record length
ID	Name	IBM IMS finance	20
Age	Age	IBM IMS finance	4
SSN	ID	UNIVAC DMS finance	20
Age		UNIVAC MS finance	4
ID	Name	UNIVAC DMS finance	24

(b)

Figure 6-8. Data directory.

The result of this process is a list of objects which are related to those in the user's original request. Each object is fully specified by using global command, management system, cluster, and object name. Thus, each object in the original request yields a list of all names by which it is known in the distributed system. A network directory (Figure 6-9) supplied an enumeration of all the places where such fully specified objects exist within the network.

This naming process is also illustrated in Figure 6-10; at the root of this tree resides a directory of programs which execute commands available to the users. Each of these programs has one or more paths to leaf nodes associated with it, i.e. the list of fully specified objects which can be accessed by a command's program. Every level in this tree corresponds to one of the components in a distributed IMS. The left portion of the tree represents management system components that can be accessed locally, while the right part of the tree holds the names of information system components which can be accessed at remote sites in the network. For that reason, the right portion of the tree must necessarily contain the machine site associated with an object. This tree is used merely to reinforce the idea of how an object name is analyzed; the information shown in this tree is, in fact, kept in several system directories (see Figures 6-7, 6-8, and 6-9).

The relationship of different subclusters and objects which exist over the

Data network directory

Subcluster internal index	Global			Equivalence PTR	Subset PTR
	Subcluster	OBJ	Site (S)		
1	Comptroller	Name	IBM S370-1	---	2
1	Comptroller	Age	IBM S370-1	---	2
2	Auditor	ID	UNIVAC 1108-3	---	---
2	Auditor	Age	UNIVAC 1108-3	---	---
2	Auditor	Name	UNIVAC 1108-3	---	---

Command program network directory

CMD PGM	MS	Site
Division payroll	IBM IMS	IBM S370-1
Division payroll	IBM IMS	IBM S360-1
Division payroll	UNIVAC DMS	UNIVAC 1108-3

Figure 6-9. Network directories.

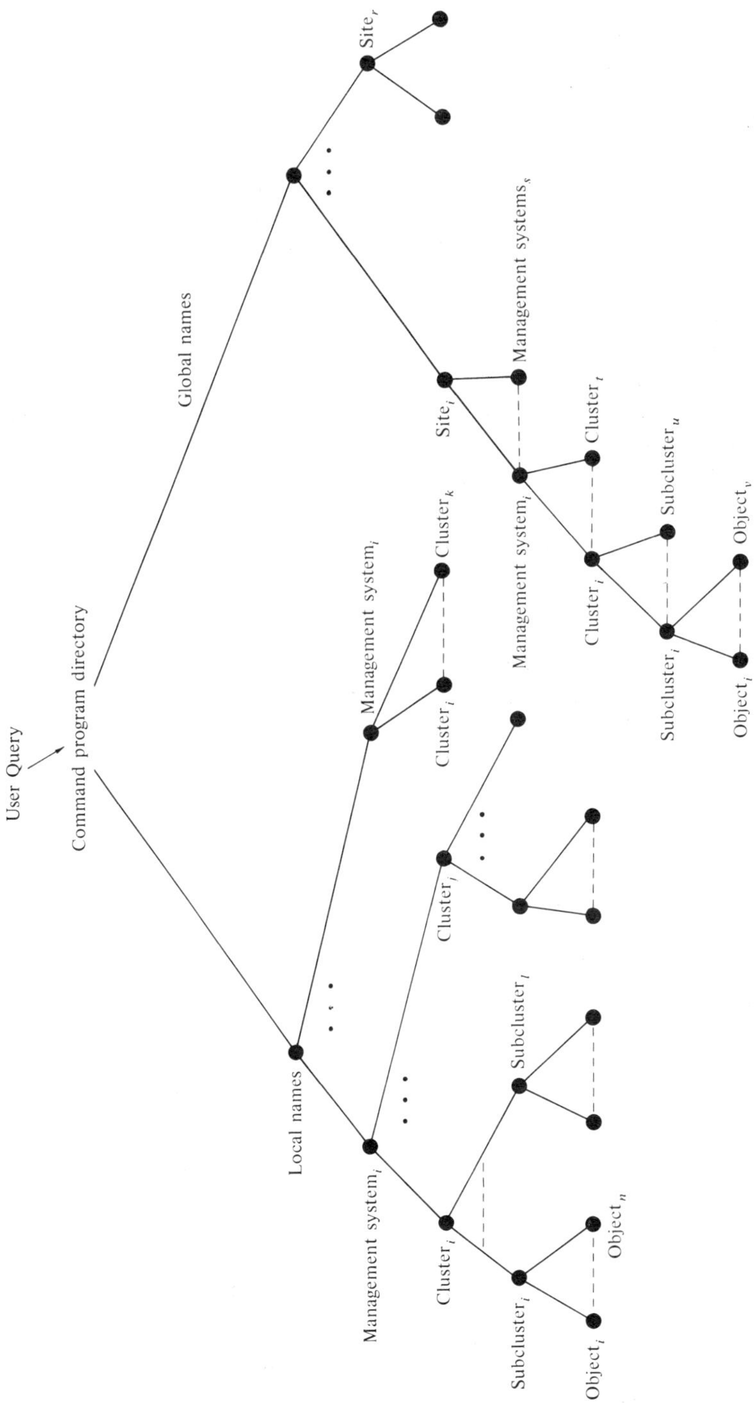

Figure 6-10. A true representation of the naming process for objects.

network is captured in the data network directory (Figure 6-9). Each subcluster is assigned an index in this directory, and has associated with it a list of the indices of subclusters which are equivalents or subsets.

2. *Generation of subcommands.* It may often happen that all the data requested by a user cannot be obtained by issuing a single command. In such a case, the original command is decomposed into subcommands through selection criteria. This selection leads to the complete specification of each object and the formation of all subcommands. Each outbound command is then represented by a list of subcommand blocks connected to the issuing task's message list header (see Figure 6-11). The results of the subcommands are combined according to the logic and qualification operations of the original command, which could not be included in the subcommands.

   For example, GET (A AND B AND C) might be split into the subcommands GET (A AND B) that is sent to DBMS.AP.S.SS1, and GET C that is sent to DBMS.APS.S.SS2. The data retrieved by these two subcommands must be ANDed in order for their data requests to be equivalent to the intended effect of the original command. Thus, the subcommands must be connected by logical operators which preserve the meaning of the original command.
3. *Translation.* This third major function of the CH routines provides a translation mechanism between the user language and different types of IMS, which are called as they are needed. An example of this translation process is given in Figure 6-12.

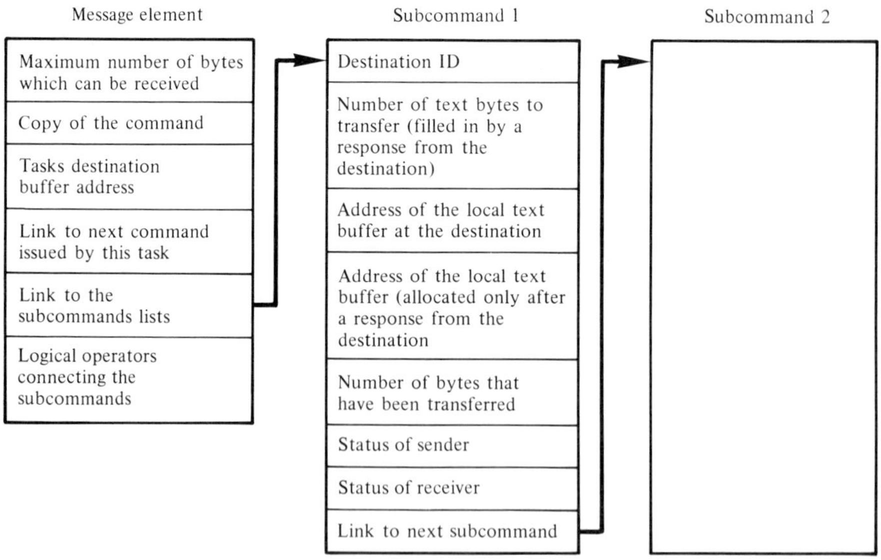

Figure 6-11. Outbound command message format.

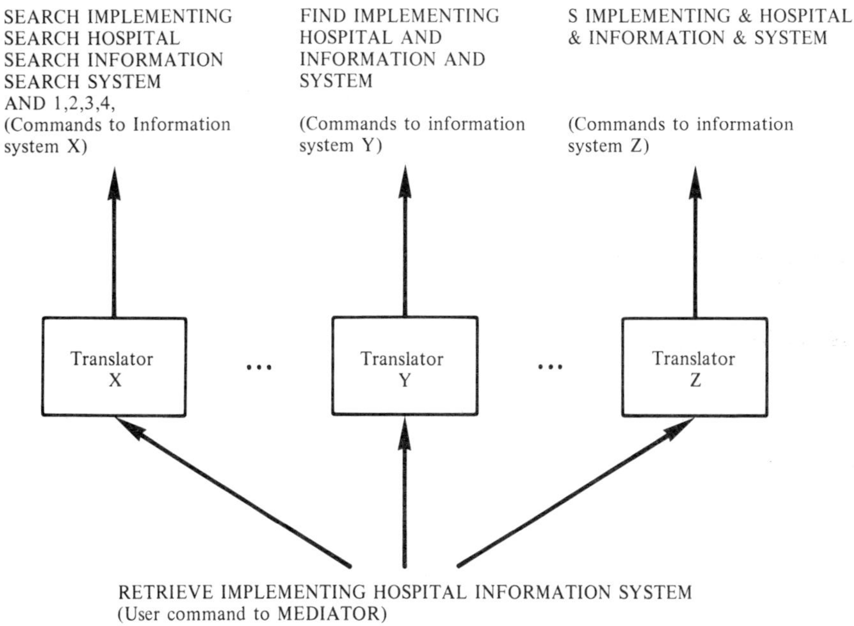

Figure 6-12. Sample translation of a user query.

As each command is built, it is put into a format that the communications system will accept. The CH is driven by two types of events: (1) user requests that have been processed by the CI and (2) inbound messages from the local communications system, which are destined for a local task in the generalized distributed IMS.

The CH establishes a message element (see Figure 6-11) for each command that it holds. It is assumed that a limit exists on the number of outstanding commands which a task is capable of issuing. The purpose of this restriction is to limit the amount of space needed to represent both subcommands and inbound commands. A command is processed by the CH in the following manner:

1. A list of all subcommands is created.
2. Responses to each of the subcommands are received and processed.
3. System buffer space is allocated for all data involved in a subcommand's transfer of data.
4. A message is sent to either start the transfer or discard the data associated with each subcommand.
5. Control of each subcommand's buffer is given to the communications system so that it may utilize a buffer to assemble data from packets received, or to fragment data being sent, into packets.
6. The accounting information for the local task is updated.

The communications system at each network site provides communication facilities to a variety of users including the MEDIATOR. The modules which compose this system must provide the following services: line control, error control, flow control, congestion control, updating network information (e.g. routing information), packet assembly, disassembly of messages into packets, and intermachine translation. The communication system interrupts the CH whenever a storage buffer is filled or emptied, or a command arrives from a remote task involved in data transfer.

NETWORK MESSAGE TRANSMISSION

It is informative to consider the sequences of messages that arise when a user engages in document retrieval through the use of MEDIATOR (se Figure 6-13):

1. A user query is submitted to MEDIATOR and decomposed into subcommands.
2. Each subcommand which has been translated into a query for an information system is sent to the designated textual management system.
3. A request to find the document identifiers associated with the desired keywords is sent to the file indices associated with the textual system's data banks.
4. The lists of identifiers are sent back to the textual management system node and are combined in accordance with the subcommand that triggered this retrieval.
5. The number of documents, along with the title, author, and publication date of each work that fulfills the subcommand, is sent back to the user.
6. After any necessary code conversion, reformatting, and the elimination of any duplicate documents, the number of hits and document information relating to all subcommands is presented to the user.
7. The user selects some or all of the documents to be retrieved.
8. Accordingly, commands are issued to the textual systems to retrieve the selected works.
9. Each textual system involved issues requests to retrieve the selected documents through the use of the document identifiers retrieved in step 4.
10. The documents' text or abstracts are retrieved.
11. Documents are sent to the MEDIATOR for any necessary code conversion and reformatting.
12. The text is stored in a user file, and the user is notified.

Let us also consider the sequence of messages over the network after a user task sends a GET command to the MEDIATOR and it is divided into several subcommands to DBMSs. (Numbers used are in reference to those of Figure 6-14.) Each of the subcommands involves objects which share a common applications program, DBMS, schema, and subschema.

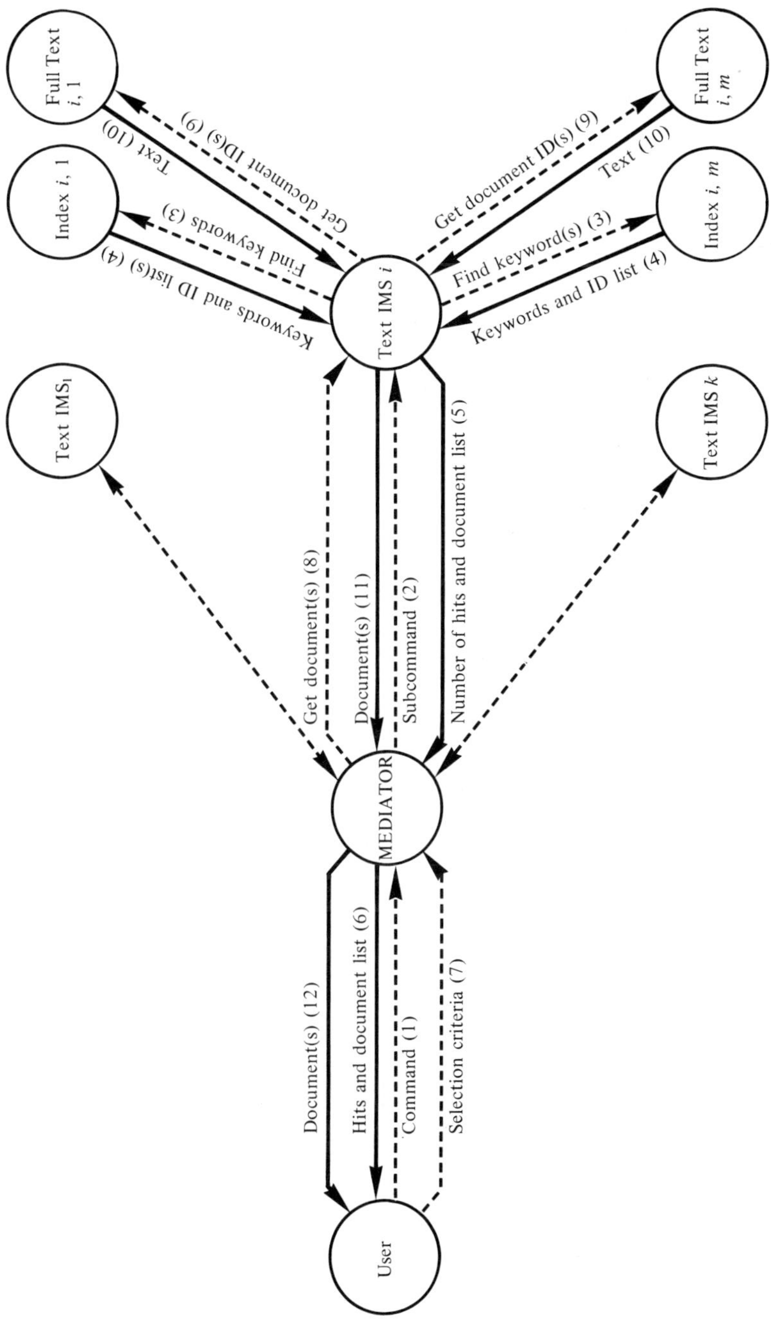

Figure 6-13. Sequences of message transactions with a query to a textual IMS.

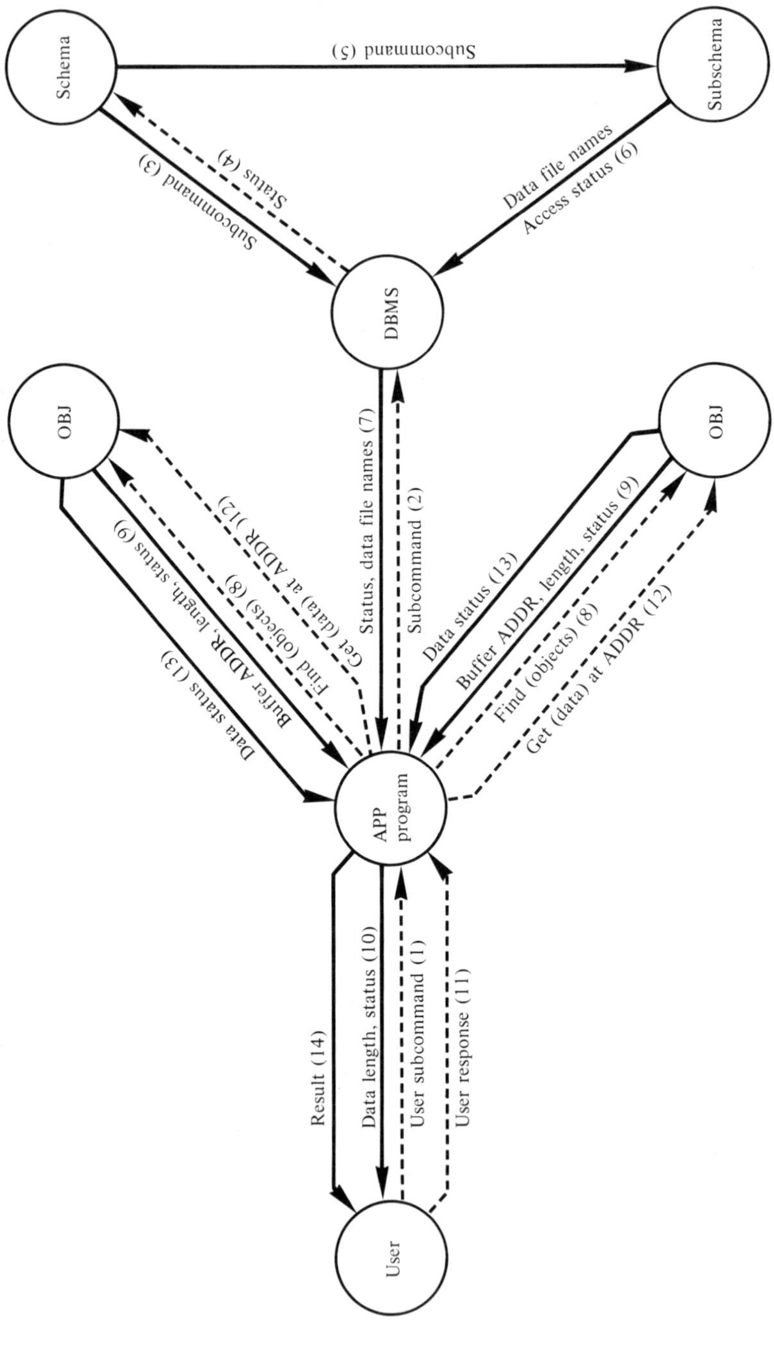

Figure 6-14. Sequence of message transactions with a DBMS command.

1. A subcommand or subquery is sent to an application program which has access to the other three components and minimizes communications costs.
2. The applications program receives the subcommand and forwards the command to the DBMS in order that the correctness of its operator can be checked.
3. The DBMS sends the command to the specified schema to verify that the user has the right to access the desired data.
4. A status that indicates the result of this verification is returned to the DBMS.
5. If the user possesses the correct access rights, then the command is forwarded to the correct subschema.
6. The subschema returns the names of the data files containing the desired objects and a status indicating the right of the user to access these data.
7. Finally, the DBMS replies to the application program with a status that indicates the availability of the objects in the schema and subschema. Also contained in this reply is the data file name(s) which contains the requested objects.
8. A message is sent to each of the data file locations which cause the named files to be opened and their contents to be buffered.
9. A reply to the applications program is generated by each of the data file locations. This response contains the address of the buffer where the data are stored, the length of the data, and an indication of their availability.
10. When responses have been received from all data file locations, the applications program constructs a 'preliminary' response to the user's subcommand. This message contains the total length of the data found and a status indicating its accessibility in each data base component (i.e. DBMS, S, SS, and data files).
11. The user task sends either a proceed or an abort signal to the applications program.
12. If a proceed signal is received, then the applications program requests the transmission of all data; otherwise, the buffers are released.
13. Data are transmitted to the application program and operated upon in accordance with the subcommand.
14. The result of the subcommand is sent to the user.

DISTRIBUTION OF COMPONENTS

MEDIATOR allows users to access any management system available in the network. To a limited extent, the users need not be aware of what management systems are available to them. Rather, they can interact by a virtual query language which MEDIATOR directs to the proper application program(s) or textual management system(s). When additional information is needed before a query can be translated into a command for a particular management system,

MEDIATOR will prompt the user in an attempt to elicit the necessary details or choices. Thus, MEDIATOR provides an intelligent interface to a distributed collection of management systems. For these reasons, MEDIATOR is ideally suited to Videotext service in which users are able to access both general interest data banks and specialized data bases. Through its virtual query language, MEDIATOR provides a global view of the data which are available to the user.

MEDIATOR is designed as an interface between either users or management system components and the network. Thus, as the components of an information management system are distributed over a network, MEDIATOR accompanies each component so that it may access and be accessed by the rest of the distributed system. A necessary ingredient for this communication is the data translation, among the objects available over the network, which MEDIATOR provides.

Each of the components in a generalized distributed IMS may be partitioned or have multiple copies over different sites in the network. Considering, for a moment, only the distribution of the data banks and clusters, it is seen that these components may be combined in four ways. These four schemes are illustrated in Figure 6-15, which graphically demonstrates when:

1. A single information management system (IMS) and its associated object clusters all reside on the samé machine m.
2. Several management systems, each with a set of associated clusters, exist on the same machine m.
3. One or more management systems and their associated clusters are partitioned over the set of machines $m'_1, \ldots, m'_i$, while one or more management systems and their associated clusters reside on a single machine m.
4. All management systems and their associated clusters are partitioned over a set of machines.

By providing some appropriate symbolism, it is possible to extend the data base viewpoint, just illustrated, to include objects.

Let α denote a set of data objects,
M denote a set of machines,
m denote a single machine,
Σ denote a set of clusters,
σ denote a single cluster, and
IMS denote an information management system.

Next some relations can be defined:

$M \geqslant \alpha$	means that the entire set of objects α is contained on at least one machine in M and α can be replicated on any other machines in M.
$M \ngeqslant \alpha$	means that the set of objects α is partitioned over the machines in M.
$\alpha \leqslant \Sigma$	means that one (=) or more (<) clusters in Σ contain a copy of α.
$\alpha \nleqslant \Sigma$	means that any cluster in Σ can contain only a subset of α.

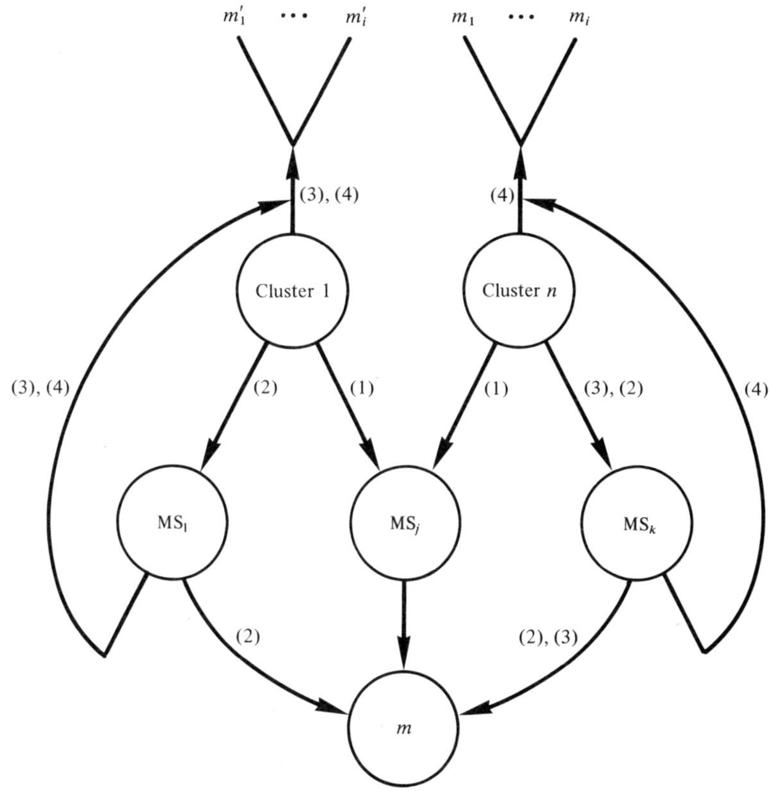

Figure 6-15. Partitioning a generalized DIMS.

Thus, the following observations can be made concerning the distribution of objects in the network:

$$M \geqslant \alpha \leqslant \Sigma \quad (1)$$
$$M \geqslant \alpha \not\leqslant \Sigma \quad (2)$$
$$M \not\geqslant \not\leqslant \Sigma \quad (3)$$
$$M \not\geqslant \alpha \leqslant \Sigma \quad (4)$$

Observation (1) states that α exists as a whole unit on one or more machines in M, and is contained as a whole in one or more clusters in Σ. Observation (2) states that again α exists as a whole unit on one or more machines in M, but the clusters in Σ contain only subsets of α. In (3), α is shown to be partitioned over the machines in M, and the clusters in Σ can contain only subsets of α. Finally, in (4), α is partitioned over the machines in M, and is contained as a whole entity in one or more clusters in Σ.

Similar observations can be made concerning how a cluster can be distributed over the network in relation to machines and management systems. To achieve this goal, we must first define some additional relations:

$m \geqslant \sigma$ means that the information defining the cluster σ is contained on machine *m*.

$m \not\geqslant \sigma$ means that the information defining σ is not contained on any single machine; rather, it is partitioned over several machines.

$\sigma \leqslant \text{IMS}$ means that cluster σ references objects in only one information management system.

$\sigma \not\leqslant \text{IMS}$ means that the cluster σ provides a global view which references objects in several IMSs.

Now the following relations can be shown:

$$m \geqslant \sigma \leqslant \text{IMS} \tag{5}$$
$$m \geqslant \sigma \not\leqslant \text{IMS} \tag{6}$$
$$m \not\geqslant \sigma \not\leqslant \text{IMS} \tag{7}$$
$$m \not\geqslant \sigma \leqslant \text{IMS} \tag{8}$$

Relation (5) states that all the information defining cluster σ is contained on one machine *m*, and that σ references objects contained in only one IMS. Relation (6) states that again all information relating to a cluster resides on one machine and that σ references objects which are partitioned among multiple IMSs. Relation (7) states that the information defining σ is partitioned over several machines and that σ references objects which are spread among several information management systems. Finally, in (8) the information defining σ is partitioned over several machines, while the cluster σ makes reference to objects that reside in just one IMS.

SITE SELECTION FOR DATA ACQUISITION

Now let us describe the ways in which an IMS, cluster (C), subcluster (SC), and a command execution program (CP) may be combined with one another. We impose the realistic restriction that only C and SC may be partitioned, and require that a CP and the data objects that it references must reside on the same machine. For each combination (i.e. distribution scheme), we can derive the minimum and the maximum number of messages that must be sent by the CP to the other components.

In Table 6-1, each component of this restricted generalized distributed IMS, C, CS, and CP is described by an ordered pair (γ, m), where γ describes the type of IMS which the component utilizes. The distribution schemes in Table 6-1 are ordered in terms of the average number of messages which must be transferred (between CP and IMS, C, and SC) in order for a subcommand to be executed at the CP. For distribution schemes 6 through 10, each message sent or received by the CP incurs an additional cost because of the translation required between α and β.

The estimated cost of sending to a destination CP.IMS.C.SC is based upon

TABLE 6-1
Distribution schemes

Distribution scheme	IMS	C	SC	CP	Restrictions	Minimum messages required	Maximum messages required
1	(α, i)	(α, i)	(α, i)	(α, i)	–	0	0
2	(α, i)	(α, i)	(α, i)	(α, l)	$i \neq l$	1	1
3	(α, i)	(α, j)	(α, j)	(α, l)	$i \notin j$	1	$1 + \|j\|$
4	(α, i)	(α, j)	(α, k)	(α, i)	$j \neq k$	1	$\|j\| + \|k\|$
5	(α, i)	(α, j)	(α, k)	(α, l)	$i \neq 1, j \neq k,$	3	$1 + \|j\| + \|k\|$
6	(α, i)	(α, i)	(α, i)	(β, i)	$i \notin j \cup k$	0	0
7	(α, i)	(α, i)	(α, i)	(β, l)	$i \neq l$	1	1
8	(α, i)	(α, j)	(α, j)	(β, l)	$i \notin j$	1	$i + \|j\|$
9	(α, i)	(α, j)	(α, k)	(β, i)	$j \neq k$	1	$\|j\| + \|k\|$
10	(α, i)	(α, j)	(α, k)	(β, l)	$i \neq l, j \neq k,$ $l \notin j \cup k$	3	$1 + \|j\| + \|k\|$

Notes.
α, β = DBMS types
i, l = single machines
j, k = sets of machines

properties of the routes from the local site to the machine(s) upon which the destination task resides. Each route has an error rate, line speed, distance, and an associated amount of traffic which may be used when estimating communication costs. It is assumed that the number of records corresponding to each object within a subcluster is only kept at the site(s) where the subcluster resides. Thus, this number is not generally available for computing an estimate of transmission costs.

A user command is assigned a priority from one of three different levels. We assume that a priority scheme exists within the network based upon factors such as a user's willingness to pay and a default command priority. Each command is decomposed into subcommands on the basis of information from:

1. The system directories, if the command is of the lowest priority
2. The system directories and possibly broadcast requests, if it is in the middle priority class.
3. Broadcast requests alone (in order to use the currently most-responsive machines containing the desired objects), if the command is of the highest priority

A description of the selection algorithm for commands of the lowest priority proceeds as follows:

Step 1. Associate with each object, or ordered set of objects, the set of global destinations CP.IMS.C.SC which contain the object. This association is performed by the CH's name analysis procedures in accordance with the restrictions imposed by names which are already partially specified.

Step 2. Starting with the largest group of objects which is connected by an AND logic operator, proceed by just finding the largest collection of objects in this group that are not contained in any subcommand and which can be found at the same IMS.C.SC. The destination IMS.C.SC is selected from the lowest possible numbered distribution scheme in Table 6-1. Each OR group which appears as part of the larger AND group must contribute one of its objects to this collection. If there is more than one choice for the CP.IMS.C.CS, then take one which minimizes both the cost and the number of different objects which it contains. This collection of objects is transformed into a subcommand for a CP which can access IMS, C, and SC. The subcommand has the same operator and disposition as the original command, and operands equal to the collection of objects that are connected by an AND logic operation. Repeat step 2 until each AND group has been completely resolved into subcommands connected by AND operators.

Step 3. For each OR-group which has not contributed to the generation of a subcommand, proceed as follows. Every operand is presently represented by either a previously generated subcommand or an object. From the objects in the OR-group, a subcommand is generated that involves just one of the objects and minimizes both cost and number of objects transferred.

The selection algorithm for a command of middle priority is the same as that just described, but with one exception. In retrieving data, if there is more than one CP.IMS.C.SC with the same cost and number of objects transferred, then the most responsive CP.IMS.C.SC is selected. This selection is accomplished by broadcasting the retrieval command to the appropriate collection of CP.IMS.C.SC.

The selection algorithm for a command of the highest priority proceeds as follows:

Step 1. For each partially specified object, broadcast a request for data representing the object.

Step 2. Take the first response for each object; this approach results in fully specified object names which utilize the currently most responsive machines.

Step 3. Based upon these responses, a command is broken into subcommands. When each subcommand is constructed, its length and address fields are already known.

When a subcommand is broadcast in an attempt to find the most responsive CP.IMS.C.SC, the communications system interrupts the CH only with the first reply. This reply is used to fill in a portion of the storage buffer and to establish communications with the designated CP.IMS.C.SC. Thus, all subsequent responses to the subcommand that was broadcast may be dealt with by the communications system through the inspection of information in the subcommands' storage buffer.

SUMMARY

MEDIATOR is designed to allow users to access both textual information systems and DBMSs. The construction of a 'user friendly' language which supports requests to multiple textual systems represents a reasonable task, since approximately 70 per cent. of the commands in different textual systems perform similar functions. It is necessary to include translators in the software of MEDIATOR; these translations map commands from the user query language into each of the individual textual systems (see Figure 6-12). Target systems selected are compatible with both the user's profile and the command issued. For example, the data banks selected must contain subjects (i.e. the cluster and subcluster) specified by the user, and the user must be authorized to have access to these data.

Often some additional parameters are required before the user's command can be transformed into an equivalent command destined for a target textual system. Each translator is therefore given the ability to interact with the user so that any needed details can be obtained. MEDIATOR may find that a user's query can be carried out in several textual management systems (as subcommands). In this situation, MEDIATOR assumes the responsibility for collecting and transforming the information returned by each subcommand before sending a response to the user. Knowledgeable users may bypass MEDIATOR's translation process by issuing commands directed to specific textual systems.

Application program names provide the command set by which MEDIATOR allows users to retrieve information from data banks. After an application program has been indicated by a user, MEDIATOR may prompt the user with a functional description of the program in order to acquire any additional parameters which are required.

It is projected that the library of application programs which presently exists across the nodes of a network will be augmented in two ways:

1. Application programs will be written for individual DBMSs which retrieve objects at various levels of granularity. Such programs attempt to supply standardized retrieval routines for the different DBMSs in the network.
2. Application programs will be composed to utilize calls to the preceding type of application program, and operate upon the retrieved objects. This type of application program provides users with a global view of the data which exist over a network. The calls which are 'embedded' in such programs are what have heretofore been described as subcommands. Before the results of

these subcommands can be combined, data translation may be required to convert the information into a common representation.

This chapter has provided the functional characteristics of MEDIATOR, a system which allows both users and IMS components to access information without regard to system boundaries. MEDIATOR acts as a friendly interface to users, providing both query and data translation. By means of this interface, the casual, nonprofessional user can easily acquire the information he desires. Since MEDIATOR acts as a focal point for the users' queries at a site, it provides a convenient place to monitor the data requested. Data which are frequently accessed can be placed in a local data bank, thus eliminating delays and costs due to translation and communication.

REFERENCES

1. Fry, J. P., and Sibley, E. H.: Evaluation of data-base management system. *ACM Computing Surveys*, **8**, No. 1, 7–42, March 1976.
2. Rothnie, J. B.: A survey of research and development in distributed data base management. *Proc. Very Large Data Bases*, Tokyo, Japan, October 1977, pp. 48–62.
3. Falor, K.: 'Distributed' doesn't mean 'random'. *Datamation*, **24**, No. 9, 226–229, September 1978.
4. Hsiao, D. K., and Madnik, S. E.: Database machine architecture in the context of information technology evolution. *Proc. of the Third Int. Conf. Very Large Databases*, Tokyo, Japan, October, 1977, pp. 63–84.
5. Wallentine, V. E., *et al.*: *An Overview of the MIMICS Design*. TR CS 77-04, Department of Computer Science, Kansas State University, Manhattan, Kansas, December 1976.
6. Myers, W.: Key development in computer technology: a survey. *Computer*, **9**, No. 11, 48–77, November 1976.
7. Marcus, R. S., and Reintjes, J. F.: *Computer Interfaces for User Access to Heterogeneous Information-Retrieval Systems*. Report ESL-R-739, MIT, Cambridge, Mass, April 1977.
8. Salton, G. R.: Automatic information retrieval. *IEEE Computer*, **1980**, 41–56, September 1980.

BIBLIOGRAPHY

Chamberlin, D. O.: Relational data base management systems. *ACM Computing Surveys*, **8**, 43–46, March 1978.

Champine, G. A.: Six approaches to distributed databases. *Datamation*, **23**, No. 5, 69–72, May 1977.

Childs, D. L.: Description of a set-theoretical data structure. *AFIPS*, 1968.

Chu, W. W.: Optimal file allocation in a computer network. In *Computer Communication Network*, Prentice-Hall, Englewood Cliffs, N.J., 1973.

Date, C. J.: *An Introduction to Data Base System*, 2nd ed. Addison-Wesley Publishing Company, Mealo Park, California, 1977.

Gasey, R. G.: Allocation of copies of files in an information network. *Proc. AFIPS 1972 Spring Joint Computer Conf.*, Vol. 40, pp. 617–625. AFIPS Press, 1972.

Gien, M.: A file transfer protocol (FTP). *Proc. of the Symp. On Computer Communications Protocols*, University of Liege, D5-1-5-7, 1978.

ISO: *Provisional Model of Open-Systems Architecture*, ISO/TC 97/SC 16 N537.

Kent, W.: New criteria for the conceptual model. *Proc. of the Second Int. Conf. on Very Large Data Bases* (Eds. P. C. Lockemann and E. J. Neuhold) pp. 1–12, 1977.

Kerschberg, L., Klug, A., and Tsichritzis, D.: A taxonomy of data models. In *Proc. of the Second Int. Conf. on Very Large Data Bases*. (Eds. P. C. Lockemann and E. J. Neuhold), pp. 43–64, 1977.

Loomis, M. S., and Popek, G. J.: A model for data base distribution. *Symp. on Trends and Applications 1976 Computer Network*, pp. 162–169. IEEE, 1976.

Maryanski, F. J., *et al.*: *Distributed Data Base Management Using Minicomputers*. Infotech State-of-the-Art Report, Mini's Versus Mainframes, 1978.

Maryanski, F. J.: A survey of developments in distributed data base management system. *Computer*, **10**, No. 2, 28–38, February 1978.

Ramamoorthy, C. V., Krishnarao, T., Ho, G. S., and Wah, B. W.: Architectural issues in distributed data base systems, *Proc. of the Third Int. Conf. on Very Large Data Bases*, Tokyo, Japan, October 6–8, 1977, pp. 121–126.

Shankar, K. S., and Chandersekaran, C. S.: Data flow, abstraction levels and specification for communication switching systems. *Proc. of the Second Int. Conf. on Software Engineering*, 1976, pp. 585–591.

Slonim, J.: *Generalized Distributed Information Management Architecture* (*GDIMA*). A Doctor's Dissertation, Department of Computer Science, Kansas State University, Manhattan, Kansas, 1979.

Advances in Distributed Processing Management, Volume 2
Edited by P. S. Fisher, J. Slonim, and E. A. Unger

Chapter 7

THE PROBLEMS OF DATA, STRUCTURE, AND APPLICATION SOFTWARE CONVERSION IN A HETEROGENEOUS ENVIRONMENT

Moon Jin Han and Paul S. Fisher
Department of Computer Science, Kansas State University, Manhattan, Kansas

A plethora of indicators demonstrates the development and utilization of data bases and data base management systems in modern organizations. In addition, a recognizable trend is to provide, within an organization, a multiplicity of machines—some as distinct systems, others as embedded computers in more general machines, systems, or instruments. With these trends, the requirement for communication becomes primordial. The value of data in terms of timeliness and availability is of central importance. Such emphasis on communication is in direct contrast to the lack of effective communication facilities. Given the need for communications, one must consider the impact of heterogeneity upon the establishment of an effective methodology for data movement. The purpose of this chapter is to review the established techniques and problems in this area.

Essentially two types of conversion are addressed in this chapter—data conversion and program conversion. In reality, both of these conversions are very important, but each can be deferred until it becomes necessary to communicate, obtain data from, or provide a program segment to any other computer environment. For a self-contained, independent organization, conversions can occur at the pleasure of management. For government agencies and medical and multisite organizations, such requirements for conversion points may already exist.

THE PROBLEMS

Data translation is defined as the process by which data are created under different logical/physical structures on one system and transferred so that they can be used by the same or a different system. In general, data conversion occurs as a result of:[1] (1) a change in the hardware environment; (2) conversion from a conventional file system to a data base system, (3) conversion from one data base system to another; or (4) a change in modified application requirements.

The data to be moved to the new system are created using unique data formats which can seldom be used in programs or systems other than those for which they were created. Every time a new generation of computers is manufactured, data from the old data bases of many old systems often have to be translated. As pointed out by Merten and Fry,[2] the most important factors contributing to the problem are: (1) implicit data definition; (2) lack of complete data definition techniques; (3) incompatibility of hardware, and (4) loss of information or significance.

Over the years, considerable research has been devoted to developing a generalized data translation methodology. At first, a few attempts were made to design a data definition language[2–8] for describing the data and storage structure of a system. There were also a few attempts to develop a generalized data translator. Currently, efforts are directed toward providing high-level tools for data conversion.[9–12] Experiments with prototype data conversion systems indicate that substantial productivity gains are possible utilizing these new tools. At present, data conversion is done infrequently because of its complexity. More conversions will be taking place more often and necessitating better tools, however.

For program conversion, a data base program is (1) a program written in a conventional programming language with embedded data manipulation statements interacting with a data base system or (2) a statement or series of statements in the query/update language of a self-contained data base system. For example, a COBOL program containing embedded CODASYL DBTG DML statements is a data base program. Queries of System 2000 are also a data base program. Program conversion may be required for various reasons, such as hardware migration, new processing requirements, or a decision to adopt a new programming language. Little progress has been made in obtaining a solution to the general problem of program conversion, while considerable effort has been made to develop special tools for a limited program conversion situation.[13,14] Many potential benefits arise when a usable data base program conversion system becomes a reality. Broadly speaking, they can be classified into (human) productivity benefits and (machine) performance benefits.[14]

Three types of data base changes affecting application programs were identified by Shneiderman:[13]

1. Alterations to the data base physical structure; e.g. the format and encoding of data or the arrangement of items within records.
2. Changes to the data base logical structure—either the deletion or addition of access paths to accommodate new performance requirements or changes to the semantics of data; e.g. modification of defined relationships between record types within records.
3. Migration to a new DBMS, perhaps encompassing a data model and/or data manipulation language different from the one currently in use.

While most commercial data base management systems provide application programs with insulation from a variety of modifications to the physical data base, protection from logical changes is minimal (particularly at the semantic level). Examples of semantic changes that affect application programs are:[27]

1. Changes in relationships between record types, such as changing a one-to-many association to a many-to-many association, or vice versa
2. Deletion or addition of data items, record types, or record relationships
3. Changes in derivable information ('virtual items') to explicit information ('actual items'), or vice versa
4. Changes in integrity, authorization, or deletion rules

The interdependence of the semantics of the data base accesses and the surrounding software greatly complicates the program analysis state of conversion.

Data Conversion—Concepts

For data conversion or translation, a user needs to describe the data structure for both source and target data and the relationships between them. Usually, two definitional languages are needed for this purpose: a data description language for source and target data and a translation description language to describe the relationships between the source and target data.

Generally, a data conversion system requires three components,[12] as shown in Figure 7-1—a reader, a restructurer, and a writer. The general function of the reader is to extract the source data and pass them to the restructurer for further processing. A data description language is needed for this process. The restructurer takes these data and produces data that can be processed by the writer. Generally, this component has the responsibility of performing the logical translations of the data and of making the data structurally compatible with the writer. A translation description language is used for this process. The writer then produces the target data according to the description of the target data structurer. A data description language is also needed for this process.[2,5,12]

The following discussion describes the technology by which data conversion is achieved. The broader approach to data conversion with a generalized system was described by Fry and his colleagues.[12]

Data exist in various and complex forms, as shown in Figure 7-2, which is an expanded form of the diagram in Figure 7-1. The diagram indicates some of the transformations which need to take place in a data conversion. It also illustrates the capabilities needed by the read and write processes in a data conversion system.

The purpose of unloading data from its source is to reduce the complex physical structure of the source data base to a very simple physical structure. The result would be a sequential data stream. The source data base contains information that interests the user. It also harbors the control information specific to a particular system. This control information is used for such data management

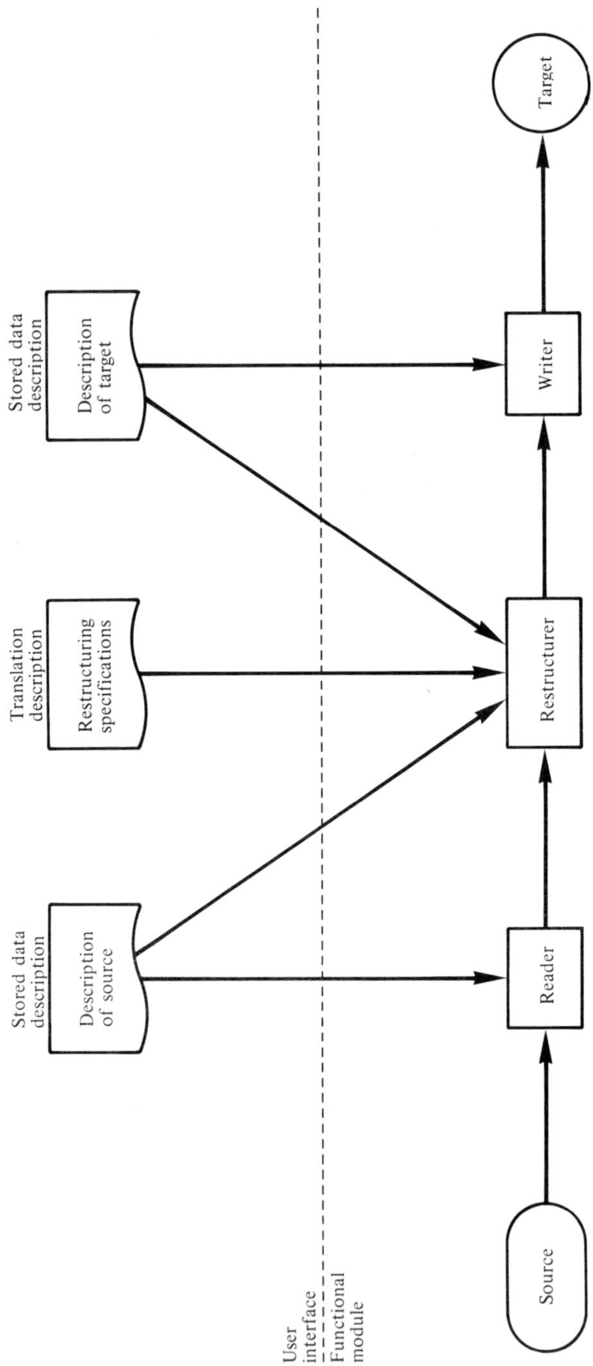

Figure 7-1. Schematic data conversion process.

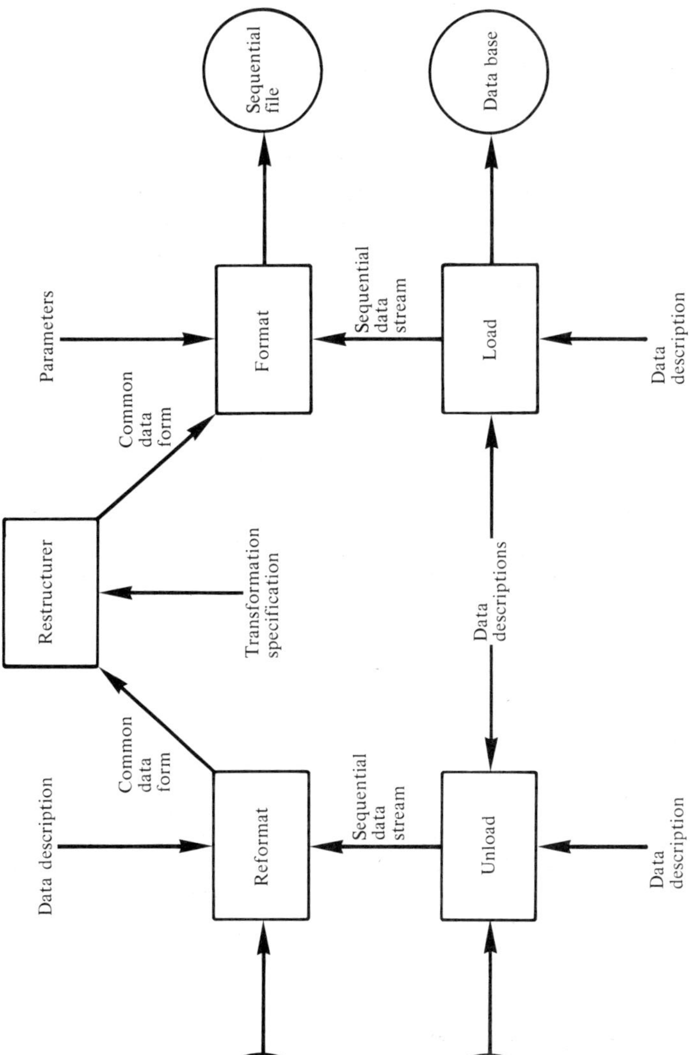

Figure 7-2. Schematic data conversion process—expanded.

functions as overflow chaining, index maintenance, and record blocking. All of this system-specific information is deleted during the unload transformation. The frequent use of pointers in a source system also makes the unloading process complex. Pointers serve two basic purposes: they represent relationships between record instances and implement alternative access paths to data. During the unload transformation, the first class of pointers maintains information that must be preserved during the transformation. The second class of pointers may be discarded without loss of information.

The reformat process creates a common data form of the source data to facilitate the restructuring step in the conversion process. In the case of a simple sequential file not under DBMS control, reformation may enter the conversion process at this point. The mapping between the input and the output of the reformat process can be considered one-to-one.

The format process and the load process are the counterparts of the reformat and unload processes, respectively, and need no further clarification. However, the use of a common data form provides additional benefits, such as easing the portability problem.

The restructuring process is the most complex part of a generalized data conversion system. The languages for this mapping process can be quite different (e.g. some procedural and others nonprocedural). The models used to represent the data in the conversion system are also quite different (e.g. some use network structure and others use hierarchical structure).

Implementation will now be briefly discussed.[9,12,15] Two techniques are used to implement the modules of a data translator—generative and interpretive. In the generative approach, the data and mapping descriptions are fed into the compiler, which generates a set of customized programs executable on a specific machine. The advantage of this approach is that efficient machine code may be generated for each application or function. The disadvantage is that two phases, code generation and module execution, are required. In the interpretative approach, the action of the system will be derived from the descriptions written in the system's language via the general interpreter implemented for the particular system. The advantage of this approach is its result—programs which are easier to understand and debug. The disadvantage is the possible inefficiency of a general-purpose interpreter.

Program Conversion—Concepts

After a data conversion, the application programs which process the original data may not run correctly against the new data. The process of modifying the programs to process the restructured data is called application program conversion or translation. Figure 7-3 represents a general approach to data base program conversion. To convert a program, it is necessary to determine the functions of the program and its semantics. Programmers need not state the assumptions about the state of the data explicitly in their program. Therefore, it will

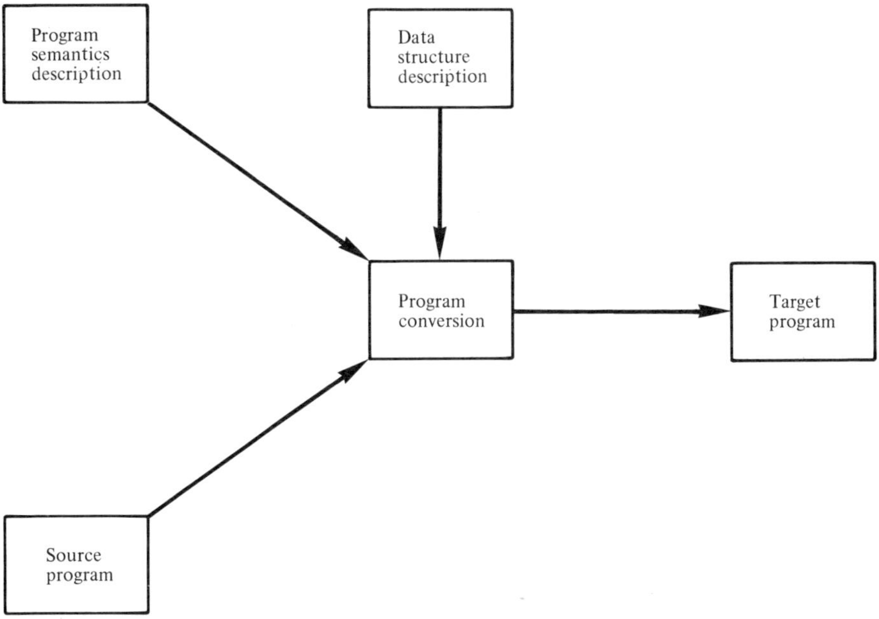

Figure 7-3. Program translations.

usually be necessary to provide more information about the semantics of the program. Also, it will be necessary to provide information about the data structure against which the program originally ran, the new structure against which it must run, and the relationship between the two. The inputs of the program conversion process are the source program, the description of its semantics, and the description of the data conversion. Program conversion determines how the data were originally accessed and how one can achieve the same access in the new structure. This process is accomplished by using the inputs and producing a new program.[13]

The main techniques in dealing with the problem of data base program conversion have been discussed in two articles.[13,14]

DML Statement Substitution

The DML statement substitution technique, which can be considered an emulation approach, preserves the semantics of the application program by intercepting individual DML statement calls at execution time and then substituting equivalent new DML calls to the restructured data base. Necessary for the generalization of this approach is the development of an emulation code for the following cases—to maintain the run-time descriptions and tables for both the original and new data base organizations, to intercept all original DML calls, and to utilize old/new data base access path mapping descriptions and rules for dynamically determining which set of DML operations on the new data base is equivalent to each specific operation on the source data base. This approach has several drawbacks although it is straightforward in concept. The drawbacks can be categorized under the general topic headings of degraded efficiency and restrictiveness. Efficiency is degraded in the emulation strategy primarily because each source DML statement must be mapped into a target emulation program which uses the restructured data base to achieve the same results. Restrictiveness occurs in the sense that this approach inhibits the utilization of the increased capabilities of the restructured data base and/or data structure through the modeling of old methods.

Bridge Program

In the bridge program technique, the source application program's access requirements are supported by reconstructing that portion of the source data base needed from the target data base. Data reconstruction is done by means of 'bridge programs.' The source program then operates upon this reconstructed portion of the data base to effect the same results that would occur in the original source data base. Reverse mapping is required to reflect updates, and each simulated source data base segment must be prepared before it is needed by the application program. This approach suffers the same types of drawbacks that are inherent in the emulation approach. Efficiency problems for complex data bases and programs performing extensive data accessing can make this approach prohibitively expensive for practical utilization.

CURRENT RESEARCH

Within the following two sections, we discuss the activities which are underway with respect to data and program conversion. Several interesting projects have been done, or are in progress, in these two areas. However, with one exception, no general systems are yet available to resolve the problems or obviate the need for a solution. As we previously indicated, the single exception dismisses the problem by maintaining only a homogeneous environment.

Research Efforts: Data Conversion

For over a decade, considerable research has been carried out on the data conversion problem, with particular emphasis on data base translation. One major focus has been the design of data definition languages for describing the structure and storage of data as an aid in the manual file translation problem.[3,4,6–8,16] We have considered this area first.

The most comprehensive work in this area has been done by members of the CODASYL System Committee. The CODASYL System Committee formed the Stored Structure Definition Language Task Group in 1970 to study the problem of data translation and to develop techniques to formulate a stored data definition language to facilitate data translation. The results of their work were presented during the 1970 SIGFIDET Data Description and Access Workshop.[16] The group was reformulated as the Stored Data Definition and Translation Task Group (SDDTTG).[3] This group is attempting to develop a general method for concisely defining commonly used existing storage structures using two data translation languages—a stored data definition language (SDDL), for describing data structure and storage structure, and a translation definition language (TDL), for describing the relationships between elements in the source structure and the target structure. The group also provides sample statements in terms of an example data translation from a COBOL file to a NIPS/360 file.

Significant work was done simultaneously at the University of Michigan and the University of Pennsylvania.

Research by Taylor[4] at the University of Michigan was directed toward the specification of the mapping of data structures. He used a formal model of the classes of data structure commonly found in data base management systems. Based on that model, Taylor developed a data definition and mapping language to detail the basic mapping policies used in data base management systems to map particular data structures to a storage medium.

Smith's research[7] at the University of Pennsylvania was directed toward the generalized data translation problem. She developed a data description language oriented toward defining data as they are to appear on various commonly used secondary storage media. The statement of Smith's language resemble assembly language macro calls, with the parameters collected in a positional format. Such a language is hard to read or write, but it is highly flexible. As a member of the SDDT Task Group, Smith[8] wrote a more detailed method for translating data to demonstrate how a program written in the stored data definition and translation task group languages can be used to drive a data translation fairly.

Sibley and Taylor[6] reviewed past work on the data definition language for describing both the logical and physical aspects of data. In order to provide a basis for continuing such work, they discussed applications of these 'generalized' data definition languages. Other attempts have also been made to build a generalized translator.[2,11,17–20]

While the emphasis has been on the language aspects of the data translation process, in 1972, Fry, Frank and Hershey[5] at the University of Michigan paid attention to the development of a software system to attack the data translation problem. They designed a model for generalized data translation to provide a framework for research, development, and implementation. Inputs to the translation process are the source data and the specifications for the data translation embodied in two declarative languages, SDDL and TDL. These two languages drive the translation process. The model for a data translator has three major components—the source and target converters, which deal with the storage structure of the data, and a restructurer, which is concerned with changes in the logical structure of the data. The translation process takes place in stages. First, a source converter extracts the source data from their physical form and converts them to a normal form. A restructurer then restructures the data into a target data base from the target normal form. To separate the restructuring process from the source and target conversion processes, a common interface, called the normal form of data, is introduced. One output is produced, namely the target data. This model served as the basis for the prototype which was implemented later. One common feature in all the preceding works is the emphasis on common languages to define data, storage, and the mapping process.

In 1974, the research work of the Data Translation Project at the University of Michigan was reported by Merten and Fry.[2] A general methodology of data translation was presented. Also described was an implementation of a prototype data translator, whose purpose was to demonstrate the feasibility of the technical approach within the framework of such a methodology.

In 1974, at the University of Pennsylvania, Ramirez, Rin, and Prywes[17] implemented a language-driven translator for the application of an automatic generation methodology in generating file conversion programs. The inputs for the system were the descriptions of the source and target files in a data description language and the relationships between source and target data in a data manipulation language. The system could have only one source input sequential file and one target output sequential file. The output was a PL/1 program capable of converting the source file to produce the target file. In 1974, Rin and Brown[18] also reported an overview of an existing software system which automatically produced file conversion programs from a user's specification in a data definition language. The paper described the structure, system design, capabilities, and application of the DDL/DML language and processor.

Another prototype generalized file translator was developed by Bakkom and Behymer at Honeywell in 1975.[11] The file translator system consists of two modules, a language processor and a file processor, as shown in Figure 7-4. The language processor reads a user statement written in DDL specification and produces a tabular encoding of the specification and a listing of the DDL specification with embedded diagnostics and a data map. The tabular encoding is used to drive the second module, the file processor, which performs the actual file conversion. This task involves the reading and identification of records from the input file, the translation of the fields on each of these records, and the writing of the resulting record to the output file. The translator uses the file data description language (FDDL) to describe the source file, the target file, and the required translation. The FDDL language is designed to describe the structure of sequential files.

At the System Development Corporation, Shoshani[19,20] developed a methodology for data base conversion that depended basically upon the logical structure of the data base by using the existing query and generation capabilities of data base management systems. The advantage of this system is independence from the internal organizational features of data bases, such as access paths and

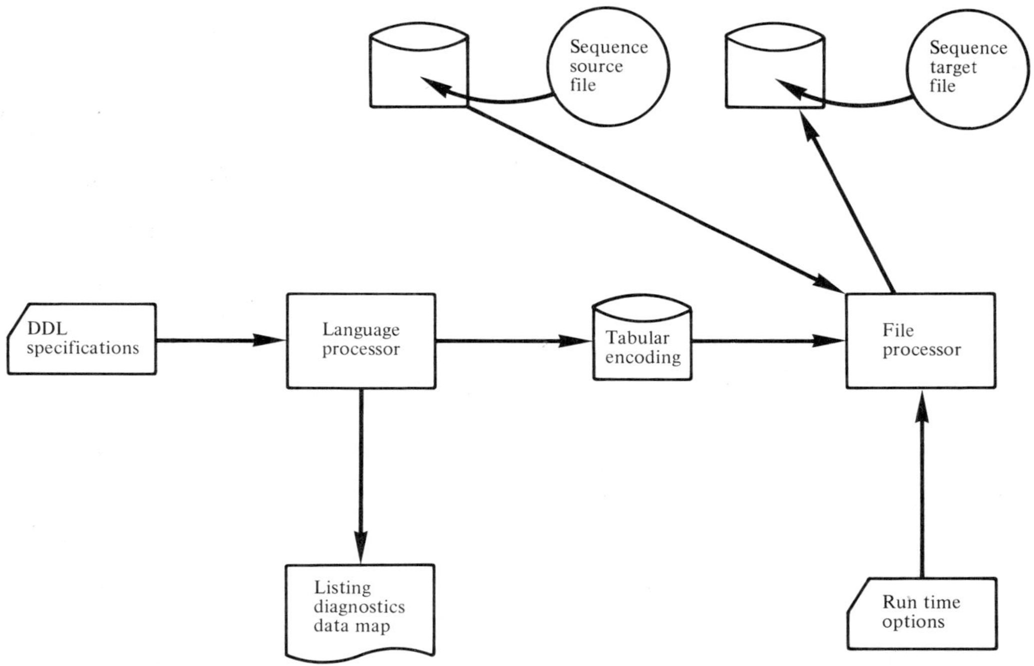

Figure 7-4. File translation system diagram. (From Bakkom and Behymer.[11])

indexing mechanisms. Their conversion system involves three processes:

1. A source reformatter, which formats intermediate source data into the standard representation
2. A logical data translator, which logically restructures the data from the source standard data form into an equivalent target standard data form
3. The target reformatter, which formats the target standard data into a data stream acceptable to generate functions of the target system.

The system needs three languages:

1. A common data description language (CDDL), which describes only the logical properties of data bases
2. A common data translation language (CDTL), which expresses logical restructuring functions, primarily in terms of field-to-field mappings
3. A common data format language (CDFL), which can specify the input and output format conventions used by the target and source DMS.

The logical translator consists of two major parts, the analyzer and the restructurer. The analyzer performs syntax legality in CDDL and CDTL statements and semantic analysis to determine which combinations of conversion types are semantically possible. The semantic analyzer constructs a translation table used by the restructurer to restructure the source records into target records. A prototype of the system was implemented and can convert one single hierarchical data base at a time.

Another major data translation research project has taken place at the IBM Research Laboratory in San Jose, California.[10,21–24] Lum, Shu, and Housel[23] developed a general methodology and a model for data conversion. The approach assumes that the source and target systems are available and play an important role in the conversion process by transforming the source data into linearized source files (sequential files) to be used as input to the conversion system. It also includes the transforming of the conversion system output into desirable target format. During actual conversion, as shown in Figure 7-5, the linearized source files are changed into a standard system internal form, i.e. IF(S1), IF(S2), . . ., suitable for reorganization. Then the restructurer produces data in a standard form, i.e. IF(T1), IF(T2), . . . Finally, the writer changes this data format into linearized target data. Two languages have been defined for this purpose—DEFINE for data description and CONVERT for mapping specification. Both languages are high level and nonprocedural, and also have capabilities for data checking in a conversion process.

The data description language, DEFINE,[21,23] was developed for describing the hierarchically structured linearized source and target data structures for their conversion model, which used this information to parse data in the read and write

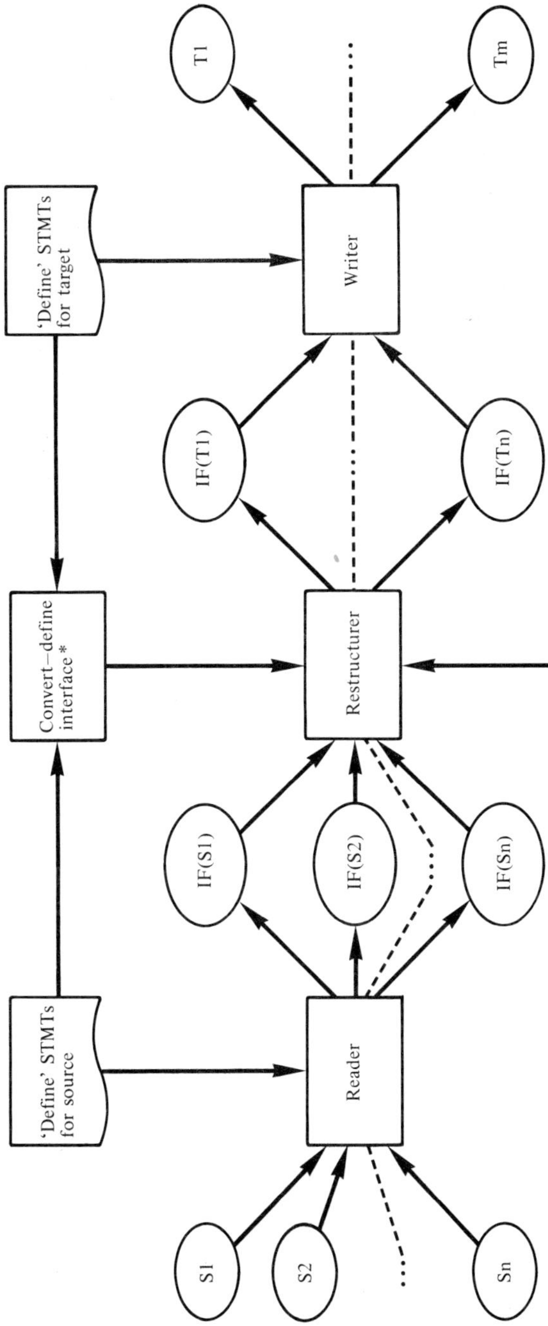

* Logical views of the fields are extracted from the define specifications.

Figure 7-5. Model of translation.

steps of the translation process and to extract the logical views of the files. A complete DEFINE program is a structured description of one or more source and target files, as outlined in Figure 7-6. The keywords SOURCE and TARGET designate whether the file is to be parsed (input to translator) or generated (output by translator).

The translation definition language, CONVERT,[23,24] was designed to operate on hierarchically structured data in tabular form, referred to as a form. The use of forms enables the user to visualize the mapping process required to compose the target(s) from the source(s). For example, from the logical views extracted from the DEFINE description of the data structurer, a user may view a conventional COBOL record with repeating groups or a tree graph (Figure 7-7a) as a form (sketched in Figure 7-7b), and proceed to write mapping statements for manipulating the data into the target description format. The data mapping and restructuring facilities are provided by a set of form operators which include SELECT, SLICE, GRAFT, CONCAT, MERGE, SORT, ELIM-DUP, CONSOLIDATE; built-in functions (SUM, MAX, MIN, AVE, and COUNT); assignments and CASE-assignments. Conceptually from a user's viewpoint, every operation starts with one or more real files (input forms) and generates a real file (an output form).

In 1976, Housel and Shu[22] asserted that the hierarchical view of data would continue to be popular for a broad class of applications and users. They proposed the use of an enhanced version of CONVERT as a high-level user interface for data base management systems for query and data manipulation.

With the advent of new software systems and expanding applications, data conversion involving extensive and selective restructuring is becoming more and more common. As a result, sophisticated data restructuring systems are emerging, such as the EXPRESS system developed by IBM Research[10] and the system developed at the University of Michigan.[9,25]

```
DATA DESCRIPTION:
  [optional data description block (DDB) declarations]
  SOURCE FILE DESCRIPTION (file a):
    [optional file description block (FDB) declarations]
    data descriptions for 'file a'
  END FILE DESCRIPTION;
  TARGET FILE DESCRIPTION (file b):
    [optional FDB declarations]
    data descriptors for 'file b'
  END FILE DESCRIPTION;
END DATA DESCRIPTION
```

Figure 7-6. DEFINE program structure.

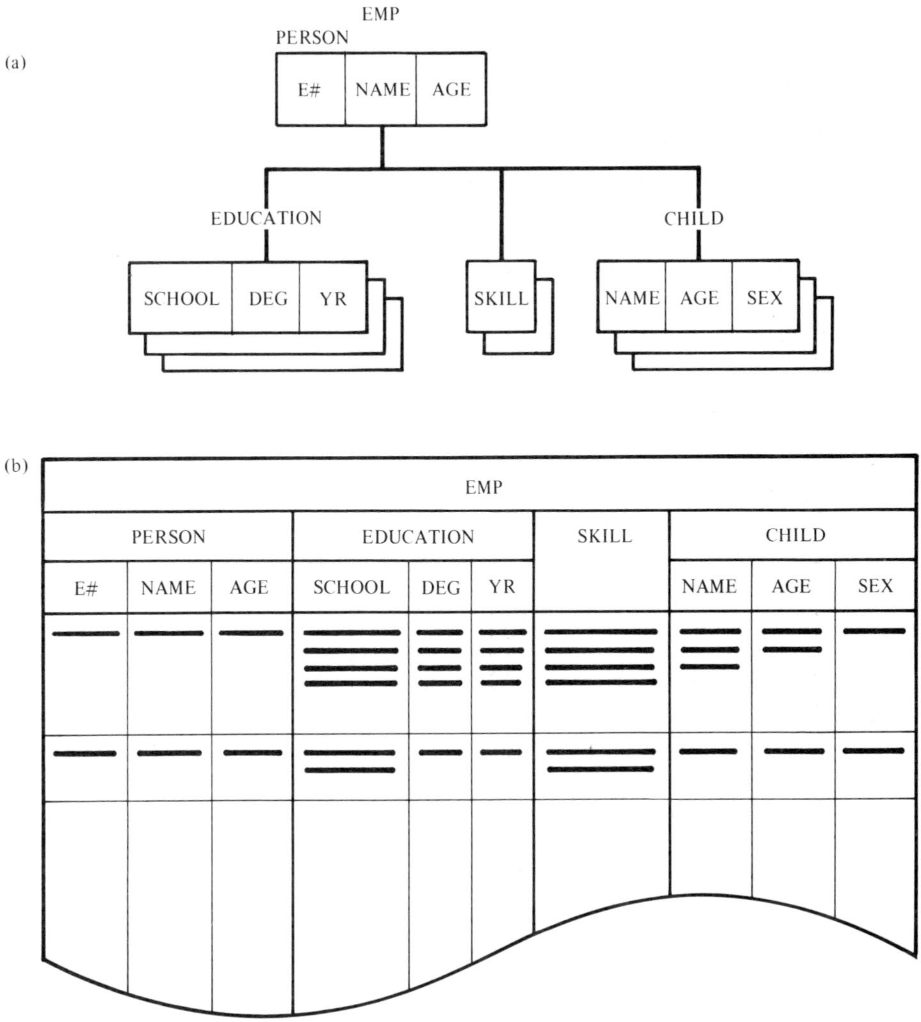

Figure 7-7. (a) A tree graph of hierarchical data and (b) a form representation of the same data.

Navathe and Fry[25] defined the semantics of the restructuring of tree-structured data bases and developed three levels of abstraction for the restructuring function. Each level of abstraction represents successively more detailed semantics of the function. At the first level of abstraction, three types of schema modification are identified—naming, combining, and relating. These three types are further divided into eight schema operations. At this level of abstraction, one considers how the schema constructs from the source are named in the target, how they are combined differently in the target, and how their relationship with one another may be changed in the target. The second level of abstraction is instance operations, which constitute the transformations on the data instances. They are divided into group operations and group relation operations. The final level is item value operations. Table 7-1 shows the three levels of abstraction and also further classifications at the first and second levels.

Swartout, Deppe, and Fry[9] focused on the development of a generalized restructuring capability for the network class of logical structures. They chose the high-level 'access path' approach to restructuring. Executing a restructuring transformation is simply the process of traversing the source data base to obtain the information needed to create the target data base and storing it according to the target logical structure. Restructuring is viewed as an operation which accesses information rather than manipulates data. Based on this approach, they formulated a network restructuring language (NRL). It is essentially nonprocedural, and its major components describe access strategies and selection criteria. The NRL describes only the information relevant to the actual transformation from source to target and assumes that the logical structures of the data bases have been previously defined and are available to the restructurer. The basic cycle of the restructurer is divided into fives phases, as shown in Figure 7-8. During the first phase, target control, the restructurer determines the next step in its traversal of the target logical structure. During the second phase, source accessing, the restructurer determines the next step in its traversal of source restructurer internal form. In the qualification phase, the restructurer implements the user's 'selection criteria.' During the fourth phase, construction, source record occurrences along the current access path are retrieved. The linking phase is the most complex in the restructurer cycle. Basically, its job is to connect the newly created target record occurrence on all appropriate target sets. Although the execution time of the restructurer is very slow, by using the access path approach it is possible to build

TABLE 7-1
An overview of the three levels of abstraction

Level No.	Name	Classified into	Representations
1a	Schematic modification	Types	Naming, combining, relating
1b	Types	Schematic operations	Renaming compression, inversion
2	Instance operations	Group instance operations	Association, tractoring, union
		Group relation operation	Collapsing, generalization, reversal
3	Value operations	—	Copy value, create null value

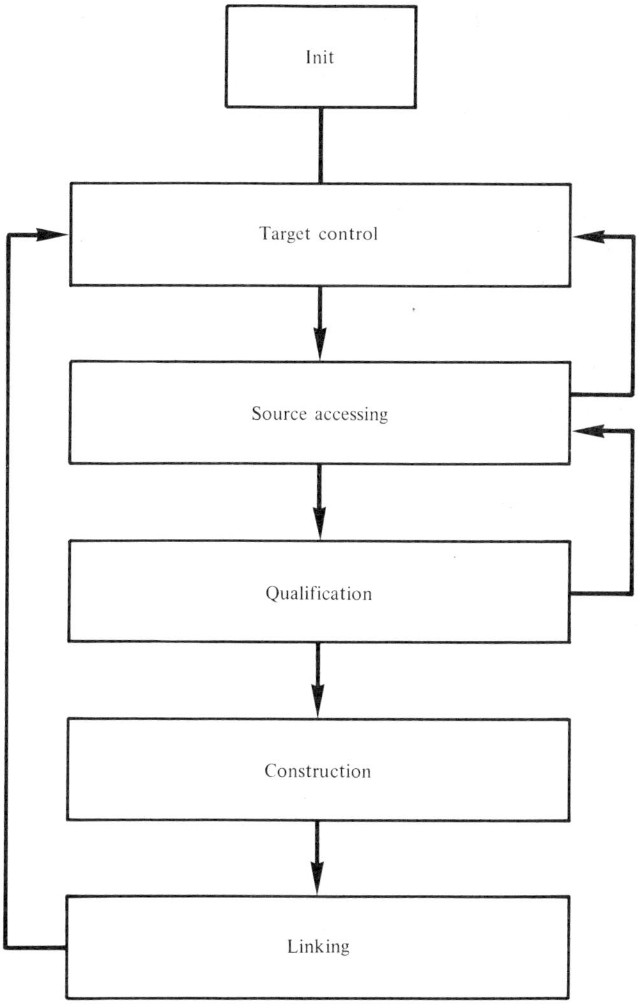

Figure 7-8. Restructurer block diagram.

general-purpose restructuring specification languages and restructuring software for network data bases.

In 1977, the EXPRESS system for data extraction, processing, and restructuring was developed by Shu *et al.*[10] at the IBM Research Laboratory. EXPRESS is an experimental prototype data translation system which can access and restructure data from multiple files and produce multiple restructured files in a single run. The model for EXPRESS is based on the approach given in an earlier paper.[23] The EXPRESS specification languages are two very high-level nonprocedural languages, DEFINE (for data description) and CONVERT (for data restructuring). Performance and usability were major concerns in the design and implementation of EXPRESS. Performance is achieved by compiling the DEFINE and CONVERT languages into customized PL/1 programs and by using the concept of pipelining to minimize I/O activities. At the same time, usability is achieved by having the system handle buffer allocation and the generation of job control statements automatically. This task is accomplished by having the compilers generate readable PL/1 code (which allows the user to follow or modify the generated code easily), and by having built-in 'user hooks' in the system (e.g. a user can intercept data from modification during reading). The modular structure of EXPRESS permits the system to be readily extended or transferred to another environment. The notion of 'pipelining' was also introduced. A CONVERT operator is defined as pipeable if it has the ability to process an input section independent of other sections to be processed. A pipeline is a series of pipeable operators.

In 1979, Bach, Coguen, and Kaplan[26] at the Bell Laboratories developed a data translation system ADAPT (which is an acronym for a data parsing and transformation) which is a generalized translation system driven by two high-level languages. One language is the description language for data parsing and generation (DDPG), which performs the actual translation of data from the source data base to the target data base. The other is the transformation programming language (TPL), which performs the actual translation of data from the source data base to the target data base. ADAPT can be used in three types of environments:

1. The static batch environment, involving an entire conversion task to a new data base application. This traditional conversion usually involves very large data bases and very large machine resources.
2. The environment involving daily scheduling of ADAPT in a batch mode to provide interfaces between large applications requiring the same data in varying formats.
3. The dynamic real-time environment where ADAPT accepts data over a network facility from a once-mechanized application and then parses and transforms the data in real time into the format and structure required by the receiving application system. Providing data in varying formats and structures in real-time to the different systems represents the most fertile area for usage of the ADAPT system. ADAPT is executed in an application which involves conversion of a very large data base (over 2 billion bytes) on an IBM 370/168 to a different data base format and structure on a PDP 11/70 or VAX 11/780.

Present data management systems are generally constructed as centralized systems serving a network of terminals. Such systems are relatively easy to construct and to manage. However, the users of data base management systems may be geographically distributed and may have a desire to have local control of their own data and data processing resources. Distributed systems become attractive for two reasons:

1. Sociological forces—the users are rarely centralized.
2. Technological forces—users install several small interconnected systems rather than a single expensive central complex, and/or install front-end processors to a preexisting central complex.[27]

Recent advancements in computer and communication technologies have made this situation possible. Through a computer network, computer resources such as software systems, hardware devices, application programs, and data can be shared among computer users throughout the country. Airlines have the most sophisticated data management system.[27] It involves: (1) multiple corporations, (2) diverse data management systems, (3) diverse terminal types, (4) diverse computer architectures, (5) diverse operating systems, and (6) activity on six continents. In addition, the systems are available on a 24-hour basis and support very respectable transaction rates. Decentralization can reduce communication costs and response times by putting the data and computing near the users. This approach may have a positive effect on both availability and reliability and makes provision for the modular growth of the system. However, several technical problems are associated with distributed systems:[27]

1. Lack of global (centralized) knowledge
2. Messages that travel more slowly, less reliably, and more expensively than in a centralized system
3. Occasional loss of messages.

Several research groups have focused their attention on this area.

In 1974, Su and Lam[28] at the University of Florida developed a semiautomatic data base translation system for achieving data sharing through a computer network. Its prototype implementations were also performed. Figure 7-9 shows the major software components and data files required in two computer systems performing data sharing. A network communication program at each node will establish the communication link. After browsing through the contents, the user can make a request to access a specific data file to system B. A common caretaker program in system B performs the following functions:

1. Communicates with the inquirer and transfers a description of the contents of a record.
2. Receives requests and calls a proper access routine and extracts the values of the field names.
3. Transmits the field names and values in a standardized format to system A for display.

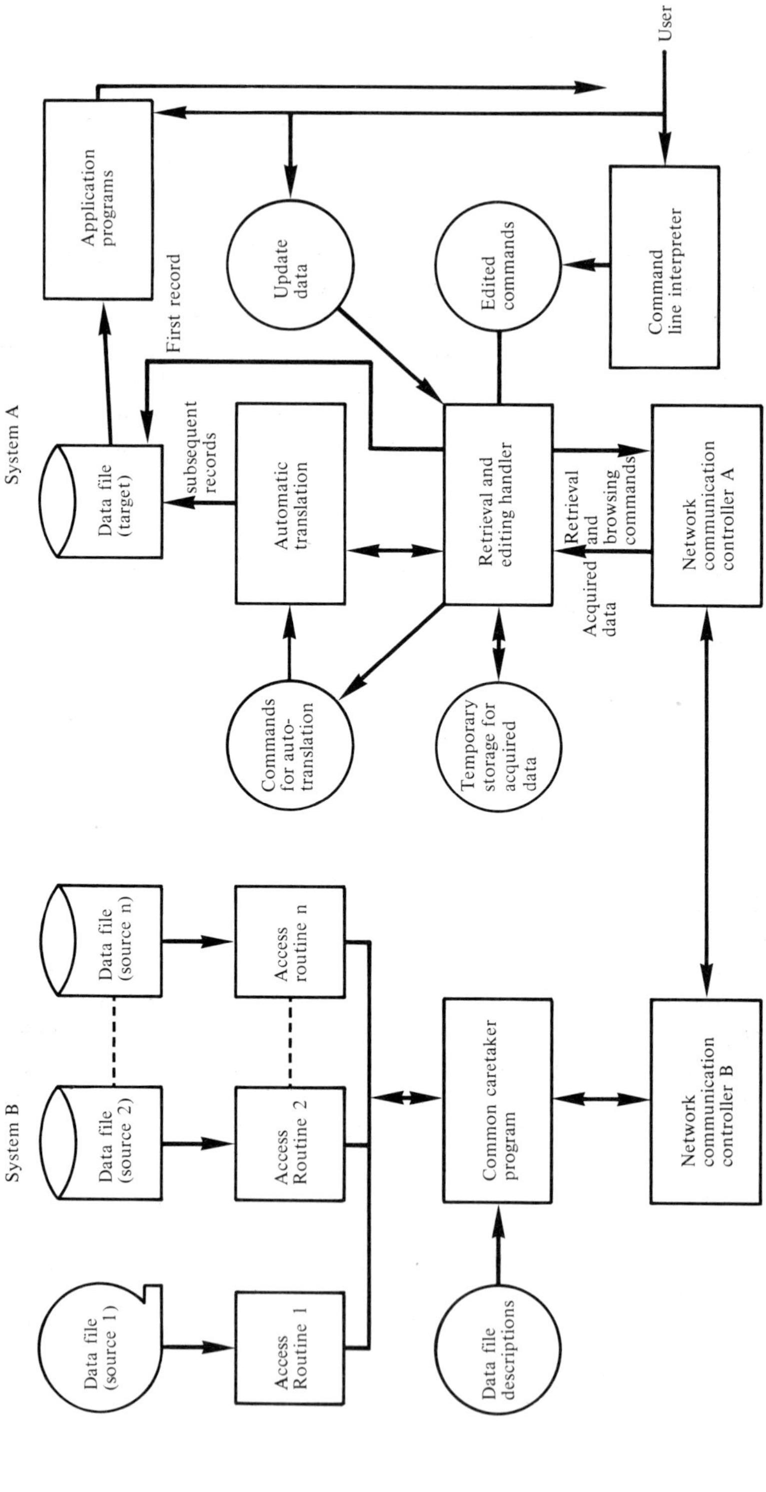

Figure 7-9. A semiautomatic data base translation system configuration.

The access routine handles only the idiosyncracies of the data set for which it is written. The data extracted from system B are stored in a temporary data file in system A. The user in system A can then use a retrieval and editing language to display and edit the data. The command line interpreter scans and edits the user's commands, and the retrieval and editing handler interprets the edited commands. The automatic translator calls up the routines to process the commands. The system takes advantage of the data conversion facility that already exists in the I/O central system of operating systems as well as in the compilers. The system is not fully automatic. The user needs to compose and design his own data structure. A prototype of the data base translation system is implemented to facilitate the testing of the on-line translation system. In the prototype implementation, the communication and translation procedures between two nodes of a network are simulated on a NOVA 800 minicomputer. The prototype system components are all implemented in FORTRAN IV, even though the individual components can be implemented in different programming languages.

In 1974, at the Computer Corporation of America, Marill and Stern[29] developed a network utility called Datacomputer which specialized in the performance of data management and storage functions within a network environment. Figure 7-10 shows the Datacomputer system logically as a box shared by a variety of external processors and accessed in a standard notation called 'datalanguage.' This high-level language includes facilities for data description, data base creation and maintenance, selective retrieval of data, and access to a variety of auxiliary facilities and services.

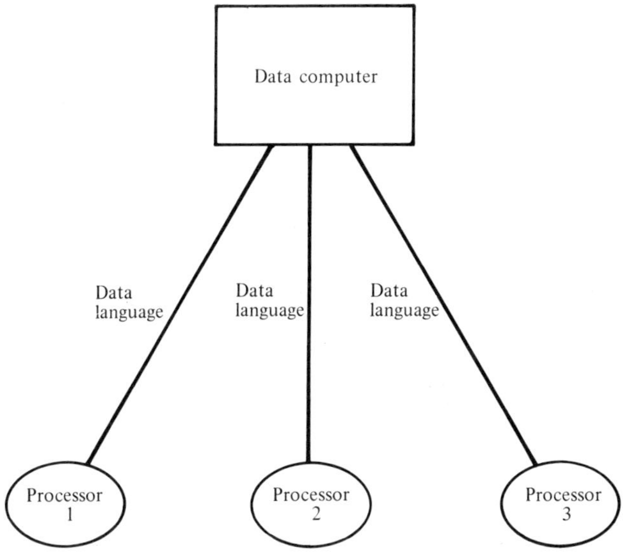

Figure 7-10. Logical view of Datacomputer.

The Datacomputer system is designed to provide several capabilities:

1. Network data sharing among different hardware:
   (a) The Datacomputer system performs data conversions between various hardware representations and data structuring concepts.
   (b) Datalanguage is designed so that self-contained requests may be shipped to the Datacomputer from the application program.
   (c) The Datacomputer communicates with the programs that run on remote machines.
2. Efficient access to large on-line files through shared use of a tribillion bit store. Two special facilities are:
   (a) Inverted file structure—the system will use the inversions to speed up its retrieval process.
   (b) Multiple staging strategies—all data are physically organized into pages which move among the three levels of storage. The Datacomputer can select among the available strategies. Examples of staging strategies are:
      (i) Move the whole file to disk and work from disk.
      (ii) Move pages from tertiary store to core, process the pages, and output directly from core.
      (iii) Break the request down so as to operate on segments of a file, and stage to disk one segment at a time.
3. Improved access control—the system responds only to a limited set of commands.
4. Economy of scale and specialization.

Figure 7-11 shows the architecture of the system. The system processor is a DEC System-10 (PDP-10). Memory is present at three levels—primary (core), secondary (disk), and tertiary (mass store). Peripherals are used for software development and for input data from tape. The system is interfaced to the best-known resource-sharing network: ARPANET (which ties together some 40-odd computers of different types) and IMP (interface message processor), which interfaces with two 50-kb/s telephone lines into the network. The Datacomputer has been offering service on the ARPANET since late 1973 using disk storage only. The applications of the Datacomputer are on-line information retrieval, file management, and large file-sharing with multihost access.

In 1977, Wong and the Computer Corporation of America[30] reported an algorithm for efficient retrieval of data from a distributed data base system. By adopting a succession of relational 'views' of the data, they isolated those problems of query processing unique to a distributed system. The algorithm is used by SDD-1, a system for distributed data bases, which is being developed by the Computer Corporation of America. SDD-1 permits the storage of data in a dispersed and redundant manner, and separates the problem of retrieving dispersed data from the problem of maintaining redundant copies of data. The distribution strategy of SDD-1 is developed by a sequential optimization proce-

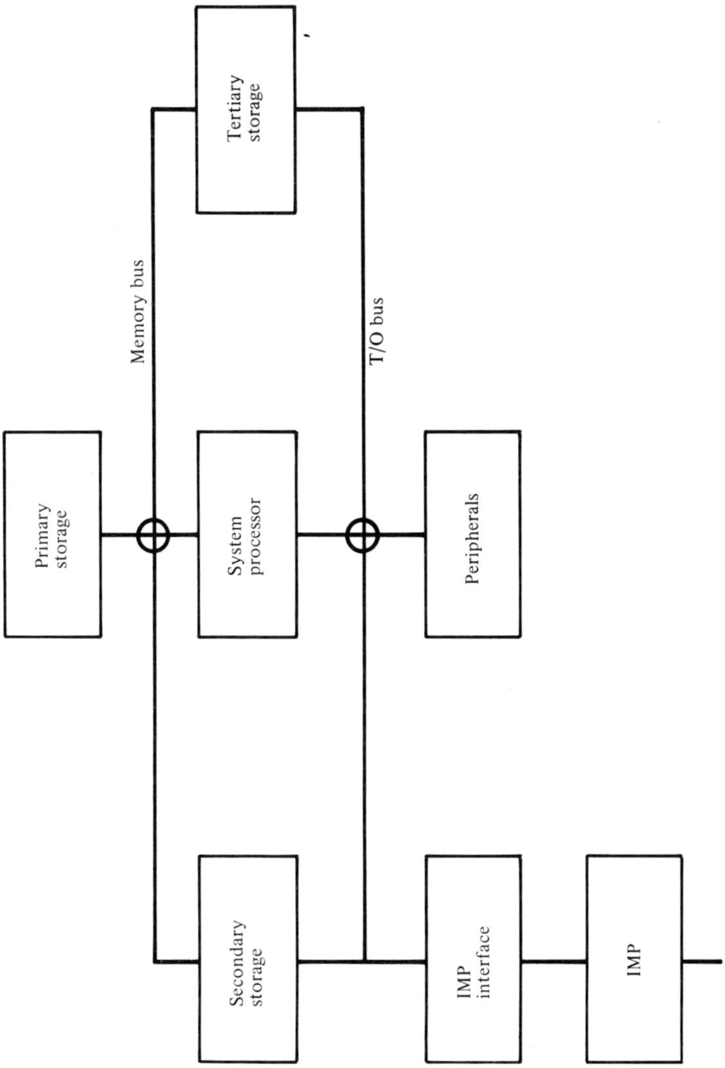

Figure 7-11. Hardware overview of system.

dure represented by a binary decision tree. Each node of the tree corresponds to a query and a set of parallel moves for that query. The method operates in the context of specified subsets of the total data base which are to be in effect during the processing of given queries, called materializations. Their retrieval methods are based on several assumptions:

1. The data model is a relational model for the duration of any one query.
2. Only fragments of relations in the data model are moved from one site to another.
3. It is unimportant where the final result is produced, as long as it is produced at a single site.

Research Efforts: Program Conversion

In 1974, Housel, Lum, and Shu[1] at the IBM Research Laboratory reported an architecture of an interactive migration system by examining the general processes involved in application migration. They used the term 'application migration' to denote the process of converting data and/or programs to run on a new or modified system. They identified four major tasks in a migration process:

1. Defining the applicatiбns by consulting knowledgeable people and existing documentation.
2. Designing data base organization by defining the logical target data base specification and considering the characteristics of the data base management system and the different applications to be included in the target system in order to produce a physical data base organization.
3. Translating the data by writing the conversion program to convert the data from source to target form.
4. Program conversion and development by writing new programs to convert old programs.

They then defined an architecture for such a conversion system which should have the following features:

1. Interactive facility where users and the system can work together
2. A central repository of information where users and the system can store and extract information as needed
3. The ability to extract information from source application programs and source environment
4. The ability to carry out the translation process automatically by using a high-level translation language.

Finally, they developed AIMS (architecture to an interactive migration system),

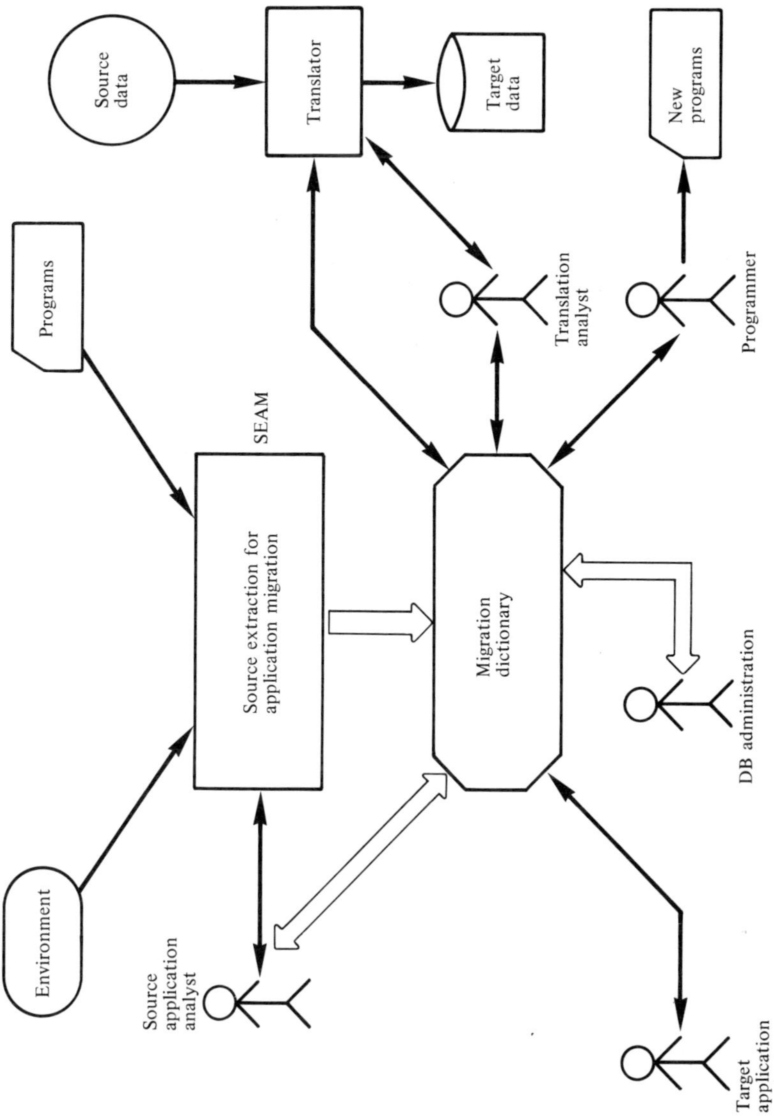

Figure 7-12. AIMS architecture to migration.

as shown in Figure 7-12. The system components are:

1. Migration dictionary. All users and other components in AIMS will interact with the migration dictionary to store and obtain information. It contains information about many items, including program, data elements, data entries, access paths, and files.
2. Source extraction for application migration (SEAM) component. This component will extract data structures, data usage, and system information from application programs, and JCL or system tables for the migration dictionary.
3. The translator component. A high-level translation language will be provided for the translating process. This translation language should have the following capabilities:
   (a) Mapping source to target
   (b) Validity checking
   (c) Nonprocedural approach but containing a mechanism to permit a user to revert to the procedural language.

In 1974, Yamaguchi and Merten[15] at the University of Michigan attempted to classify and analyze various classes of translation processes. Four approaches to overcome incompatible data were presented:

1. Standardization approach—standardization of software and/or hardware systems. Partial standardization of software, especially the standardization of data formats, would be extremely desirable, but it would be more difficult than standardizing the programming language because of the close relation between data and hardware.
2. Program translation approach—translation of either the source program, to which the data are compatible, or the target program, to which the data are incompatible, into a program which satisfies target program specifications and operates on the data properly. This approach may not be practical due to the cost, time, and complexity.
3. Data translation—translation of data from one system to another. Most of the current efforts focus on this approach since the data and storage structures of generalized data base management systems are considered to be the basis of the data incompatibility problem.
4. System translation—translation of both data and the program. Yamaguchi and Merten assert that this approach will be the ultimate approach to data compatibility. The two major merits are first, system translation which may reduce some complexity in data or program translation; second, it may obtain better results in terms of efficiency.

In 1976, Gerritsen and Morgan[31] at the University of Pennsylvania (Wharton

School) discussed the dynamic restructuring of data bases which was being implemented as part of the WAND (Wharton alerting network data base) system. The WAND system is an experimental subset of the CODASYL DBTG Specification, with special features added to the data base manager and the DML for the alerting or monitoring of data bases, for processing, and for easy restructuring. The WAND approach permits several generations of structure to coexist. Hence, a translation occurs only as data are accessed. Each generation of structure is described in a generation data structure (GDS) schema, which has a generic structure of its own. The restructuring data definition language (RDDL) can specify the transformation to be made to the current schema. The system processes the RDDL into a new set of entries for the GDSS, and a new source language copy of the overall schema is generated. The RDDL contains three major classes of entries—INCORPORATE (adds entries to a schema), EXCISE (removes entries from a schema), and CHANGE (changes entries of a schema).

In 1977, Housel[23] at the IBM Research Laboratory presented a model for program conversion in which the data conversion mappings are used to dictate the necessary transformations required for rewriting the source programs. The program conversion process consists of four steps:

1. Decompiling the source application programs to an abstract representation.
2. Substituting the inverse of the source to target data mapping into the abstract representation of the application programs in order to express them in terms of the target data structures.
3. Simplifying the result of step 2.
4. Recompiling the simplified results into the desired host language and data manipulation language of the target system.

Several observations are identified for this model. First, all source and target system dependencies are handled in the decompiling and recompiling steps. Second, these steps are independent of the program transformation steps (2 and 3). Third, the program conversion transformations are carried out in abstract form. Their model uses a sample mapping language (ML) for specifying the abstract representation of source programs as well as for specifying the data translation operations. The language is a subset of CONVERT plus some of Codd's relational operators. The ML operators were designed to have simple semantics and convenient algebraic properties to facilitate program transformation. The ML was based on a hierarchical data model in order to maintain algebraic simplicity.

In 1978, Shneiderman[13] at the University of Maryland addressed conversion of network data base programs under schema transformation. The goal of his research was to define the set of transformations for which automatic conversion was possible. Subgoals included the development of new schema definition and data manipulation languages. The formal tasks include:

1. Data base describes the data as they exist in the data base. Both record and set instances are described.
2. Schema describes the syntax and semantics of the schema. The schema is a formal description of the record and set types.
3. Programs describe the allowable operations on the data. By referring to schema level names and instance level literals, the user can describe the operations required.
4. Transformations describe the operations on the schema. These transformations cause changes in the data base and revisions to the programs operating on the data base.

The possible schema transformations include SPLIT, BIND, EXPAND, COMPRESS, PARTITION, MERGE, ADD-SORT, and DELETE-SORT.

In 1978, Fry *et al.*[12] surveyed the data- and program-related conversion problem extensively. The group was looking into various aspects of these problems. For the problem of the conversion of data organizations, they surveyed concepts, tools, and technology currently available. For conversion problems, they:

1. Discussed current approaches employed in industry, i.e. the DML statement substitution and bridge program, and current research works aimed toward developing more generalized tools.
2. Identified current research directions for future research:
   (a) Semantic description of data base and application programs. Future research needs to be conducted to model and describe the semantics of application programs, study semantic changes and their effect on application programs, and derive transformation rules for program conversion.
   (b) Equivalency of source and target programs. It is not clear how one can prove that a target program still preserves the original intent of the source program.
   (c) Decompilation with this technique means that a data base application program is first transformed into an operationally equivalent higher order language (decompilation process) or an abstract representation and then returned to a usable language level in a converted form (compilation process). Research suggests that this would be the preferred method to effect DML/host language program conversion.
   (d) Conversion aids. A system can be built to analyze application programs to assist the conversion analysts to identify and isolate program segments affected by the data changes, detect inefficient code, produce a program execution profile, and detect, in some cases, the program code which depends on the programmer's assumption of data values, ordering of records, and other factors.

(e) Optimization of target program. It is necessary to investigate a global optimization or simplification to improve the converted program.

3. Analyzed the major tests that were done with each of the prototype conversion systems, including the Penn translator, the System Development Corporation translator, the Honeywell translator, the Michigan data translator, and XPRS.
4. Listed some questions that remain to be answered concerning the technical feasibility of building generalized systems, discussed some of the unanswered questions with respect to usability of the current data conversion systems, and analyzed how some implementation issues would affect the cases where a generalized conversion system can be applied.
5. Specified guidelines for both reducing the need for conversion and for simplifying conversions which are required, in order to lessen the conversion effort:

(a) Application design guidelines:

(i) The design decisions which should be made to alleviate the conversion problem.

Requirements analysis: many of the decisions affecting the long-term effectiveness of the application system are made during this stage of system development. It should focus on information needs and should minimize constraints imposed by the physical environment.

The following underlying principles were used as program design guidelines:

—Design for maintainability: implies that the application should be written in a high-level language with a syntax that permits good program structure.

—Design for the application: concentrates on what results are desired rather than on the implementation details of achieving these results.

—Data independence: insulates the application program from the way the data are physically stored. This notion is extremely important in program design.

—Layered design: designs the application as a series of layers, each of which communicates with the system at a different level of abstraction.

The goal of the program design was summarized:

—to provide the highest possible application interface to the program.

—to maximize program independence from the characteristics of the mainframe, peripherals, and data base organization.

—to maximize portability of the application program through the use of high-level languages.

—to maintain a clean program/data interface.

(ii) Equally important to intelligent design is a set of programming techniques and standards which prohibit programmers from introducing dependencies in code.

(b) Data base design is still an art at the present time. The data base designer should be aware of contrivances and therefore be in a position to evaluate the relative effects of a design decision. An accurate logical design can still be data dependent. Some examples of induced dependencies in logical data base design which may impact upon conversion are:
   (i) owner-coupled set in DBTG
   (ii) storage of physical pointers in an information field of a record
   (iii) combining of segment types to reduce the amount of I/O required to traverse a data base.

(c) DBMS utilization and selection. Selection of a DBMS can have a major impact on conversion requirements. A high-level DBMS is characterized by powerful functions and a high degree of data independence from the point of view of the application. DBMS prospects should evaluate the data independence characteristics of a proposed product.

6. Discussed impact of future technologies and standards on conversion:
   (a) Hardware and architectural technologies. Improvements in hardware technologies create more need for data and program conversion. Three approaches to data management hardware technologies have been pursued to help simplify the conversion problem in recent years:
      (i) The specialized data management machine is based on the idea of using an associative memory device.
      (ii) The back-end data management machine is a special processor dedicated to managing storage and data bases on behalf of a host computer. The motive is to offload the data management function from the host to a specialized machine that can execute this function at a much lower cost.
      (iii) Another hardware technology development is the group of mass storage devices, such as video disks. For supporting data management functions, there is a growing use of minicomputers.
   (b) Software development trends. The concept of data independence has led to the development of data access and manipulation languages that depend on the logical data model only. The various data models will exist for many more decades.
   (c) Standards development. Standards that are oriented to determine the nature of the DBMS are hard to bring about, even in a highly controlled environment. A standard that is more likely to be accepted is one that affects only the way of interfacing to a DBMS.

7. Assessed impact on conversion problems:
   (a) Hardware development will increase the need for generalized conversion tools.

(b) The reduction in hardware costs will make conversion cost more acceptable.
(c) Special hardware DBMS machines will simplify the conversion process.
(d) Software advances will not eliminate the need for conversion but can simplify the conversion process.
(e) Multiplicity of logical models are likely to exist.
(f) Standards will not eliminate the conversion problem.
(g) Standards can greatly simplify conversion.

In 1979, the Data Base Program Conversion Task Group of the CODASYL Systems Committee[14] investigated the application program conversion problem. The purpose of their work was to identify the significant research problems associated with converting data base programs and to provide a general framework on future research. The paper presents a survey of current approaches and research efforts. The current approaches fall into two major categories:

1. The manual approach, which is labor intensive and costly. It represents the state of the art in many installations.
2. The computer-aided approach, which can be further divided into operational and experimental approaches:
   (a) Operational computer-aided strategies. A few are employed by industry to perform actual conversion, including proprietary vendor products, parameterized computer aids, and vendor conversion teams. Fixed-price conversion contracts are available from some vendors for assembly language-to-COBOL and COBOL-to-COBOL conversions of non-data-base programs.
   (b) Experimental strategies have been developed by research laboratories and universities, such as DML emulation strategy and bridge program strategy.

   Current research aims are toward developing more generalized tools for computer-aided conversion, but this aspect is still in its infancy.

The work describes some of the difficulties in converting current data base programs. The two major problems are:

1. Inadequate representation of application requirements. The most significant deficiency in the existing models is their inability to model integrity constraints to the degree needed.
2. Execution time variability. Data base programs can change their behavior relative to the data base during execution.

The CODASYL Systems Committee also presented a global model of a program conversion system based on more explicit and high-level data base and program descriptions. Their system is shown in Figure 7-13. It is intended to be interactive

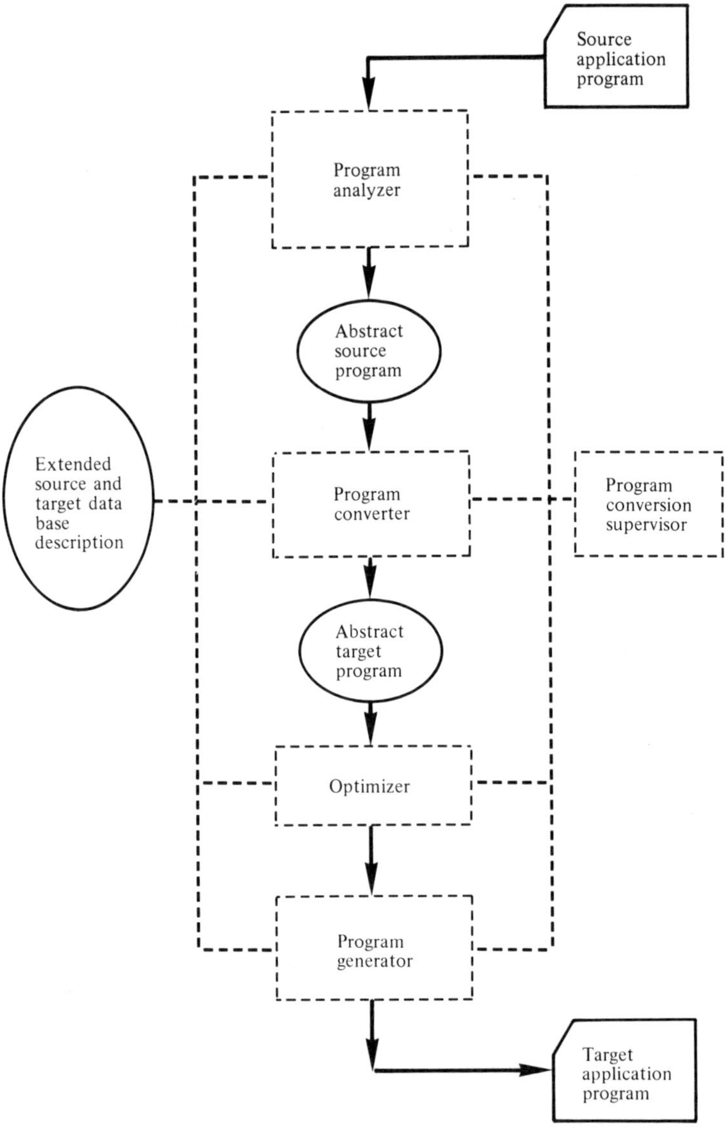

Figure 7-13. Data base program conversion framework.

and controlled by a conversion analyst interacting with the program conversion supervisor. The conversion analyzer analyzes the source and target data bases to classify the types of changes made and to encode the descriptions in suitable internal representation. The program analyzer, which uses the source data base description, matches candidate language templates against the source application program and produces the internal representation of the program. This is used by a program converter to select the proper transformation rules for use in mapping the source program representation to the target program representation. The optimizer processes the target program's representation for improving access paths, algorithms, and data handling. The program generator produces a target program.

CODASYL also summarized the research efforts undertaken by the University of Florida, the University of Maryland, and the University of Michigan. Finally, they proposed some problems to be investigated in future research:

1. Improved description of data base and application programs
2. Equivalence of source and target programs
3. Analysis, transformation, and synthesis of programs
4. Optimization of application program representations.

CONCLUSION

The problems involved with conversion of data, structure, and application software are difficult, as this chapter has shown. The very nature of the problem deals with exacting details in environments which are changing in terms of hardware, system, and communication software. Many changes are independent in effect for the topic of this chapter; however, alterations in standards and modifications in I/O facilities can make a significant impact. Thus, a solution, in order to be long term, must provide for perturbation within the environment. In terms of data and structure conversion, this requirement would imply a language which allows design of the conversion system for each desired application. This feature would work well for static conversions, but in the dynamic environment of a network the process is less effective. Within a dynamic environment the technique of utilizing a network data language would appear more reasonable. However, it is not nearly as amenable to modification in static environments.

In considering the problem of program conversion, it appears that the best solution is to provide an independent data access method in a high-level language. Access to the data base can then be done by invoking the necessary commands by calls from the application software, such as is done in many present systems. The drawback to such an approach is that it requires the data to come to the program location in order to be examined for suitability. When data transmission speed is a limiting factor, this approach places a heavier burden upon the communication capabilities of the network. A better solution would be to transmit a request for data to the location of that data. Then only data which are appropriate are sent to the requesting process for consumption. Such an approach has been taken by some of the systems discussed. It does require more total processing time within a network.

The solution to these problems is clearly desirable. Unfortunately, the manufacturers of hardware facilities are not actively engaged in providing solutions to these problems. Further, with the exclusion of a very few commercial concerns, all solutions are still in the realm of research and development. Thus, the organization that finds itself in this situation will also find itself solving its attendant problems.

REFERENCES

1. Housel, B. C., Lum, V. Y., and Shu, N. C.: Architecture to an interactive migration system (AIMS). *Proc. of the ACM SIGMOD Workshop on Data Description, Access, and Control*, pp. 157–170. Ann Arbor, Michigan, 1974.
2. Merten, A. G., and Fry, J. P.: A data description language approach to file translation. *ACM Proc. SIGMOD Workshop on Data Description, Access and Control*, Ann Arbor, Michigan, May 1974, pp. 191–206.
3. Fry, J. P., Smith, D. C. P., and Taylor, R. W.: An approach to stored data definition and translation. *Proc. 1972 ACM-SIGFIDET Workshop on Data Description, Access, and Control*, Denver, Colorado, November 1972, pp. 13–55.
4. Taylor, R. W.: *Generalized Data Base Management System Data Structures and Their Mapping to Physical Storage.* Ph.D. Dissertation, The University of Michigan, Ann Arbor, Michigan, 1971.
5. Fry, J. P., Frank, R. L., and Hershey, E. A., III: A developmental model for data translation. *1972 ACM-SIGFIDET Workshop*, pp. 77–106, 1972.
6. Sibley, E. H., and Taylor, R. W.: A data definition and mapping language. *Comm. ACM*, **16**, No. 12, 750–759, December 1973.
7. Smith, D. P.: *An Approach to Data Description and Conversion.* Ph.D. Dissertation, Moore School Report 72–20, University of Pennsylvania, Philadelphia, Pa., 1972.
8. Smith, D. P.: A method for data translation using the stored-Data definition and translation task group languages, pp. 107–124. *ACM Proc. SIGFIDET Workshop on Data Description and Access*, 1972. Denver, Colorado.
9. Swartout, D. E., Deppe, M. E., and Fry, J. P.: Operational software for restructuring network data bases. *Proc. of the 1977 National Computer Conf.*, Vol. 46, pp. 499–508. AFIPS Press, Montvale, N.J., 1977.
10. Shu, N. C., Housel, B. C., Taylor, R. W., Ghosh, S. P., and Lum, V. Y.: EXPRESS: a data extraction, processing, and restructuring system. *ACM Trans. on Database Systems*, **2**, No. 2, 134–174, June 1977.
11. Bakkom, D. E., and Behymer, J. A.: Implementation of a prototype generalized file translator. *Proc. of the 1975 ACM SIGMOD Int. Conf. on Management of Data* (Ed. W. F. King), pp. 99–110. ACM, New York, 1975.
12. Fry, J. P., *et al.:* An assessment of the technology for data- and program-related conversion. *Proc. of the National Computer Conf.*, Vol 47, pp. 887–907. AFIPS Press, Montvale, N.Y., 1978.
13. Shneiderman, B.: A framework for automatic conversion of network database programs under schema transformation. *Third Jerusalem Conf. on Information Technology* (Ed. J. Moneta). North-Holland, Amsterdam, 1978.
14. Database Program Conversion Task Group of the CODASYL Systems: Database program conversion: a framework for research. *IEEE*, **1979**, 289–312.
15. Yamaguchi, K., and Merten, A. G.: Methodology for transferring programs and data. *Proc. of the 1974 ACM-SIGFIDET Workshop on Data Description, Access and Control*, pp. 141–156. ACM, New York, 1974.
16. Storage Structure Definition Language Task Group (SSDLTG) of CODASYL Systems Committee: *Proc. 1970 ACM-SIGFIDET Workshop on Data Description, Access and Control*, Houston, Texas, November 1970, pp. 368–380.

17. Ramirez, J. A., Rin, N. A., and Prywes, N. S.: Automatic generation of data conversion programs using a data description language. *Proc. of the ACM SIGFIDET Workshop on Data Description, Access, and Control*, pp. 207–225. ACM, New York, 1974.
18. Rin, N. A., and Brown, M.: *An Overview of a System for Automatic Generation of File Conversion Programs.* Technical Report on Research on Automatic Program Generation, Department of Computer Sciences, University of Pennsylvania, Philadelphia, Pa., 1974.
19. Shoshani, A.: A logical-level approach to data base conversion. *Proc. of the 1975 ACM/SIGMOD Int. Conf. on Management of Data*, pp. 112–122. ACM, New York, 1975.
20. Shoshani, A., and Brandon, K.: On the implementation of a logical data base converter. *Proc. of the Int. Conf. on Very Large Data Bases*, Framingham, Massachusetts, September 1975, pp. 529–531.
21. Housel, B. C., Lum, V. Y., and Shu, N. C.: Data translation, part II: DEFINE; a non-procedural language for defining information easily. *Proc. of the ACM Pacific 75 Conf.*, April 1975, pp. 62–70.
22. Housel, B. C., and Shu, N. C.: A high-level data manipulation language for hierarchical data structure. *Proc. of Conf. on Data: Abstraction, Definition, and Structure*, Salt Lake City, Utah, March 1976.
23. Lum, V. Y., Shu, N. C., and Housel, B. C.: A general methodology for data conversion and restructuring. *IBM J. of Research and Development*, **20**, No. 5, 483–497, 1976.
24. Shu, N. C., Housel, B. C., and Lum, V. Y.: CONVERT; a high-level translation definition language for data conversion. *Comm. ACM*, **18**, No. 10, 557–567, 1975.
25. Navathe, S. B., and Fry, J. P.: Restructuring for large databases: three levels of abstraçtion. *ACM Trans. of Database Systems*, **1**, No. 2, 138–158, June 1976.
26. Bach, M. J., Coguen, N. H., and Kaplan, M. M.: The ADAPT system: a generalized approach towards data conversion. *IEEE*, **1979**, 183–193, 1979.
27. Gray, J. N.: *A Discussion of Distributed Systems.* Research Report, RJ2699(34594) 9/13/79, IBM Research Laboratory, San Jose, California 95193.
28. Su, S. Y. W., and Lam, H.: A semi-automatic data base translation system for achieving data sharing in a network environment. *ACM SIGFIDET Workshop on Data Description, Access, and Control*, May 1–3, 1974, pp. 227–247.
29. Marill, T., and Stern, D.: The Datacomputer—a network data utility. *National Computer Conf.*, 1975, pp. 389–395.
30. Wong, E., and Computer Corporation of America: Retrieving dispersed data from SDD-1: a system for distributed databases. *Proc. of the Second Workshop on Distributed Data Management and Computer Networks*, May 25–27, 1977.
31. Gerritsen, R., and Morgan, H.: Dynamic restructuring of databases with generation data structures. *Proc. of the 1976 ACM Annual Conf.*, pp. 281–296, ACM, New York, 1976.

SECTION III

LOCAL DISTRIBUTION

Advances in Distributed Processing Management, Volume 2
Edited by P. S. Fisher, J. Slonim, and E. A. Unger

Chapter 8

APPLICATION ANALYSIS FOR NODAL AUTONOMY

Charles T. Baker

International Business Machines Corporation, Poughkeepsie, New York

Many of the advantages that are expected of distributed data processing systems require a high degree of autonomy for each of the nodes in the system. For example, the overall availability of a system is enhanced when a distributed implementation has highly autonomous nodes—since the failure of one node has little impact on the surviving nodes. However, a distributed data processing system is a single system; it supports a set of related applications that have interdependencies among the nodes. Thus, each node depends to some extent upon another node or some other node depends to some extent upon it. It is this combination of interdependence and autonomy that characterizes a distributed data processing system and distinguishes it from other multiple processor configurations. In this chapter are considered means for obtaining a practical balance between nodal autonomy and nodal interdependence that is essential for a well-designed system.

NODAL AUTONOMY

Two aspects of nodal autonomy must be considered by the system designer—system autonomy and application autonomy. System autonomy, which is not of concern in this chapter, involves the system management functions. These functions, such as problem management, change management, and operations management, each can be centralized, partially distributed, or completely distributed. The options that are selected determine the system autonomies of the nodes.

A node has a substantial degree of application autonomy if it can perform a substantial amount of application work without depending on the application services or application data of other nodes. Application autonomy is determined by the degree of dependency of the application functions at one node on the application data at other nodes. As these dependencies decrease, the nodal autonomies increase. The degree of dependencies can be changed by changing the assignment of the applications and their data to the nodes in the system. To do this effectively, one must have a means for measuring and classifying dependencies, which will be discussed subsequently. Only on-line applications will be considered.

INTERNODAL DEPENDENCIES

Internodal dependencies arise when an application program at one node requires application data from one or more remote nodes, in addition to its local data. An example occurs in distributed on-line retail banking systems where an individual may have a savings account record at one node and a checking account record at another node and where bank policy requires that both account records remain at the nodes where they originally were established. At any time, an individual may request that funds be transferred from his savings account to his checking account, or vice versa. Moreover, this operation may be performed with a customer-operated automatic teller machine that displays both account balances to the individual before and after the transaction is completed. The internodal dependency involves both the accessibility of the remote data and the assurance that the revised data are consistent—the correct amount must be debited to one account and credited to the other account. The assurance of distributed data consistency is not a trivial problem.

LOGICAL DISTRIBUTION

Concern here is with those properties of a set of related applications that are pertinent to the task of designing a distributed data processing system. To facilitate the discussion, logical distribution, which reflects this chapter's immediate interests, is defined.

A *logical distribution* is a partition of a collection of related applications and their data into a maximum number of groups that have a specified low level of interdependence. A logical distribution is composed of at least two groups. Every proper subset of the logical distribution has an interdependency with at least one group not in the subset.

Because of its interdependencies, a logical distribution represents a single application environment; consequently, any implementation of these applications, either centralized or distributed, will be a single data processing system. If the implementation is distributed, a central coordination of communication structures, key data structures, and key applications will be required, for without central coordination no assurance exists that the dependencies among the groups will be supported.

MEASUREMENT OF INTERGROUP DEPENDENCIES

What is needed is a procedure for developing a logical distribution from a collection of related on-line applications and their data. Such a procedure requires classifications and quantitative measures of the intergroup dependencies of the logical distribution. Many different measures of dependencies can be defined. One of the system designer's tasks is to select the measure that is most appropriate for his applications.

An on-line application is composed of a set of application programs. An application program, or transaction, is usually activated by an individual at a terminal. Dependencies among the groups of a logical distribution are composed of transaction dependencies. A *transaction dependency* is that part of an intergroup dependency that is due to a single transaction type. Transaction dependencies can be measured in many ways.

A transaction dependency has an *orientation*, since its application program is contained in one group of the logical distribution and some of its data are in another group. This situation is asymmetrical; hence, the asymmetry, or orientation, must accompany the transaction dependency measure.

It is important to note the distinction between a transaction dependency and a transaction message routing function. A transaction dependency exists between two groups of a logical distribution when the dependent transaction requires data from both groups. If a physical implementation of the logical distribution puts one of these logical groups into one physical node and the other logical group into a different physical node, then the physical implementation must support the transaction dependency across the two physical nodes.

A transaction message routing requirement exists when a transaction is entered at one physical node and must be processed at a different physical node. Here the transaction is *routed* to the proper node. Usually the routing decision is based upon either the transaction type code or a data value, such as an account number. Note that a transaction that has been routed to a remote node may also be a dependent transaction; i.e. it may require data from both the remote node to which it has been routed and from one or more other nodes.

Perhaps the simplest measure of a transaction dependency is the frequency of its use during a given period, such as a 24-hour day. Given this statistic, one must determine whether the usage is high or low. One way to perform this task is by comparison with the total number of transaction executions in the entire system. For example, if the dependent transaction were used 100 times a day in a system that processed 100,000 transactions per day—a 0.1 per cent. level, one might assume that this transaction dependency is low. On the other hand, if the dependent transaction were used 20,000 times per day—a 20 per cent. level—one might say that the transaction dependency is high. In practice the system designer must decide what is high and what is low.

The complete intergroup dependency is determined by the collection of transaction dependencies that are present between the two groups. In the foregoing example, one would add the usages per day of the individual transactions to obtain the complete dependency between the two groups. Clearly the complete dependency has an orientation. Also, since dependent transactions can be in any group, each pair of groups of the logical distribution can have two complete dependencies—one for each orientation.

Another measure of a transaction's dependency involves the pattern of its usage throughout the workday. A labor attendance transaction, for example, would be used heavily at the beginning and end of a work shift; thus, its dependency might be high at the ends of the shift and low at other times.

The required currency of the remote data can also be a basis for the measurement of a transaction's dependency. Some applications do not need up-to-the-minute data; they can function satisfactorily with data that are not truly current. For example, a salesman's inquiry about the status of an order usually can be answered with data that may be up to 24 hours old. The salesman does not need up-to-the-minute data. Dependencies of this kind are weaker than those that require truly current data.

The timing requirements connected with distributed data consistency can also lead to a measure of a transaction's dependency. In an earlier example of a distributed retail banking application, it was noted that the results of a funds transfer between two bank accounts must be displayed immediately to the individual that entered the transaction. This application has a requirement for the immediate consistency of distributed data. A less demanding distributed retail banking transaction would involve the withdrawal of funds from a remote node via an automatic teller machine (ATM). Here the dollar amount must be debited from the remote account and from a local ATM total record that controls the amount of money contained in the particular ATM that is used. Clearly a data consistency requirement exists for the two records. However, the required consistency need not be immediate, since the bank's customer does not need to see the ATM total; he requires only a display of his checking account total. Hence, a transaction of this type has a lesser degree of internodal dependency than the transaction in the earlier example, which required an immediate display of the updated totals at each of the two nodes.

The amount of remote data that a transaction could require also can be used as a measure of a transaction's dependency. Here all of the remote data that conceivably could be called by the transaction are measured since no way exists to predict which data it actually will use.

In addition to quantitative measures of internodal dependencies, several possible classifications of on-line transactions are pertinent to the development of logical distributions. For example, some dependent transactions may require read-only reference to remote data, while other types of dependent transactions may need to updata remote data. This difference suggests one basis for the classification of transactions, where the transactions with the read-only reference requirement have a weaker dependency, since they do not have any distributed data consistency requirement.

Dependent on-line transactions can also be classified by their deferability; i.e. some transactions cannot be deferred. The salesman's inquiry, for example, should not be deferred, since he may have a customer present who needs the information immediately. Other transactions may be deferred; manufacturing order entry transactions often can be deferred for hours, since their data may not be needed until the next production schedule is prepared.

The foregoing is not an exhaustive list of the means for classifying and measuring dependent on-line transactions. Additional factors may arise as applications are analyzed and logically distributed. The intent here is to illustrate some of the key concepts; the system designer will apply or extend these concepts for his specific applications.

It must not be assumed that all of the foregoing types of interdependencies must enter into every application system analysis. Although the system designer must be aware of such interdependencies, only a few of them should be relevant to a given application. Indeed, if the system designer finds that many types of interdependencies must be included in his analysis, he may question the appropriateness of a distributed implementation for his applications.

TYPES OF DATA DISTRIBUTION

Data can be distributed in two ways. The first is based upon data values in the records. It is called file splitting. For example, the checking account files and the savings account files of a retail banking application could be distributed according to the locations of the branch banks where the accounts were opened. However, the system designer must be alert for any relations that may exist among the records, such as the relation between a savings account and a checking account for the same individual. In this case, if the accounts were opened at different branches, the relation could span two groupings of a logical distribution. For some implementations this relation could lead to a distributed data consistency control problem when funds are transferred between the two accounts.

The second way to distribute data is by separation. Using this approach, the system designer assigns entire data bases to groups of the logical distribution. For example, in a manufacturing application the work-in-process data base would be assigned to a plant floor operations group, and the production planning data would be assigned to a production planning group. Again, as with data splitting, the designer must be alert for relations that exist among the data bases that are being separated, since such relations can lead to implementation problems, such as data consistency assurance.

DISTRIBUTION PROCEDURE

At present, a pragmatic, trial-and-error, iterative procedure is required to produce a logical distribution, although more theoretical methods may be used as current research and development work matures.[1–3] The first step of the procedure is data-gathering, which includes collecting information about the number and types of data bases, data base structure, and relations among the data bases. Information about the application programs, or transactions, is also required.

This information includes the data usage of the transactions (ideally at the data field level), the nature of the data usage—read-only or update—and the frequency-of-use statistics. Equally important is information about the nature of the application set, particularly those properties of the application environment that could provide a basis for a distribution. For example, a retail banking system might be distributed on a geographical basis whereas a manufacturing plant might be distributed by function, e.g. order entry or production planning.

The degree of detail of the data that are gathered depends on the stage of development of the application set. If the development is in an early stage, the data cannot be very detailed and the logical distribution will be in a gross, preliminary form. As the system design evolves, more detailed data become available and the logical distribution can be refined. After the system has been implemented, the logical distribution can be further refined with operational data. Postimplementation analyses can be used to adjust the system to its actual workload and to aid subsequently in system expansion and modification.

The iterative procedure that is followed to produce logical distributions is shown in Figure 8-1. With this procedure, after the data have been gathered, one begins by postulating a set of application groupings. The postulated groups are based upon the information that the system designer has obtained about the application environment during the data-gathering phase. For example, in a manufacturing plant the designer might define a three-group structure that consists of an order entry group, a production planning group, and a production operations group.

After the application groupings are defined, the next step of the procedure is to assign applications to the groups. At this point a complete application, which consists of a set of application programs, is assigned to one group only.

Next the data bases are assigned to the application groupings. These assignments are based upon the system designer's knowledge of the applications and the data they require. They can also be based upon a measure of the application's daily aggregate use of a data base, measured in transactions per day.

At this point in the procedure it would be possible to calculate the intergroup dependencies, since all of the application programs and all of the data have been assigned to groups. However, the application assignments involve putting each complete application into only one group—a relatively gross level of distribution. Occasionally a few application programs are most closely related to data in a group other than that to which they were first assigned. Hence, the logical distribution may be improved by moving any such application programs, which leads to the transaction assignment step of the procedure.

In the transaction assignment step, the original assignment of applications to groups is ignored and each application program is assigned to the group that contains the data that are most closely related to that program. The 'closeness' of the program's relation to its data can be measured either by the frequency with which it uses the data, or by any other measure that the system designer chooses. At the completion of this step one has a logical distribution that can be evaluated by

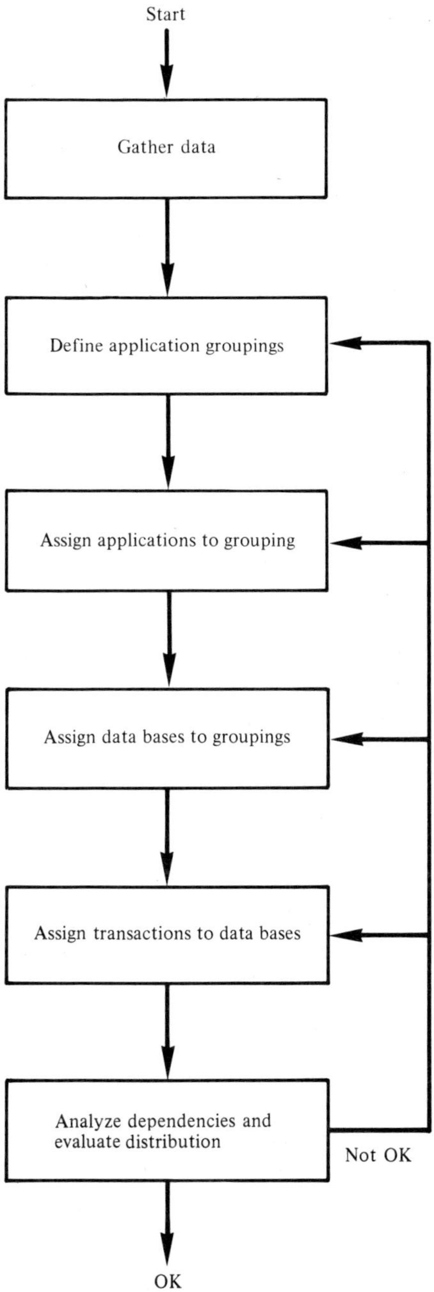

Figure 8-1. Procedural steps for producing logical distribution.

calculating the interdependencies among all of the groups. The procedure can be reiterated until an acceptable logical distribution is attained.

ILLUSTRATIVE DISTRIBUTIONS

First, the use of the procedure for logical distribution is illustrated with an analysis of data that were obtained from an existing on-line operations planning and control system in a steel mill. This centralized system is based upon the IBM information management system, IMS/VS Version 1.1.4. The purpose of this analysis is to explore the feasibility of distributing such a system. (This analysis originally appeared in Baker article.[4])

The second illustration is based upon the same steel mill system. Here, however, one is working with data as they would have appeared in the early stages of the system's development prior to implementation.

THE STEEL MILL SYSTEM

Two categories of production activity are supported by the on-line system: primary steel production and steel plate production. Primary steel production starts with the introduction of molten pig iron, scrap steel, and other raw material into a basic oxygen furnace. After a 45-minute process cycle, the furnace produces a 'heat'—300 tons of molten steel—with a specified chemical composition. After several intermediate processing steps, the heat is formed into slabs, an intermediate product that weighs roughly 17 tons and is up to 8 inches thick, up to

TABLE 8-1
Application set

Code	Application
A	Primary steel production reporting
B	Primary steel production planning, 1
C	Chemical analysis
D	Work-in-progress reporting
E	Shipping data services
F	Plate metallurgical services
G	Order receipt
H	Order position
I	In-process inventory maintenance
J	Finished inventory maintenance
K	Plate production reporting
L	Shipping
M	Slab inventory maintenance
N	Slab requirements planning
O	Slab scheduling
P	Primary steel production planning, 2
Q	Labor incentive accounting
R	Primary steel production planning, 3

TABLE 8-2
Data base, description, and size for steel mill application

Code	Item	Millions of bytes	Code	Item	Millions of bytes
DB01	Metallurgical, check analysis	19.1	DB29	Slab inventory, 8	2
DB06	Primary steel orders, 1	10.7	DB30	Primary steel orders, 2	0.5
DB07	Slab inventory, primary steel	10.7	DB31	Chemical analysis	34.2
DB08	Slab orders, 1	5	DB32	Slab inventory, 9	66.2
DB09	Slab orders, 2	1.6	DB33	Plate production sequence	1.7
DB10	Metallurgical grade practice	0.5	DB34	Plate production reports	12.4
DB11	Primary steel terminal	0.5	DB35	Slab incentive, 1	5.2
DB13	Slab orders, 3	0.5	DB36	Slab incentive, 2	11.5
DB14	Metallurgical specifications	5.0	DB37	Plate inventory, 1	11.4
DB15	Plate orders, 1	1.2	DB38	Plate inventory, 2	0.3
DB16	Plate orders, 2	45.8	DB39	Shipping services	14.6
DB18	Physical test, 1	26.2	DB40	Shipping, 1	1.2
DB19	Physical test, 2	7.4	DB41	Shipping, 2	0.7
DB20	Slab inventory, 2	20	DB42	Shipping, 3	0.7
DB21	Slab inventory, 3	2	DB43	Shipping, 4	0.3
DB24	Slab inventory, 4	1.5	DB44	Shipping, 5	1
DB25	Slab inventory, 5	39.1	DB45	Shipping, 6	1
DB26	Slab inventory, 6	2.5	DB46	Shipping, 7	0.3
DB27	Slab pusher	7	DB47	Primary steel production	14.6
DB28	Slab inventory, 7	0.7	DB49	Finished inventory	1.7

6 feet wide, and 20 feet long. Slabs are the end product of primary steel production. Steel plates, which are a finished product of this mill, are produced by a series of rolling and shearing operations. A steel plate is defined (arbitrarily) by its thickness, which must equal or exceed 0.19 inch. A steel plate can be as much as 160 inches wide and up to 60 feet long.

The steel mill data system is composed of 16 applications, listed in Table 8-1. Each application is composed of a set of transactions—application programs. The system has 271 transactions and 284 batch programs. The transactions are used approximately 37,000 times a day.

The 400 million bytes of on-line data in the steel mill system are organized into 40 physical IMS data bases, 18 of which are isolated in that they have no IMS logical relations to other data bases. The remaining 22 data bases are organized into nine clusters. Logical relations connect the data bases within each cluster, but no logical relations connect any cluster to any other cluster. The descriptions, codes, and sizes of the data bases are given in Table 8-2.

DISTRIBUTION OF THE EXISTING SYSTEM

The volume and complexity of the relationships that must be analyzed in the IMS steel mill applications are substantial. Thus, a detailed analysis of the steel mill system is impractical without data processing support. To this end a set of

TABLE 8-3
Update activity for each data base by application programs

Data bases	Application codes*																	
	A	B	C	D	E	F	G	H	I	J	K	L	M	N	O	P	Q	R
DB01	0	0	312	0	0	0	0	0	0	0	0	0	0	0	0	0	0	0
DB06	0	122	0	0	0	0	0	0	0	0	0	0	0	0	0	1,055	0	886
DB07	0	122	0	0	0	0	0	0	0	0	0	0	0	0	0	453	0	1,267
DB08	0	127	0	0	0	0	0	0	0	0	0	0	0	1,581	2,537	1,910	0	886
DB09	0	44	0	0	0	0	0	0	0	0	0	0	0	0	0	1,161	0	886
DB10	0	0	0	0	0	0	0	0	0	0	0	0	0	1,369	0	207	0	0
DB11	0	257	0	0	0	0	0	0	0	0	0	0	0	0	0	3,019	0	0
DB12	0	0	0	0	0	0	0	0	0	0	0	0	0	0	0	0	0	0
DB13	0	0	0	0	0	0	0	0	0	0	0	0	0	1,465	0	0	0	0
DB14	0	0	0	0	0	390	0	0	0	0	0	0	0	0	0	0	0	0
DB15	0	0	0	0	5	0	97	239	0	0	0	0	0	0	0	0	0	0
DB16	0	0	0	54	245	14	143	239	0	0	0	0	0	0	0	0	0	0
DB18	0	0	0	0	0	2,358	0	0	0	0	0	0	0	0	0	0	0	0
DB19	0	0	0	0	0	2,358	0	0	0	0	0	0	0	0	0	0	0	0
DB20	0	0	0	0	0	0	0	0	0	0	0	0	187	0	0	0	0	0
DB21	0	0	0	0	0	0	0	0	0	0	0	0	187	0	0	0	0	0
DB24	0	0	0	0	0	0	0	0	0	0	0	0	187	0	0	0	0	0
DB25	0	0	0	968	0	1	0	0	0	0	21	0	2,579	1,465	2,885	0	0	0

DB26	0	0	0	0	0	0	0	0	0	0	0	0	1,419	0	0	0	0	0
DB27	0	0	0	0	0	0	0	0	0	0	0	0	1,108	1,539	2,537	0	0	0
DB28	0	0	0	968	0	0	0	0	0	0	21	0	1,193	1,413	569	0	0	0
DB29	0	0	0	0	0	0	0	0	0	0	0	0	1,683	1,413	2,070	0	0	0
DB30	0	390	0	0	0	0	0	0	0	0	0	0	0	0	0	0	0	1
DB31	0	0	341	0	0	0	0	0	0	0	0	0	0	0	0	0	0	0
DB32	0	0	0	2,263	0	416	0	0	572	17	45	1,439	0	0	299	0	0	0
DB33	0	0	0	192	0	0	0	0	0	0	0	0	0	0	237	0	0	0
DB34	0	0	0	1,719	0	0	0	0	452	0	66	0	0	0	0	0	0	0
DB35	0	0	0	0	0	0	0	0	0	0	0	0	0	0	0	0	153	0
DB36	0	0	0	0	0	0	0	0	0	0	0	0	0	0	0	0	153	0
DB37	0	0	0	1,747	0	0	97	0	500	17	24	929	0	0	299	0	0	0
DB38	0	0	0	833	0	0	0	0	513	0	24	221	0	0	299	0	0	0
DB39	0	0	0	0	1,453	7	0	0	0	0	0	22	0	0	0	0	0	0
DB40	0	0	0	0	0	0	0	0	252	0	0	1,742	0	0	0	0	0	0
DB41	0	0	0	0	0	0	0	0	442	0	0	874	0	0	0	0	0	0
DB42	0	0	0	0	0	0	0	0	252	0	0	883	0	0	0	0	0	0
DB43	0	0	0	0	0	0	0	0	442	0	0	864	0	0	0	0	0	0
DB44	0	0	0	0	68	403	0	0	252	0	0	1,156	0	0	0	0	0	0
DB45	0	0	0	0	68	403	0	0	252	0	0	1,434	0	0	0	0	0	0
DB46	0	0	0	0	0	403	0	0	252	0	0	910	0	0	0	0	0	0
DB47	44	0	0	0	0	0	0	0	0	0	0	0	0	0	0	185	0	0
DB49	0	0	0	0	0	0	0	0	76	92	0	0	0	0	0	0	0	0

*Application codes are defined in Table 8-1.

programs were prepared that provide a comprehensive analysis of the data that are generated by IMS utility programs.[5]

The first step of the procedure is to form the application groupings. This step involves several considerations. The first and most obvious consideration is that the data system supports two major categories of production activities: primary steel and steel plates. This arrangement gives one major partitioning. A second major partitioning is based upon the type of work activity: planning and operations. The distinction between planning and operations is based on the time horizon of the activity. Slab scheduling, for example, prepares the sequence of slab consumption several days in advance. It is a planning activity. Plate production reporting, however, is done within an 8-hour interval. It is an operations activity. At this point the application groupings are: plate production planning, plate production operations, primary steel production planning, and primary steel production operations. Next, the data that were gathered from the system are used for further defining the application groupings. These data are given in Table 8-3, which shows the update activity of each application for each data base. An analysis of these data, which include cluster analysis, together with our knowledge of the application characteristics, leads to the identification of an additional group—order services—and the separation of the primary steel production operations group into three parts: primary steel production reporting, chemical analysis, and primary steel labor incentive accounting.[6] This step completes the definition of the application groupings.

The next step is to assign the applications to the groupings of the logical distribution. Preliminary assignments are made by using the data in Table 8-3. The final assignments in this example required extensive discussions with persons familiar with steel production and finally a review with members of the data processing staff that developed the system. The final assignments of applications are shown in Figure 8-2.

The fourth step of the procedure is to assign data bases to the logical groupings—by using the data in Table 8-3. The results are shown in Figure 8-3. Since Table 8-3 is composed of update data, a data base is assigned to the application group that contains the applications that make the most updates on that data base. An additional constraint involved IMS logical relations. The assignment of data bases to application groups was such that no logical relations link any groups. Thus, logical relations are wholly contained in each group.

This step of the procedure produces the basic structure of the logical distribution. For this reason, the data base assignments were based upon update activity, thus tending to minimize the number of dependencies that involve updates. This approach becomes significant when implementations are considered, since one of the implementation options involves the use of copies of data to provide local (within the group) support for dependencies. Clearly, it is desirable to minimize the need for data copies that must be updated, since this copying function can involve difficult control problems.

At this point, a set of groups exists, each of which contains applications and

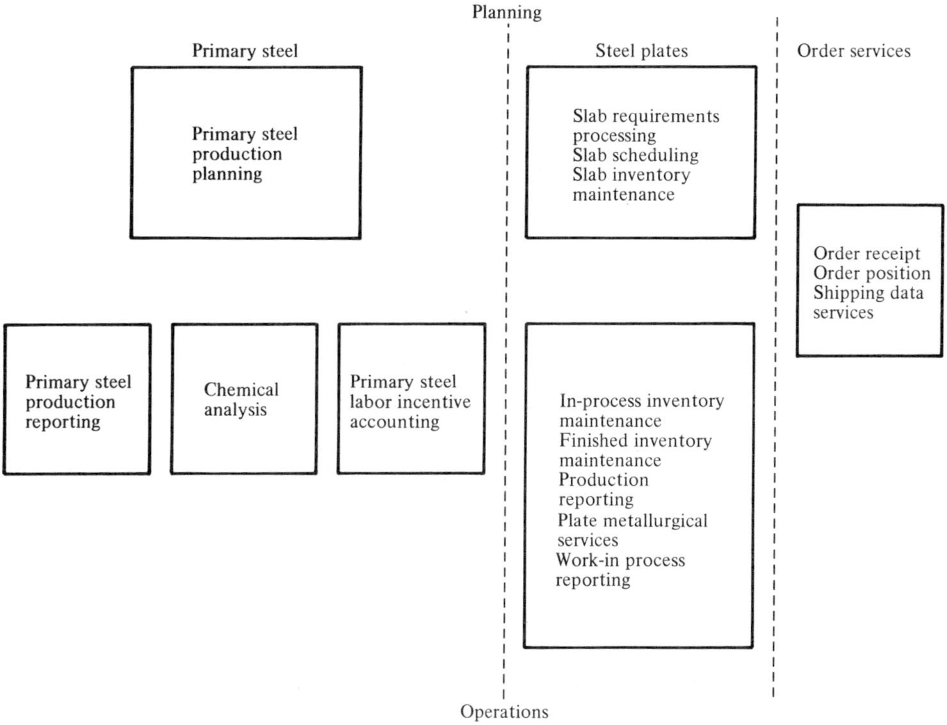

Figure 8-2. Assignments of applications to groups for logical distribution.

data bases. In the next step of the procedure the initial assignment of applications to groups is ignored, and the transactions are assigned to the groups according to their total use of the data in the group. The transaction is put with the data that it uses most heavily. This assignment yields a grouping of transactions that strongly resembles the initial application groups but differs in that a few transactions are in different groups. The resulting number of transaction occurrences per day in each group is shown in Figure 8-4.

The intergroup dependencies must now be analyzed and evaluated as the final step of the procedure. This task requires the definition of an interdependency measure. For this example, measure is used that is related to two of the options that are available for the implementation support of the interdependencies—data communications and data copies. For data communication support to be practical, the communication traffic should not be heavy. For data copy support to be practical, the amount of data that are copied should not be high. For the steel mill system, the number of dependent transaction usages per day is used to indicate the data traffic. The amount of remote data that could be used by all of the dependent transactions is used to indicate the maximum amount of the data that would be copied.

The dependency between each pair of groups is calculated from the set of

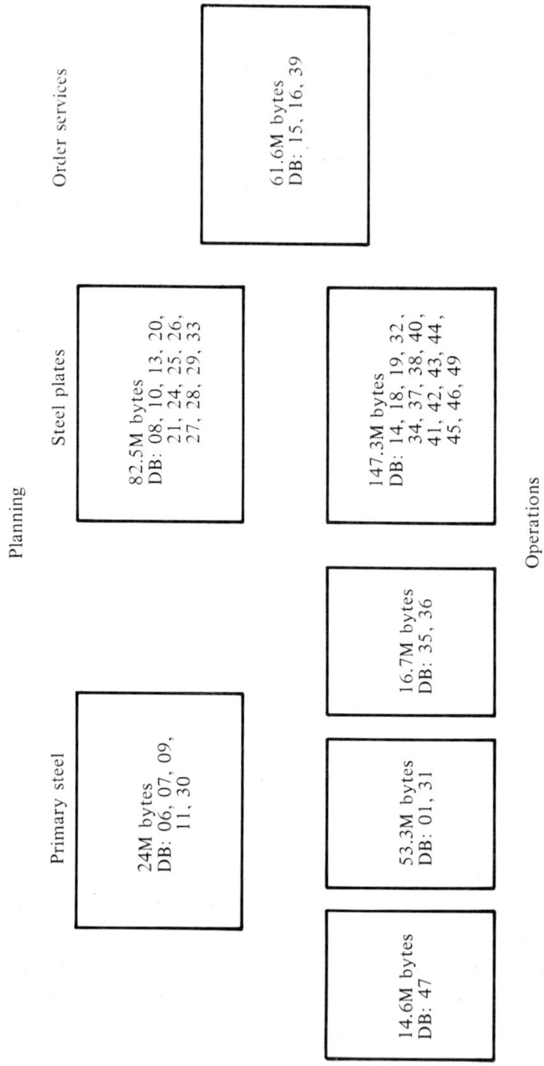

Figure 8-3. Assignments of data bases to logical groupings of Figure 8-2.

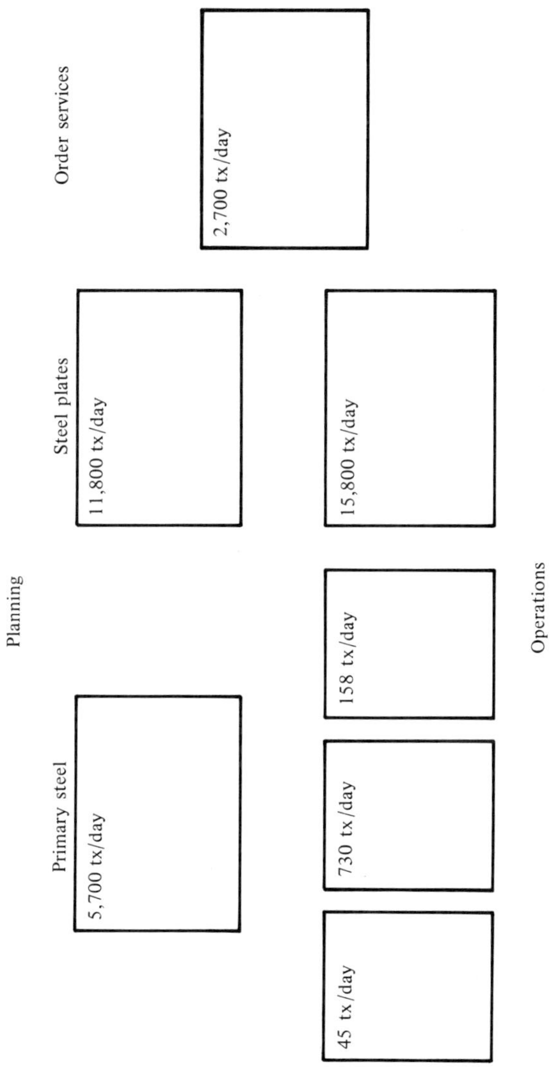

Figure 8-4. Daily transaction volume for each grouping of Figure 8-2.

transaction dependencies that occur between the groups. A *transaction dependency* is that part of an intergroup dependency that is due to a single transaction type. It is characterized by an orientation and two numbers. The orientation relates the local group, where the transaction is situated, to the remote group, where the dependent data are located. The first number, called the active component, gives the frequency of use of the transaction in usages per day. It is called the active component of the transaction dependency because it represents a part of the activity of the system. The second number, called the passive component, is the number of bytes of remote data that must be accessible by the transaction. It is called the passive component because its value is independent of the activity of the transaction.

Transaction dependencies are put into four categories with reference to an active threshold and a passive threshold. In the following examples, the active threshold is 500 transactions per day (tx/day), and the passive threshold is 4 million bytes:

1. Active component = 1000 tx/day
   Passive component = 0.1 million bytes
   Classification = high, low (HL)

2. Active component = 20 tx/day
   Passive component = 10 million bytes
   Classification = low, high (LH)

3. Active component = 20 tx/day
   Passive component = 0.1 million bytes
   Classification = low, low (LL)

4. Active component = 1000 tx/day
   Passive component = 10 million bytes
   Classification = high, high (HH)

The purpose of these categories is to classify and measure the transaction dependency. In the HL category the transaction requires little remote data, so the transaction dependency is low. In the LH category the transaction is not used very often, so the transaction dependency is again low. Clearly, the LL dependencies are low. The HH dependencies are high since they are used frequently and require a large amount of remote data. This aspect leads to one condition for the logical distribution; it may not contain any HH transaction dependencies.

The dependency between two groups of a logical distribution is usually due to more than one transaction type. Hence, the transaction dependencies can be consolidated. This consolidation is accomplished within the transaction dependency categories by adding the active components and by measuring the set theoretic union of the passive components. For example,

Transaction type A

Active = 600 tx/day
Passive = 0.15 million bytes

Transaction type B

Active = 500 tx/day
Passive = 0.1 million bytes

Assume that A and B could use 0.05 million bytes of remote data in common. Their consolidated dependency is

Active = 1,100 tx/day
Passive = 0.2 million bytes

After the transaction dependencies are consolidated within their respective categories, the consolidated dependencies are classified using the same thresholds. This consolidation leads to a further condition for the logical distribution—a consolidated dependency cannot be in the HH category.

It is now possible to describe a dependency between two groups of the logical distribution. This description consists of an orientation and the three consolidated dependencies, HL, LH, and LL. The schematic representation of an intergroup dependency is shown in Figure 8-5.

It is evident that the values of the thresholds determine the number of groups in the logical distribution, the extent of a group's autonomy, and the strength of its dependencies. The threshold values are determined judgmentally, after a thorough familiarity with the applications has been attained.

A graph of all of the dependencies of a distribution is a useful visual aid for

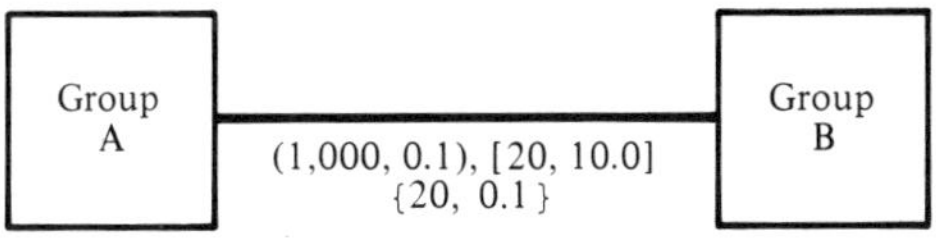

Key:

( ) : HL, active component = 1,000 tx/day
passive component = 0.1 million bytes

[ ] : LH, active component = 20 tx/day
passive component = 10 million bytes

{ } : LL, active component = 20 tx/day
passive component = 0.1 million bytes

Figure 8-5. Intergroup dependencies for the active and passive components of the daily transactions.

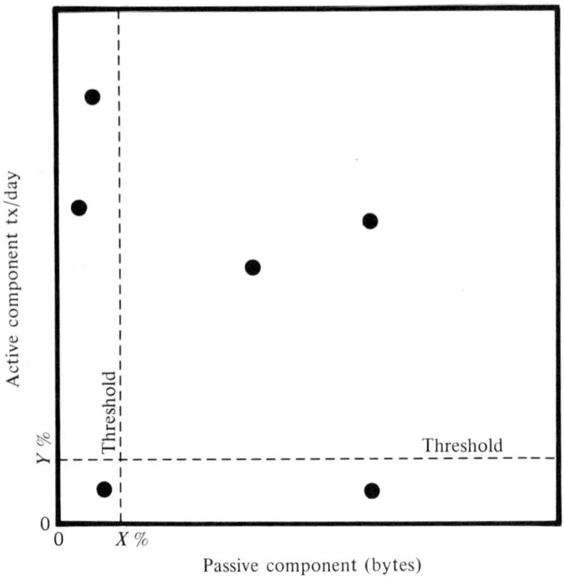

(a)

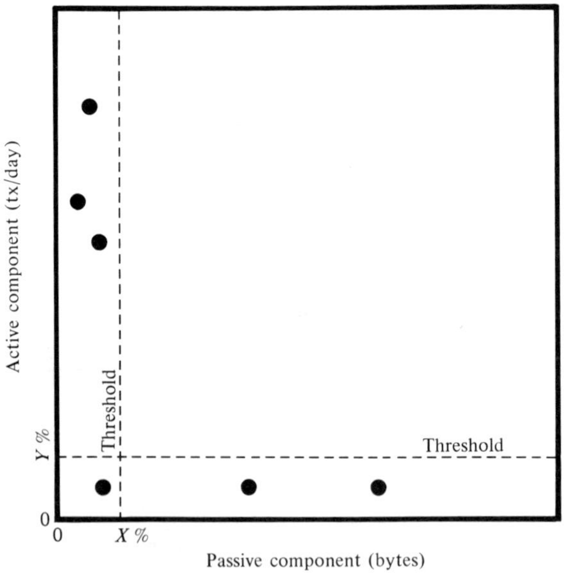

(b)

Figure 8-6. Graphic representation of six dependencies for two possible logical distributions.

these analyses. The example in Figure 8-6 shows six dependencies for two variations of a logical distribution. The variations usually involve the relocation of a few transactions. The percentages shown in Figure 8-6 are percentages of the total on-line bytes and the total number of on-line transactions per day. Comparison of Figure 8-6(a) with (b) shows that in Figure 8.6(b) the points are closer to the horizontal and the vertical axes. It is the closeness of the points to the axes that characterizes the better distribution and leads to the judgmental determination of the threshold values. In the steel mill system analysis, a 1 per cent. threshold was used. This figure put the active threshold at 370 transactions per day and the passive threshold at 4 million bytes.

The results of the calculation of the active components of the transaction dependencies are listed by transaction code and show the frequency of daily occurrence, remote data segments accessed, and type of access: read-only or update. The results are grouped by intergroup dependency. A sample list is shown in Table 8-4, which is for the intergroup dependency from the primary steel planning group to the steel plate planning group. A summary table for all active components of the intergroup dependencies is shown in Table 8-5.

The next step in the procedure is to calculate the passive components of the transaction dependencies. The data required include a description of the data bases—number of child segment occurrences per parent, field descriptions by segment type, field sizes, and hierarchical structure. Also required is a list of field usage by transaction type.

TABLE 8-4
List of active components

Tx code	Tx/day	Segments accessed				
SP1 C80	61	DB081 R	DB082 R	DB083 RU		
SP1 C82	5	DB081 R	DB082 R	DB083 RU	DB084 RU	
SP1C84	14	DB081 R	DB082 R	DB083 RU	DB084 RU	
SP1C90	14	DB101 R				
SP1T26	5	DB081 R	DB082 R	DB083 RU	DB084 RU	
SP2P65	268	DB081 RU	DB082 RU	DB083 RU	DB084 RU	DB101 RU
SP2P74	17	DB101 R				
SP2P80	810	DB081 R	DB082 R	DB083 RU		
SP2P82	47	DB081 R	DB082 R	DB083 RU	DB084 RU	
SP2P86	207	DB081 RU	DB082 RU	DB083 RU	DB084 RU	DB101 RU
SP3T22	838	DB081 R	DB082 R	DB083 RU	DB084 RU	
SP3T29	48	DB081 R	DB082 R	DB083 RU	DB084 RU	
	2,334	= Active component of dependency				

Dependency: from primary steel planning group to steel plate planning group.
Data usage key: R = read-only; RU = read or update.
Key to DB code: DB08¹ ← Segment 1.

TABLE 8-5
Summary of active components of intergroup dependencies

	To						
From	Primary planning	Steel plate planning	Order services	Chemical analysis	Plate operations	Primary steel labor incentive accounting	Primary steel production reporting
Primary steel planning	0	2,334	0	0	0	0	185
Steel plate planning	2,938	0	3,079	470	353	0	0
Order services	0	0	0	279	260	0	0
Chemical analysis	0	496	0	0	0	0	0
Plate operations	0	951	2,223	805	0	0	0
Primary steel labor incentive accounting	0	0	0	0	0	0	0
Primary steel production reporting	0	0	0	0	0	0	0

The starting point of the calculation is the list of active components, as in Table 8-4. These transactions are put into two groups: those whose occurrences exceed the active threshold and those whose occurrences do not. The passive components are first calculated for the group with occurrences that exceed the active threshold. If a passive dependency exceeds the passive threshold, another iteration is required. If all passive dependencies in the group fall below the passive threshold, the group is consolidated. If the passive component of the consolidated dependency exceeds the passive threshold, another iteration is required. Otherwise, one continues with the remaining transaction dependencies.

The passive components of the remaining transaction dependencies are now calculated. These components are either LL or LH dependencies, since their active components are all less than the active threshold. Those in the LL category are consolidated. If the resulting consolidated dependency is HH, another iteration is required. Otherwise, one can continue with the remaining LH transaction dependencies, which are consolidated. If the resulting consolidated dependency is HH, another iteration is required. Otherwise, the logical distribution is finished.

The actual calculations of the passive components first are made with a single data base record. This calculation yields the maximum number of bytes that a transaction type could require and is expressed as a percentage of the data base record size. This percentage is applied to the size of the entire data base to give the size of the passive component of the transaction dependency for that data base. The procedure is repeated for each data base that is accessed by that transaction type. The sum of the individual data base components gives the total passive component of the transaction dependency.

The final logical distribution was produced after more than ten iterations of the procedure. The changes in successive iterations included the redefinition of application groups, movement of individual transaction types from one group to another, and the movement of individual data bases from one group to another.

The logical distribution is shown in Figure 8-7. The distribution has 14 consolidated dependencies—eight HL, four LL, and two LH. Figure 8-8 is a plot of these dependencies. Note that one group, primary steel labor incentive accounting, has no on-line dependencies. It is included in the logical distribution because of its batch processing dependencies, which are not part of this analysis.

In the foregoing example, a logical distribution has been developed for an existing centralized on-line operations planning and control system in a steel mill. Such a distribution can be used in several ways. It can provide a basis for the physical distribution of the centralized system, it can provide insight into the basic structure of that system, and it can also be used as a guide for the development of new and distributed systems in other similar steel plants. However, the analysis is based upon an existing system. What about systems that do not yet exist? Can a logical distribution be developed prior to implementation? The answer is 'yes', but a logical distribution prior to implementation will have less detail and will be less accurate than a postimplementation distribution.

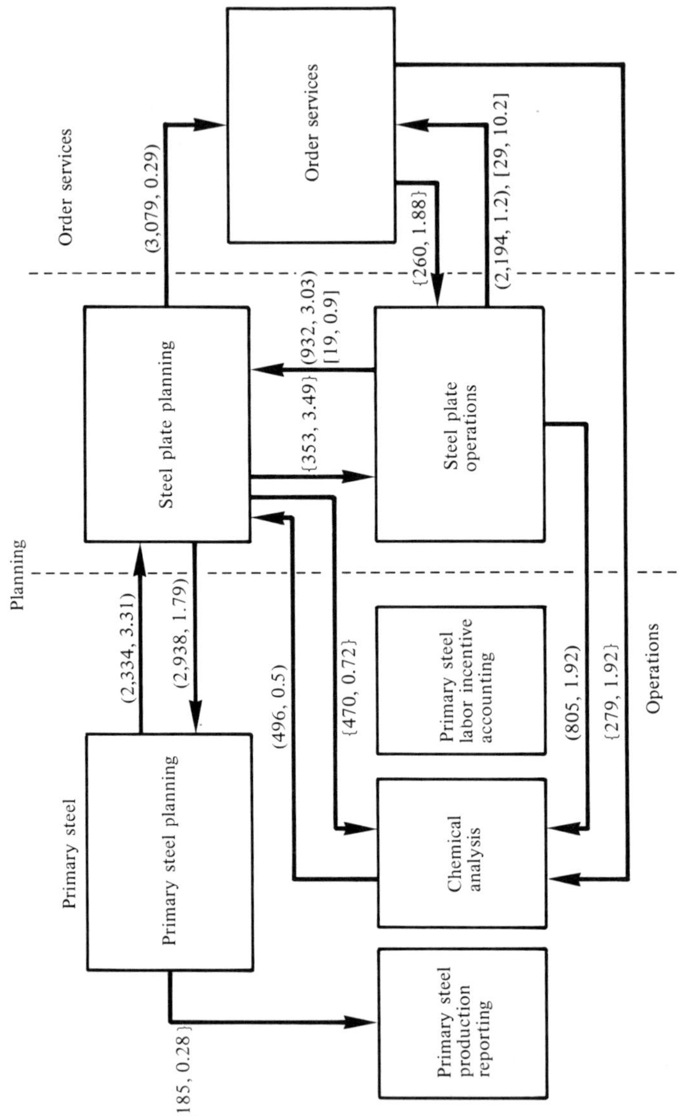

Figure 8-7. Logical distribution of dependencies by group.

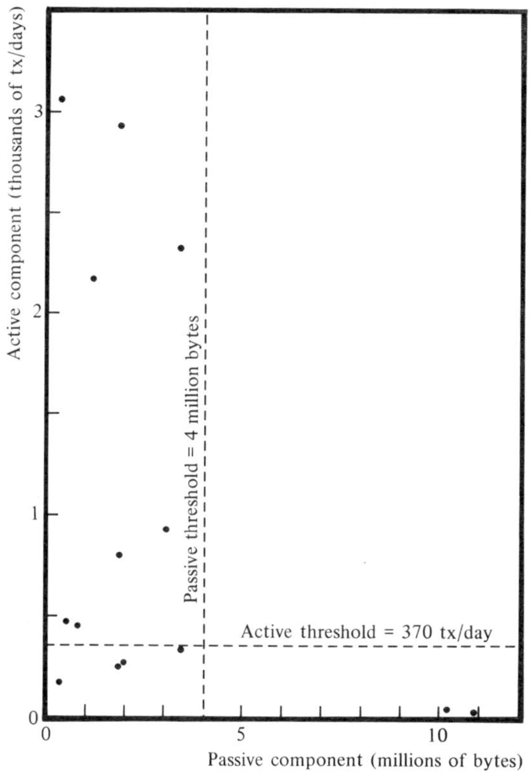

Figure 8-8. Plot of 18 dependencies of Figure 8-7.

LOGICAL DISTRIBUTION PRIOR TO IMPLEMENTATION

The procedure for logical distribution that was applied to an implemented system can also be applied to estimates of the system data prior to implementation. The same types of system data are required. Since these data are estimated, they are less detailed and less voluminous than the data from an implemented system. Hence it may be feasible to do a preimplementation analysis manually. This kind of analysis can be illustrated with data from the same steel mill system used in the preceding example. However, the data have been put in a form that would have occurred in an earlier preimplementation stage of development. Some applications and some data are not yet identified. Individual application programs are not identified and data base structures are not yet specified. The data are identified merely as clusters of data, where each cluster may ultimately become one or more data bases. The data in this form are given in Table 8-6, which shows the relation of application clusters to data clusters in terms of their estimated daily usage. Total activity is estimated at 40,000 transactions per day.

To develop the preimplementation logical distribution, the procedure of Figure

TABLE 8-6
Daily transactions of data clusters versus application clusters

	Application clusters								
Data clusters	Primary steel planning	Primary steel production reporting	Chemical analysis	Slab requirements processing	Slab scheduling	Plate production reporting	Plate metallurgical tests	Shipping	Order services
Primary steel orders	250	0	0	0	0	0	0	0	0
Slab inventory	2,000	0	0	10,000	5,000	900	500	500	0
Slab orders	6,000	0	0	2,000	1,000	0	0	0	0
Metallurgical specifications	0	0	0	0	0	0	500	0	0
Plate orders	500	500	0	0	0	1,000	100	0	1,000
Metallurgical tests	0	0	0	0	0	0	5,000	0	0
Slab schedule	0	0	0	0	250	500	0	0	0
Chemical analysis	0	0	1,000	0	0	0	0	0	0
Shipping	0	0	0	0	0	2,000	1,500	4,500	0
Plate inventory	0	0	0	0	500	2,000	0	1,000	250

8-1 is applied to the data in Table 8-6. However, at this phase of the system development, it is possible to use a simple dependency measure, namely usages per day. This approval leads to the structure in Figure 8-9, where a 10 per cent. threshold—4,000 tx/day—was used.

Examination of Figure 8-9 shows that a primary steel operations group will be separated from the other applications, since all but one of this group's dependencies are for read-only reference to data that are static. (Once recorded, primary steel production data are not changed.) The remote updates that are made by the primary steel production planning system are orders for future production, not current production. These updates could be deferred if necessary, with no impact on current production operations. For these reasons, it can be concluded that the primary steel production operations applications could be separated as one group of a logical distribution. Note that sufficient information is not available to break this group into three parts as was done with the implemented system.

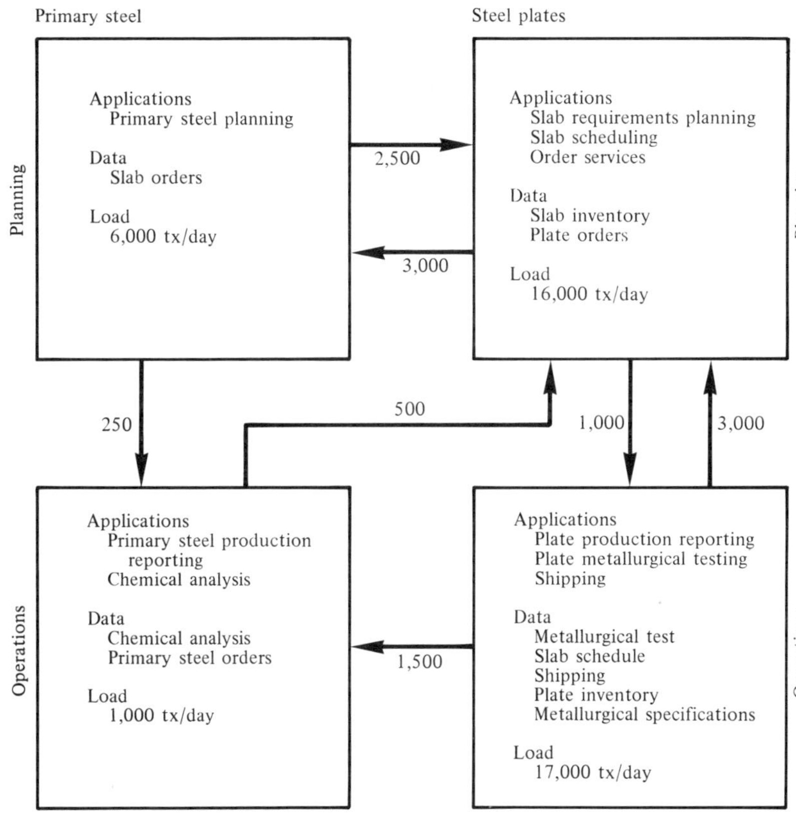

Note. Intergroup dependencies are measured in transactions per day.

Figure 8-9. Logical distribution of functions with expected loads.

Referring again to Figure 8-9, one sees that the three remaining groups of the logical distribution are connected by dependencies at the 10 per cent. level. The largest of these dependencies is 3,000 transactions per day, or 7.5 per cent. of the estimated total transaction activity. This level of dependency appears to be sufficiently low for this early phase of the system development. Hence, one can tentatively accept the structure of Figure 8-9 as the logical distribution. One can then proceed with the system development and expect that as more details are defined, the tentative logical distribution will be refined. Thus, one does not expect always to obtain a refined logical distribution at the outset of the system design. The refined distribution evolves from a more crude distribution that is tentatively accepted early in the development cycle.

LOGICAL DISTRIBUTION AND DISTRIBUTED SYSTEMS

This chapter is concerned with the techniques for organizing a set of related applications and their data into a logical distribution, the purpose of which is to

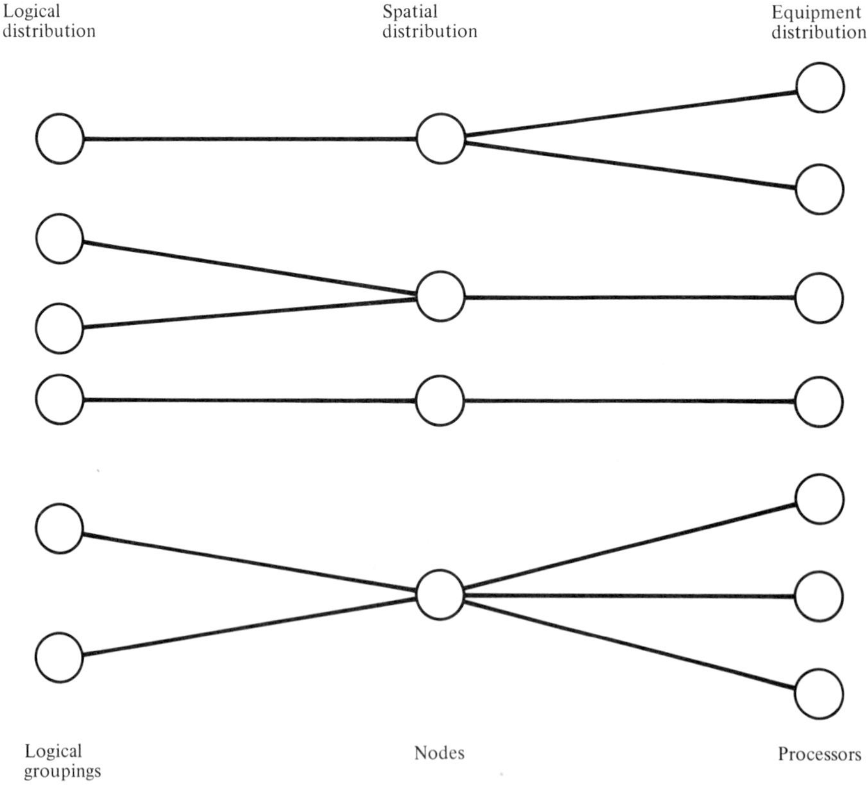

Figure 8-10. Relations between applications, data, nodes, and equipment.

provide a means for controlling the strength of the interdependencies among the nodes of a distributed system and thus to assure a satisfactory degree of autonomy at each node. To see how a logical distribution provides this function, its relation to a distributed system is examined, as illustrated in Figure 8-10.

Figure 8-10 depicts the relations among three sets of elements: the logical distribution, which is a set of groups of applications and data; a spatial distribution, which is a set of nodes or volumes of space; and an equipment distribution, which is a set of processors with their associated control software. Figure 8-10 shows that each group of the logical distribution is assigned to one node only and that each processor of the equipment distribution is assigned to one node only. The total collection of logical groupings, nodes, and processors, together with the relations among them, comprises a distributed data processing system. With this structure, it can be seen that the controlled interdependencies of the logical distribution determine the nodal interdependencies and thus the nodal autonomies of the distributed data processing system.

USE OF LOGICAL DISTRIBUTION

A logical distribution can be used in several ways. It can provide a basis for a physically distributed system, either in the original application environment or in similar environments. Some of the groups of the logical distribution would probably be combined for a physically distributed implementation. Such combinations, which are called derived distributions, can be made in many ways. Considerations that affect the choice of combination are load balance, total amount of data copied, availability, and administrative convenience, where local user groups have their own processors. Other uses of the logical distribution include the organization of application development activities and application maintenance.

One can illustrate the evolution of a derived distribution from the logical distribution with a hypothetical example. Suppose that the steel mill management wanted their system divided into two systems: one for primary steel and the other for plates and order services. The obvious division on this basis is shown in Figure 8-11(a). Note, however, that this derived distribution requires the support of six dependencies across the interface between the two systems. However, four of these dependencies are related to one small grouping in the primary steel system—the chemical analysis grouping. If this grouping were moved out of the primary steel system and into the plate/order services system, it would then be necessary only to support two, rather than six, dependencies across the interface. The new derived distribution is shown in Figure 8-11(b). It could provide a reasonable basis for a distributed implementation.

DEPENDENCY SUPPORT

Once a derived distribution has been defined, decisions must be made about the means for supporting its dependencies. The two choices are: data communications

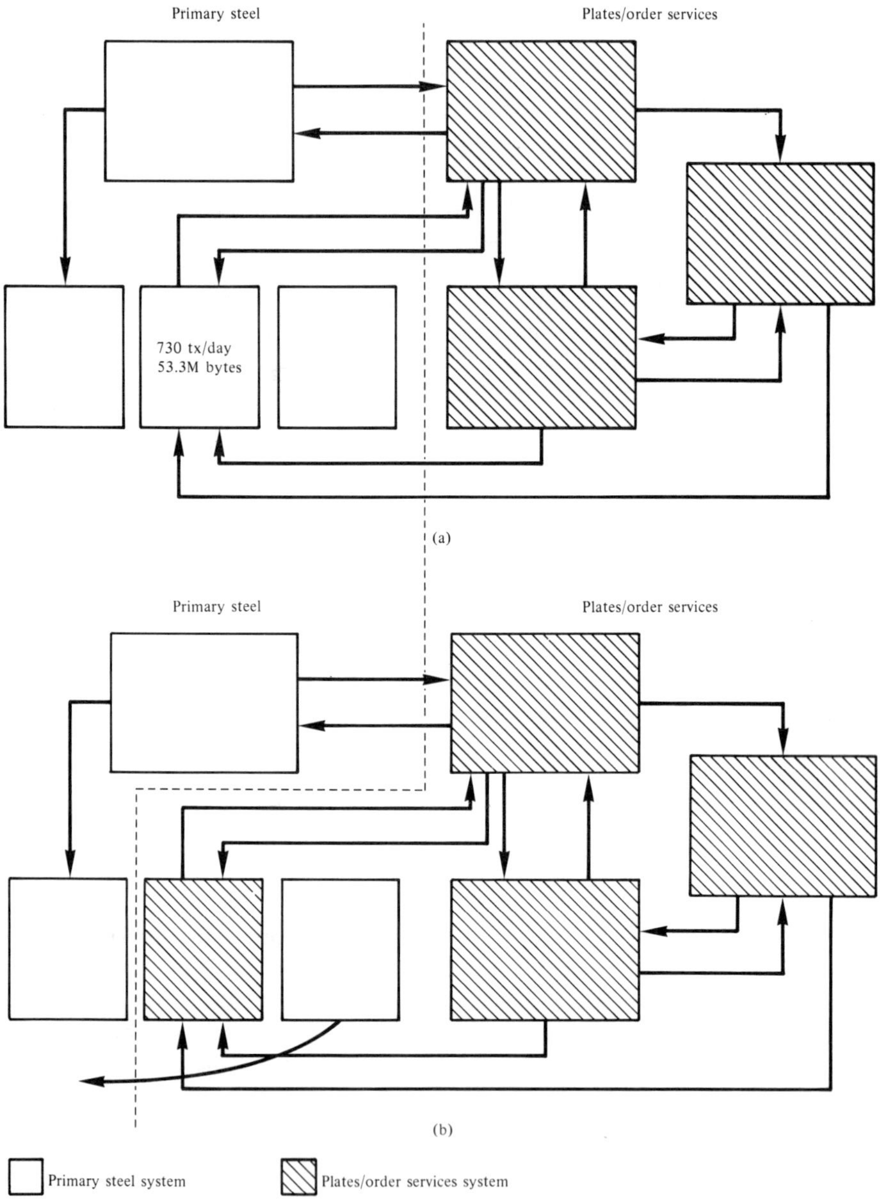

Figure 8-11. An example of derived distribution where (a) represents obvious division and (b) represents reduction in dependencies.

or data duplication, each of which has advantages and disadvantages. An important advantage of data communications support is data currency and integrity; since the data are not duplicated, just one valid set of records exists in the system. However, data communications support has potential disadvantages, which include questions of availability and excessive response time, due either to communications delay or to file overload—too many people using the same file.

The pros and cons of the use of data duplication as a means for supporting dependencies are the converse of the data communications considerations cited previously. Duplication of data raises questions about data currency and integrity, particularly when copies are updated. However, the use of copies enhances the autonomy of a logical grouping and therefore improves system availability, local management control, and response time.

It is evident that the selection of data communications or data duplication to support the dependencies of a derived distribution can be a complex problem that involves many trade-off decisions. The logical distribution and its various alternative derived distributions can aid system designers by clarifying their options.

When dependencies are supported by the duplication of data, questions of data consistency and integrity must be considered, particularly when updates are applied to the copies. To pursue this question with the steel mill, consider the logical distribution as in Figure 8-12, where the active components of the dependencies are separated into read-only usages and update usages. Examination of these data shows that in 9 of the 12 HL or LL dependencies, the update part of

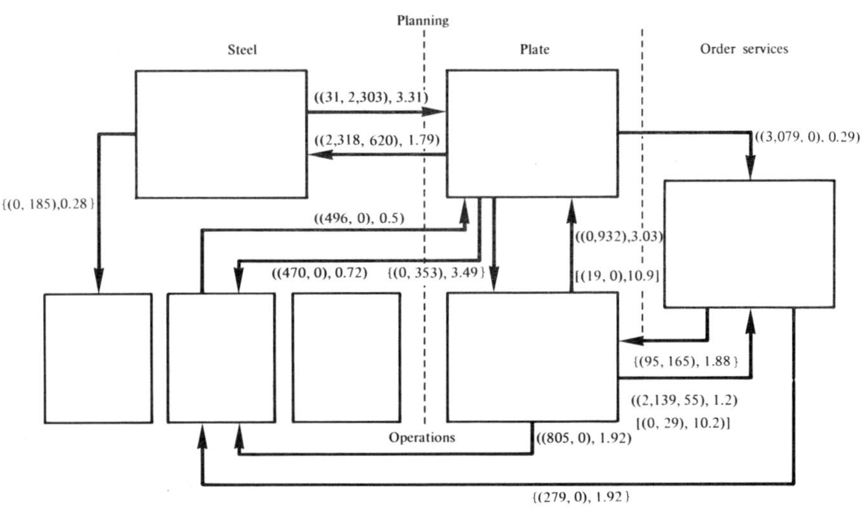

Key. ((Read-only tx s/day, update tx s/day), bytes)

Figure 8-12. Logical distribution in terms of read only and update components.

the active component of the dependency is either zero or below the 1 per cent. threshold. For these 9 dependencies, one can post an interim update to the copy and send the update transaction to the master data base, where the true update is applied. Periodically the copy is refreshed from the master, after which the preceding interim updates are discarded. The data copies will also support the read-only usages. With this arrangement, the update control of the data is maintained by the node that contains the master data base.

The significant update HL dependencies that remain are between primary steel planning and plate planning, and between plate planning and plate operations. For both interfaces, one finds the same result: it is never necessary for a given item of data to be updated simultaneously by two or more logical groupings. This concept can be illustrated using the two planning systems.

Consider Figure 8-13. Here the plate planning system is generating net slab requirements and posting them to the net slab requirements master file, which is an IMS physical data base that is organized by steel grade. The primary steel planning group uses a copy of the net slab requirements file and develops new steel orders—orders for the production of heats of steel. The system has a natural

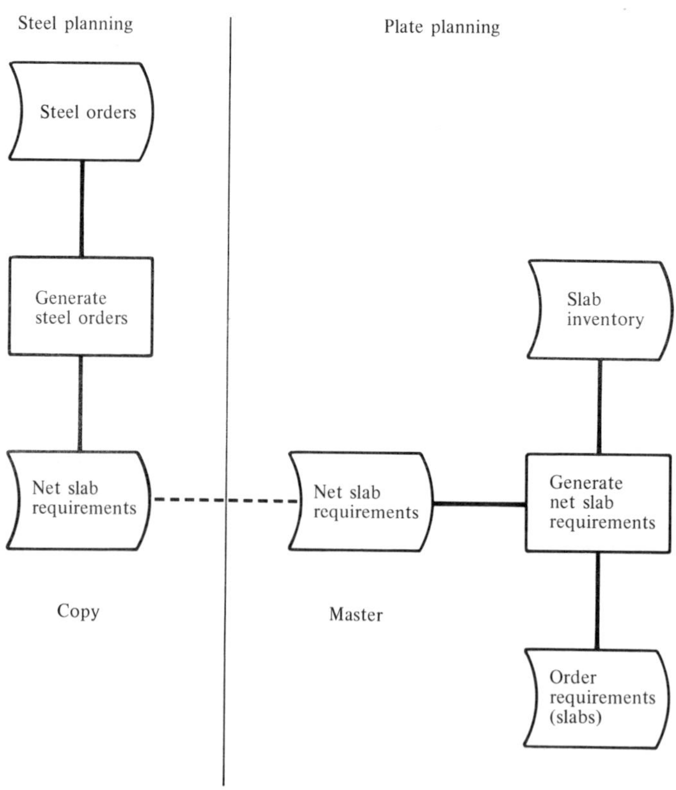

Figure 8-13. Information flow in steel and plate planning systems.

logical sequence that results in the update authority for a given data item being passed back and forth between the two planning systems, thus precluding the need for any simultaneous updating by the two systems. The logical flow is described with reference to Figure 8-14.

Update copy control is maintained by a system of flags in the root segments. The plate planning system can read any data but may update only those data base records that have their flags set to one. Net slab requirements are developed within one steel grade at a time. When the slab requirements are completed for a grade of steel, the data base record, with its flag set to one, is sent to the primary steel system where it is put into the copy file. The same record is stored in the master file with its flag set to zero.

The same logical control applies to the primary steel planning system. Only those data base records in the copy that have their flags set to one can be updated. After the new steel orders have been prepared, by grade, the updated net slab requirements data base record is returned to the plate planning system, with its flag set to one. It is also put into the copy data base with its flag set to zero. Thus, the most current version of the data base record, updated by the primary steel planning system, has returned to the plate planning system, ready for another processing cycle.

From the foregoing discussion, it can be seen that the update authority for any one data base record passes systematically back and forth between the two planning systems. No need exists for simultaneous updates. In this way the copy updating is controlled naturally by the application requirements. A similar logic applies to the copy update activities across the interface between the plate planning and plate operations groupings.

The two remaining LH dependencies are between the plate operations group and the plate planning group, with 19 read-only references per day, and between the plate operations group and the order services group, with 29 updates per day. Both LH dependencies can be supported by data communications facilities and service programs that are installed at the remote nodes. The remote read-only service program receives the data request parameters from the local node, reads the requested data, and sends it to the local node. The remote update service program receives the update data from the local node and posts it to the order service data bases. These updates are reports of the mill's shipments—they are deferable and do not present a near-instantaneous multinode data consistency requirement. After each of these updates has been successfully posted, an acknowledgment is returned to the local node by means of a conventional communications protocol.

It is evident that the steel mill system does not have strong data consistency requirements for its dependency support functions as it uses the alternating update arrangement between the two planning systems. When one system lacks update authority for the record of a particular grade of steel, its operators have no interest in those data. Thus, when those data become inconsistent owing to the other system's updates, no harm is done. When the updated record is returned

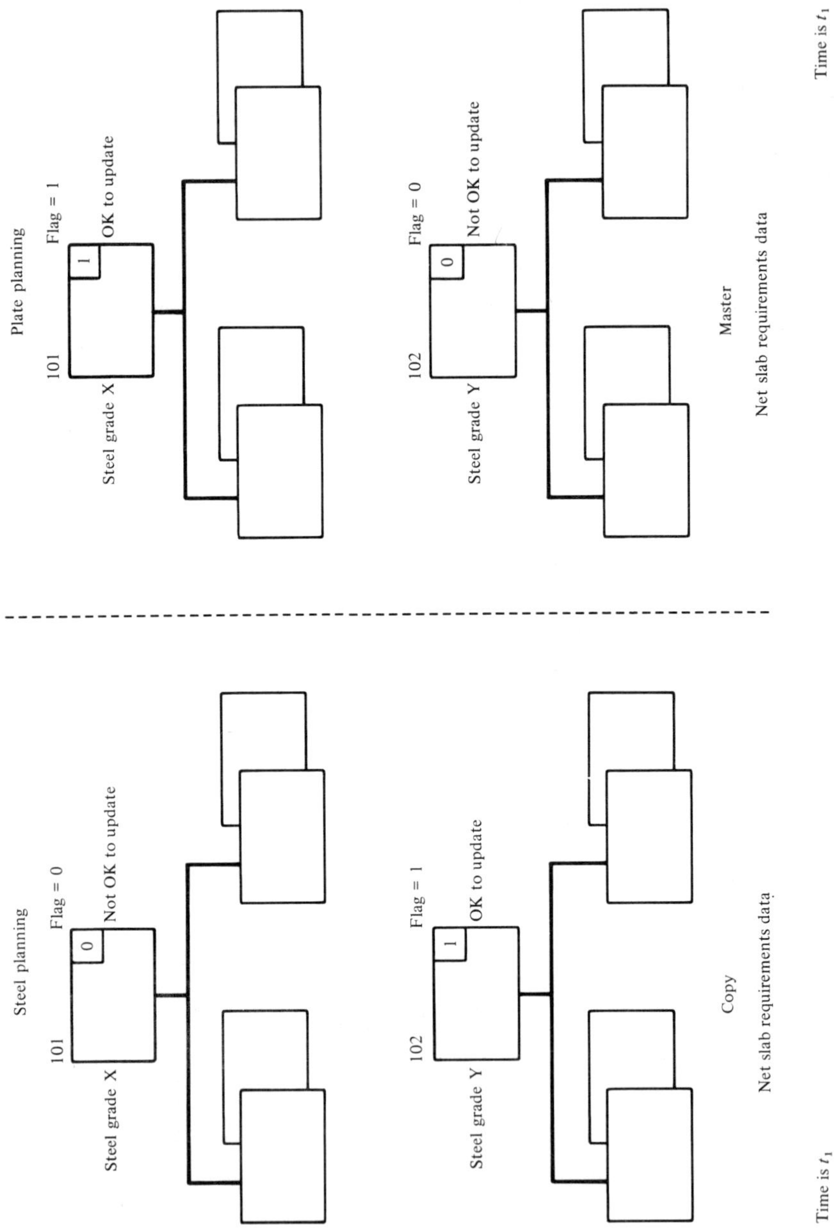

Figure 8-14. Logical flow control for update between the two planning systems.

together with the update authority, that grade of steel is ready for another cycle of planning. At that time the data become of interest to the operators.

In the remaining HL or LL dependencies where data may be copied, they consist of production reports, chemical and metallurgical test results, and shipping notices, for example. None of these items require near-instantaneous consistency between copies and master files. With the interim post-to-copy procedure that is described, the master files probably would have a consistency lag of 1 minute or less, which is acceptable for such applications. Thus all of the steel mill system's HL and LL dependencies can be supported by data duplication functions that do not have near-instantaneous consistency control facilities. As noted, the two LH dependencies can be supported by data communications functions.

A requirement for near-instantaneous data consistency is present in the distributed retail banking system that was described previously. An example occurs when an individual uses an automatic teller machine to transfer funds from an account in one node to an account in another node. When the individual finishes the transaction, he must have a display of the new balances for each account—a near-instantaneous consistency requirement.

When faced with near-instantaneous multinode data consistency requirements, the system designer must first determine the stability of the relations among the records that are involved. In the banking example, the relation is stable if both accounts belong to the same individual, since it is the fact of account ownership that establishes the relation. If the involved relations are stable, the system designer may seek to require that all such related records be maintained at one node. This requirement eliminates the multinode consistency requirement. However, other problems may arise when such steps are taken. Again in the banking example, if all such related records are put into one node, there is a problem with the individual's account numbers. Must new account numbers be issued when the account records are moved from one node to another? Or could pointers be put in the data bases to show where the records were moved? In the banking example, practical solutions exist for this problem, but ready solutions may not be available for other applications.

The system designer must seek to minimize the requirements for near-instantaneous multinode data consistency. This task is essential because of the complexity and overhead of the dependency support functions that must be used. Such considerations are part of the evaluation step of the procedure for logical distribution. The minimum requirements for near-instantaneous multinode data consistency should be composed of only those cases in which the relations among the involved records are not stable. Once these requirements have been determined, the system designer must select a means for dependency support. A typical approach involves data borrowing.

With data borrowing the local node processes a transaction to the point at which it is determined that remote data are required. The local node then suspends the transaction synchronously—the transaction's resources are retained and the processing step at the time of the suspension is recorded.

When the local process is suspended, a remote data request message is sent to the remote node. The remote node responds with a message that contains a copy of the requested data. Upon receipt of this message, the local node resumes processing of the local transaction. When the processing is finished, the local node sends the borrowed and updated data back to the remote node where they are replaced in their data base. As the local transaction terminates, it activates a protocol that checks both nodes to assure that all of the processing has been completed successfully, thus assuring multinode data consistency.[7]

It is evident from the foregoing discussion that one can have several different types of interdependency support requirements and a corresponding set of support functions. It is probably unreasonable for the system designer to select only one support function for use as a universal solution for all interdependency requirements. A more satisfactory approach would be to select those support functions that are best suited to the interdependency requirements at hand.

SUMMARY

A major goal of distributed system design is to bring data processing functions and data closer to their users than is possible with a centralized design. The expected advantages of this arrangement, such as enhanced availability and improved responsiveness, have been expressed at length in the literature on distributed data processing. Many of these advantages depend on the system designer's attainment of a substantial degree of autonomy for each of the nodes in the system. It is to be noted, however, that a node of a distributed system does not function in an isolated, stand-alone mode. Other nodes depend on it, or it depends on other nodes. If these interdependencies are too strong, many of the expected advantages of the distributed system are lost. It is essential, therefore, that such a system be designed so that the nodal interdependencies are at an acceptably low level. One approach to this task has been illustrated in this chapter.

ACKNOWLEDGMENT

The author is indebted to H. S. Arora, B. Roth, and R. M. Gale for their aid and constructive comments about the material in this chapter.

REFERENCES

1. Jenny, C. J.: *Partitioning and Allocating Computational Objects in Distributed Data Processing*. Research Report RZ 984, IBM Corporation, 1979. Available through the local IBM branch office (ITIRC No. 79A 7097).
2. Lawson, T. and Mariani, M. P.: Distributed data processing system design—a look at the partitioning problem. *COMPSAC 1978 Proc.*, IEEE, New York, 1978.
3. Bochmann, G. V.: Design and implementation of distributed systems. *Proc. of the Sixth Int. Conf. on Very Large Data Bases*, pp. 75–101, IEEE Catalog Number 80CH1534-7C. IEEE Computer Society, Long Beach, Calif., 1980.

4. Baker, C. T.: Logical distribution of applications and data. *IBM Systems J.*, **19**, No. 2, 171–191, 1980.
5. Gale, R. M.: *A Methodology for Determining Logical Nodes in a Distributed Data Processing System.* Technical Report TR 00.3023-1, IBM Corporation, 1979. Available through the local IBM branch office (ITIRC No. 79A 6109).
6. Späth, H.: *Cluster Analysis Algorithms.* New York, 1980. Halsted Press (John Wiley), 1980.
7. Sevcik, K. C.: Concurrency control in distributed systems. *Proc. of the Sixth Int. Conf. on Very Large Data Bases*, pp. 275–317, IEEE Catalog Number 80CH1534-7C. IEEE Computer Society, Long Beach, Calif., 1980.

SECTION IV

GEOGRAPHICAL DISTRIBUTION

Advances in Distributed Processing Management, Volume 2
Edited by P. S. Fisher, J. Slonim, and E. A. Unger

Chapter 9

MANAGEMENT ISSUES IN A GEOGRAPHICALLY DISTRIBUTED SYSTEM

E. A. Unger
Department of Computer Sciences, Kansas State University, Manhattan, Kansas

W. T. Cottrell
U.S. Army, CACDA, Ft. Leavenworth, Kansas

P. A. Viglucci
U.S. Army, Ft. Devons, Maryland

> ... as hardware and applications are being distributed, so must the data processing management function and its reporting relationship be redeveloped. Our central control mechanisms no longer apply ... in short, we find managers and professionals are uncertain of their proper role in the distributed environment.
> G. H. Hoxie and D. M. Shea[1]

The information processing concepts developed and the supportive technological advances in the late seventies have made geographically distributed computing environments possible. The adaptation of current management methodology to distributed environments and the introduction of sound management philosophy, structure, and technique supportive of the geographically distributed system is essential. Management issues, not technical issues, are the real challenges in geographically distributed computing systems. The purpose of this discussion is to address the issues and the challenges present in a restrained model of geographically distributed systems. This constrained model is predicated upon current plans for the U.S. Army's mobile battlefield computer system, but correlates well with management systems in any large institution or enterprise. The emphasis will be directed to the creation of communication and control techniques which can assure system integrity, responsiveness, resiliency and efficiency while allowing functional autonomy in the dispersed processing units.

For the purpose of this chapter, a network is defined as a collection of interconnected computing systems. The computing systems will be referred to as nodes, and the communication interconnections as paths and switching elements. Paths are the medium through which messages are transferred between and among nodes. Switching elements are entities (physical and virtual) which can provide intervening intelligence between the sending and receiving units. The intervening intelligence will include that logic which determines the appropriate path or paths the message is to take to arrive at its proper destination(s).[2] Within the paradigm network the message-switching will be assumed to be handled within and among network system processors.

The model network will be assumed to support distributed processing, communication between three or more nodes, distributed data bases, and network-wide rules.[3] The next section of this chapter defines the model network to encompass most of the features of extant and conceptualized state-of-the-art distributed systems. The third section provides further background information by addressing life cycle management. It focuses attention upon the magnitude of complexity associated with acquisition, development, and installation of systems that are available or are being designed for use in distributed environments.

In the fourth section management issues which are unique to the distributed environment within the context of the model network are defined, and in some cases solutions are suggested. These issues are categorized as follows: (1) essential information, (2) partitioned authority, (3) standardization, (4) data management, (5) security management, (6) network resiliency, performance, and integrity, and (7) maintenance management.

The final section encapsulates the suggestions for management strategy discussed herein and summarizes those topics which require further study.

THE RESTRAINED MODEL NETWORK

A paradigm or notion of a geographically distributed network which restrains the information common to the nodes and restrains the paths of communication is proposed. Within this idealized and, in a sense, simplified environment, the issues of management concern within a geographically distributed network will be discussed. The model can be envisioned as a matrix of network compatible nodes. Two *network compatible nodes* can communicate a pool of information common to the sending and receiving nodes along predefined paths. Two nodes or processors may be *homogeneous* in the sense that all the hardware/firmware/software/data components of these nodes are compatible. The model allows network interconnection of network compatible nodes.

The basis of the logical matrix structure is the division of the information into two categories: (1) that required for structured decision-making (tactical) and (2) that required for unstructured decision-making (strategic). Network compatible nodes will be logically connected in what is to be considered the horizontal plane of a matrix when peer nodes are connected (see Figure 9-1). The vertical logical

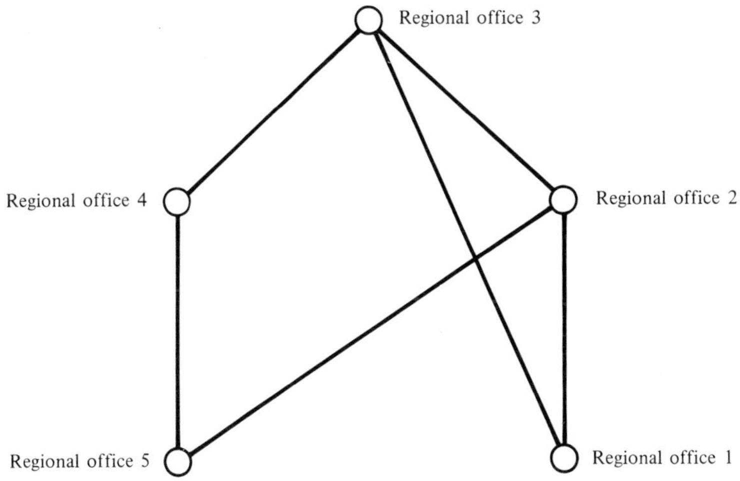

Figure 9-1. Horizontal interconnection of peer nodes for information flow in structured decision-making (tactical).

interconnections represent physical interconnection within the network between nodes that have a hierarchical relationship with one another. Generally, the horizontal interconnections represent data flow for tactical processing whereas the vertical interconnections represent data flow for strategic processing (see Figure 9-2). Although internodal, data flow between homogeneous nodes can occur. Figure 9-2 can easily be interpreted to represent the state, regional, and national office network nodes for a corporation along the vertical axis.

A node is considered to consist of a number of logical (perhaps) physical processors. Interconnection between homogeneous internodal processors is allowed (see Figure 9-3). Examined from a management perspective, such interconnections can provide support for resiliency and integrity but complicate security management.

The model allows the application of the structural abstractive principles espoused by E. W. Dijkstra.[3a] Thus, a network can, at a higher level of abstraction, be considered a node. Clearly, super networks, i.e. networks of networks, are accommodated by the model. Each node will contain the logical processor (perhaps an independent physical processor) for communication between nodes. It is through this processor that information for strategic decision-making must flow and through which other information may flow. Each node has one or more logical information processors to support the functional processing at that nodal site. Additionally, a data base processor and associated data bases may exist within the definition we have adopted for distributed processing. Each of these processors is able to communicate at least with the network processor, but intranode compatibility and homogeneity are not requisite. This freedom allows a realistic view because computer systems are in place before distribution is

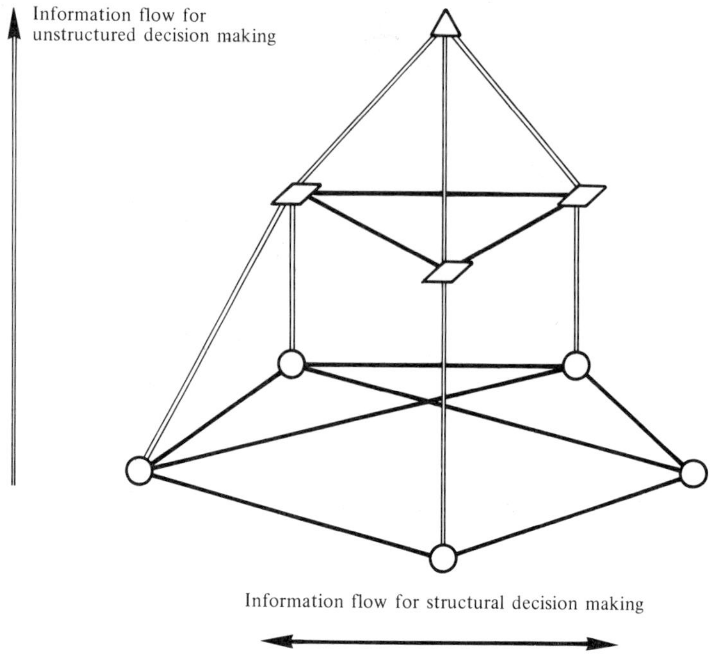

Figure 9-2. Information flow for structured and unstructured decision-making.

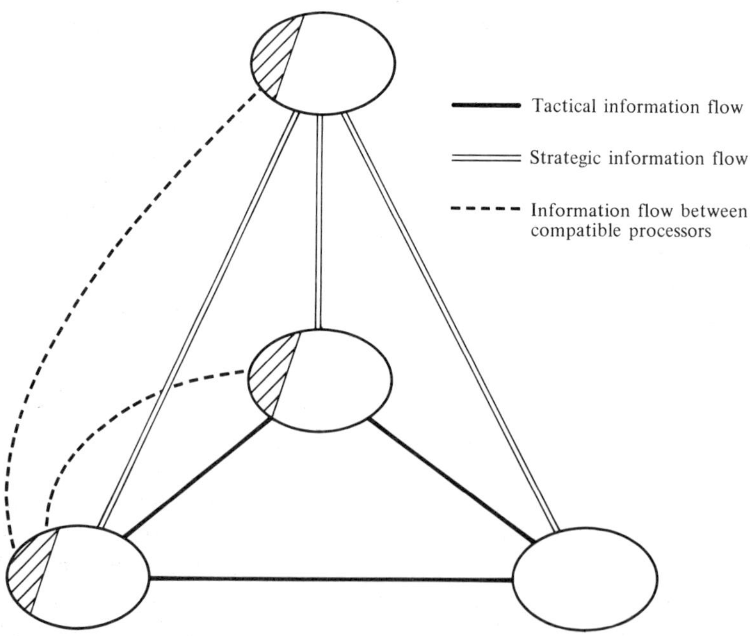

Figure 9-3. Internodal connection between compatible processors.

introduced into most institutions. As an aside we would observe that most contemporary networks have been built from existing computer sites. The sites have been managed by local managers prior to network inclusion and exhibit a good deal of intranodal compatibility. The model node demands only communication compatibility between the network processor and other processors within the node. It is likely that communication is possible between the data base processor and one or more information processors (see Figure 9-4).

The data base processor is conceptually a bifunctional unit supporting those functions provided locally at the node and also supporting the network informational (strategic) needs. The network data base by definition will be in a form compatible with all other network data bases in the system. For this data base to be effected with efficiency, a common set of compatible information is dictated for internodal flow (both tactical and strategic). We term this set the minimal essential elements of information (MEI).

Thus, the model will generally have two physical data bases, one for the network information and at least one other to support the local processing

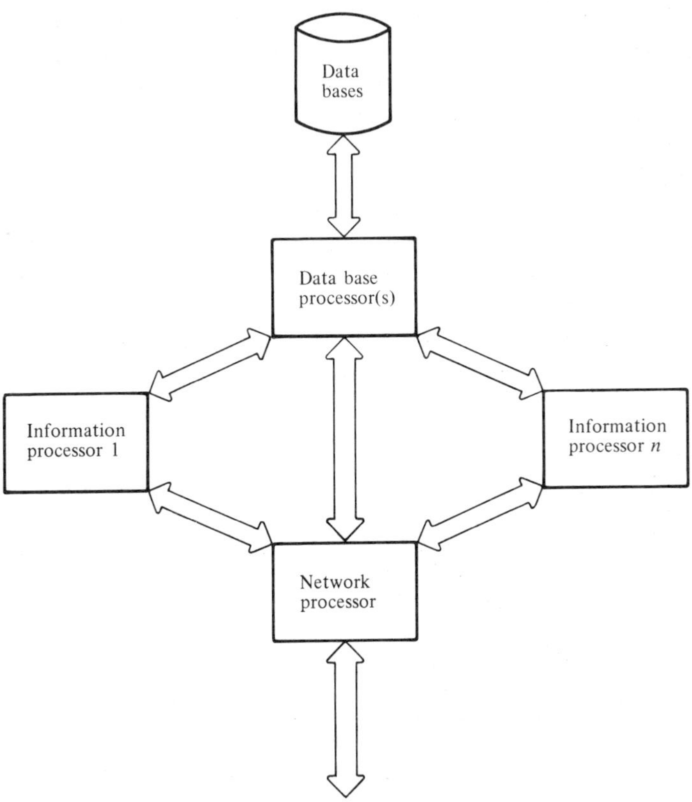

Figure 9-4. Model node.

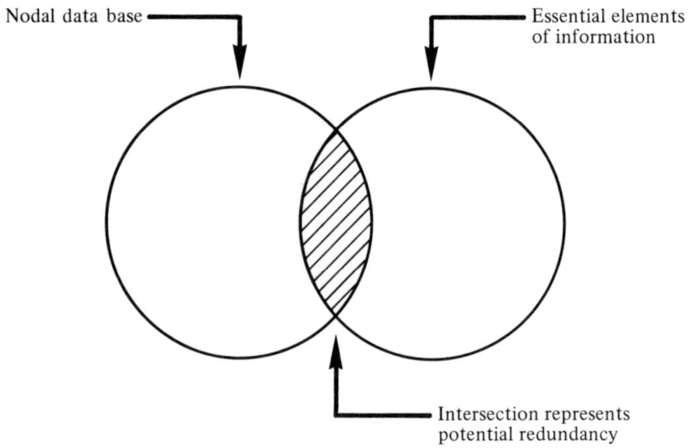

Figure 9-5. Nodal data redundancy.

requirements. Redundancy is anticipated when the intersection of these two data bases is not null (see Figure 9-5).

To support this bifurcated data model adequately, it is proposed that the network processor drive the data base processor to maintain and manipulate the network data base using the local data base information when necessary. Thus, the currency of nodal MEI is network-determined.

Current research indicates that transmittal of data base processing programs to the data site followed by transmission of the retrieval/processing result is more economical than transmission of unprocessed data to a processing program.[4,5] Taking this result to the logical extreme, the authors add the restriction that query requests on the MEI be handled identically (compatibly) by all nodes. Conceptually this approach results in a network-compatible data base management system (see Figure 9-6). In practice it is anticipated that many of these logical processors will map to one physical processor.

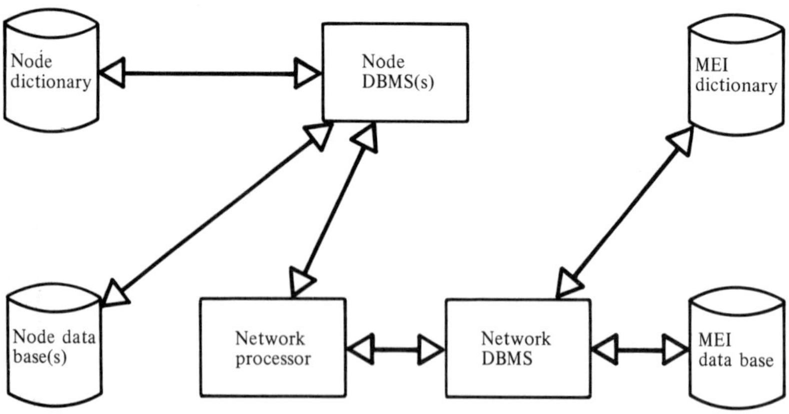

Figure 9-6. Node data base model.

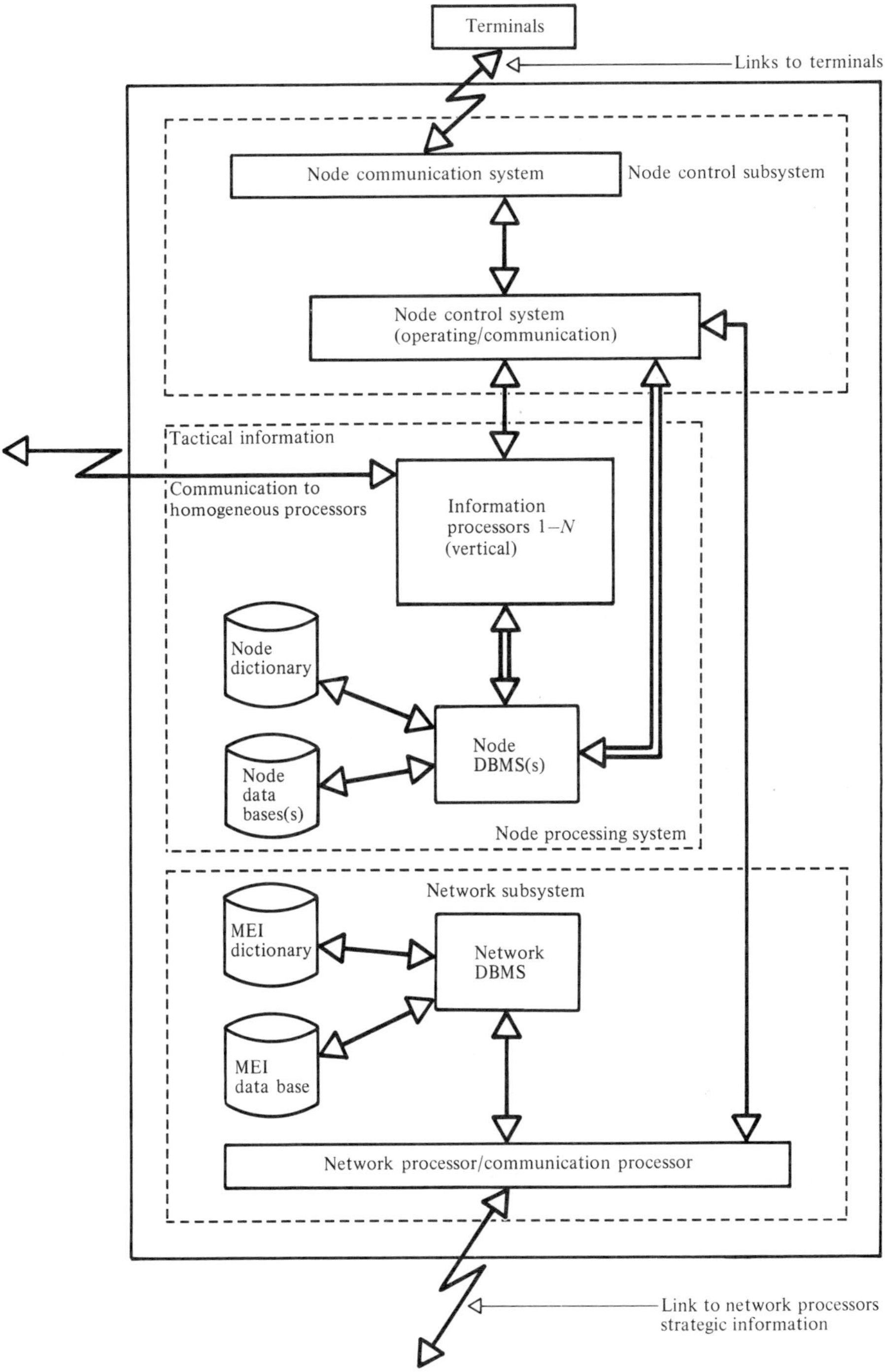

Figure 9-7. Model node.

The final node model or paradigm can be described in terms of three subsystems: the network subsystem, node processing subsystem, and node control subsystem. The model node is depicted in Figure 9-7.

MINIMUM ESSENTIAL INFORMATION

The concept of minimum essential information is derived from the military concept of essential elements of information. Historically, military commanders and staffs have identified a set of information items as critical to their decision-making processes within a conflict situation. This set varied from situation to situation, but current military thought has now evolved sufficiently to conclude that a universal set of essential information or essential elements of information exists. The universal set is conceived to fulfill the information needs of the tactical decision-makers.[6] This set will be the information base for the Army's tactical distributed processing system, execution control, and subordinate system (ECS2) for use on the battlefield.

This concept assumes the existence of a set of critical information which is needed by top management to reduce uncertainty. Management has to have access to these critical data in a timely fashion, be assured of their integrity, and be able to use them easily to make good decisions. In order to achieve these goals within a distributed system, we will further restrain the model to allow only a minimal set of essential information to be transmitted between network processors (strategic system). The minimum essential information (MEI) is the union of the pairwise intersections of the information needed by each of the model decision-makers to make tactical decisions (internal information) plus information from the surrounding environment (external information) needed only by strategic decision-makers. Some internal information will appear both as nodal data and in the MEI set; the level of aggregation and form may vary depending on its locations. The entire MEI is conceived to exist at each network node; each node generates a portion of the MEI and shares this portion with all other nodes. Ascertaining the minimum set of essential information will require high-level management direction and encouragement. A method of selecting and maintaining a viable MEI will be discussed in a later section of this chapter.

SYSTEM LIFE CYCLE MANAGEMENT

To manage any complex system, whether it be hardware/software/data or an integral combination of these elements, requires an effective methodology which addresses the changing issues over the system's life cycle. This section proposes a method for use in system life cycle management in a geographically distributed environment. It can be used with new subsystems or for upgrading existing subsystems.

System life cycle management can be defined as those activities necessary to plan, organize, and control major corporate resources, i.e. personnel, money, and time, to ensure efficient system matriculation throughout its life cycle.[7] The four major phases in this cycle are conceptual, validation, full-scale development, and production/maintenance. This section emphasizes the first phase because of its critical nature to the successful progression through the other phases.

Five major functions must be performed during the system life cycle: concept development, system development, education, logistics management, and testing. The concept development function consists of specification of the general system requirements, objectives, and, to some extent, organization for the future (or revised) system. This function involves close and effective communication with both the user community and the system development team.

The system development function consists of:

1. Preparation of general specifications which reflect user needs and desires
2. Preparation of technical specifications which reflect system constants and parameters
3. Preparation of a cost/benefit analysis delineated by need, desire, and the generality/flexibility trade-offs reflected in the technical specification
4. Development, coordination, and maintenance of schedules required to produce the system, e.g. critical path analysis
5. Negotiation and administration of all contracts consummated with suppliers and participants in the project effort
6. Maintenance of estimated versus actual cost/time comparisons

The education function consists of the identification of requisite skills for system use and the delineation of the impact on corporate resources. Programs to educate concerned individuals in both of these areas must be developed and implemented.

The system test function consists of the development and conduct of appropriate testing procedures to ensure that the system meets its specification.

The conceptual phase is initiated when a perceived and expressed need or desire for system improvement is present. This need/desire evolves through a well-structured definitional process in the conceptual phase. A well-structured approach to defining and documenting what someone thinks is to recognize that the person's need/desire can aid his thought process and, thus, his understanding of the problem. It also is a substantial improvement over verbal and unstructured problem statement/solutions as the method increases the integrity of communication and the information versus noise ratio within the organization.[8] From Cleland's work,[9] the following activities have been included in this phase:

1. Investigation. This activity involves the problem definition, technical specification of system requirements, economic feasibility, and environmental impact analysis. Also included is the study of alternate ways of accomplishing system objectives, human and nonhuman resources required to support the system, and delineation of interfaces to other systems.

2. System formulation. This activity involves the definition of initial system designs by function specification of interfaces to other systems, establishment of the system organization, and specification of subsystems and their interface protocol.

These two activities may be accomplished in sequence and repeatedly if one activity requires further detailing of the other (see Figure 9-8):

1. Requirement documentation. This activity involves the formal specification of the system within a documentation format which will allow a prototype model to be built if necessary. A team effort by the concept developer and the system developer is necessary for this phase and the next.
2. System development plan. This activity involves a specification of resources necessary to develop the system or a prototype of it. It also provides a point at which the viability of the operational and technical potential can be judged. The system education manager and logician should be included in this activity. The system development plan is the responsibility of the system developer but must be coordinated with individuals responsible for the four other functions. The plan should include analysis of technical options, development, testing, implementation, production, education and logistics support, and life cycle plans for the remaining life cycle phases.

The logician should provide support requirements and potential difficulties in terms of current and proposed logistic procedure so that this high-level design and all requirements of it can meet the requirements of, for example, portability and security.

The educational planning commences in this phase and continues through the entire life cycle of the system in varying levels of intensity. The educational manager has the responsibility to ascertain system design features which will contribute negatively to human performance. Human factor engineering should have an important influence on system design. Planning at this stage for education should also result in efficient progression through all phases.

The second phase of the system life cycle is the validation phase. This phase involves the creation of prototype modules and perhaps a system for use in effectiveness and efficiency evaluation. A second activity is modification using the test results (see Figure 9-9). This activity should result in the creation by concept and system development teams of a formal system specification document(s) which includes a recommended best technical approach based upon testing results, cost/benefit analysis, trade-off analysis, e.g. simplicity versus flexibility, and a cost/time analysis of technical approaches, human factors, logistical support, and time constraints. The supporting analysis should be documented, preferably in tabular form.

The third phase is the full-scale development phase (see Figure 9-10). This

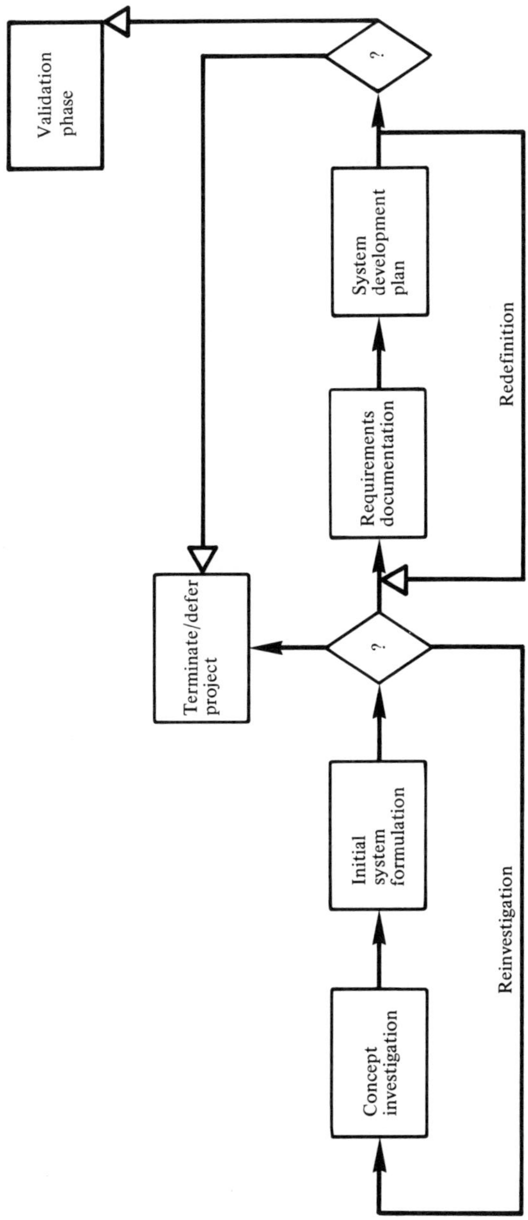

Figure 9-8. Conceptual phase of the system life cycle.

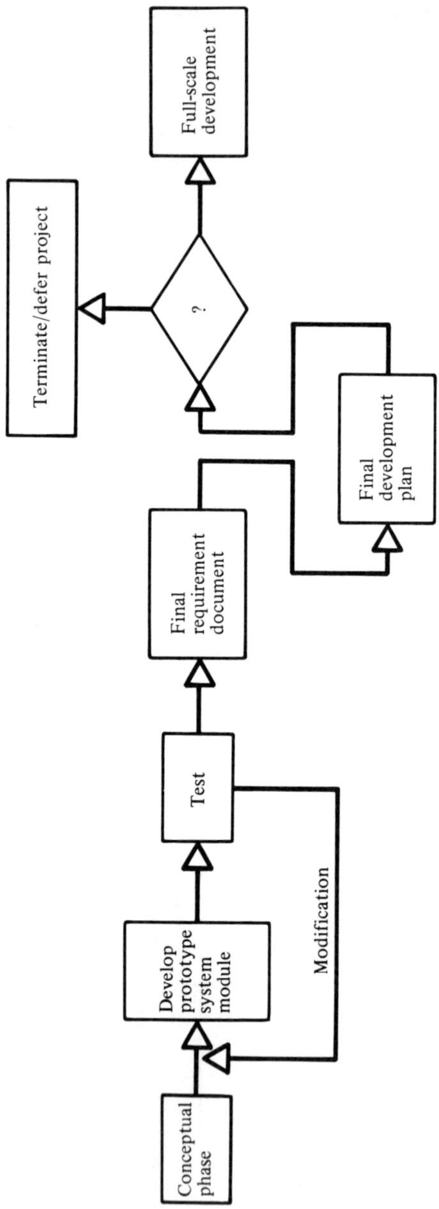

Figure 9-9. Validation phase of the system life cycle.

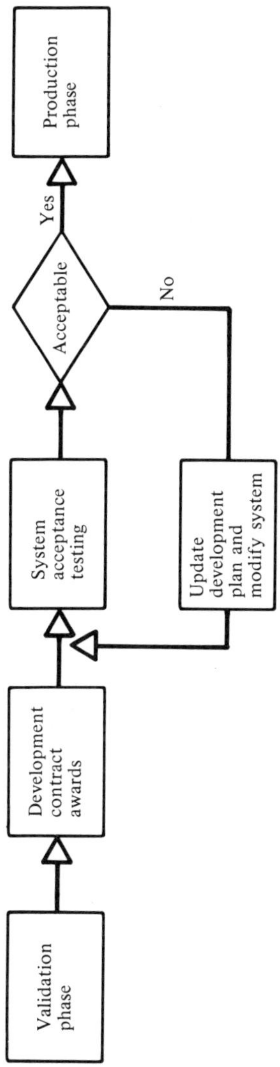

Figure 9-10. Full-scale development.

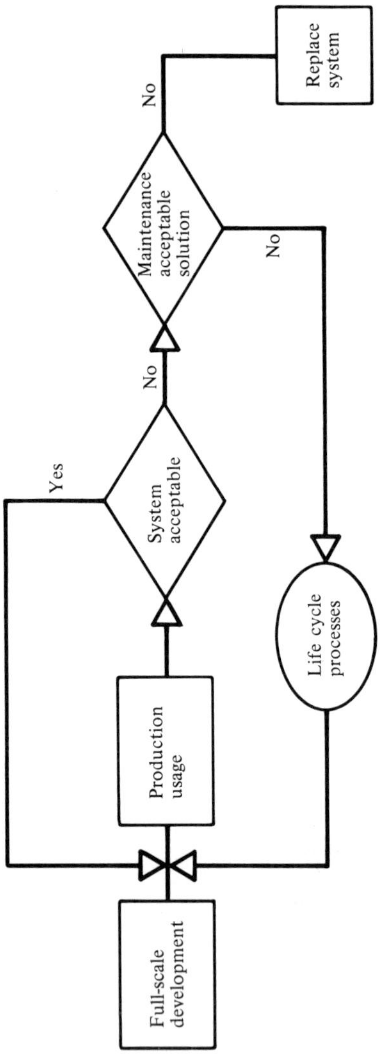

Figure 9-11. Production and operation phase of the system life cycle.

phase is initiated with the letting of a contract for system development (even in-house). It is the responsibility of the life cycle team to develop an acceptance schedule and test for the system and to negotiate with the contractor any changes which need to be made to the system.

The final phase is the production and operation phase which occurs after the system is procured, accepted, and installed (see Figure 9-11). Maintenance occurs during this phase, and such changes should be handled as carefully and as formally as those for the original system specification. Maintenance cost traditionally has amounted to as much as 70 per cent. of the total system cost.[10]

The system life cycle management strategy advocated herein is a well-organized method grounded on the written specification. It has the potential of providing management with the checkpoints and the information necessary to guide the development of systems which solve complex problems in a cost-effective manner. The strategy encourages coordination and communication among those units which are responsible for research and development, logistics, production, and education. Four definable benefits are:

1. Uncertainty is reduced. Generally systems are becoming larger and more complex. The selection and acquisition of the components which comprise the system assemblage is thus a difficult task, the decisions of which must be remade as new concepts and products are interspersed into the marketplace.
2. Objectives are the focal point. A good plan for system development serves to focus the organization's objectives as well as the system's objectives.
3. System control is improved. Points at which system decisions must be made are provided by this method.
4. Economy is enhanced. This method ensures that interacting and impacted systems are considered, and thus the cost of incoherence is reduced.[11]

MANAGEMENT ISSUES

This section of the chapter has the primary purpose of raising issues which impact management decision-making in a geographically distributed environment and are unique to that environment. Within that scope we propose two additional strategies for use within the model network: a partitioning of data and a partitioning of responsibility/authority. These two strategies further simplify the extremely complex problems of managing a geographically distributed network. Both contributed strongly to the effectiveness of the network, i.e. performance, resilience, security; the second contributes also to the effectiveness of management interaction and the motivation of nodal managers.

The organization's environment is conceptualized as a three-dimensional matrix; along the axes are represented definable organizational decision-making levels, management function, and the information (data) created/processed/required by the decision-making levels.[12] This matrix is depicted in Figure 9-12. The major management functions are planning, organizing, staffing, and controlling.

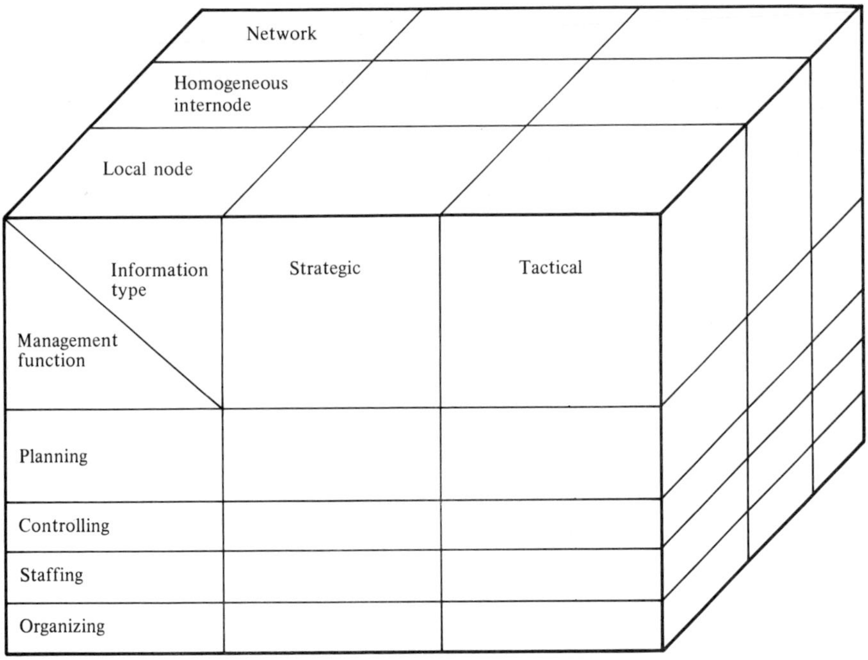

Figure 9-12. A structure view of management authority.

Sanders states: '. . . the success of any business is determined by how well its executives perform these activities (management functions). And how well these functions are carried out is dependent, in part, upon how well these information needs of managers are met.'

The partitioning of information to reflect this matrix creates three sets of data: strategic network, previously called the minimum essential information (MEI); the local node data (tactical and strategic); and the data transferred between homogeneous nodes for tactical purposes. The partitioning of responsibility and the incumbent authority for the management functions are allocated parallel to the subsetting of the data.

Minimum Essential Information

This concept assumes that a set of critical information is required by top management to reduce the uncertainty of strategic decision-making. The model network rests the authority for this data and all factors which impact it with network (central-high level) management. The nodal managers have responsibility and authority for a subset of data, the data control procedures, and management factors which impact that subset of data. Two nodal managers with homogeneous nodes may communicate tactical information. Since the nodes are homogeneous, the data formats will be compatible and minimal management communication is required to establish procedures; this management function is left to the nodal managers involved. The MEI set can be determined by forming the union of the intersections to the data entities needed by each nodal manager to make tactical decisions; in addition, strategic decision-makers may need other entities, especially those relating to the global external environment. Frequently decision-makers think that they use much more information than in reality they do use to make strategic decisions. Thus, ascertaining the minimum set of essential information will require direction and encouragement from a high management level. The U.S. Army currently has limited its essential information to 121 entities in the automated battlefield decision support system (ECS2).

This minimum set of essential information will exist at each node within the network. Each node will generate or originate a subset of the MEI information which will be shared with other nodes under network control. The existence of the MEI at each network node provides backup and network resiliency; it also adds location flexibility to top management and makes strategic information available to all tactical decision-makers.

As the network grows in levels, e.g. through the conglomeration process, the MEI for each subnet can be aggregated, as the tactical information was, to form hierarchies of MEI. At this juncture, as with multiple battlefield commanders, the subnet MEIs (SMEIs) may vary slightly from one another to accommodate management style (see Figure 9-13).

The initial step in ascertaining the MEI is to establish a data dictionary of all corporate data items, their relationships to one another, a semantic profile of each, and storage representations. Information required from external sources should also be similarly codified.

The second step is to eliminate syntactic and semantic redundancy. Following this step, the union of the pairwise intersections of nodal information will form the initial basis for the MEI. Examination of the corporate objective and associated problem areas by the strategic decision-makers will allow the delineation of additional entities necessary to effect good decisions.[13] Strategic problems are generally unstructured, one of a kind, and require data to assess the future. Such information includes competitor profiles, future technology, economic indicators, and market structures. These data often contain more noise (are less certain) and as such may have to contain accuracy/integrity indicators.

The final step to make such a concept really work within an organization is to develop a corporate information policy. Recognition of information as one major corporate asset which must be controlled, protected, and used judiciously is indicated by a clear and comprehensive statement of information policy. Such a policy should be designed to ensure that the MEI remains standard throughout the organization, both in syntax and in semantics. The policy must be rigid enough to enforce consistency and yet sufficiently flexible to accommodate changing environments and management styles.

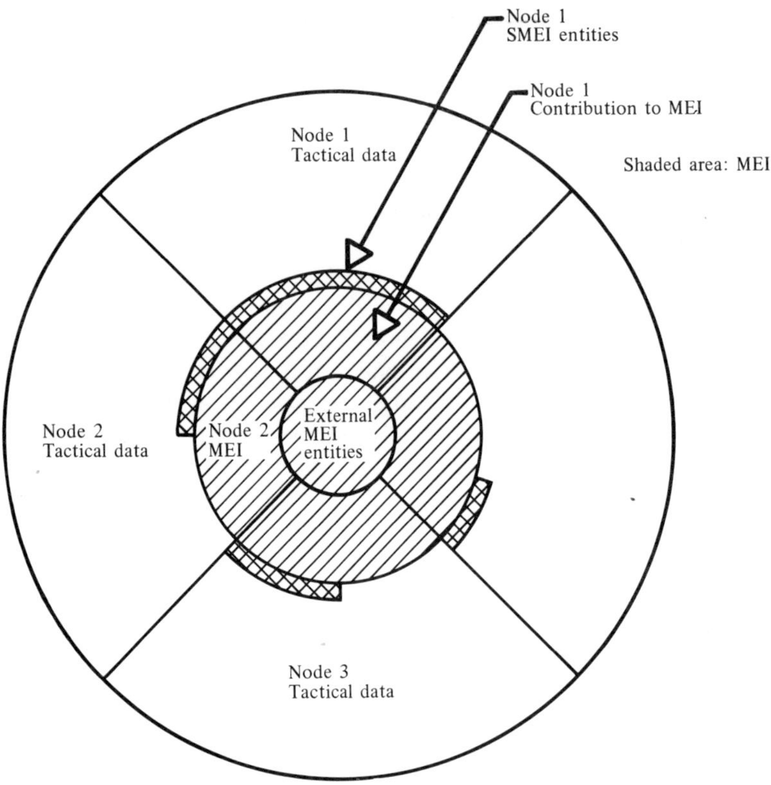

Figure 9-13. Network partitioning of data.

Partitioned Management

The key to successful management is '. . . that all resource planning and ongoing operations are based on formal goals which demand "excellence", not adequacy,' so notes Starita[14] while presenting the successes achieved by the Bank of Montreal in their management of a large multivendor environment. It is a sound philosophy but one that is not unique to computing and in fact is the rule in almost all successful business. Establishing a sound management philosophy is a necessity; but providing the organization structure, the management principles, disciplines, policies, and tools is essential and entails a significantly larger effort than establishing the philosophy.

This section addresses the structures, principles, disciplines, and tools necessary to manage a geographically distributed processing system, and merges them with the problem resolutions previously discussed. In viewing network management, Cotton[15] concentrates on 'managing organization' rather than the 'sponsoring organization' and notes, '. . . they may be the same and if the sponsoring organization really wants the network to succeed, it is better that they be the same.' This concept is really adaptable to distributed systems where the organization is composed of multiple independent divisions and where their information processing operations require integration to satisfy corporate needs. Grobenstein and Uhlig[16] provide a method for network management built around a wholesale/retail concept. This concept is also readily adaptable to distributed processing where the member nodes provide vertical (retail) information processing, and the integration of that processing constitutes the corporate horizontal (wholesale) information processing functions. The approach taken to network management is based on the following two premises:

1. When node managers lose local control and become dependent on externally controlled node or network facilities, they lose control of and, therefore, responsibility for efficient and effective local and network shared processing.
2. A network management structure is needed to develop and maintain policies and standards for network operations and performance and effective management controls based upon levels of autonomy to assure that the network functions as an integral corporate entity.

The elements that comprise this partitioned approach are:

1. Local data processing management staffs responsible for node (vertical) functions and its slice of the corporate processing responsibilities.
2. A corporate-level regulatory committee (steering group) made up of node and corporate staff members responsible for establishing the corporate processing goals, policies, standards, and long-range data processing planning, with emphasis placed on corporate-oriented network use and involvement.
3. Corporate level management of network systems. The management and organization of the information processing system must be such that management can control the system and not allow the system to control management. Also, the nature and characteristics of the distributed processing system do not define the corporate organization, but the corporate organization defines the processing environment.[12]

The responsibility and appropriate incumbent authority within a geographically distributed system may be centralized, decentralized, or partitioned. Centralized control is essential if the distributed system supports cross-departmental functions or if one function is supported by multiple nodes.[17] It also simplifies standardization, it inhibits incoherence by controlling the network growth process, and it provides a richer career path environment for all network personnel. In contrast, the decentralized control puts the responsibility and authority for action closer to the nodal end user of the system; it tends, thus, to make the system and personnel more responsive to the nodal end user; it creates nodal management positions which are attractive to good managers because of the responsibility/authority level; and, thus, it provides an environment with more growth potential for the people. Decentralization thus provides, at the node, more of the factors important to data processing professions as they evaluate positions.[18]

A compromise between these two extremes is advocated for use within the paradigm network. The strategic information, MEI, and associated hardware, software, and personnel would be fully controlled by a centralized high-level network management team. Responsibility/authority for nodal information associated hardware, software, and personnel would be delegated to the nodal managers. Decisions involving MEI entities generated and controlled by a nodal manager would be indirectly managed by the network manager; i.e. the network copy of the entity, its integrity, security, and currency would be under network control (see Figure 9-14).

If all the problems of management, even in the nodal network, could be handled neatly within the proposed scheme, the problem would be simpler than in reality it is. Thus, the rest of the chapter addresses a number of management areas and raises issues of concern to those involved in a planned, evolving, or existing geographically distributed network.

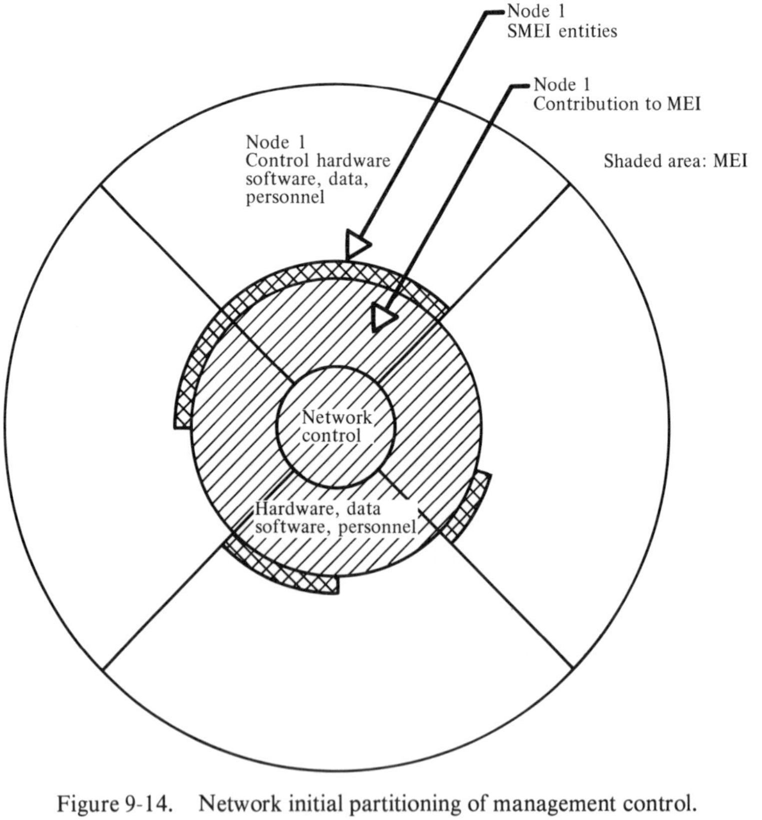

Figure 9-14. Network initial partitioning of management control.

- Amount of internodal, interfunctional access
- Desired level of system resiliency and reliability
- Stability of organization's structure
- Volatility of user requirements
- Impact of future technology
- Desired level for standards control, data control, project management, operational control, maintenance
- Intensiveness of interaction between corporate division members

Figure 9-15. Key factors in partitioning of authority.

- Data control should be distributed with the data.
- Generalized information policy and standards increase value of data assets, performance maintenance, security, backup, resiliency, and nodal management activity.
- Incoherency will develop unless checked by standards and policy.
- Heterogeneous systems require local systems programming staffs.
- Each node should have but one point of control in corporate structure.
- Nodal management activities will vary depending on, for example, work composition, data partitioning, and system structure and performance.

Figure 9-16. Guidelines for partitioning management.

The degree of corporate control is dependent on a number of key considerations given in Figure 9-15.[19] The management disciplines that these impact are processing management, performance management, problem management, change management, capacity management, exigency management, security, integrity and auditing management, and accountability management.[20] Once the implications of the key considerations upon these management disciplines have been determined, the decomposition of corporate activities can be effected. Some general guidelines are given in Figure 9-16. The best perspective that management can take as decisions on the partitioning of authority are considered is that management should establish the objective; technology should never dictate corporate objectives.

Standardization

One curious paradox of the computing industry is that standardization efforts occupy a good deal of professional time and yet few standards have been accepted and are practiced industry-wide. To support this thesis, we turn to Gruenberger's[21] list of successful standards (see Figure 9-17).

It is unrealistic to expect great advances in standardization in the near future. However, as Shepherd[22] notes: '. . . distributed processing must not become an excuse for uncontrolled proliferation of incompatible hardware and software if serious problems are to be avoided.' Within an organization, management must be aware of the incoherency problems stemming from the use of system nonstandard data, hardware, and software.

In addition to recommending the network compatible nodes of the model and the establishment of the MEI, standardization efforts in data representation, system security, and system support services are advocated.

Data standardization reduces the costs associated with data translation and

- Punch card dimensions
- Width of magnetic tape
- Use of the diamond for the flowchart decision symbol (it took 22 years to set this standard)
- FORTRAN and COBOL
- Keyboard positions for the English letters

Figure 9-17. Successful standardization efforts. (From Gruenberger.[2])

reduces the complexity of system and human communication schemes. The establishment of a uniform security management policy and program reduces the complexity introduced by the multivendor, hardware, heterogeneous software, and distributed management control present in most geographically distributed systems.

System support services includes such management concerns as vendor interaction, system maintenance, and emulation/simulation packages required for backup and compatibility. The more standardization generally reduces the number of vendors involved and, thus, decreases the possibilities of having to mediate between vendors to pinpoint component malfunctions. It also reduces the time that management must spend interacting with vendors and gives the organization a larger power base with which to negotiate.

System (data/personnel/hardware/software) performance is enhanced as the number of heterogeneous components is reduced. Defining overall acceptable system performance criteria, e.g. cost and performance, can more easily be accomplished and measured if the complexity introduced by nonstandard components is reduced. Within the model, however, management can measure whether the nodes are meeting their local and vertical (stove-pipe) processing requirements independent of measurement of the effectiveness of horizontal (network) processing performance.

In summary, distributed systems do not require standard compatible components but their absence complicates the management function in the following areas:

1. Data representation and control
2. Data and system security
3. Measuring and improving system performance
4. System backup and recovery planning
5. Multivendor interaction

The concern, when an effort to standardize is effected, is the rigidity that such efforts may impose upon an organization which must respond to changing technology.

Data Management

Data management distills to the issue of control and administration. The authority for the establishment of data control policy, as with most authority within a geographically distributed system, may be centralized, decentralized, or partitioned.

Lorin[19] describes six factors which must be considered when authority for data management is established:

1. Volatility of applications software
2. Volatility of hardware and system software
3. Program development, resource availability, and location
4. Volatility of network configuration
5. Nodal management skill availability
6. Heterogeneity of the current network

Data control policy is, thus, affected by system structure, application autonomy, and personnel management philosophy.

Partitioned data control authority is advocated within the model network as a compromise between the centralized and decentralized approaches. Basic to the model is sharing the MEI throughout the network. Effective sharing of the generation and maintenance of the MEI includes the issues of control of all hardware, software, protocols, data formats, translation algorithms, maintenance schedules, backup responsibility, and data integrity. Responsibility and authority for these data should be centralized at the highest level. Control would generally be inflexible in its accommodation of local environments and managerial styles. The degree of local control would have to be ascertained, based upon the necessity for nodal interaction, but as much nodal responsibility/authority as possible is encouraged.

Security Management

A security management policy for a geographically distributed system will depend on the cost to the organization of security breaches. The factors involved vary little from those considered when remote terminals are added to a central facility. The critical issue is the cognizance and accessment of the security breach costs for all nodes within the network.

Network security can be divided into three categories: physical security, administrative control, and computer system and network security. Physical security is generally still the most effective measure against deliberate attempts to breach security.[23] Administrative control includes those procedures utilized to ensure correct system operation; included are personnel screening procedures, programming and operations practices, duty assignment schedules, and periodic auditing. Computer and network security is designed to control and monitor access to programs and data by unauthorized users. Included in this last category are data encryption techniques, user identification schemes, data security profiles, and audit trails.

Winkler and Donner[24] describe the types of attacks on data security in four categories as unauthorized disclosure, modification, restriction, or destruction. Unauthorized disclosure occurs through exposure, the accidental disclosure of information to unauthorized persons, or through interception, the deliberate seizure of data by unauthorized persons. Unauthorized modification occurs through alteration, the accidental change of data, or through deception, the deliberate change of data. Unauthorized restriction occurs through interruption, the accidental denial of proper access, or through disruption, the deliberate denial of proper access. Unauthorized destruction occurs through erasure, the accidental expunging of data, or through elimination, the deliberate expunging of data.

Until recently, security was overlooked by vendors of hardware/software.[25] With the advent of distributed processing, this lack of security features has led to acute problems. At the Computer Security and Privacy Symposium in Phoenix, April 1979, Edward H. Coughan said: 'We're always in a catch up mode.' Robert E. Kukrall of Honeywell Information Systems echoed the same feeling: 'The minicomputer explosion and the geographic distribution of networks and terminal-based systems, also contribute to the problem of designing and implementing effective controls. Physical surveillance is difficult, if not impossible, in such an operating environment, and indicates an increasing need for controls built into the application.'[26]

Security issues are usually not addressed as an integral area of concern by the system project manager. Usually no positive mechanism/program is present to ensure that automation security parameters are identified early in the system's life cycle. A prime example of this situation is the Department of the Army where security is particularly pressing. However, when systems are being developed, normally the requirement documents only state that the provisions of Army regulation 380-380 will be met. From this, each system developer then 'meets' these provisions in his own way. Additionally, no established measure is available to determine whether in reality these provisions have been met.[27]

Security management starts with the development of a corporate security policy formulated by analyzing corporate needs, regulatory and legal constraints, and possible threats. Once established, this policy outlines the security management structure, management responsibility and authority, and general standards for the network. This policy must be refined, by each lower level down to the nodal level, into security programs utilizing the appropriate network security controls.

The policies of a computer installation depend not only on the corporate-directed policy but also on the existing hardware and software. For example, a corporate policy might not be practical if there is no division level method to support it.[28] The security policy is further complicated when dealing in a heterogeneous network, both in hardware and processing, that requires a system high-security level enforced from system concept development to system implementation and operation.

The primary corporate decision concerning security is where to establish security control. Centralized or decentralized, Wood[28] suggests that a factor for determining which policy to follow concerns the concept of ownership and administration of the data bases. The owner of a data base is considered to be the activity responsible for creating the data. In the absence of a clearly defined owner for a data base, the DBA or security administrator can be considered the owner and, thus, responsible for security, integrity, and privacy of the data.

Five major components are present in a good security policy: formal security requirements, security analysis, security manager(s), security testing, and security certification. In the concept and development phases of the system life cycle, the possible threats should be clarified and the cost of security measured, and these results used to determine the level of security present in a system. A security manager should be made a part of the project management team to design and verify system security. Security should be tested periodically during the entire life cycle of a system. For highly sensitive systems, verification of a system security through deliberate penetration efforts by an uninvolved person or team is good insurance.

Network Resilience and Performance

Management of a network involves the challenge of establishing high system resilience while maintaining acceptable-to-good system performance under current tight budget constraints.

It must be determined what good system performance is for each of the nodal functions and for the network functions. In establishing this standard, performance can be divided into two areas: internal performance and external performance. Internal performance refers to the efficiency of the system components, e.g. bit transfer rate and operating system overhead. External performance refers to the results of the service.

At least three general categories for system measurement must be considered when establishing performance guidelines for a network: psychological, throughput, and cost/benefit. The psychological guidelines reflect the network performance as perceived by the user, e.g. acceptability and uniformity of response time and learning required to use the system. Throughput is the ratio of work/unit time and measures user access/utilization of the system. Cost/benefit is a measure of the quality of the other two factors in fiscal terms.[15]

Deviations of performance from accepted norms must be monitored and receive management response if the system is to remain acceptable to the users. The paradigm system is structured such that performance measures can be established in three areas which minimally impact each other. They are network MEI system, nodal local performance, and internodal performance between homogeneous/compatible nodes.

A resilient network is one with the following four major attributes:

1. It is able to detect and recover from a given maximum number of errors.

2. It is reliable to a sufficiently high degree that the user can ignore the possibility of service failure.
3. If the service provides perfect detection and recovery from n errors, error $n + 1$ is not catastrophic; a best effort is made to continue service.
4. The abuse of service by one user should have a negligible effect on other users of the service.[29]

Resilience is introduced primarily through standardization and redundancy. Standardization provides nodal backup possibility. Redundant data and software decrease the probability of losing processing capability either temporarily or permanently. Redundancy can be costly both in terms of storage and in terms of data transmission and update time. A resiliency criterion can be developed for the hardware by ascertaining each subsystem component's mean time to failure and mean time to repair. When a node fails, that failure must be detected;[30] the network must then respond to user service needs in as user-transparent a manner as possible. Finally, the node must be reintegrated into the system. Rothnie and Goodman[8] espouse a persistent communication method which is designed such that delivery of a message to a node is guaranteed even if the receiver is down when the message is sent and the sender is down when the receiver recovers. Another method easily used in the model network involves prespecification of a nodal backup(s) through redundancy. The node recovers by using the backup for updating when the node is fully recuperated; it is reintegrated into the system.[31] It is beyond the scope of this chapter to outline these methods and to develop backup and redundancy to assure a level of resilience; the reader is referred to Akins's report[31] for details.

Within the model network, resiliency and performance are partitioned generally as the data are partitioned. Complete redundancy occurs for the MEI; redundancy for a nodal function is envisioned as the responsibility of the nodal managers.

Maintenance

Adequate maintenance for software and hardware within a geographically distributed network is a crucial element which must be considered carefully during all phases of the life cycle, especially design and development. Some of the factors which must be considered are system maintenance, personnel and training, support and test equipment, replacement subsystems and parts, transportation and handling, facilities, manuals, support funds, and system management information.[32]

Maintenance will be considered from the hardware and the software perspective within the model network, as difference maintenance methodologies are advocated.

Hardware maintenance may be essentially centralized or essentially decentralized; examples of each scheme are in practice today, e.g. IBM, and the

	Centralized	Decentralized
Advantages:	Economy of scale (test and support equipment) Fewer and concentrated technicians Reduction of replacement inventory Efficiency of management	More responsive to user Faster response and more resilient effect in network
Disadvantages:	Slower response and less resilient Less responsive to user	Proliferation of personnel and equipment Distributed inventory and generally larger inventory More costly

Figure 9-18. Hardware maintenance evaluation.

U.S. Army. Except for the compatibility of the network interface, no imposed homogeneity of hardware is imposed on the system; therefore, each node should retain as much hardware maintenance capability and autonomy as possible (see Figure 9-18).

Software maintenance is an extremely costly and critical support problem. A major result of a recent study[33] of Army software systems was '... unless the management problems are corrected and the technical problems brought under control, it is doubtful that the Army can provide adequate support to its battlefield automated system in wartime or crisis situations.'[20] This report also cited many problems discovered in current Army software maintenance. These problems, which are not unique to an Army battlefield system, are summarized in Figure 9-19.

After study of the problems and the centralized versus decentralized approaches, a hybrid approach to software maintenance within the model network is advocated. Network software, common nodal functional software, and internodal communication software should be centrally developed and maintained. Unique functional node software should be maintained at the node. However, systems should be designed for maintenance and tailoring. For example, within a structured modular network, system modules should be able to be appended to handle the unique node needs. However, existing modules should be changed at the node only under very inflexible guidelines. Rationalizations for

- Lack of procedures, guidelines, and standards for maintenance, resulting in implementations which vary from node to node
- Lack of planning for later maintenance by system developers, lack of documentation, and inadequate personnel training, making maintenance difficult and costly.
- Application of inappropriate hardware maintenance concepts to software maintenance
- Upgrading of noncompliant systems to meet standards
- Continuing system evolution with a lack of coordination
- Inadequate response to problems by central system development and maintenance team
- Lack of coordination of systems development which must function together at some nodes
- Failure to focus on crisis support (e.g. hospital and air traffic control systems)

Figure 9-19. Software maintenance problems: a decentralized approach.

this hybrid approach include:

1. Software changes can be easily transmitted electronically.
2. Fewer software technicians are required (save on the systems which are centrally maintained).
3. Management control is better.
4. Node control of unique node systems is possible.
5. Node software technicians can detect and document errors, apply change patches, install changes, and upgrade systems.

This approach will work effectively only if systems are designed to be easily maintained.

CONCLUSION

The full benefits of geographically distributed processing systems are reaped only when the systems are well managed. The complexity or potential complexity of these systems as they are created, especially when they are created by interconnection of existing systems, requires a realignment of management structure and philosophy. This chapter has proposed a new perspective on this problem by commencing with a partitioning of organization information needs into two categories, strategic (planning and unstructured decision-making) and tactical (routine processing and structured decision-making). A model or paradigm network is then established to support this information-partitioning, Management authority/ responsibility is similarly partitioned with the particular management structure dependent on a number of factors.

This perspective on management was inspired by current U.S. Army proposals for an automated battlefield decision support system (ECS2).

REFERENCES

1. Hoxie, G. H., and Shea, D. M.: Ten hot buttons facing management. *Infosystems*, **1977**, 60–100, September 1977.
2. Anderson, G. H. and Jensen, E. D.: Computer interconnection structures: taxonomy, characteristics, and examples. *Computing Surveys*, **7**, No. 4, 197–213, December 1975.
3. Tsichritzis, D. and Lochovsky, P.: *Data Base Management Systems*. Academic Press, New York, 1977.

3a. Dijkstra, E. W.: Notes on structured programming, in *Structural Programming*. APIC Studies in Data Processing, No. 8. Academic Press, New York, 1972.

4. Hevner, A. R. and Yao, S. B.: *Query Optimization in Distributed Database Systems*. Private communication, 1980.
5. Unger, E. A., Fisher, P. S. and Slonim, J.: Evolving to a Distributed Data Base Environment. *Computer Communications*, **5**, No. 1, pp. 17–22, 1982.
6. *Technical Interface Concept (TIC) on the Corps Battlefield: E-Systems*. Greenville Division, November 30, 1979 and March 14, 1980.

7. Army: *Life Cycle Systems Management for Army Systems.* Department of the Army Pamphlet No. 11/25, May 1975.
8. Rothnie, J. B. and Goodman, N.: An overview of the preliminary design of SDD-1: a system for distributed data bases. *Proc. Second Berkeley Workshop on Distributed Data Management and Computer Networks*, May 1977.
9. Cleland, I. and King, Wm. R.: *Systems Analysis and Project Management.* McGraw-Hill, New York, 1975.
10. Orr, K.: Private communication, 1976.
11. Grubb, D. and Cotton, I. W.: Rating performance. In *Data Communications.* McGraw-Hill, New York, 1975.
12. Sanders, D.H.: Managing data communications. *Datamation*, **1978**, 43–47, November 1978.
13. Steiner and Miner: *Management Policy and Strategy.* Macmillan Publishing Company, New York, 1977.
14. Starita, D. I.: Managing a large multivendor operating environment. *Datamation*, **1979**, 147–152, September 1979.
15. Cotton, I. W.: *Issues in Network Management 1978.* Computer Networks: A Tutorial, 1978.
16. Grobstein, D. L. and Uhlig, R. P.: *Wholesale/Retail Specialization in Resource Sharing Networks.* Computer Networks: A Tutorial, 1978.
17. Lorie, R. A.: Distributed processing: an assessment. *IBM Systems J.*, **18**, No. 4, 1979.
18. Fitz-Enz, J.: Who is the DP professional? *Datamation*, **1978**, 125–128, September 1978.
19. Lorie, R. A.: Distributed processing: an assessment. *IBM Systems J.*, **18**, No. 4, 1979.
20. Smith, J. M.: Distributed systems management—a key to success. *Proc. COMPCOM 80*, September 1980, pp. 16–22.
21. Gruenberger, F.: Fruitcakes, nuttier than. *Datamation*, **1978**, 135–137, November 1978.
22. Shepherd, A. J.: A British example of distributed computing. *Datamation*, **1978**, 87–91, March 1978.
23. Scharf, J. D.: *Computer Network Security: An Assessment of the State of the Art.* Unpublished Master's Report, Kansas State University, 1980.
24. Winkler, S. and Lee Danner: Data security in the computer communications environment. *Computer*, February 1974.
25. Sanders, D. H. and Birkin, S.: Computers and Management in a Changing Society. McGraw-Hill, New York, 1974.
26. Myers, E.: A game of catch up. *Datamation*, **1979**, 76–79, May 1977.
27. Fifth Battlefield Automation Appraisal (BAA V), Fort Huachuca, Arizona, July 1980.
28. Rothnie, J. B. and Goodman, N.: An overview of the preliminary design of SDD-1: a system for distributed data bases. *Proc. Second Berkley Workshop on Distributed Data Management and Computer Networks*, May 1977.
29. Alsberg, P. A. and Day, J. D.: A principle for resilient sharing of distributed resources. *Proc. of the second Int. Conf. on Software Engineering*, 1976.
30. Randall, B. and Treleaven, R. W.: Reliability issues in computing systems design. *CACM*, **10**, No. 2, June 1978.
31. Akins, W. P.: Data Security and Data Independence in a Mobile Military System. Unpublished Master's Report, Kansas State University, 1979.
32. Department of the Army: *Field Manual 54-10*, April 1977.
33. Department of the Army: *Post-Deployment Software Support (PDSS) Concept Plan for Battlefield Automation Systems*, May 1980.

34. Hoffman, L. J.: Modern Methods for Computer Security and Privacy. Prentice-Hall, Englewood Cliffs, N.J., 1977.
35. Stewart, W. J., and Wecker: Network management in decnet. *Proc. COMPCON 80, Twenty-first IEEE Conf.*, September 1980, pp. 108–114.

Advances in Distributed Processing Management, Volume 2
Edited by P. S. Fisher, J. Slonim, and E. A. Unger

Chapter 10

SYSTEM RESILIENCY IN A MOBILE NETWORK

William P. Aikens
U.S. Army, Fort Huachuca, New Mexico

Elizabeth A. Unger
Department of Computer Science, Kansas State University, Manhattan, Kansas

The introduction of computer hardware components that are small, light, and capable of withstanding the battlefield environment has precipitated a remarkable number of potential applications for the military. Systems are in development to manage intelligence collection, support intelligence analysis, support command and control functions, record and disseminate radiation dosages, manage communications links, control weapons systems, account for supplies, control movements, and provide personnel data. Nearly every aspect of the functioning army has been examined for its automation potential. In addition to the hardware advances are several processing techniques that offer even greater potential to the army. These techniques include networking, distributed processing, data base management systems, and distributed data base management systems. In contrast to the immediate recognition of the hardware advantages, several of these techniques have not yet been applied to army applications. This chapter concentrates on distributed processing and its applicability to mobile military systems.

Strategic versus Tactical Systems

This chapter is concerned with tactical systems. These systems are relatively small and mobile. They support forces that are physically present on the battlefield. Strategic systems support the National Command Structure, the CIA, and other agencies. They are relatively large systems that are located in secure areas in the United States. The problems faced by strategic systems are similar to the problems faced by commercial and academic installations—problems which have been widely investigated and discussed. The problems that apply to tactical systems are currently unique to the military. Tactical systems face unusual environmental, reliability, security, and maintainability problems that have not been thoroughly investigated to date. In some cases serious feasibility issues must be resolved before tactical computer systems can be installed with confidence.

Definitions

The following definitions are used throughout this chapter:

1. *Distributed processing.* So much confusion surrounds this term that a thorough definition would merit publication. Enslow[1] has identified five components for distributed processing: a multiplicity of general-purpose resource components that can be allocated dynamically, a physical distribution of these resources through a communication network, a high-level operating system to control the distributed components, system transparency, and cooperative autonomy. This explanation is closer to a checklist than a definition. The real key to distributed processing is the autonomy component. The capability for components to cooperate and yet maintain their own identities is unique to distributed processing. Distributed processing can only be achieved in certain environments. The environments are those identified by Enslow and are based upon the degrees of hardware, data base, and control decentralization. Multiple processors or multiple computers, replicated cooperating or multiple fully cooperating control, and some scheme of distributed files, replication, or partitioning are the necessary environments to achieve distributed processing. Katzan[2] describes a distributed system as one 'in which there are several autonomous but interacting processors and/or data stores at different geographical locations.' Distributed processing then is the capability for a group of dispersed, independent, but (cooperating) components in particular environments to provide users with processing resources as required.
2. *Distributed data base management system (DDBMS).* The concept of a DDBMS is even less clear than distributed processing. Maryanski and colleagues[3] imply that a DDBMS is a generalized interface for different DBMS conventional systems. They state that a DDBMS '. . . would reside on a heterogeneous computer network with different data base systems available at various processors.' This setup may be an evolutionary step toward realization of a DDBMS, but it is not a fair definition of the DDBMS itself. A DDBMS should provide the data base management services on a system basis rather than a nodal basis. These services include the usual data definition and data manipulation capabilities of conventional systems plus the capabilities unique to a distributed system. These unique capabilities include the means to distribute data (partitioned or replicated), distribute directories, manage updating of replicated data, and rollback and recovery. These unique capabilities are the reasons why a true DDBMS is not currently practical. When they do become available, then a DDBMS will provide its services throughout the distributed system rather than managing the efforts of a collection of DBMSs located at different nodes.
3. *Network.* Anderson[4] has defined networks as being made up of a combination of computer interconnections. The interconnections are constructed

from paths and switching elements. Paths are the medium by which messages are transferred between the other system elements. Switching elements are entities which may be thought of as 'intervening intelligence' between the sender and receiver. A network is a combination of paths and switching elements.

4. *Mobile system.* A mobile system is one in which all elements of the system can be moved without external support. User areas, power sources, and all associated hardware are installed in trucks. A mobile system can operate at a variety of locations with a minimum of time required to move the system from one location to another.
5. *Tactical system.* A tactical system is a mobile system that must have the additional capabilities of cross-country movement and the ability to operate in a variety of environments. These environments include the various weather conditions that can be encountered and the fact that an enemy force is actively trying to locate and destroy the system.

Use of Computers in the Military

The following overview traces the use of computers by the military in general terms. A general framework assists in understanding the need for distributed systems and the external problems that already exist.

Several single-machine systems have been in use for some time, the most noteworthy being the Field Artillery Data Analysis Center (FADAC). FADAC provides ballistic computational support to artillery units. These single-machine systems are self-contained and are not required to interface with any other system.

Systems that have been recently installed or are about to be installed are characterized by several micro- or minicomputers that are linked together to form a single system. Examples of this configuration include the tactical operating system (TOS) and the all source analysis system (ASAS).[5–7] These systems utilize the capabilities associated with networks. Users may be geographically dispersed and may enter and leave the network of their own volition. Each of these systems performs services for a single functional area. TOS provides support for command and control while ASAS provides support to the intelligence activities.

The next logical step in the development of military computer systems is the design and installation of systems that will support more than one functional area. Current research has recognized this need. However, to date, resources are being spent in developing patchwork arrangements to tie the existing systems together. This action has not been successful. The existing systems were developed independently. Choices of hardware, software, data standards, and communication standards were all made independently. As a result it has proved difficult to tie these existing systems together. In addition, each of the functional areas is controlled by a different organization. None of these organizations is inclined to surrender some of its independence in order to achieve a truly integrated system.

This chapter uses a notional system as a basis for investigating the possibility of achieving better data security, data independence, and system resiliency in a tactical system. The system is fully integrated by functional area. It supports command and control, intelligence, and logistics simultaneously. The likelihood of such a system being developed does not depend on research or the state of the art. It does depend on the organizational politics cited previously.

POSTULATED DIVISION SYSTEM

Description of a Typical Military System

The system used is representative of several developing military computer systems. These systems include the tactical operating system (TOS), which provides command and control support; the combat service support system (CS3), which provides logistics support; and the all source analysis system (ASAS), which will provide intelligence support. Each of these systems provides its support in an independent manner. The interfaces between them are, in most cases, handled manually rather than electronically. This interface policy is partially due to security policies but principally due to uncoordinated development of the separate systems by separate elements. The model described in this chapter incorporates features of all of the existing systems. It has been developed as a paradigm from which to discuss distributed processing. The model is developed through three separate views. While not an actual system, it incorporates the general requirements for a military system at the division level.

Organizational View

The current organization of an army division has evolved over the last 15 years. Today's organization is shown in Figure 10-1. The traditional line and staff functions are annotated. The line organizations generally are the 'doers' for their respective functional areas. Their information requirements are of a flow (I/O) rather than of a processing nature. They report information to be analyzed and used to support current and future decisions and receive information based on their current or expected mission. The staff organizations are characterized as 'planners.' They receive and evaluate reports from internal and external sources and apply updates to the data bases as appropriate. They also do extensive analysis in preparing reports and orders for future operations. An explanation of the functions of each element can be found in the Appendix. This view of the organization is the official copy of the organization of reference. When changes to the organization itself are considered or applied, they are usually done based upon this view. In many cases, the staff and line organizations and functions overlap. These overlaps occur in the performance of a variety of functions. For example, elements from the G2 and G3 Division Artillery and Intelligence Battalion combine to form the Tactical Operations Center (TOC) and the Tactical Command Post (TAC CP).[8] This combination renders the organizational view nearly useless when examining information flows.

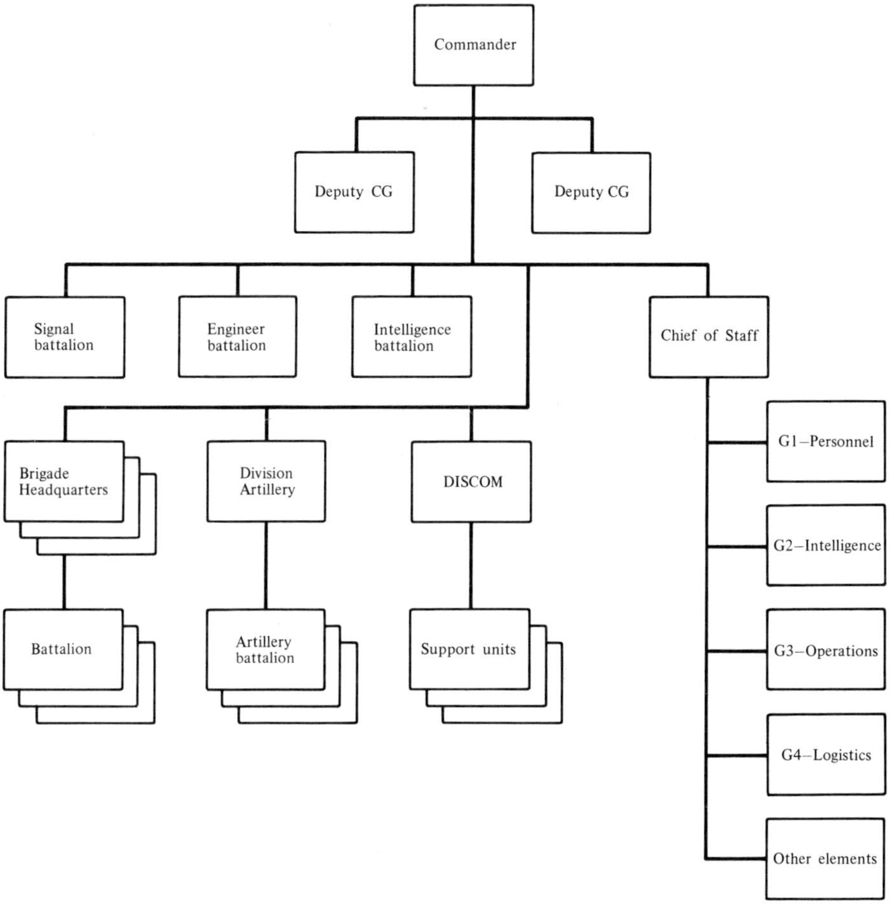

Figure 10-1. Organization of an army division.

User View

Figure 10-2 illustrates a user view of the organization within the framework of the user functions. A mapping of the current systems onto the user view is shown in Figure 10-3. The logistics system (CS3) is separate functionally and geographically. The command and control and intelligence systems share locations but their functions operate independently. This arrangement has caused or will cause a proliferation of manual interfaces. A more appropriate system is suggested next. Called the Postulated Division System (PODS), it incorporates the command and control, intelligence, and logistics functions into a single distributed system. The PODS consists of three nodes.

The JUMP node is a relatively small configuration used by the commander to control his forces. It is usually located close to the front lines. It is that portion of the PODS that provides support to the Tactical Command Post (TAC CP). Its

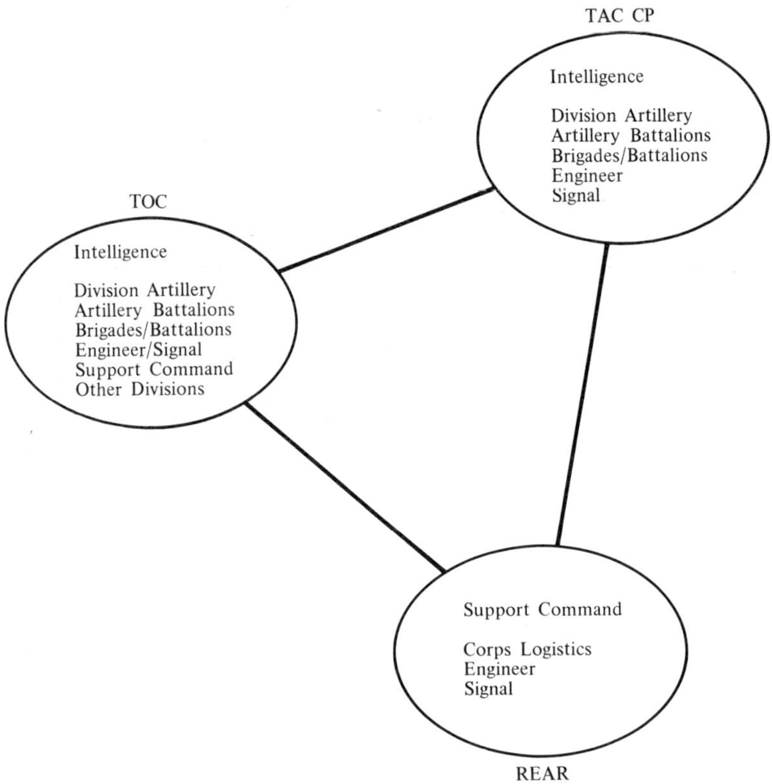

Figure 10-2. User view of the organization.

geographic location dictates a small size and high mobility. Yet the commander requires access to any information in the distributed system.

The MAIN node provides service to the division staff and other elements of the Tactical Operations Center (TOC). Its capabilities and size are both larger than the JUMP.

The REAR node provides the logistic and administrative services as a part of the distributed system. Its size and function dictate a safer location and less frequent movement.

Other entities provide information to, or receive information from, the division system. For purposes of discussion, all elements connected to the division system may be viewed as terminals from at least one of the nodes in the system. In actuality, several of these elements are networks themselves, but the simplistic view is more manageable for this chapter. One interesting aspect of this view is the restructuring or reordering of relationships when compared to the hierarchical view. Brigade headquarters and their subordinate battalions are treated as like elements by the division system. This speeds information flow but can disrupt traditional command relationships.

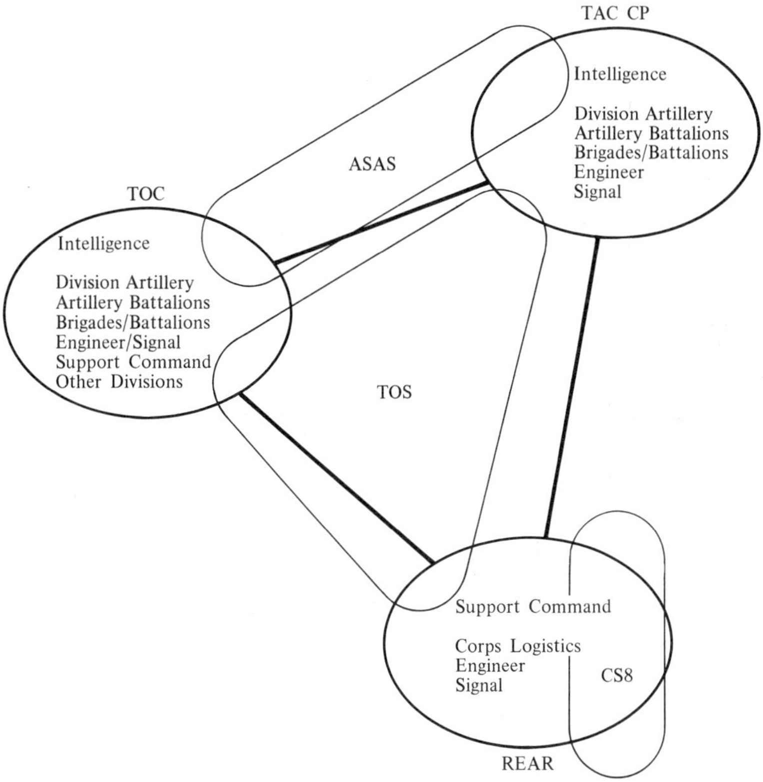

Figure 10-3. Mapping of current systems onto user view.

System View

The system as seen by a system designer is shown in Figure 10-4. The nodes have different functions and capacity and therefore are likely to be heterogeneous. The network structure is the DDC (direct, dedicated, complete) architecture of Anderson's taxonomy scheme.[4] Communication in all cases is by radio link rather than cable. Approximate geographic dispersion is indicated in Figure 10-4. These distances are very dynamic, as will be seen. Note that while a reflection of the user view does exist here, there is little that resembles the hierarchical view.

General Need for System Resiliency

The division system is entirely mobile. However, this feature indicates that the system is easily moved, not that the system operates while moving. In order to maintain continuous service, a modified leapfrog technique is used. One node (usually the JUMP) leaves the network and moves to a new location. After the JUMP returns to operation, other nodes leave the network, move and return to the network. An estimated frequency of movement is shown in Table 10-1.

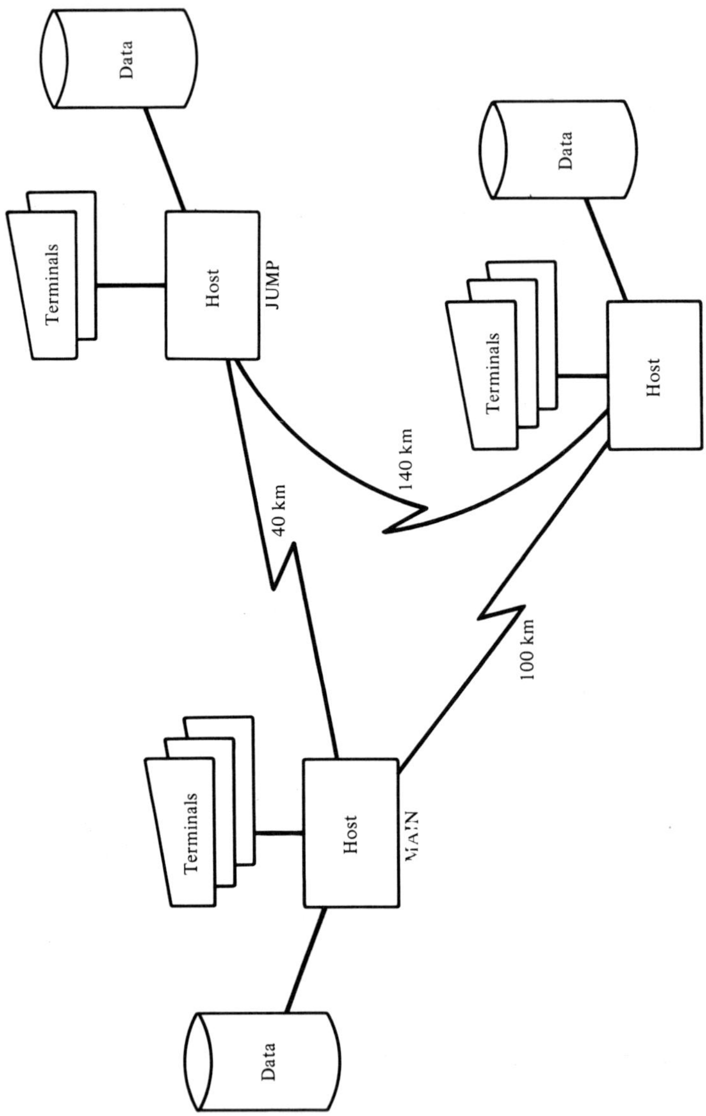

Figure 10-4. View of system by a system designer.

TABLE 10-1
Frequency of node movement

Node	Frequency
JUMP	2 per day
MAIN	1 per day
REAR	2 per week

While total movement time varies, an average 'away from the network' time is 4 hours. In addition to the normal component failures experienced by commercial and academic networks, a military network must anticipate the loss of a node due to enemy action. In this case, there is little hope that the data resident on the affected node can ever be recovered. The network must be capable of sustained operation without one or more nodes if necessary. Further, maintenance of the communications is difficult on a battlefield. Any node may find itself operational but unable to communicate with the rest of the network. In those situations the node must be able to operate in some independent or autonomous manner until a connection with the network can be restored.

SYSTEM RESILIENCY

System resiliency is the ability of a distributed system to continue operations despite component failures. This general definition raises more questions than it answers. The ability to continue operations despite component failures can affect system design, software design, hardware configuration, hardware selection, and data base design. If a system is to be truly resilient, then this capability must be recognized as the system is initially described and designed. In most existing systems, the need for system resiliency was recognized after design was well underway or even after the system was already in operation. The methods used to achieve varying degrees of system resiliency have been patches and, as such, have usually provided the additional capability at great cost, if at all.

The central difficulty in achieving a high degree of system resiliency is the need to ensure that *data base consistency* is not violated as a result of component failures;[9] i.e. the user must be able to access the required information regardless of component failures. Components in this context may be individual pieces of equipment but are usually construed to be a complete node in the network.

In order to preserve this data base consistency, Rothnie, Goodman, and Bernstein[9] identify five broad areas that must be considered. These areas are reliable broadcast, operation with missing nodes, restarting a node, failure detection, and partitioning.

Reliable Broadcast

Reliable broadcast is the capability to ensure positively that a message sent to more than one node will, in fact, reach all addressed nodes. The sending node must be aware that the message has reached all destinations. Most communications systems available today do not support reliable broadcasting.

Operation with Missing Nodes

The system must continue to function despite the absence of one or more nodes; the critical condition becomes what to do with updates for a node that is missing. Most systems treat the missing node as if it does not exist. This action can create unacceptable delays if one node must have access to the missing node. Some mechanism must be available to continue operation of the remaining nodes while accumulating the essential transactions for later use by the missing node.

Restarting a Node

Once a failed node has been restarted, its data bases must be brought to a current state. Transactions that would have been directed to this node must now be applied. The principal technique in use is called 'persistent communication' by Rothnie. This term implies that any message sent will be received at some time, regardless of the condition of the destination node at the time of transmission or the sending node at the time of reception. Another alternative worth investigating is the 'recuperating node.' A recuperating node is defined as follows:

> After a failed node has returned to operation, it is placed in a special status within the network. While in this status all accumulated transactions are applied without interruption from current (and perhaps higher priority) tasks.

When the recuperating node is up to date, its status changes from recuperating to fully participating. The feasibility of the recuperating node has not been investigated. It has some obvious advantages, as will be seen later in this chapter.

Failure Detection

In order to operate with missing nodes, or to know that a node has failed, one must have a means for quickly and efficiently detecting a node failure. Most provisions today are based on a time out condition. If a node does not respond in a predetermined time, then the node is deemed to be nonoperational. While this concept serves adequately from a system operator's view, it may be poor or even unacceptable from the user or organizational point of view. For critical real-time functions the user may need a failure detection algorithm that will both recognize failures and reroute transactions to other nodes as appropriate. There is little evidence of a link between failure detection and operation with missing nodes to ensure a smooth transition. If a distributed system is to provide reliable service to the user, system turbulence must be held to a minimum when a node is failing or has failed.

Partitioning

This area overlaps restarting a node and operating with a missing node. However, the point of view has changed from a node to the data. The weak and strong consistencies of SDD-1 also are applicable to this area.[9] How can consistency (all nodes have current data) be maintained in an environment of failed, recuperating, operating nodes? The design decisions on what data elements will be stored at which nodes will have a great impact on the operation of the network. Data that are strictly partitioned will be relatively easy to restore after node failure but will be totally unavailable if their node fails. Conversely, replicated data will be more likely to be available in a network with missing nodes, but updating recuperating nodes will be more complex. The current philosophy of Rothnie, Goodman, and Bernstein[9] is:

> In general, the correct action to take when a partition is repaired depends on the semantics of the database, the topology of the partition, and the transactions which have been run during the partition. The integration process is likely to require human decision making assisted by automatic conflict detection and some limited automatic conflict resolution.

If human decision-making is required during the restoration process, then in a turbulent network it is quite possible that users will spend a significant amount of time restoring nodes.

Specific System Resiliency Requirements

Although the division system used here is only theoretical, some of the specific requirements for system resiliency are readily identified. The requirements are based upon the user view but must be implemented in the system view.

The system's 'normal' state will be one in which nodes are missing. Individual node availabilities based on Table 10-1 are:

$$\begin{aligned} \text{JUMP} &= 1-(8/24) &&= 0.6667 \\ \text{MAIN} &= 1-(8/24) &&= 0.6667 \\ \text{REAR} &= 1-(16/168) &&= 0.90476 \end{aligned}$$

In addition, certain nodes will be out of the network due to communication failures, hardware component failures, and destruction. No firm estimates are available for these factors. A conservative estimate is that 10 per cent. of the time a node will not be available for one of the three reasons noted previously. This figure could approach 20 per cent. in a violent battle situation. This estimate is based on the time that a node is available (not moving); therefore the total probability that a node is available is the sum of the probabilities for availability based on movement requirements and other factors. Thus, the total availability for the JUMP node becomes:

$$P(\text{JUMP}) = 1 - ((0.3333) + (0.10)) = 0.5667$$

The probability that the entire network is available can be estimated if the availabilities of individual nodes are independent events. Network availability then is the product of the probabilities for each of the nodes in the network.

$$P(\text{NETWORK}) = P(\text{JUMP}) * P(\text{MAIN}) * P(\text{REAR})$$

By using the probabilities already developed, the total network availability becomes:

$$P(\text{NETWORK}) = (0.5667) * (0.5667) * (0.8048) = 0.258$$

Thus the division system will operate with missing nodes at least 75 per cent. of the time. A means of achieving system resiliency in this area is essential.

If the total network is available only 25 per cent. of the time, then some means to save all pending updates until a node is recuperating or to direct all changes to a designated replication for later transfer to the affected node must be developed.

In most cases a node failure will be directed; i.e. a node will fail or leave the network in order to relocate. In those cases the network can be warned of the failure, and a failure detection mechanism is unnecessary. When a failure is due to a communications loss, hardware failure, or destruction, then some means must be available to detect failures. This action should include failure detection, automatic rerouting of retrievals and updates, and informing the other nodes (and the users of other nodes) of the outage. Although this action is not trivial, it is essential. An automatic failure detection may be the first indication that the node from which the commander is directing the battle is not available. This situation must be recognized quickly so that a deputy commander can assume command (even for short periods of time). This rapid succession of command keeps battlefield confusion at a minimum.

Based upon the node and network availabilities already developed, it is obvious that some portions of the data base must be replicated. The general replication requirements are shown in Table 10-2. Design considerations will also include identification of applications software that will require replication. This software replication will be necessary to permit an individual node to continue to operate independently if necessary.

Existing Methods for Managing System Resiliency

Most efforts to achieve system resiliency have been based on exception processing; i.e. the normal state of the network will be one in which all nodes are operational. In addition, the algorithms in use are communications-oriented rather

TABLE 10-2
General replication requirements

Type of information	Node		
	JUMP	MAIN	REAR
Friendly unit status	30/100/0	70/30/70	60/60/40
Enemy unit status	40/100/0	100/40/60	20/100/0
Intelligence analysis	30/100/0	100/40/60	10/100/0
Logistics data	20/100/0	40/100/0	100/40/60
Planning information	35/100/0	65/30/70	35/30/70

A—percentage of total data base held by node.
B—percentage of node's data that are replicated.
C—percentage of node's data that are unique.

than function- and system-oriented. As a result, the algorithms tend to concentrate on the technical neatness of a particular situation rather than concentrating on how best to continue functional service to the user. In order to compare existing methods with the needs of the division system, two such methods will be used as examples: the algorithms used in the ARPA and MERIT networks.

The approach taken in the MERIT network is based on the assumption that in most networks it will be impractical to have direct connections between each possible node pair.[11] Tajibnapis then develops a method to maintain network topology information at each node. Thus, at any given time a node that originates a message can route the message along the shortest path to the destination. The topology information is maintained in distance and route tables. When a node notes the absence or presence of a neighboring node, the distance and route tables are updated and a special class of message (NETCHANGE) is sent throughout the network. This technique is strictly designed to manage the topology of the network. Within that view, no apparent provision exists for positively identifying the 'new' neighbor. While Tajibnapis indicates that further research is required in the areas of flow control and congestion control, he does not mention the capability for the network (or individual nodes) to continue operation in a partial network.[10] This lack can probably be attributed to the nature of the MERIT network whereas each node in the PODS is a 'voting member.' The difference in degree of participation is significant. For this reason the MERIT scheme does not provide a solution for the division system.

The methods used to manage the ARPA network are, in most cases, more elegant than those used by MERIT. The network has member nodes with different capabilities and roles in the network. Some members are classed as terminal interface message processors (TIP) whereas most members are interface message processors (IMP) having one or more hosts resident.[12] While this is closer to the topology of the division system, the methods used to manage the network are centered on the same concerns as in the MERIT scheme. Topology, message routing, etc., receive the greatest attention—for the same reasons that they receive maximum attention in the MERIT network. Both of these networks were built around existing centers. These centers became member nodes but retained their original roles at their respective locations. When a network such as the division system is postulated as a single cohesive distributed network, then the means required to manage the network tend to be expressed in terms of the network as a whole rather than in terms of individual nodes.

FUTURE WORK

In order to achieve a degree of system resiliency in a system such as the division system, further research is required in several areas: recuperation nodes, recognition of node failure/restoration in a systematic manner, efficient accommodation of essential transactions for missing nodes, and better identification of design requirements for such a system. While each of these areas is a potentially rich one for research, little evidence exists that significant effort is being directed at any of them. If a system such as the division system is to be realized, then the need for this research must be recognized in the near future.

APPENDIX

Commander—The individual who controls and is responsible for the 16,000-man division.

Deputy CG—Two general officers who are used in various roles chosen by the commander. They may perform line or staff roles.

Chief of Staff—The manager of the staff units. This individual controls and coordinates the various staff units.

Staff Elements—Perform planning tasks in their respective areas. The 'other' block includes such specialized staff officers as the Division Surgeon and the Division Chaplain.

Signal Battalion—Provides long-range communications to the division on an area basis. Communications support includes data, record traffic, and messenger service.

Engineer Battalion—Provides construction and barrier support to all units of the division.

Intelligence Battalion—Provides systems for collection and processing of intelligence information for the division.

Brigade Headquarters—An intermediate line entity that controls 2 to 5 battalions depending on the situation.

Division Artillery—The command and control unit that coordinates all fire support. This support includes the artillery battalions, air strikes, and naval gunfire.

DISCOM—Division Support Command controls the supply, maintenance, and medical activities available to support the division as a whole.

Battalion—The basic line building block of the division. This group usually contains 600 to 800 men and associated equipment.

Arty Battalion—A line unit that provides artillery fire support to a brigade.

Support Units—A collection of maintenance, supply, and medical battalions that perform support roles for the division as a whole.

REFERENCES

1. Enslow, J. B. and Goodman, N.: An Overview of the Preliminary Design of SDD-1: A System for Distributed Databases, *Proc. 2nd Berkeley Workshop on Distributed Data Management and Computer Networks*, 38–57, May, 1977.
2. Katzan, H., Jr.: *An Introduction to Distributed Data Processing.* Petrocelli Books, New York, 1978.
3. Maryanski, F. J., *et al.*: *Distributed Data Base Management Using Minicomputers.* Computer Science Department, Kansas State University, TR CS 77-22, October 1977.
4. Anderson, G. A., and Jensen, E. D.: Computer interconnection structures: taxonomy, characteristics, and examples. *Computing Surveys*, **7**, No. 4, 197–213, December 1975.
5. Hilsman, W. J. (Major General): C31 communications vital in integration of the force-multipliers. *ARMY*, **29**, No. 3, 31–33, March 1979.
6. Mahaffey, F. K. (Major General): C31 for automated control of tomorrow's battlefield. *ARMY*, **29**, No. 3, 26–30, March 1979.
7. Stubblebine, A. N., III (Brigadier General): C31 for automated focus on intelligence picture. *ARMY*. **29**, No. 3, 34–36, 1979.
8. Starry, D. A. (General): A tactical evolution—FM 100-5. *Military Review*, **LVIII**, No. 8, 2–11, 1979.
9. Rothnie, J. B., Goodman, N., and Bernstein, P. A.: The redundant update algorithm of SDD-1: a system for distributed databases (the fully redundant case). *First Int. Conf. on Computer Software and Applications*, November 1977.
10. Rothnie, J. B., and Goodman, N.: A survey of research and development in distributed database management. *Proc. Third Int. Conf. on Very Large Data Bases*, October 1977, pp. 48–61.
11. Tajibnapis, W. D.: A correctness proof of a topology information maintenance protocol for a distributed computer network. *Communications of the ACM*, **20**, No. 7, 477–485, July 1977.
12. Ornstein, S. M., *et al.*: The terminal IMP for the APPA computer network. *AFIPS Conf. Proc.*, **49**, 1972.

Advances in Distributed Processing Management, Volume 2
Edited by P. S. Fisher, J. Slonim, and E. A. Unger

Chapter 11

MODELING AND SIMULATION OF THE PERFORMANCE OF DISTRIBUTED DATA MANAGEMENT SYSTEMS

V. E. Wallentine
Department of Computer Science, Kansas State University, Manhattan, Kansas

W. J. Hankley
Department of Computer Science, Kansas State University.

The local and geographic distribution of an organization's data, and its needs for access to and processing of that data, have given rise to commercially available computer networks which can provide distributed data management. However, the wide variety of available solutions creates a management problem. From the available systems and configurations, the information systems manager must select a hardware configuration, a software configuration, and a data distribution which achieves acceptable performance of the total data system. Unfortunately most vendors, and even in-house systems analysts, provide only intuitive judgments of performance. It is thus the manager's role to understand the concepts of performance of distributed systems and the tools that can be used to obtain performance projections.

This chapter is addressed to the information system manager. The first section presents the components and concepts of distributed data systems from the viewpoint of developing simple models which can characterize the performance of the real, more complex systems which they represent. The relationship between response time (delay) and throughput and their role as indicators of overall system performance are explained. The objective is to explain enough of the operation of the hardware and software to enable readers to understand the impact of specific data distribution and configuration decisions. The level of detail of the models considers host processors, data base machines, communication subnets and processors, generalized communications lines, and various data instances (buffers)—which are all viewed as resources—and software components for data bases, communications, and applications—which are viewed as processes which compete for resources.

The second theme of this chapter is that the simple models of distributed data systems are suited for discrete event simulation of their dynamic behavior. Once its component models are validated, a simulation program can serve as a tool for predicting performance of future configurations and distributions of data. Simulation can also be used to gain understanding of the dynamics and interactions within a system that would otherwise be too big and too dispersed to observe and to be subject to experiments. Such simulations are within the size and complexity to be an in-house tool for management analysis. To illustrate this statement, an example of a simulation system and an example of a network model are explained to show their structure, size, and performance. The simulation system has been used to study an actual distributed data base configuration. The final discussion contains a warning of some of the continuing problems of simulating large distributed data management systems.

ELEMENTS OF COMPUTER NETWORKS AND THEIR IMPACT ON THE PERFORMANCE OF DISTRIBUTED SYSTEMS

Computer Network Hardware Components

This section contains a discussion of the components of a computer network and provides the reader with a foundation in network terminology. (For more detailed information, please refer to the text of Davies *et al.*[1]). These components are illustrated in Figures 11-1 and 11-2 for the reader to reference while digesting the definitions given in this section.

A *computer network* is a collection of computers which are connected together by a *communications system.* In our terminology, terminals must be connected to a processor on the network or they must contain a processor with enough intelligence to interface to the communications system. The processors which execute applications programs are called *host* computers. Specialized processors attached to the host are called *DBMS machines.* These machines are tailored to data base management system (DBMS) functions and may be attached to the host to offload the DBMS routines[2] to relieve the host computer of the DBMS computational load. Host computers are interconnected via a communications system which may be a locally implemented system or a geographically distributed system. A *local computer network* can typically connect hosts which are within several kilometers of one another, whereas a *global network* can connect hosts which may be dispersed around the world. The distinction between local and global is determined by the mechanisms of the communications system.

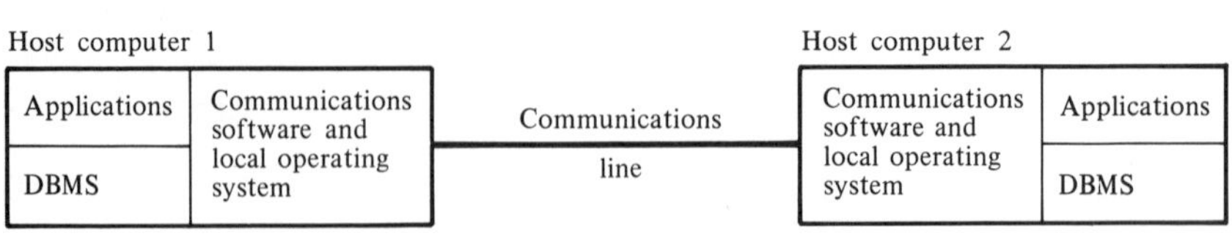

Figure 11-1. Simple point-to-point computer network.

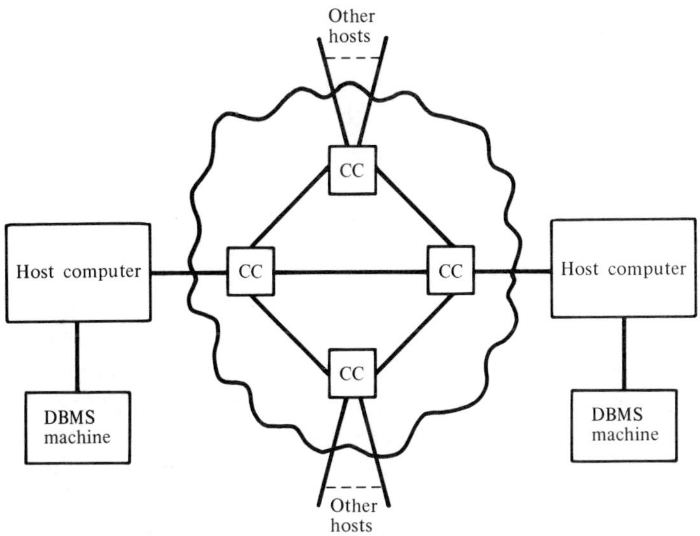

Figure 11-2. Elements of a computer network.

Figure 11-1 illustrates a simple form of a computer network. In this example, two host computers are connected via a simple communications system—a line. This *line* will have *bandwidth*, *propagation time*, and *error rate* characteristics. The speed or bandwidth of a line is measured in bits per second; and for a telephone line these rates are typically 2,400 to 50K bits per second. For short lines, such as twisted wire pairs, coaxial cable, and fiber optic cables, the bandwidth can reach 10 megabits per second. Propagation time refers to the time that it takes a bit to travel the length of the line, which is measured by (length of line)/(speed of light) in seconds. It becomes a delay factor in performance when lines are long, such as in satellite links, where propagation delay is typically 272 ms (45,000 miles). It is relatively unimportant for lines less than 10 miles, where it is less than 0.054 ms. When data is transmitted across this line, errors on the line may invalidate the data. It is then retransmitted until it is correctly received. In terms of performance a message of data is *delayed* at the source host until its first bit is propagated down the line, the message has been transmitted to the destination, and an acknowledgment has been sent back to the source. Errors increase the delay because of retransmission. Since errors force retransmission, considerable loss of *effective bandwidth* can occur if a large message must be retransmitted. Therefore, many communications systems transmit large messages in several small *packets* so that only a packet must be retransmitted on error instead of the whole message. Furthermore, many small messages (less than or equal to the size of a packet) between several applications on the host computers may be competing for the line. All short messages would have to wait for one long message. Packetizing thus permits lower delay for individual packets.

Small (or low) delay for entry of data onto the communications line is desirable for interactive traffic, such as that which emanates from interactive terminals attached to hosts. For transferring files between the host computers, it is also important to have high *throughput*; i.e. once part of a file (message) has started to flow into the communications line, that file on the destination host is not usable until the whole file has been received. In order to improve throughput, the *communications software* in the source host can continue to transmit packets of a message from a specific application (file transfer) at the expense of low-delay traffic. This flow control policy decision is inherent in the software.

In a global network (Figure 11-2) the communications system is typically an interconnected set of *communications controllers* (CCs) or *nodes* which comprise a communications subnet. These nodes can be connected via land lines, satellite channels, or radio channels, and they transmit packets of data from a source host to a destination host via a path of nodes. These subnet nodes use a *store-and-forward* technique in which each node stores a packet and then forwards it via a *line* to the next node. A node stores the packet until the next node in the path correctly receives it and has acknowledged this fact to the sending node. This arrangement is the basic architecture of the currently emerging *public data networks*.

The communications subnet of a public data network breaks up a large message of data into smaller packets (approximately 1,000 bits in ARPANET[3]) before sending them across the lines between the nodes. The store-and-forward technique thus effects a 'pipelining' of packets of a message across the subnet—possibly a packet at each node/line combination. These packets can also be routed dynamically to avoid *congestion* at the busy subnet nodes. These factors—line errors which force retransmission, routes through the subnet, and concurrent use of the subnet for the pipelining of packets of a message—will strongly impact the performance of the communications system.

Local networks are connected via lines that must be relatively short—up to 10 kilometers. These lines are typically coaxial cable as in ETHERNET,[4] twisted wire pairs, or computer buses. A taxonomy of these systems is presented by Anderson and Jensen.[5] A common form of local networks is the *ring network*, as in the distributed computing system of Farber[6] at the University of California at Irvine, or a *loop* network, such as the Spider network at Bell Labs.[7] In each case small microcomputers form the interface of the host to the communications system. In this case all routing is performed by these microprocessors with or without a central routing switch (see Figure 11-3). The most prevalent local network architecture is a coaxial cable on which only one host interface can transmit one data message at a time. This message is *broadcast* to multiple host interfaces which listen for a message with their specific address. Collisions between transmitting interfaces are detected and retransmission is the recovery strategy. Sensing a carrier busy flag (the coaxial cable is transmitting) reduces the number of collisions on transmission. This basic architecture of ETHERNET is also the architecture of NET/ONE.[8] This architecture is illustrated in Figure 11-4.

Networks can be interconnected by *gateways* so that users on one network can

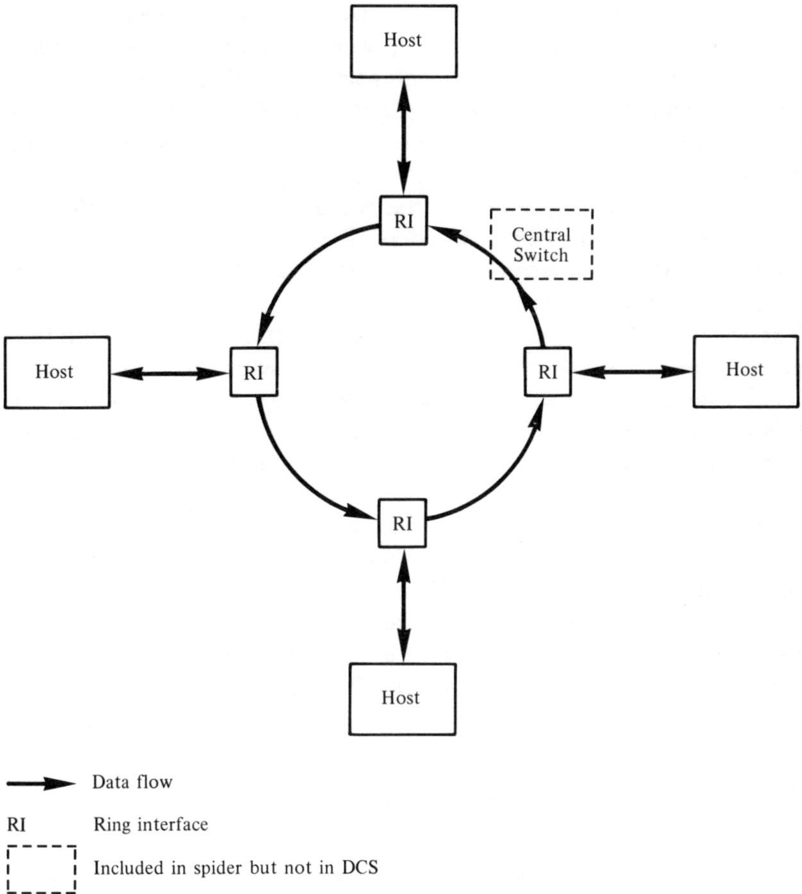

Figure 11-3. Ring network architecture.

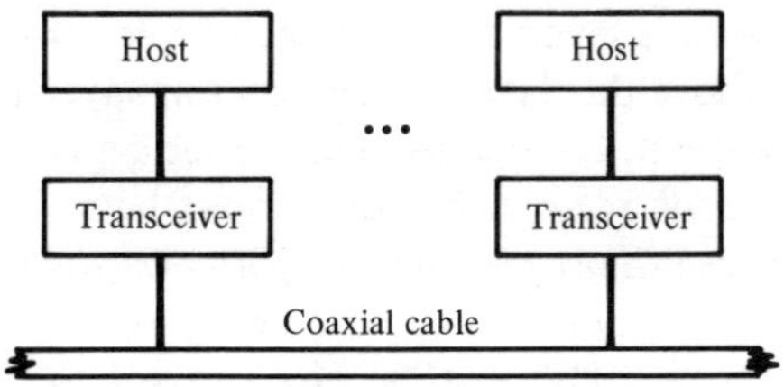

Figure 11-4. ETHERNET architecture.

access resources on other networks. For example, users on local networks can only access local hosts on a coaxial cable because the cable is limited by distance. However, if data is to be used at geographically distributed locations, interconnection of remote hosts via a public data network (PDN) is many times cheaper than connection via long-distance phone line. A local network can interface to a PDN as a host. PDNs can typically interface at the node processors within the network. Each of these gateway interfaces must provide data transfer *protocol* matching between the individual networks. These networks can then be 'chained' together via gateways to present the source and destination host computers with a single network view of data transfer.

The level of detail of computer networks presented in this chapter is fairly superficial for a network implementor,[1] but it is sufficient in most cases for a modeler's view of a computer network. We have presented the concepts of *error*, *retransmission*, *delay*, and *throughput* of packets or messages. These measures of performance are of interest to the performance modeler of a network. They are also important for *point-to-point* connections (as in Figure 11-1) as well as local networks and can be provided by a vendor or measured on a real system under a real traffic load or projected from a simulation model (as described in a later section of this chapter). Even the PDN architecture can be characterized by these measures even if internetwork gateways are involved. The performance of applications software on hosts in a computer network will depend on these measures of computer network performance. Ways of using these measures in modeling performance are discussed later.

Computer Network Software Components

In the previous section, computer network components were described. In this section the software components which drive or control the hardware will be described. This software controls the allocation of physical resources—lines, nodes, and hosts—to the transmitting of data between application and DBMS *processes* which are distributed across the network. Since software controls resource allocation, it can be used to change performance of a network. It also uses resources to carry out its function, thereby reducing the amount of *effective* (usable) *processor* and communications *bandwidth* which can be allocated to production computing and transmission. Thus, it may be necessary to incorporate its functions in a modeling effort.

Software in a network is layered so that each layer performs a set of functions such that all layers above this layer depend on this layer and this layer depends only on the layers below it. Each layer must reside on each host, and each layer must establish a *protocol* between its counterpart layer in the other host. Each layer of software on each host executes its part of a *distributed algorithm*. The corresponding layer in the other host is executing its part of that algorithm, and they are exchanging status information which drives the distributed algorithm. This exchange of status is necessary because the two ends of the protocol exist on machines with disjoint memories. Four layers of software are illustrated in Figure 11-5. The remainder of this section will consider the function of these layers and the impact of each layer on performance.

The lowest level of software—*data link control* (DLC) in Figure 11-5—controls the allocation of the communications subsystem to the transmission of data between sender and receiver processes which are distributed across the network of hosts. Its primary functions are error detection and recovery (retransmission), data *flow control* between source and destination hosts, and efficient use of the communications subsystem. This level of software can be as simple as an alternating send/receive protocol between two hosts, where the communications system is a point-to-point half-duplex telephone line. A slightly more sophisticated DLC is present in the broadcast form of ETHERNET where multiple-host interfaces listen for their address on the cable and transmit in a contention mode. If the communications system is a packet switch as in PDNs, the DLC may be a *full-duplex* protocol, such as the X.25 standard protocol,[9] which transmits data in both directions simultaneously. Each of these DLC types attempts to maximise the effective bandwidth of the communications system to provide high throughput between hosts while also providing low delay for small packets.

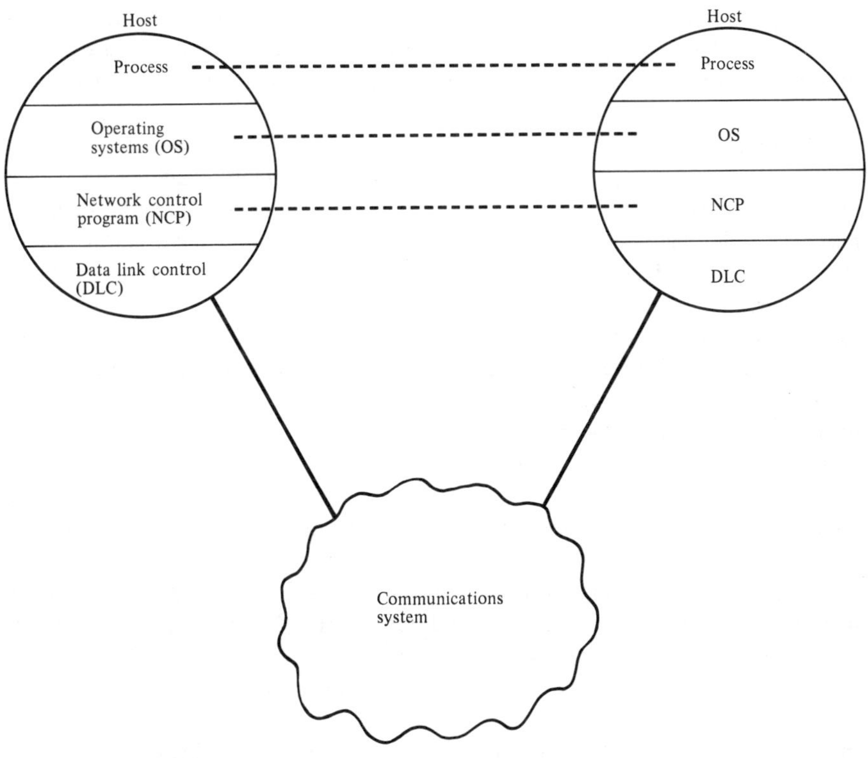

Figure 11-5. Layering of software protocols in a computer network.

DLC protocols keep the communications system busy by *buffering* packets which are ready to be transmitted. This buffering serves to accommodate the difference in the rate at which packets are supplied to the DLC and the rate at which packets can be transmitted to and received correctly at the destination host. Differences in these flow control procedures can be adjusted in order to balance the number of buffers necessary to keep the line busy against the amount of memory necessary to hold the buffers. Since both line time and memory are expensive in cost and delay of packets is expensive in performance, this balancing is a policy decision in the design of computer networks; performance modeling can give a good indication of how this trade-off should be made.

The number of buffers needed to keep the line busy is proportional to the time it takes to receive acknowledgments of correctly received packets at the destination host. Thus, it is related to the propagation delay, the transmission speed, the error rate, and the retransmission strategy. The longer the delay, the greater number of buffers and the greater the *queuing* or *admission delay* for entry onto the communication system. Statistics on the *length of* this *queue* and the *time in queue* are valuable measurements of network performance and should thus be output from a simulation model. They are good indicators of the predicted performance of various DLC procedures under consideration in a proposed system. This admission delay can also be used to test the ability of a public data network to accommodate a proposed additional load since many of these packet switch communications networks avoid internal congestion by delaying new packets—increasing the admission delay.

The effective bandwidth of the communications system is reduced by a DLC protocol because each packet must contain some control information. This packet overhead consists of addressing or routing, priority, acknowledgments, sequence numbers, redundancy checks for error detection, and possibly other control status that is being exchanged between the two DLC layers. Simulations of this overhead and its resultant reduction in throughput (lowered effective bandwidth) can establish guidelines for the performance of a proposed DLC.

The layer above the DLC is called the *network control program* (NCP) as in ARPANET, and the protocol implemented between two NCPs is called the host-to-host protocol (*end-to-end* protocol). Its functions are to provide unique *interprocess communication* paths or *associations* on which processes can transport messages, to provide flow control of messages between processes which are distributed across the network, to provide message buffering, and to allocate (multiplex) the available bandwidth of (presented by) the DLC among the process associations (data streams). The host-to-host protocol establishes the process-to-process data stream (association), and reallocates that association when the processes have finished exchanging messages.

The effect on performance of the policies applied at the NCP layer can be measured by the queuing statistics used at the DLC, the difference being that the measurements and control procedures are concerned with distinct process-to-process data streams. Thus, measurement of throughput and delay (response on process interactions) can be related to buffer usage by specific (application) processes. The projected data transmission resource and performance requirements can be used to 'size' applications processes to a particular protocol and/or host computer. The NCP as well as the DLC uses communication and host resources to establish its protocol. These requirements are additive overhead and thereby further reduce the effective processor and bandwidth capacity. This overhead can be modeled to predict the excess processor and line resources needed to accommodate them.

The operating system (OS) is only a layer in the sense that it is used to establish the processes in each host and to allocate the necessary resources (e.g. memory, tasks, and files) for them to run. This function must be handled in a synchronized way so that communicating processes are active at the same time. The individual OSs exchange process resource description information, thus placing more communications loads on the system. It also uses host processor resources for its own purposes, such as task-switching. The excess processor power needed to accommodate this overhead can be predicted from a simulation model. The relationship to overall degradation in performance of distributed programs (processes communicating across a network) in some cases can be related to the OS overhead.[10]

Processes are the active entities in the system which carry out application and DBMS programs. They implement distributed algorithms by exchanging data with other processes. For example, assume that a user sitting at a terminal is issuing queries of a data base. An implementation might be that the terminal is being controlled by a query process on the host processor to which the terminal is connected. Assume further that the data base is on another host. When a request to retrieve data is issued by the user, the query process experiences the following delays before a *response* can be sent to the user.

1. The local OS must request the remote OS to bring up a DBMS process and then notify the local OS. This delay is a round-trip message—from the source host to the destination host and back to the source host—across the system.
2. The NCPs must establish an association between the query and DBMS processes—another round-trip delay.
3. The query process sends a message to the DBMS process; the DBMS process accesses the data, and then sends the data to the query process. Depending on NCP and DCL protocols, one or two round trips take place on the communications system. Each round trip encounters delays due to competition from other currently active associations and to the admission delays to the communications system.
4. Response to the user is accomplished only after all the aforementioned delays. This delay is called *response time.*

Modeling processes and their competition for processor and communications facilities permit simulation experiments which project user response time to be related to processor and communications loads. They also permit size estimates of new facilities for already existing or new applications.

Data Distribution

Our modeling efforts, described in the next section, represent communication software, application, and DBMS functions as processes, and their performance is evaluated as a function of delay in communications between distributed processes. In a distributed data management system, placement of data and data dictionaries is of prime importance in the performance of the distributed data management algorithm. The delay inherent in distributing a query process and a DBMS process was discussed in the last section. The comparison of query and DBMS processes running on the same host with that of the distributed form of the last section can be quite illuminating. In a simple experiment of response time on a real system,[11] response time for a single host was half a second. For the distributed version it was 20 seconds. This experiment used slow lines which turned out to be the dominant delay. A simulation model of basically the same system[10] indicated that high-speed lines alleviated the delay problem. In Figure 11-1 this simulation model is illustrated, except that only applications on one host were run and the other host ran only DBMS processes—a *back-end DBMS*. Further simulations with the same model indicated the proper relationship of communications software overhead, OS task switch times, multiprogramming level, and line speeds. The important issue is that when obvious bottlenecks to performance (in terms of response time and throughput for the preceding model) are eliminated in simulation experiments, other factors may become dominant. Thus, by experimentation overall performance can be 'tuned' for a model workload before a real system is constructed.

The results of simulations using the previous simple example model were not intuitively obvious before the simulation experiments. The performance of the more complex model of data distribution in the next section is even less obvious and thus requires more careful modeling to achieve good results. The remainder of this section will focus on other distributed data management protocols and their impact on response time.

Figure 11-6 shows a system in which application programs on each host may access data on their own host as well as data on all other hosts. A conceptually simple implementation is to provide an application process which has interprocess communication paths to server processes on each of the other hosts. These server processes execute DBMS access routines. The model of the next section represents these real processes by model processes so that the model is very close in structure to the real system. The application program can operate one of many different protocols. Several of these are described next.

The first protocol is for the application program to request data from each of the server processes in a serial manner. As soon as a server responds with the data, the application ceases to ask for data. Thus, the total delay is the sum of the

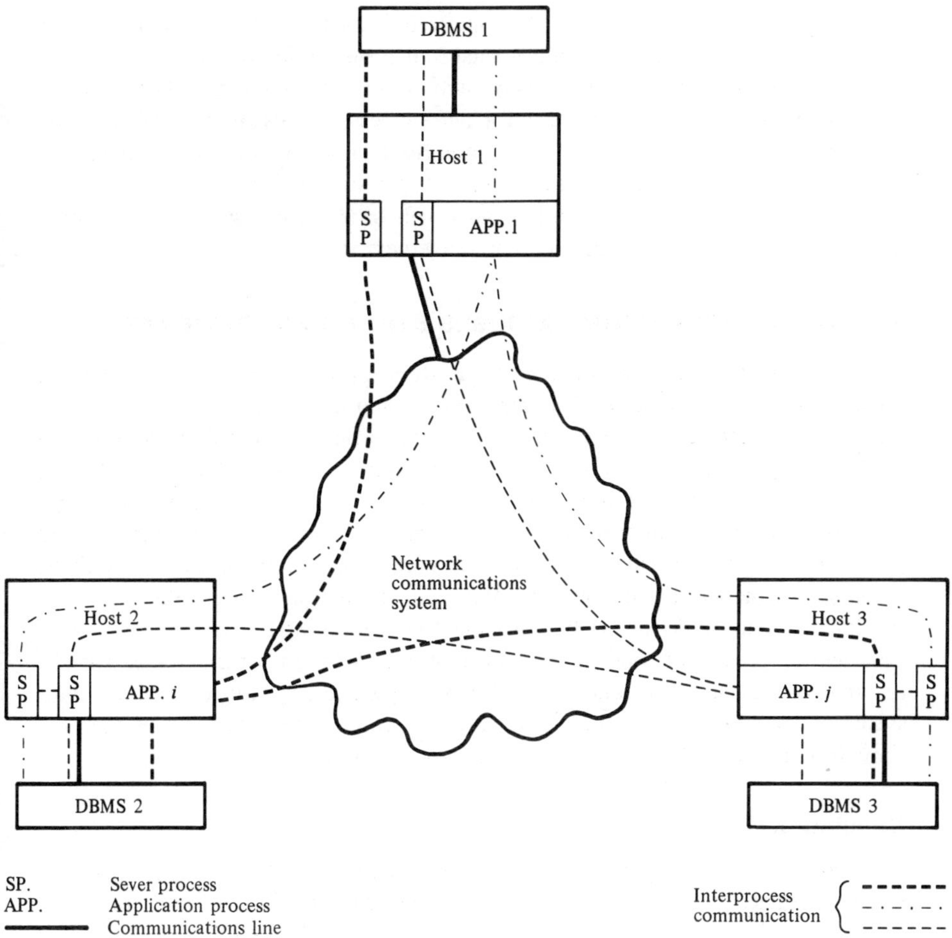

Figure 11-6. Distributed data base.

delays to each server process which is polled. Another application protocol may issue requests to all server processes at the same time. In the latter protocol the delay is the longest delay for a single-server process DBMS access. If the data are evenly distributed across the hosts, the second protocol will produce the shortest (access) response time at the expense of using a good portion of the effective bandwidth of the communications system. If the data are predominantly on the first server process interrogated, then the minimal communications bandwidth is used for essentially the same access time.

Other protocols for this system can be envisioned. For example, one server process could hold a data dictionary which describes the location of each part of the data. In this protocol the application process sends the data request to the data dictionary process. This process then requests data from the designated server process locations. The delay is thus at least four transmission times.

The performance of the overall distributed system is a function of the frequency of the application program requests for data access, the distribution of data, the load on the individual hosts, and the additional load on the communications system as well as the delay times inherent in a distributed program. In the next section more measurements of importance will be described in the context of a simulation model of a distributed data management system.

NETWORK SIMULATION—MODELS AND MEASUREMENTS

Development of simple models of a data system allows a manager to understand the performance of the real system; and it is a mechanism for the prediction of the effect of changes to the system, either by formal analysis of the model or by simulation of the model. Simulation is particularly suited as a management tool because simulation experiments can be specified as a management parameter and intermediate results can be obtained which explain and justify the overall performance results. Yet simulation also holds pitfalls. Without a balance of model abstraction and validation, simulation experiments can be on one hand too unwieldly or on the other hand not representative of the real system. This section presents a view of the concepts of simulation, which is necessary to be able to specify simulation experiments—particularly for distributed data systems—and to interpret their results. The section concludes with an example simulation model with a summary of cost, size, and complexity of results.

Simulation Concepts

A data management network is by nature a discrete event system. Its operation is characterized by the occurrence of distinct data operations (e.g. initiation, receipt, transfer, and completion) which each begin at a discrete time and each last a finite duration. This behavior may be captured by a discrete event simulation. An essential vocabulary for describing simulation experiments covers concepts of a simulation clock, processes and transactions, resources, synchronization and events, and delays.

A simulation 'runs' by advancing increments of simulation time on the underlying reference time counter, called the clock. It determines the granularity of time and the maximum duration of the simulation. For example, if the clock is implemented as a signed 16-bit counter and the time unit is taken as 0.1 second, then the maximum simulation period is approximately

$$(65{,}000) \times (0.1) = 6{,}500 \text{ seconds} \approx 100 \text{ minutes}$$

and operations of less than 0.1 seconds' duration might be ignored in the simulation.

The definitions of processes, transactions, and resources are all interrelated

```
CYCLE FOREVER;
      ACCEPT TRANSACTION FROM INPUT QUEUE
            {TRANSACTION IN STATE S}
      SEIZE REQUIRED RESOURCES
            {MAY BE DETERMINED BY TRANSACTION TYPE};
      DELAY PROCESSING TIME INTERVAL
            {MAY BE DETERMINED BY TRANSACTION TYPE};
      RELEASE RESOURCES;
      OUTPUT TRANSACTION TO NEXT QUEUE
            {TRANSACTION IN NEW STATE S};
      DELAY PROCESS RECOVERY TIME INTERVAL;
END OF CYCLE BODY;
```

Figure 11-7. Typical process simulation logic with one input queue.

with one another. *Processes* model the operating functions within a data system; *transactions* represent the entities of data flow; and *resources* are passive entities over which processes compete for use. Processes execute by servicing transactions, thus mapping them from one state to the next. An example of process simulation logic is represented in Figure 11-7. Typically, the process competes for some limited resource for which it may have to wait and must be held before the process can execute. Then, serving a transaction is simulated by merely waiting some increment of simulation time which corresponds to the real process operation time. The intriguing reality of a simulation arises in part from its stochastic behavior. This randomness may be created in two primary ways:

1. By specifying a statistical distribution for the 'arrival' (i.e. creation) of transactions which are new inputs to the system.
2. By specifying a statistical distribution for the delay time intervals for processes.

These distributions must be determined from measurement or analysis of the physical system which is modeled.

No unique choice specifies what are processes and what are transactions. Rather, these choices may be determined by the viewpoint of the person who builds the model, for example:

Views of simulation of supermarket

	View 1	View 2	View 3
Processes	Checkouts, butcher	Shoppers	Shoppers, managers, butcher
Transactions	Shoppers	Carts	Carts
Resources	Manager	Checkouts, manager, butcher	None
Synchronization	Driven by transactions	Driven by transactions	By transactions and by signal for manager

Note. Manager validates shoppers' checks.

Views of communications line simulation

	View 1	View 2
Processes	Communication software	Messages
Transactions	Messages	None
Resources	Communication lines and processors	Same
Synchronization	Driven by transactions	Enforced by holding resources

In a 'process view' the simulation program describes the logic of the functions that seem naturally to be physical processes and it maintains some data store for the states of the transactions. Alternately, in a 'transaction view' the program describes the logic of the sequences of operations for patterns of flow of transactions, which are viewed as active entities; process logic is subsummed in the coding of the transactions. Neither view is definitely better than the other. Each yields some intermediate results in a slightly different form. Either may yield a smaller, more efficient simulation depending on the relative number of distinct process cases versus the number of distinct transaction patterns. We advocate a process view in the example given later (such as view 1 of the communication line) because we feel that this view yields intermediate results that are easier to relate to the actual system function.

In all simulations, the active entities (processes) require some mechanism for *synchronization.* Common mechanisms include:

1. Processes wait for queued transactions.
2. Processes wait to acquire use of resources.
3. Processes wait for *events* which are explicitly signaled by other processes.

In the example simulation, all three of these are used. The first closely resembles the behavior of data-driven network software; the second mimics network sharing of physical resources (CPUs, lines, buffers); the third models synchronization between directly communicating software components.

Given all of the preceding concepts, one can proceed to the original objective—to determine model *performance.* Two kinds of information can be gathered—trace information which is viewed as qualitative, and *statistics*, which are quantitative. Selective traces of a simulation give the time sequence of the states of selected entities (processes, transactions, or resources). This information is necessary for qualitative judgment of the reasonableness (or the unreasonableness) of the simulation. Unfortunately, the abundance of tracing data can be overwhelming. Data can be used only if limited or if displayed in some graphic dynamic mode (e.g. as moving dots on a network diagram).

Statistics which can be gathered include:

Resources	Usage (which process), time of use
Transaction queues . .	Length, time of waiting in the queue
Processes	Active time, number of transactions processed (number of each kind), time waiting for resources, time waiting for transactions
Counters	These record values computed by the simulation program. Cumulative counters record totals, e.g. total simulated failures of a component. Mean counters record averages, e.g. the average duration time of a recurring sequence (Tend—Tstart) for some operation.

For each quantity, an average, a maximum, and a minimum are easily measured. Variance is commonly reported also, but it is more costly to obtain. One potential danger is that statistics may require an adjustment for partial results during the time interval in which results are reported.

Implementation

Three kinds of alternatives are available for programming a simulation:

1. Write the entire program directly in some available high-level language (e.g. FORTRAN). This alternative is foolish.
2. Write the program in some specialized simulation language (e.g. SOL,[12] SIMULA,[13] or SIMSCRIPT.[14]). We somewhat advise against this decision as it involves an additional language for programmers to learn, maintain, and explain.
3. Write the program in the available high-level language (e.g. FORTRAN or PASCAL) using existing simulation extension packages (e.g. GASP[15] for FORTRAN and PASCAL-PLUS[16] or SIMPASCAL[17]). We advocate this approach.

As illustration of one simulation package, we mention SIMMON, which was developed at Kansas State University as an extension for Concurrent PASCAL (CPASCAL).[18] CPASCAL is a PASCAL-like language which supports logically concurrent execution of program components, called (concurrent) processes, and sharing of data structures, called monitors. (Queuing of data flow items can be programmed using monitors, but it is not directly supported in CPASCAL.) Because of its concurrent processes, CPASCAL is an easy environment in which to implement discrete simulation. SIMMON is a monitor (i.e. a shared package) which maintains a simulation clock counter and provides callable procedures for simulation primitives including:

1. Naming of processes and resources.
2. Delaying of a simulation time interval.
3. Requesting to seize a resource and release of the resource.
4. Signalling event I and wait for any events i1 . . . i*n*.

Definition, storage, and queueing of transactions is left to the simulation program, with the intent that synchronization can be controlled explicitly using events. Capabilities for measurement of performance include:

1. Operations on internal counter variables (e.g. for recording queue lengths and transactions).
2. Reporting of tracing and statistics for processes, resources, events, and counters.

The SIMMON monitor comprises about 1,000 lines of CPASCAL source code not counting user declaration of processes and data structures for transactions. The maximum numbers of processes, resources, events, and counters are all defined constants, so that the monitor can be recompiled for specific size configurations as needed. The monitor comes in two versions: an interpreted form with a 16-bit clock and a fully compiled form with a 32-bit clock.

Simulation Example

Let us consider an example program. The purpose of the example is not to present all of the details of the program, but to show enough structure to be useful as a comparison in the simulation of other data systems.

We recently studied a conjectured three-node distributed data system using the CPASCAL SIMMON package.[19] The objectives of the study were:

1. To investigate data queues within the line control software.
2. To investigate the effect on performance of separate processors for line control and data base control.
3. To investigate the effect of varying user and system buffer sizes.

A two-node form of the system was available for physical experimentation and for modeling and evaluation of model parameters. Based upon the two-node system, a nominal model was created and is represented in a typical configuration in Figure 11-8. It consists of three distributed nodes, each connected by communication lines. In full form, each node consists of a 'front-end' CPU (CPU(i)), a communication controller (CC(i)), and a back-end data base machine (DM(i)). Each CPU(i) hosts various numbers of user tasks (USER(i)) running in an interactive query mode, and a query handler process (RQSTR(i)) which accepts queries from user tasks, distributes the queries to the appropriate data machine, and returns the

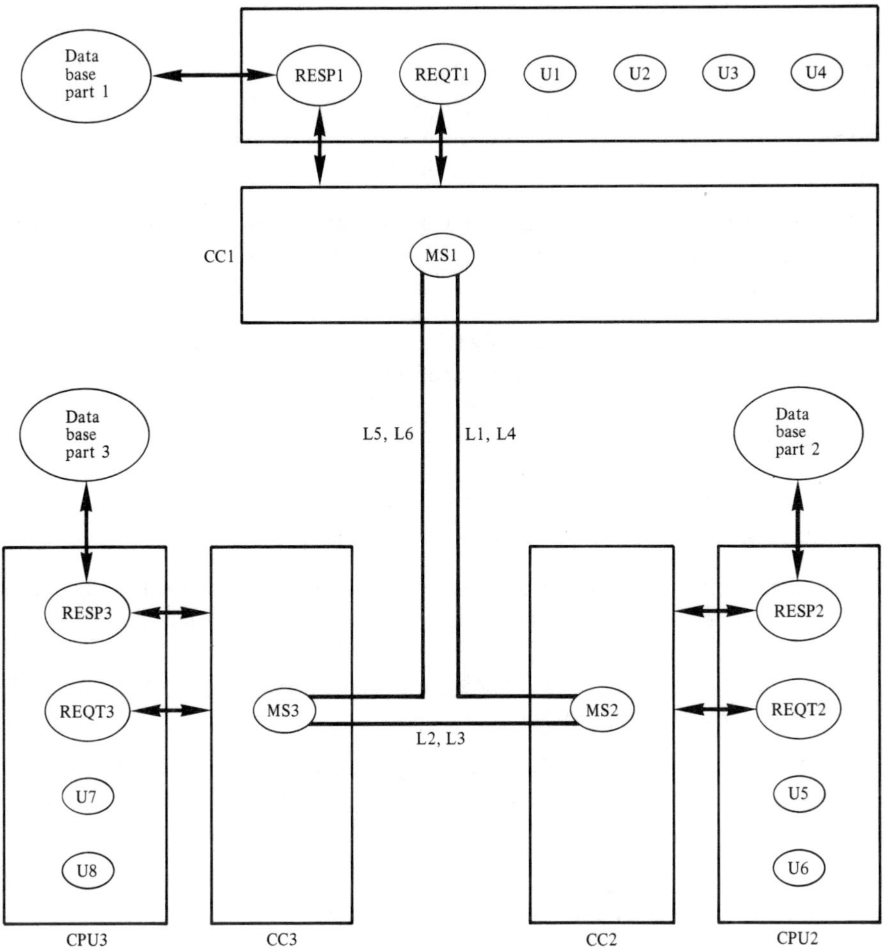

Figure 11-8. Communications logical view of sample network.

responses to the user tasks. Each data base machine runs a data server process (RESPR(i)) which computes the response for each query.

For the simulation, we initially selected the processes as:

USER(i)	User tasks
RQSTR(i)	Requested tasks
MS(i)	Communication message system tasks
RESPR(i)	Data base responder tasks

and the resources as:

CPU(i)	Node CPUs
CC(i)	Communications control CPUs
L(ij)	Communication line subsystems
DM(i)	Data machine CPUs

Then the transactions represented data queries and responses traveling through the system. No physical data are moved. Rather, transactions are represented as a record with fields:

STATE	Usually the name of an input queue
FROM	The name of the original sender process (RESPR(i) or USER(i))
TARGET	The name of the ultimate target process (USER(i) or RESPR(i))
DATA_LEN	The length of data represented
CMD_CODE	A code to indicate request type or end of data

The maximum number of transactions was limited, based upon the maximum possible number of outstanding requests and the average number of buffers per response.

To implement transaction handling, a queuing monitor was written in CPASCAL with primary entries:

SEND	Queues a transaction to a specified process
RECEIVE	Waits for a transaction in the input queue (from any source, assuming only a single input queue)

```
MASTER_PROCESS:
1. INITIALIZE ALL OTHER PROCESSES
2. WAIT TOTAL SIMULATION TIME
3. REPORT STATISTICS AS REQUIRED
4. END SIMULATION
```

(a) Main process logic.

```
USER (i):
INITIALIZE PARAMETERS FOR i-th USER INSTANCE;
cycle forever
    1) consume T1 CPU seconds then
       SEND a request with CMD=0
    2) Cycle1 RECEIVE response buffer with CMD=0
       until receive last buffer with
       CMD=101 endcycle1
    3) wait human reaction time, random {T2 to T3}
end cycle

THE INTERNAL USER PARAMETERS ARE:
    T1   CPU usage time 1 unit = 0.01 seconds
    T2   bounds on interaction time 50 = 0.50 sec.
    T3   bounds on interaction time 100 = 1.00 sec.
USER_BUF_LEN... USER BUFFER LENGTH
                DIFFERENT USER INSTANCES SET FROM
                80 BYTES TO 2000 BYTES
```

(b) Structure for user (*i*) logic.

```
RQSTR (i):
1. INITIALIZE PARAMETERS FOR i-th RQSTR
2. cycle forever
     2.1  RECEIVE a request from USERi
     2.2  consume TRQSTR1 CPU seconds computation time
     2.3  randomly select a target machine "R" for the data base item
     2.4  SEND request to RESPRi on network node R
     2.5  if local_data then RECEIVE response_length
          else
          cycle 1
          2.5.1  RECEIVE response buffer from RESPRi
          2.5.2  consume TRQSTR2 CPU seconds
          until CMD=101 endcycle1 fi
     2.6  cycle2 SEND buffer to user with CMD=0
          until SEND last buffer with CMD=101
          end cycle2
endcycle

THE RQSTR PARAMETERS ARE:
MACHINE.....................NETWORK NODE NUMBER
TRQSTR1.....................computation time to analyze a
                            request; nominally 1 unit = 0.01 second
TRQSTR2.....................time to process one buffer of data
                            from a RESPR; nominally 1 unit = 0.01
                            second
RQSTR_BUF_LEN.....REQUESTER BUFFER LENGTH,
                            INSTANCES SET FROM 256 TO 1024
```

(c) Structure for RQSTR (*i*) logic.

```
RESPR (i):
1. INITIALIZE PARAMETER FOR i-th INSTANCE
2. INITIALIZE RECEIVE REQUEST ON ALL NETWORK NODES
3. cycle forever
     3.1  accept the RECEIVE request on machine R
     3.2  consume TRESPR1 CPU seconds on node R
     3.3  if local-data then SEND response with
          CMD=-RESPONSE_LENGTH
          else
          cycle 1
          3.3.1  if last-buffer-of-data then CMD=101
                 else CMD=0 fi
          3.3.2  SEND response buffer to REQSTR
          3.3.3  wait until SEND is completed
          until last-buffer-sent endcycle1 fi
     3.4  reissue RECEIVE on node R
endcycle

THE RESPR PARAMETERS ARE:
MACHINE .....................NETWORK NODE NUMBERS
CPU OR DM....................MACHINE ON WHICH DATA BASE EXECUTES
TRESPR.......................FIXED COMPUTATION TIME FOR DATA RESPONSE,
                             INITIALLY 100 UNITS = 1 SECOND,
                             BUT SUBJECT TO EXPERIMENTAL VARIATION
LENGTH_VEC...................DISCRETE DISTRIBUTION OF EIGHT DIFFERENT
                             RESPONSE LENGTHS, DETERMINED FROM
                             APPLICATION STATISTICS
```

(d) Structure for RESPR (*i*) logic.

Figure 11-9. Design of some distributed data system processes.

The transactions were actually maintained in a table and the queue behavior was programmed using event variables and counter variables so as to obtain simulation statistics.

The first design of some of the processes is shown in Figure 11-9 (a) to (d). The master process initializes and terminates each simulation. The user processes consume CPU(i) time—to represent input operations—and delay time—to represent human generation of each next query. Loading of the data system can be varied by changing the speed of generating queries and by changing the number of instances of user tasks.

The requester logic is a data dictionary, a traffic manager, and a buffer manager. User requests for data are sent to the appropriate responder, whose location is given in the data dictionary; the response data are buffered. Note that in order to determine the buffering, the user buffer sizes are available as global data. Each of the responder processes accepts requests from users (via requesters) and then returns response data. Local data on the same node are moved as a block transfer; the remote data are buffered. To simulate multithreaded data

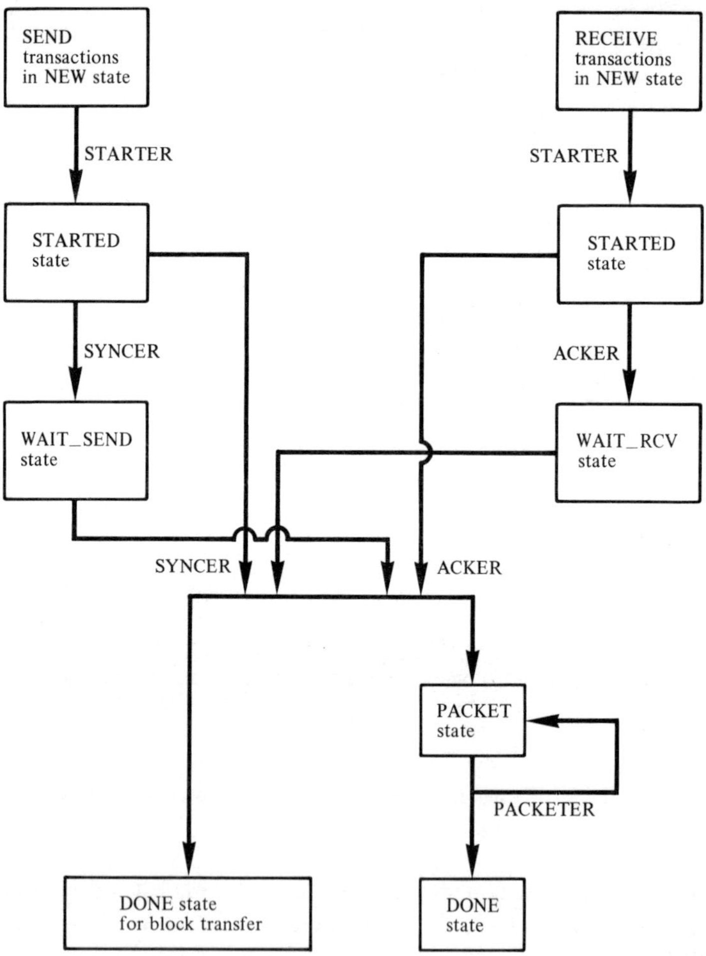

Figure 11-10. State diagram of message system transactions.

machines, one responder process was dedicated to each user task and allowed to 'float' between machines. Thus, RESPR1 would serve a request from USER1 on any of the machines DM1 or DM2 or DM3. That method trades code simplicity for additional process instances, which was deemed acceptable for the small, initial stage of the simulation.

Initially, the communications functions were viewed as a single abstracted MS process. However, in order to view the internal structure in more detail, the MS model was expanded to four subprocesses to handle synchronizing of messages and movement of individual packets of data. (This refinement is the inverse direction that one might seek in other simulations. More commonly, it is desirable to abstract a subnet or subsystem into fewer abstract processes.) On each communication controller the software processes are:

STARTER(i)	. . . .	Starts initial processing of each request; consumes TSTART time on CC(i)
SYNCER(i)	. . . .	Matches receive (send) requests with
ACKER(i)	. . . . .	Waiting send (receive) requests if available; otherwise puts requests in a waiting state
PACKETER(i)	. . .	Moves packets of 128 bytes over appropriate line $L(i,j)$ using both TPACKET time on CC(i) and TLINE time on $L(i,j)$

Together these move SEND and RECEIVE requests through a sequence of six states (NEW, STARTED, WAIT_SEND, WAIT_RCV, PACKET, and DONE), as shown in Figure 11-10. The figure shows the one case in the simulation wherein a process (the SYNCER and ACKER) state and WAIT_SEND or WAIT_RCV).

In total, the nominal simulation model with eight user tasks comprised 32 processes and space for 80 active transactions—a modest size simulation. The source program consisted of:

1,300 lines	. . .	Communication logic
300 lines	. . .	Processes
300 lines	. . .	Initialization and printing
1,000 lines	. . .	SIMMON monitor
200 lines	. . .	Global types and constants

In the interpreted form for a 16-bit machine, it compiled into about 40K bytes of virtual code. It ran (interpreted) in a 40K-byte data space in 'real' time, i.e. 5 minutes of simulated time for six CPU executed in 5 minutes in a time-shared environment. This execution time was reduced by a factor 3 on the 32-bit compiler version. The programming effort was small, about 1 man-month, and easily dwarfed by the associated tasks (parameter evaluation, validation, experiments, and documentation), which lasted for several months. These tasks are summarized next. Performance information consisted of traces—which were measured in inches of pages—and statistics summaries which were four one-page tables, one each for counters, processes, resources, and events. In spite of that brevity, it was necessary to restructure the data to a form better suited to show performance trends. Numeric results dealt with utilization of resources and throughput and delays for transactions. To illustrate from the example configuration: while process operations were in the 10-ms range, transaction times ranged from 10 seconds to 1 minute; the busiest parts of the network were the lines with 60 per cent. utilization, with delays of 10 ms per packet, and the communication CPUs with 30 per cent. utilization.

Parameters to be evaluated for the example model consisted of such features as time usage constants for holding resources, buffer sizes, size of response data, and error rates, together with their distributions. In general, parameters might be evaluated based upon a combination of analytic component models, experiments with the physical system, and guesses. For example, the time delay parameters were determined by running several 'open loop' measures of the physical system suppressing interfering processes. One case consisted of generating requests which were queued but not otherwise processed, yielding TRQSTR1 for the requested processes. Another consisted of starting message system requests without further processing, yielding TSTART for the STARTER process. A third consisted of sending packets with no synchronization of responses, yielding TPACK for the PACKETER processes. In all these cases we were satisfied with a discrete time value rather than a time distribution. Other constants followed from the design of the physical system, e.g. the buffer sizes and packet size. The line error rates were determined from published models of line characteristics. We merely converted bit error rate to equivalent packet error rates, which is overly conservative. The existing data base model specified a skewed distribution of response data sizes based upon the class of the user. This model was implemented by using a uniform selection of size values from tables of discrete values set for each responder, e.g. 10, 20, 50, 100, 200, 500, 1,000, and 10,000.

Validation consists of controlled tests of the program to show correctness of its logic and performance—although the validation does not guarantee correctness of later experiments. Validation tests that we checked for the example were:

1. All process time was accounted. For each process, the total simulation time is divided between delay times (which models active time of the process), time waiting for resources (which models contention times), and time waiting for transaction (which models idle time).
2. All user requests were accounted and matched with a response.
3. In a tracing mode, specific transactions and events were followed through a complete cycle of query and response for several user tasks.
4. The model was configured in several reduced forms, and throughput and response measures were compared with the corresponding measured data

for the physical two-node system. Configurations were all for two nodes without a data machine, for one or two users. Experiments covered all remote data, all local data, and several fixed length responses.

5. Runs of varying total simulation time were observed to check for settling of transient behavior of queues.
6. Runs were made with different seeds for the random number generator, with different initial state of the MS processes, and with different initial delays of all the processes so as to show that initial conditions did not affect the results.

We observed that even after the program was compiled and run, the validation tests exposed several small errors which had some effect on the reported statistics (including an error in the statistics report itself).

Experiments are the objective of any simulation. For the example system, the primary experiments were:

1. Running the program with and without the DMs and with and without the CCs. When the special CPUs were removed, the processes were made to use the host CPUs.
2. Running the program with different line speeds.

For these cases, the results were qualitatively intuitive, but the simulation did provide quantitative comparisons.

Documentation should not be the last item. It can be of greater value before the simulation experiments than afterward, by providing the organization of thoughts and design that can prevent wasted time in programming and experiments.

SUMMARY

In this chapter we have attempted to overview a methodology that the information manager can use to evaluate the performance of distributed data management systems. We have presented short tutorials on computer network hardware and software in order to establish the elements of distributing computing which are important performance measures. We then proceeded with a tutorial on simulation modeling followed by a detailed example of a simulation model of a distributed data base system. This example is used to illustrate the experimental nature of performance evaluation and the suitability of simulation experimentation to the projection of performance of proposed distributed systems. The success of performance projection with simulation tools is, however, not assured. It depends on the ability of the system analyst to construct meaningful experiments. If he is knowledgeable of the real system, a sequence of simulation experiments should converge to an optimum performance by isolating, one by one, the values of the tuning parameters.

REFERENCES

1. Davies, D. W., Barber, D. L. A., Price, W. L., and Solomonides, C. M.: *Computer Networks and Their Protocols*, John Wiley and Sons, New York, 1979.
2. Maryanski, F. J.: Backend data base systems. *Computing Surveys*, **12**, No. 1, March 1980.
3. Heart, R. E., Kahn, R. E., Ornstein, S. M., Crowther, W. R., and Walden, D. C.: The interface message processor for the ARPA network. *AFIPS Conf. Proc. SJCC*, **36**, 551, May 1970.
4. Metcalfe, R. M., and Boggs, D. R.: ETHERNET: distributed packet switching for local computer networks. *Comm. of ACM*, **19**, 395, July 1976.
5. Anderson, G. A., and Jensen, E. D.: Computer interconnection structures: taxonomy, characteristics, and examples. *Computing Surveys*, **7**, No. 4, 1972, December 1972.
6. Farber, D. J.: A ring network. *Datamation*, **21**, 44, February 1975.
7. Fraser, A. G.: A virtual channel network. *Datamation*, **21**, 51, February 1975.
8. Bass, C., Kennedy, J. S., and Davidson, J. M.: Local network gives new flexibility to distributed processing. *Electronics Magazine* (*McGraw-Hill*), September 25, 1980.
9. Series X recommendations. *The Orange Book*, Vol. VIII. 2, International Telecommunications Union, Geneva 1977.
10. Maryanski, F. J., and Wallentine, V. E.: A simulation of a backend data base management system. In *Pittsburgh Modeling and Simulation Conf.*, April 1976, pp. 243–248.
11. Housh, R. D.: *An Implementation of a Distributed Data Base Management System*. M.S. thesis, Department of Computer Science, Kansas State University, Manhattan, Kansas, 1978.
12. Knuth, D., and McNeley, J. L.: SOL—a symbolic language for general purpose system simulation. *IEEE Trans. on Computers*, August 1964.
13. Dahl, O. J., and Nygaard, K.: SIMULA—An ALGOL-based simulation language. *Comm. of ACM*, **9**, No. 9 September 1966.
14. Kiviat, P. J., Villaneuoa, R., and Markowitz, H. M.: *The Simscript II programming Language*. Prentice-Hall, Englewood Cliffs, N.J., 1968.
15. Pritsker, A. A., and Kiviat, P. J.: *Simulation with GASP II*. Prentice-Hall, Englewood Cliffs, N.J., 1969.
16. Welsh, J., and Bustard, D. W.: Pascal-Plus—another language for modular multiprogramming, *Software-Practice and Experience*, **9**, No. 11, 947–957, 1979.
17. Deminet, J.: SIMPASCAL. *Pascal News*, **17**, March 1980.
18. Wallentine, V. E., Hankley, W. J., and McBride, R. A.: *SIMMON—A Concurrent Pascal Based Simulation System*. Tech. Rpt. CS-79-05, Department of Computer Science, Kansas State University, Manhattan, Kansas, 1979.
19. Hankley, W. J., Wallentine, V. E., Skidmore, A., and McBride, R. A.: *NETSIM: A Distributed Network Simulation Program*. Tech. Rpt. CS-79-02, Department of Computer Science, Kansas State University, Manhattan, Kansas, 1979.

INDEX